Routledge Revivals

A History of Emigration

A History of Emigration

From the United Kingdom to North America 1763-1912

Stanley C. Johnson

First published in 1913 by Frank Cass and Company Limited by arrangement with Routledge and Kegan Paul Ltd.

This edition first published in 2018 by Routledge
2 Park Square, Milton Park, Abingdon, Oxon, OX14 4RN
and by Routledge
52 Vanderbilt Avenue, New York, NY 10017, USA

Routledge is an imprint of the Taylor & Francis Group, an informa business

© 1913 Taylor & Francis

All rights reserved. No part of this book may be reprinted or reproduced or utilised in any form or by any electronic, mechanical, or other means, now known or hereafter invented, including photocopying and recording, or in any information storage or retrieval system, without permission in writing from the publishers.

Publisher's Note
The publisher has gone to great lengths to ensure the quality of this reprint but points out that some imperfections in the original copies may be apparent.

Disclaimer
The publisher has made every effort to trace copyright holders and welcomes correspondence from those they have been unable to contact.
A Library of Congress record exists under ISBN:

ISBN 13: 978-0-367-00258-9 (hbk)
ISBN 13: 978-0-367-00259-6 (pbk)
ISBN 13: 978-0-429-40051-3 (ebk)

Printed in the United Kingdom
by Henry Ling Limited

EMIGRATION FROM THE UNITED KINGDOM TO NORTH AMERICA 1763-1912

A HISTORY OF EMIGRATION

From the United Kingdom to North America
1763-1912

STANLEY C. JOHNSON

FRANK CASS & CO. LTD.
1966

Published by Frank Cass & Co. Ltd.,
10 Woburn Walk, London W.C.1
by arrangement with Routledge and Kegan Paul Ltd.

First Edition	1913
New Impression	1966

Printed in Holland by
N.V. Grafische Industrie Haarlem

TO
DR. KNOWLES
OF THE LONDON SCHOOL OF ECONOMICS
AND
SIR CHARLES LUCAS, K.C.B., K.C.M.G.,
I AM GREATLY INDEBTED FOR
MANY VALUABLE
SUGGESTIONS   S. C. J.

September, 1913.

CONTENTS

CHAPTER I
PRELIMINARY SURVEY, 1763–1815 . . . 1

CHAPTER II
HISTORICAL SURVEY, 1815–1912 . . . 14

CHAPTER III
THE CAUSES OF EMIGRATION 38

CHAPTER IV
UNASSISTED AND ASSISTED EMIGRATION . . 68

CHAPTER V
THE TRANSPORT OF EMIGRANTS . . . 101

CHAPTER VI
IMMIGRATION RESTRICTIONS 131

CHAPTER VII
THE RECEPTION OF IMMIGRANTS . . . 158

CHAPTER VIII
THE DESTINATION OF BRITISH EMIGRANTS . 176

CONTENTS

CHAPTER IX
LAND SYSTEMS AFFECTING THE IMMIGRANT IN NORTH AMERICA 197

CHAPTER X
COLONISATION SCHEMES 227

CHAPTER XI
THE EMIGRATION OF WOMEN 255

CHAPTER XII
THE EMIGRATION OF CHILDREN . . . 272

CHAPTER XIII
THE ECONOMIC AND SOCIAL VALUE OF EMIGRATION AND IMMIGRATION 295

CHAPTER XIV
PROBLEMS OF EMIGRATION 327

APPENDIX I
STATISTICAL TABLES RELATING TO EMIGRATION 344

APPENDIX II
BIBLIOGRAPHY 356

INDEX 379

SUMMARY

Chapter I. Preliminary Survey, 1763–1815

Effects of Treaty of Peace on emigration, *p.* 1. Volume of early emigration from United Kingdom, *p.* 2. Loyalist migration to Nova Scotia and Canada, *p.* 5. Glengarry emigrants, *p.* 6. Lord Selkirk's emigrants, *p.* 8. Colonel Talbot's emigrants, *p.* 11. Effects of Napoleonic wars on emigration, *p.* 12.

Chapter II. Historical Survey, 1815–1912

Outline of movement during period 1815–1912, *p.* 14. Sources of information respecting emigration, *p.* 16. The Select Committee of Emigration, 1826–7, *p.* 16. Parliamentary grants in aid of Emigration, *p.* 19. E. G. Wakefield's theories, *p.* 20. Lord Durham's enquiry in 1838, *p.* 22. The Great Famine in Ireland, *p.* 25. The Colonial Land and Emigration Commissioners, *p.* 25. Canadian schemes, *p.* 27. The Emigrants' Information Office, *p.* 29. Sir H. Rider Haggard's proposals, *p.* 30. The work of emigration societies, *p.* 32. The Poor Law Commission, *p.* 34. Mr. Burns and the Imperial Conference of 1911, *p.* 35.

Chapter III. The Causes of Emigration

Growth of population contrasted with growth of emigration, *p.* 38. Distress in Ireland, *p.* 40; Scotland, *p.* 40; England, *p.* 41. The consolidation movement, *p.* 42. The change from arable to pasture land, p. 44. Depopulation in Scotland, *p.* 45. The unsatisfactory lot of the farm-hand, *p.* 46. The recurring agricultural depressions, *p.* 47. The potato crop and Irish emigration, *p.* 52. The Industrial Revolution, *p.* 53. The case of the weavers, *p.* 54. The introduction of steam-power, *p.* 56. The growth of foreign industrial competition between 1836 and 1845, *p.* 57. The question of artisan emigration, *p.* 57. The Stockport operatives, *p.* 58. Distress in Paisley, *p.* 59. The ribbon weavers of Coventry, *p.* 59. The depression of 1886, *p.* 59. Recent emigration classified, *p.* 60. The work of inducing emigration, *p.* 61. Feudal changes: their effects on emigration, *p.* 64. Prepaid passages, *p.* 65. Atlantic rate wars, *p.* 65. Industrial conditions in the country of reception, *p.* 67.

x   A HISTORY OF EMIGRATION

CHAPTER IV. UNASSISTED AND ASSISTED EMIGRATION

Unassisted emigrants outnumber the assisted, *p.* 68. The proofs we have that this is so, *p.* 69. Assistance available in early times, *p.* 69. Prepaid passages, *p.* 70. The practice of transporting redemptioners, *p.* 71. Philanthropic assistance, *p.* 72. Aid provided by landlords to ejected tenants, *p.* 72. The movement set on foot by Baroness Burdett Coutts, *p.* 72. Mr. Tuke's enterprise : followed by that of Lady Gordon Cathcart and Mr. Rankin, *p.* 73. The work of the Charity Organisation Society, *p.* 76. The East End Emigration Fund, *p.* 76. The Church Army, *p.* 76. The Self-Help Society, *p.* 77. The Salvation Army, *p.* 79. Other help provided by minor philanthropic agencies, *p.* 79. The effect of the Dominion Land Act on charitable assistance, *p.* 80. The work of trade unions, *p.* 80. Governmental assistance, *p.* 85. The emigration votes of 1819, 1821, and 1825, *p.* 80. The Poor Law Commission of 1832, *p.* 86. The Union Chargeability Act of 1865, *p.* 87. The Further Amending Act of 1849, *p.* 92. County Councils, *p.* 94. The Purchase of Land Act, 1891, *p.* 96. The Unemployed Workmen Act, 1905, *p.* 97. The Dominion expenditure, *p.* 99.

CHAPTER V. THE TRANSPORT OF EMIGRANTS

Absence of legislation controlling Atlantic passenger traffic, *p.* 101. Result of increase in outflow, *p.* 102. The first passenger Act passed in 1803, in the face of much opposition, *p.* 102. The Act often evaded, *p.* 103. Amended Acts passed in 1823 and 1825, *p.* 103. Outcry against the legislation resulted in its repeal, *p.* 104. The uncontrolled passages : the hardships they imposed on the emigrants, *p.* 104. A new Act enforced in 1828, *p.* 105. The aim of the British Passenger Acts compared with that of the United States Acts, *p.* 106. The appointment of the Colonial Land and Emigration Commissioners, *p.* 109. The Royal Commission of 1851, *p.* 114. The experiences of Mr. Vere Foster, p. 116. The troubles incidental to embarking and landing, *p.* 117. The emigrant staff of inspectors at Liverpool; much overworked, *p.* 118. Castle Garden at New York, *p.* 118. New York legislation in 1855, *p.* 118. The prevalency of shipwrecks : the responsibility of shipowners on these occasions, *p.* 119. The case of the *Robert Isaacs*, *p.* 120. The change from sail to steam, *p.* 120. The position of Atlantic passenger transport in 1860, *p.* 122. The Merchant Shipping Act of 1894 and 1906, *p.* 123. The Atlantic journey to-day, *p.* 126.

CONTENTS

Chapter VI. Immigration Restrictions

Preliminary survey, *p.* 131. The first measure of restriction: passed by New York State, 1824, *p.* 132. Abuses which arose as a consequence of the measure, *p.* 133. The introduction of a Head-Tax in 1832, *p.* 134. How the tax was expended, *p.* 134. The drawbacks to this legislation, *p.* 134. Appointment of the first board of Immigration Commissioners of the State of New York, *p.* 135. Their early decrees, *p.* 136. Seasonal taxes introduced in Canada, 1848, *p.* 136. Constant changes in the restriction code of Canada, *p.* 137. Arrangements of Ontario for attracting population, *p.* 138. Decision of the Supreme Court of the United States affecting restriction, *p.* 138. The action of the steamship companies, *p.* 138. Final arrangements between the two bodies, *p.* 139. Current United States restrictions, *p.* 140. Regulations drawn up by the Commissioners of Immigration, *p.* 141. Contract labour, *p.* 144. Paupers not welcome, *p.* 146. Weaknesses of the immigration laws, *p.* 148. Effect of such weaknesses on the community, *p.* 148. Current restrictive measures of Canada, *p.* 150. Spirit in which the measures were and are enforced, *p.* 156. The future of the restrictive policy, *p.* 157.

Chapter VII. The Reception of Immigrants

Early information is wanting, *p.* 158. The available sources, *p.* 158. Reasons for supposing that immigrants between 1783 and 1820 were comfortably settled, *p.* 158. Those arriving after 1820, not so fortunate, *p.* 159. The hardships of the sea-passage, the cause of much suffering after landing, *p.* 160. Outbreak of cholera in Lower Canada in 1832, *p.* 160. The executive government of Canada established a temporary quarantine station in the same year, *p.* 160. The temporary hospital became a permanent institution where diseased newcomers were isolated, *p.* 161. The present system of Marine hospitals in Canada, *p.* 161. People suffering from certain curable complaints are detained for treatment: the steamship companies being financially responsible, *p.* 162. The New York Commissioners built a detention hospital at Ward's Island in 1847, *p.* 162. Provision now afforded at Hoffman and Swinburne Islands, *p.* 162. The work of the Bureau of Labour in New York, *p.* 163. The trials endured by immigrants on landing, *p.* 165. The appointment of Canadian officials to check the abuses of crimps and runners, *p.* 164. Arrangements of to-day in connection with disembarking, *p.* 165. The efforts made officially to disperse immigrants throughout the less-populated areas, *p.* 165. Free inland passages given in Canada and the United States, p. 166. The institution of information and employment bureaux, *p.* 166. Their management, *p.* 166. Comforts afforded to incoming settlers, *p.* 166. Fraudulent use of free inland tickets leads to their abolition, *p.* 167. Political grounds for giving no such assistance now, *p.* 167. Crown Lands Department in Ontario and farm vacancies, *p.* 168. Canvassers appointed by the Dominion Government to introduce workers to employers, *p.* 168. The work of charitable societies, *p.* 169. The assistance they have given when an immigrant has been landed at wrong port or shipwrecked, *p.* 170. Their work to-day contrasted with formerly, *p.* 170. The British Welcome League, *p.* 171. The Salvation Army, *p.* 171. The Church Army, *p.* 171. The Imperial Home Reunion Association, *p.* 171. Canada's plans for popularising agriculture, *p.* 173. Experimental farms, *p.* 173. Agricultural colleges, *p.* 174. Demonstration farms of the Canadian Pacific Railway, *p.* 175.

CHAPTER VIII. THE DESTINATION OF IMMIGRANTS

Preference shown in early times for the United States, *p.* 176. Reasons for this preference due to the advanced state of the Republic as compared with Canada, *p.* 177. Activity in the States but apathy in the British provinces, *p.* 177. Lord Durham's account of the two countries, *p.* 177. Land surveys and grants in the United States far more satisfactory than in Canada, *p.* 179. Conditions of the coinage, *p.* 180. Lack of ready money in Canada, *p.* 179. The tendencies of the Artificer's Acts, *p.* 179. Destination of Irishmen, *p.* 183. A change of preference in destination has gradually appeared, *p.* 183. The phenomenal progress of Canada within recent years, *p.* 184. Its climate, lands, and transport facilities for producing wheat, *p.* 185. Exodus from the United States into the Dominion, *p.* 185. The growth of settled areas in North America, *p.* 188. The work of the new arrival as compared with the older inhabitant, *p.* 195.

CHAPTER IX. LAND SYSTEMS AFFECTING THE IMMIGRANTS IN NORTH AMERICA

Early grants of land were made in a reckless manner, *p.* 197. The consequences resulting from such a policy, *p.* 197. Anxious to reduce the National Debt, the United States entered on a plan of selling the free lands at a reasonable price, *p.* 198. Revised conditions of sale enforced by Congress, 1800, *p.* 198. The

CONTENTS

Graduation Act, 1854, *p*. 200. Lands held for special purposes, *p*. 200. Treatment of resident Indians, *p*. 201. The Pre-Emption Acts: their history, *p*. 202. The Homestead Act, 1862, *p*. 203. The benefits following the United States land policies, *p*. 203. The Timber Culture and similar Acts, *p*. 204. Land available in the United States at the present time: methods of obtaining it, *p*. 205. The various railroad holdings, *p*. 205. Settlers in the United States from the United Kingdom, numerous, *p*. 207. Early forms of Land Tenure in British North America, *p*. 208. The work of Governors Murray and Carleton, *p*. 209. Appointment of an Executive Council at York, *p*. 212. The Crown Reserves and the Canada Company, *p*. 214. Mr. Richards' tour of inspection, *p*. 218. Free grants discontinued in 1832, *p*. 218. Lord Durham's report on Canadian land systems, *p*. 219. The practices of the jobbers, *p*. 219. Provisional enactments in favour of Ontario, *p*. 221. The Public Lands of the Dominion Act, 1872, *p*. 221. Settlement clauses, *p*. 222. Land available in Canada: and methods of obtaining it, *p*. 222. The Dominion Lands Act, *p*. 224. The growth of land companies, *p*. 225. Figures relating to land sales in Canada, *p*. 226.

CHAPTER X. COLONISATION SCHEMES

Lieutenant-Colonel Cockburn's colony of disbanded soldiers, *p*. 227. Mr. Vansittart's South African settlement, *p*. 228. Peter Robinson's settlement in Canada, *p*. 229. The Swan River scheme, *p*. 232. Edward Gibbon Wakefield's theories, *p*. 233. The South Australian Act of 1834, *p*. 233. Fielding's successful settlement in New Zealand, *p*. 234. Father Nugent and Mr. Sweetman's unsatisfactory operations in the United States, *p*. 235. Lady Gordon Cathcart's settlement in Canada, *p*. 236. Mr. Rankin's colony, *p*. 238. The Wolseley Settlement in Cape Colony, *p*. 238. The Crofters' Colonisation Scheme of 1888–9, *p*. 240. The Barr Colony, *p*. 243. Sir H. Rider Haggard's recommendations, *p*. 244. The recent schemes of Sir Thomas Shaughnessy, *p*. 247. The relative merits of different fields for colonisation purposes, *p*. 248. The reason for so many failures in the past, *p*. 251.

CHAPTER XI. THE EMIGRATION OF WOMEN

Women emigrants are of two classes: the escorted and the unescorted, *p*. 255. Special arrangements for the latter class, *p*. 255. The London Female Emigration Society: the first to

A HISTORY OF EMIGRATION

safeguard women's interests, *p.* 255. The Irish Poor Law unions, *p.* 256. Their action to lessen the disproportion between the sexes, *p.* 256. The work of the Colonial Land and Emigration Commissioners, in connection with women emigrants, *p.* 256. The British Ladies' Emigration Society, *p.* 257. Miss Rye and Miss Lewis, *p.* 257. Mr. Vere Foster's parties, p. 257. More sympathy attracted to the women's cause in 1880, *p.* 258. Inception of many small societies working solely for women and girls, p. 258. The British Women's Emigration Association, *p.* 258. Its volume of business, *p.* 259. The classes it assists, *p.* 259. Its loan fund, *p.* 260. Its emigration routine, *p.* 261. Other societies at home, *p.* 262. Institutions in Canada, *p.* 263. Domestic service, *p.* 264. Milliners, dressmakers, etc., *p.* 266. Openings for the better class women: nurses, teachers, *p.* 266. The value of emigration, specially referring to women and girls, *p.* 268.

CHAPTER XII. THE EMIGRATION OF CHILDREN

The employment of pauper children in factories, *p.* 272. Abuses in the system led to its partial abolition, *p.* 272. Emigration turned to in place of factory employment, *p.* 273. With an increased population, other children also emigrated in considerable numbers, *p.* 273. The sufferings of child-emigrants, *p.* 274. Children first openly emigrated in 1830, *p.* 274. The emigration of girls to Australia in 1848, *p.* 275. The London Ragged Union sent boys and girls to Australia also in 1848, *p.* 275. At this time, the Colonial authorities showed anxiety to receive them, *p.* 275. The Central authorities, at home, viewed the exodus with disfavour and forbade it, *p.* 276. Many Boards of Guardians continued the practice illegally, *p.* 276. The enterprise of Miss Rye and Miss Macpherson, *p.* 278. The Doyle enquiry, *p.* 279. The Local Government Board, in 1883, once more sanctioned child-emigration, *p.* 281. Joint action of the Board and the Canadian authorities in 1888, *p.* 282. Conditions regulating juvenile emigration, *p.* 282. The Act of 1891, *p.* 284. The province of private societies, *p.* 285. Dr. Barnardo's Homes and other societies, *p.* 285. Reception in Canada, *p.* 286. Dominion inspection system, *p.* 287. Reports on the system, *p.* 288. Growing tendency to send children elsewhere than Canada, *p.* 290. Mr. Sedgwick's plans in New Zealand, *p.* 290. The value of juvenile emigration, to the Colony, to the child, to the Mother Country, *p.* 291.

CHAPTER XIII. THE ECONOMIC AND SOCIAL VALUE OF EMIGRATION AND IMMIGRATION

The effect of emigration on an expanding population, *p.* 295. Its effect on decaying industries, *p.* 296. The views of trade unions, *p.* 296. Poor law unions: the benefits they reaped by providing emigration assistance, *p.* 297. Recent emigration from Norwich, *p.* 297. The practice of emigrating the unfit, *p.* 299. The effect of such a process on the remaining population, *p.* 300. Natural emigration takes away surplus population without draining the Mother Country unduly, *p.* 300. This is seen not only in the United Kingdom, but also in France and Germany, *p.* 300. British emigration is largely recruited from the agricultural districts whilst over-population is felt in the towns, *p.* 301. Superabundant labour of to-day: its poor adaptability to the present needs of the Colonies, *p.* 302. The standard of comfort does not necessarily fall when population increases, *p.* 304. Emigration often robs a country of its most useful workers, *p.* 305. Marshall and Farr's estimate of the monetary value of an emigrant, *p.* 306. The money which departing emigrants take with them, *p.* 308. The savings which retired British workers bring back to the United Kingdom, *p.* 310. Emigration aggravates the disproportion between men and women, both at home and in the colonies, *p.* 311. The effect of immigration on North American population, *p.* 311. The extent to which the United States and Canada are indebted to immigration for their population, *p.* 312. The estimate of Dr. Jarvis, *p.* 312. The estimate published by the Census Bureau, *p.* 313. The industrial distribution of immigrants, *p.* 314. Farming, *p.* 314. Mining, *p.* 316. Unskilled and moderately skilled labour, *p.* 316. The work undertaken by the immigrant population, *p.* 316. Fewer demands now than formerly for unskilled immigrants, *p.* 317. The Report of the Ford Investigation Committee, *p.* 317. British workers who temporarily visit the United States, *p.* 318. A great section of the immigrant population is a burden, *p.* 319. Pauperism, illiteracy, sickness, vice, and crime are largely the product of immigration, *p.* 320. The political status of the male foreigner, *p.* 321. Does the individual immigrant gain by quitting the Mother Country ? *p.* 322. Either he or his children usually do, *p.* 322. Hardships attending his life, as reported in early reviews, *p.* 323. More favourable accounts given in contemporary Government publications, *p.* 324. The transmission of vast sums to friends and relations, a sign of success on the part of the immigrant, *p.* 324. The value of emigration at the time of the Irish Famine, *p.* 324. Success, a factor dependent on the individual, often influenced by his conjugal state and the size of his family, *p*. 326.

CHAPTER XIV. PROBLEMS OF EMIGRATION

Can the Homeland afford to spare its emigrants? *p* 327. Those who go to foreign states, a loss, *p*. 327. Those who go to the Colonies help to strengthen the Empire, *p*. 328. But help to drain the Mother Country, *p*. 328. United Kingdom and Germany compared, *p*. 329. Imperial Defence, *p*. 331. Canadian restrictive code, too harsh, *p*. 332. Swiss emigration laws, *p*. 336. Italian laws, *p*. 336. Hungarian laws, *p*. 336. Russian laws, *p*. 336. Belgian laws, *p*. 337. Should the Home Government take an active part in forwarding emigrants and financing their movement? *p*. 337. The respective merits of emigration and colonisation, *p*. 339. Concluding remarks, *p*. 341.

A HISTORY OF EMIGRATION

CHAPTER I

PRELIMINARY SURVEY: 1763–1815

By the Treaty of Peace, which was signed at Paris on February 10th, 1763, Great Britain gained possession of the whole of North America situated east of the Mississippi River, with the exception of the town of New Orleans and the neighbouring district. She thus retained the original thirteen states, and added to her dominions the territory of Canada with all its dependencies and the island of Cape Breton.

For some few years prior to these diplomatic arrangements, the original British Colonies had been welcoming a steady inflow of immigrants from the Mother Country, and, as these maritime states suffered little or no change of administration following on the terms of peace, the human stream continued to find its way into them unaffected by the redistribution of political power between France and England. No authoritative data concerning the statistics of this migratory movement were preserved or even collected, but it is safe to say that its strength was by no means insignificant. A writer in the *Gentleman's Magazine*[1] of 1774 gave figures to show that in the five years 1769–1774 no less than

---

[1] *Op. cit.*, p. 332, vol. 44.

43,720 people sailed from the five Irish ports of Londonderry, Belfast, Newry, Larne and Portrush to various settlements on the Atlantic seaboard. These points of departure were thus responsible for an annual outgoing of at least 8740 souls. Scotland was contributing even more,[1] at this time, to the exodus than was Ireland, whilst England was also furnishing colonists, but to a lesser degree. From these facts it seems fair to assume that the home emigration to the English states across the Atlantic resulted in a displacement of quite twenty thousand souls per annum.

The majority of the settlers within this area were drawn from the Highlands of Scotland and from Ireland generally. The *Scots Magazine* for the years 1771–1775 contains a number of references to the emigration of these early times. " We are informed," runs one paragraph,[2] " that upwards of five hundred souls from Islay and the adjacent islands prepare to migrate next summer to America under the conduct of a gentleman of wealth and merit whose predecessors resided in Islay for many centuries past, and that there is a large colony of the most wealthy and substantial people in Sky making ready to follow the example of the Argathelians in going to the fertile and cheap lands on the other side of the Atlantic Ocean." Another quotation[3] says : " In the beginning of June, 1772, about forty-eight families of poor people from Sutherland arrived at Edinburgh on their way to Greenock in order to imbark[4] for North America. Since that time, we have heard of two other companies, one of a hundred, another of ninety, being on their journey with the same intention. The cause of this emigration they assign to be want of the

---

[1] Vide *Annual Register, Scots Magazine, Gentleman's Magazine*, etc., of a contemporary date.
[2] Vol. 33, p. 325 year 771.   [3] Vol. 34, p. 395, year 1772.
[4] The original spelling is preserved.

PRELIMINARY SURVEY: 1763-1815

means of livelihood at home through the opulent grasiers ingrossing the farms and turning them into pasture." Perhaps a still more interesting quotation is the following:[1] "In the beginning of September, the Lord Advocate represented to the commissioners of the customs, the impropriety of clearing out any vessels from Scotland with emigrants for America: in consequence of which, orders were sent to the several custom-houses injoining[2] them to grant no clearances to any ship for America which had more than the common complement of hands on board." Summarizing the substance of these and other passages of a contemporary date, we may state that, between 1763 and 1775, emigration to the old British Colonies in North America was regularly and constantly practised, that those who joined in the exodus were sometimes in possession of considerable sums of money,[3] that changes in agricultural economy were usually the cause of the unrest, and that the local authorities feared, but with little reason, that the outward streams might eventually depopulate the country.

When Canada and its dependencies were placed under British rule, it became an obvious advantage for a proportion of our colonists to settle within this newly acquired territory. We find, therefore, that the Royal proclamation of 1763 authorised the free granting of land, within this area, to officers and soldiers who had served in the war; it also encouraged British settlers, generally, by providing a General Assembly.

The first to take up military settlements were the Frasers and Montgomeries, who chose Murray Bay as the site of their new homes; this they did in 1763. Farming was their chief occupation, but in 1775 they

---

[1] *Scots Magazine*, vol. 37, 1775, p. 523.
[2] Original spelling.
[3] "425 people sailed from Maryburgh and took at least £6000 with them."—*Scots Magazine*, vol. 35, p. 557.

formed the first battalion of the Royal Highland Emigrants. Speaking of this regiment, the *Scots Magazine* for 1775[1] said : " A ship sailed lately from Greenock for America with shoes, stockings, plaids, belts, etc., for a regiment of emigrants now raising by Government in America to be called the Royal Highland Emigrants. Mr. Murdoch Maclean of Edinburgh is appointed captain in them." Quickly following on the settlement of the Frasers and Montgomeries was that of a party of British colonists who had previously made their home in the New England states ; they encamped at Maugerville, on the banks of the St. John River.[2] A third group of colonists came from Belfast and Londonderry, where they had been engaged in the wool trade. In 1767, the whole of Prince Edward Island was allotted to sixty-seven proprietors, chiefly Scotch, on condition that they should settle European Protestants or British Americans on their domains, a condition which they fulfilled by stocking the land exclusively with Highlanders, most of whom were of Roman Catholic faith, and with Dumfries men.[3] In 1772–4, a number of Yorkshire Methodists settled at Sackville, New Brunswick and Amherst, Nova Scotia.[4] Many other records of colonisation in Canada may be mentioned, but it has been shown, with sufficient insistence, that the inflow from England, Ireland, and especially Scotland, during this period, was of an important nature.

Though Canada had received great numbers of emigrants from the United Kingdom, these were few in comparison with the crowds of men and women who entered this territory after the war broke out. The extent of this complex movement is but imper-

---

[1] Vol. 37, p. 690.

[2] J. D. Rogers, *Historical Geography of the British Colonies* (Lucas), vol. 5, part 3, p. 81.

[3] J. D. Rogers, *Historical Geography of the British Colonies* (Lucas), vol. 5, part, 3, p. 54.   [4] *Ibid.*, p. 57.

PRELIMINARY SURVEY: 1763-1815

fectly understood. It is known, however, that the Loyalist migration into British territory flowed in two great streams, one by sea to Nova Scotia and the other overland to Canada. In this second stream were many Highland families which had only recently settled in the Colony of New York—Macdonells, Chisholms, Grants, Camerons, M'Intyres and Fergusons. Prominent among these Highland families were the Macdonells, who were Roman Catholics from Glengarry in Inverness. In 1773, they had settled in the Mohawk Valley, but, when hostilities began, had flocked to the Loyalist banner; they afterwards went to Ontario and made their new homes in a country to which they gave the name of Glengarry.[1] This site was probably chosen because it bordered on the edge of Lower Canada, and so enabled the Highland Catholics to enter into a bond of religious sympathy with the adjacent French Catholics.

Treating the movement in greater detail, it may be said that the Loyalists first entered the provinces of Nova Scotia and New Brunswick in 1783, and in the following year mustered 28,347 souls. The older settlers of British descent in this area, it may be mentioned in parenthesis, only totalled fourteen thousand. Cape Breton Island attracted, roughly, three thousand settlers, whilst other streams of exiled humanity poured into the peninsula of Gaspé and the seigniory of Sorel. In Upper Canada and the present province of Ontario, the refugees numbered some thirty thousand, but it is probable that this estimate includes at least a small proportion of re-emigrated Loyalists from the maritime provinces, as the total movement was not supposed to exceed forty thousand in all.[2]

The Loyalists were drawn from almost all the original states, but Virginia and New York, their

---
[1] J. Murray Gibbon, *Scots in Canada*, pp. 63-5.
[2] Cf. Sir Charles Lucas, *History of Canada*, 1763-1812, pp. 225-6.

stronghold, provided the main body ; Connecticut also furnished an important element ; whilst Pennsylvania sent a slightly lesser number than Connecticut. From the town of Philadelphia, alone, three thousand people fled when the British Army withdrew.

As a body, the United Loyalists fared badly in the early years of their settlement. Some drifted away, many complained of the long winters, and, had it not been for Government gifts of land, seed, food, clothing and money, their plight would have been disastrous. Later, the more determined ones attained success and " made of New Brunswick and Nova Scotia sound and thriving provinces of the British Empire."[1]

The actual settlement of the Loyalists forms in itself an important chapter of colonial history, but the welcoming of these refugees from the south to the sparsely populated lands of Canada is to be remembered most for its effect on succeeding generations of emigrants. We must remember that, until the arrival of the Loyalists, most of the lands situated more than a few miles from the chief waterways were uninhabited, uncultivated, and more or less forbidding. But the Loyalists went in of sheer necessity and formed, as it were, the nucleus for later settlers. Thus, it is not too much to say that they laid the foundation for the westward extension of Canada as we know it to-day.

In 1785, the men of Glengarry, Canada, induced a party of five hundred Scotch Glengarries to come and join them. In the *Gazette* of Quebec, under the date of September 7th, 1785, their coming was heralded as follows : " Arrived, ship *McDonald*, Captain Robert Stevenson, from Greenock with emigrants, nearly the whole of a parish in the north of Scotland, who emigrated with their priest (the Reverend Alexander Macdonell Scotus) and nineteen cabin passengers,

---

[1] Sir Charles Lucas, *History of Canada*, 1763–1812, p. 224.

PRELIMINARY SURVEY: 1763-1815

together with five hundred and twenty steerage passengers, to better their case." The success of these men of Glengarry induced others to follow. Apparently, Alexander Macdonell conducted a second party to Canada in the year 1791. In 1793, Captain Alexander M'Leod took out forty families of M'Leods, M'Cuaigs, M'Gillwrays and M'Intoshes from Glenelg and placed them on land at Kirkhill, whilst a large party of Camerons from Lochiel, Scotland, settled in 1799 at Lochiel, Canada.[1] Other Highlanders went to Cape Breton Island, to the Niagara district, and to the shores of Lake Erie.

In 1803, Lord Hobart, Secretary of State for the Colonies, wrote from Downing Street to Lieutenant-General Hunter, Lieutenant-Governor of Upper Canada, the following letter:[2]

A body of Highlanders, mostly Macdonells, and partly disbanded soldiers of the Glengarry Fencible Regiment, with their families and immediate connections, are upon the point of quitting their present place of abode, with the design of following into Upper Canada some of their relatives who have already established themselves in that Province.

The merit and services of the Regiment, in which a proportion of these people have served, give them strong claims to any mark of favour and consideration which can consistently be extended to them: and with the encouragement usually afforded in the Province, they would no doubt prove as valuable settlers as their connections now residing in the District of Glengarry of whose industry and general good conduct very favourable representations have been received here.

Government has been apprised of the situation and disposition of the families before described by Mr. Macdonell, one of the Ministers of their Church, and formerly Chaplain to the Glengarry Regiment, who possesses considerable influence with the whole body.

He has undertaken, in the event of their absolute deter-

---

[1] J. Murray Gibbon, *Scots in Canada*, p. 70.
[2] Reprinted in *Scots in Canada*, p. 70.

mination to carry into execution their plan of departure, to embark with them and direct their course to Canada.

In case of their arrival within your Government, I am commanded by His Majesty to authorise you to grant in the usual manner a tract of the unappropriated Crown lands in any part of the Province where they may wish to fix, in the proportion of 1200 acres to Mr. Macdonell, and two hundred acres to every family he may introduce into the Colony.

The Highlanders in question, arrived in due course, and were settled close to the lands taken by their kinsmen in 1783 and 1785.

Among the earliest organisers of colonisation schemes in the nineteenth century may be placed Lord Selkirk. This Scotchman banded together a number of thrifty farmers of his own race who had given up their highland territories, and escorted them to Prince Edward Island, where they were comfortably located on a settlement vacated by the French. The Government freely placed tracts of land at their disposal, but proffered no financial support. What money was necessary came either from Lord Selkirk or was derived from sales, held in the Old Country, of the settlers' stock.[1]

Three vessels were chartered to carry the eight hundred odd colonists across the Altantic, and these reached their destination on the 7th, 9th, and 27th of August, 1803. Selkirk took passage in one of the regular liners, and arrived in the island shortly after the first party had landed. The following account,[2] written by himself, is interesting in that it gives a capital insight into the early life of his settlers:

I lost no time in proceeding to the spot, where I found that the people had already lodged themselves in temporary wigwams, constructed after the fashion of the Indians, by

---

[1] *Edinburgh Review*, vol. 7, pp. 180-90.
[2] Observations on the Present State of the Highlands of Scotland, 1805. The passage has been reprinted recently in *Scots in Canada*, p. 51, etc.

setting up a number of poles in a conical fashion, tied together at top, and covered with boughs of trees.

The settlers had spread themselves along the shore for the distance of about half a mile, upon the site of an old French village, which had been destroyed and abandoned after the capture of the island by the British forces in 1758. The land, which had formerly been cleared of wood, was overgrown again with thickets of young trees, interspersed with grassy glades. I arrived at the place late in the evening, and it had then a very striking appearance. Each family had kindled a large fire near their wigwams, and round these were assembled groups of figures, whose peculiar national dress added to the singularity of the scene.

Provisions, adequate to the whole demand, were purchased by an agent; he procured some cattle for beef in distant parts of the island, and also a large quantity of potatoes, which were brought by water carriage into the centre of the settlement, and each family received their share within a short distance of their own residence.

To obviate the terrors which the woods were calculated to inspire, the settlement was not dispersed, as those of the Americans usually are, over a large tract of country, but concentrated within a moderate space. The lots were laid out in such a manner that there were generally four or five families and sometimes more, who built their houses in a little knot together; the distance between the adjacent hamlets seldom exceeded a mile. Each of them was inhabited by persons nearly related, who sometimes carried on their work in common, or, at least, were always at hand to come to each other's assistance.

The settlers had every inducement to vigorous exertion from the nature of their tenures. They were allowed to purchase in fee simple, and to a certain extent on credit; from fifty to one hundred acres were allotted to each family at a very moderate price, but none was given gratuitously. To accommodate those who had no superfluity of capital, they were not required to pay the price in full till the third or fourth year of their possession.

Selkirk remained in the colony for a month, and then set himself the task of exploring the inland tracts of Upper Canada. Twelve months later he returned and made the following report:[1]

I found the settlers engaged in securing the harvest which their industry had procured. They had a small proportion of grain of various kinds, but potatoes were the principal crop; these were of excellent quality and would have been alone sufficient for the entire support of the settlement. . . . The extent of land in cultivation at the different hamlets I found to be in the general proportion of two acres or thereabouts to each able working hand; in many cases from three to four. Several boats had also been built, by means of which a considerable supply of fish had been obtained, and formed no trifling addition to the stock of provisions. Thus, in little more than a year, one year from the date of their landing on the island, had these people made themselves independent of any supply that did not arise from their own labour.

So great was the success of Selkirk's first attempt at colonisation that he made plans for a second scheme in 1811. In this year he leased lands from the Hudson's Bay Company, some two thousand square miles in extent, and stretching from Manitoba to Minnesota. To this colony many shiploads of dispossessed Scotch farmers were sent, but neither he nor his officers fully appreciated the difficulties which were to confront them. Selkirk did not seem to realise that the establishment of a colony in the then unknown West was quite a different matter to organising an encampment on the accessible shores of Prince Edward Island. From the very outset, the second expedition proved disastrous. Not only were the colonists improperly equipped for carrying on agricultural pursuits in such remote parts, but the position of their settlement brought them into conflict with the North-West traders. The newly acquired farmlands, it must be explained, lay across the trading routes leading into the interior and, therefore, constituted a menace to the hunting expeditions of the half-breeds. As a

---
[1] Quoted from *Scots in Canada*, pp. 54, 55.

PRELIMINARY SURVEY: 1763-1815

consequence, these latter determined to rid the locality of the new-comers, which they did in 1815 by pillaging and burning the farms belonging to Selkirk's tenantry. More than a half of the sufferers, however, took up settlements in other parts of the country, chiefly around St. Thomas and London in Ontario, but their ultimate fate is uncertain.

Closely following the schemes of Selkirk came that of Colonel Talbot, a member of the Lieutenant-Governor's staff in Canada. From various parts of the United Kingdom, but specially from Scotland, he collected some two thousand men, women and children, probably during the year 1813, and settled them at Port Talbot on Lake Erie. To this nucleus of settlers he annually added other emigrants, until in 1823 it was reported that he had under his control no less than twelve thousand souls. The financial burden of his undertaking was probably borne jointly by the British Government and the Canadian Legislature, the former finding the passage money, and the latter providing the food supplies. On this matter, however, some uncertainty exists, but it is recognised that his followers were too poor to provide for themselves, whilst Colonel Talbot, we know, received payment for his services. As to the success of the scheme, the Report says that the people who emigrated were of the poorest description, but, when last heard of, were as independent and contented a band of yeomanry as any in the world.[1]

---

[1] The following is interesting in that it is a copy of a leaflet which was handed to each of Talbot's original settlers :—
"On application made to the superintendent of the land granting department of the district in which he proposes to settle, the colonist will obtain a ticket of location, for a certain quantity of land; furnished with this, his first care ought to be to select a proper situation for his house. This should be placed, as near as may be, to the public road on which his lot abuts, and contiguous, if possible, to a spring or run of water. Having chosen his spot, he then sets about clearing a sufficient space to erect his house on, taking care to cut down all the large trees within the distance of at least 100 ft. The dimensions of the house are generally 20 ft. by 18 ft., and the timber used in constructing the walls, consisting of the rough stems of trees cut into those

Selkirk and Talbot had few contemporary imitators, for between 1806 and 1815 Napoleon was harassing Europe, and men found employment in connection with military and transport operations, not needing, for the time, the possibilities which a colonial life offered them.

The period of 1783-1815 is important, in that it paved the way for the movement which was to assume such notable proportions during the nineteenth and twentieth centuries. Without the inrush of Loyalist settlers to Canada in the closing years of the eighteenth century, the map of British North America, to-day, would probably present a very different aspect. It was these sturdy men and women who broke down the barriers of forests and wildernesses which seemed impenetrable, and opened the course for later settlement. In comparison with the volume of the present outflow, the emigrants of this early period were, of course, insignificant in numbers, but they were pioneers and made history and must be valued accordingly. Their actual labours, commercial and agricultural, were of no great moment, for they had many difficulties with which to contend. In Lower Canada, financial conditions were oppressive: land tenure, everywhere, bred discontent, whilst discord with the rebel neighbours of the south proved a constant source of danger.

---

lengths, is not to exceed 2 ft. in diameter; the height of the roof is commonly about 13 ft., which affords a ground-room and one overhead; the house is roofed in with shingles (a sort of wooden tiles) split out of the oak, chestnut, or pine timber; a door, windows, and an aperture for the chimney at one end, are next cut out of the walls, the spaces between the logs being filled up with split wood, and afterwards plastered both inside and out with clay and mortar, which renders it perfectly warm. When once the necessary space for the house is cleared and the logs for the walls collected on the spot, the expense and labour of the settler in erecting his habitation is a mere trifle; it being an established custom among the neighbouring settlers to give their assistance in the raising of it; and the whole is performed in a few hours. The settler having now a house over his head commences clearing a sufficient quantity of land to raise the annual supply of provisions required for his family."

Major-General T. Bland Strange, in the *United Service Magazine*, May, 1903, pp. 151-2, writes:

The British effort at military colonisation, after the conquest by Wolfe, proved futile. The Fraser Highlanders were disbanded and settled at Murray Bay, on the St. Lawrence, but as no Scotch lassies were provided, they married the lively little French girls, whose creed, language, and nationality they adopted; the only traces of their Highland descent are their names and red hair. At the close of the Peninsular War, individual naval and military officers settled in what was called Upper Canada, but no systematic effort was made to encourage the settlement of the rank and file—quite the contrary, from that day to this, everything has been done to discourage it. Under the administration of Mr. Cardwell, the garrisons were withdrawn from all the Colonies suitable for settlement by white soldiers. The old Royal Canadian Rifles, composed of Volunteers from various British regiments, were struck off the Army list, as also the old Cape Mounted Rifles, and the emigration of officers was checked by a Royal warrant subjecting them to loss of pension, should they elect to serve under any Colonial Government. At the close of the Crimean War, the only soldiers assisted to emigrate, and given grants of land, were the German Legion whom we settled in South Africa, though they never fired a shot for us; some of their descendants probably fought against us in the late war. Our own British-born soldiers of the Crimean War and Indian Mutiny were, in many cases, left to die in the workhouse, as the shorter periods of service then introduced deprived them of the right of pension. At the close of these wars, the reductions in our arsenals and dockyards drove large numbers of mechanics, some of whom were ex-soldiers and sailors, with their families to the United States, whose industries, especially of war material, largely benefited thereby. According to Lord Charles Beresford something similar is now going on in his constituency at Woolwich.

The earlier settlement by the Pilgrim Fathers was on independent lines, assisted in the Southern States, as later in Australia by the transportation of convicts, sometimes for slight offences, who in many instances became good citizens.

CHAPTER II

HISTORICAL SURVEY: 1815–1912

THOUGH emigration from the United Kingdom to North America had begun on a limited scale in the early part of the seventeenth century[1] and had grown in volume during the eighteenth, no official returns relating to the extent of the exodus were made until 1815. In this year, the great war, in which England had for so long been engaged, terminated, and men turned to emigration as though it were the one panacea for all social ills.[2] In 1815, the outflow to North America stood at 1889 persons; it then grew annually with slight fluctuations until 1852, when the enormous total of 277,134 was reached, an exodus which is, considering the volume of people from which it was drawn,[3] probably without parallel in the history of any civilised country. The years 1846 to 1854, inclusive, were remarkable for their high rate of departures, but, after 1854, a sudden and, with some fluctuations, a continued shrinkage took place until in 1861 the numbers dropped to 62,471, the smallest emigration since 1844. The Crimean War, 1854–6, and the Indian Mutiny, 1857–9, which caused an increased demand for young men in the army and navy, were largely responsible for the falling off in the returns of this period. Between 1861 and 1869 the exodus took an upward tendency, and, in this latter year, acute distress at home made

---

[1] Colonisation Circular, 1877, p. 7.
[2] Cf. J. D. Rogers, *Historical Geography of Canada* (Lucas), p. 67.
[3] Census of 1851. England, Wales, Scotland, and Ireland; population given as 27,309,346.

HISTORICAL SURVEY: 1815-1912

the figures rise to 236,892, and they remained somewhat high until 1873.[1] The middle seventies proved a period of diminished emigration, but the ebb was soon followed by a copious flow, for, in the year 1882, the important total of 349,014 was reached. Recent times have shown somewhat high figures; in fact, for every year since 1903, with the exception of 1908, an exodus to North America of over three hundred thousand has been returned. In 1910, the outward stream numbered 499,669, and, in 1911, 464,330 souls.

The above figures require some qualification. The early records refer almost entirely to men and women of British nationality; the later ones speak of the volume of traffic as carried by the Atlantic transport concerns and so contain an important foreign element. It is thus misleading to make comparisons without duly allowing for this change in the composition of the exodus.[2] A second point to note is that, at the present time, the outward passengers are largely counter-balanced by the inward passengers, but, prior to the sixties, the inward passengers were few compared with the outward. Thus, net emigration to-day is found by subtracting the incoming from the outgoing stream,[3] but net emigration until about the year 1860 was the total outflow with few or no deductions whatever. A third point to note is that the total population of the three kingdoms has grown considerably since the year 1815; it is thus misleading to compare, say, the 277,134 emigrants of the year 1852 with the 499,669 emigrants of 1910 without taking into consideration the gross populations of these two years. Table 5 in Appendix II, which deals with this matter, states that the proportion of emigration to the population was 0·84 per cent between 1853 and 1855, but only 0·39 per cent in the period 1906-

---
[1] Cf. Appendix.   [2] Vide Appendix I, Table 2.
[3] Vide Appendix I, Table 3.

1910. Thus the exodus from the Mother Country was, in reality, more remarkable in the earlier than in the later period.

Of the 983,227 emigrants who left the United Kingdom for all destinations, prior to 1840, 499,899, or more than half, went to British North America; of the remainder, 417,765 went to the United States, and 58,449 to the Australian Colonies, including New Zealand. Since 1834, however, the total annual migration to the United States has always exceeded that proceeding to Canada, but it must be mentioned that when British emigrants as distinct from all emigrants from Britain are considered, it will be found that, on two occasions since 1880, Canada has welcomed more men and women than the United States. This happened in the last two years of the period, 1910 and 1911.

The history of emigration in the nineteenth and twentieth century may be traced from the Government reports and papers which have, from time to time, been published. The first of these documents, which was devoted solely to a consideration of the present subject, was the report of the Select Committee which sat in 1826 to consider emigration from the United Kingdom. From this report we learn that the Government first gave its serious attention to the matter in 1820. In that and the following years many debates were held in both Houses of Parliament to discuss its value as a remedy for the social distress which then existed in the home-country.[1] As a result of these debates, the select committees of 1826 and 1827 were appointed.

The Committee of 1826 reported generally on the evidence placed before it, and stated that there was a greater amount of labouring population in the United Kingdom than could be profitably employed,

---

[1] Cf. Hansard, Parliamentary Debates, Vol. XII, p. 1358; Vol. XIV, p. 1360; Vol. XVI, pp. 142, 227, 475, 653.

HISTORICAL SURVEY: 1815-1912

and that the British Colonies afforded a field where the excess could be disposed of with advantage. The Committee of 1827 entered further into detail and pointed out more specifically the nature and extent of the assistance which it would recommend to be given to emigration from national resources. The Bishop of Limerick, who appeared before the earlier body, said :

> The evil is pressing and immediate. It calls, therefore, for an immediate remedy. Take any system of home relief, it must be gradual in its operation : before it can be brought to bear, the present sufferers will have died off, and others will have supplied their place, but not without a dreadful course of intermediate horrors. Now, Emigration is an instantaneous relief, it is what bleeding would be to an apoplectic patient. The sufferers are at once taken away : and, be it observed, from a country where they are a nuisance and a pest, to a country where they will be a benefit and a blessing. Meantime, so far as displaced tenants are taken away, the landlords, aided by existing laws, and especially by the Act now about to be passed (Sir Henry Parnell's Act), will have it in their power to check the growth of population, somewhat in the same way as, after removing redundant blood, a skilful physician will try to prevent the human frame from generating more than what is requisite for a healthful state.[1]

The Committee called a considerable number of witnesses and repeatedly put the following question to those giving evidence : " Were the Government to advance an indigent man his passage money and provide him with a homestead, could he be expected to repay the loan at the rate of £5 per annum, commencing after his fifth year of residence ? " Most witnesses replied in the affirmative, with the result that the committees suggested that the Treasury should advance a sum of about ten thousand pounds, with which it was proposed to form a loan fund for emigrants. The essence of this report is contained in the following extract : " Your Committee cannot

---
[1] Page 142 of first Report.

but express their opinion that a more effectual remedy than any temporary palliative is to be found in the removal of that excess of labour by which the condition of the whole labouring classes is deteriorated and degraded. The question of emigration from Ireland is decided by the population itself, and that which remains for the Legislature to decide is, whether it shall be turned to the improvement of the British North American Colonies, or whether it shall be suffered and encouraged to take that which will be and is its inevitable course, to deluge Great Britain with poverty and wretchedness and gradually but certainly to equalise the state of the English and Irish peasantry. Two different rates of wages and two different conditions of the labouring classes cannot permanently co-exist. One of two results appears to be inevitable : the Irish population must be raised towards the standard of the English or the English depressed towards that of the Irish. The question whether an extensive plan of emigration shall or shall not be adopted appears to your Committee to resolve itself into the simple point whether the wheat-fed population of Great Britain shall or shall not be supplanted by the potato-fed population of Ireland ? "

Resulting from the advice contained in this report, a letter was sent to Colonel Cockburn on January 26th, 1827, from Downing Street, stating that His Majesty's Government required him to survey three hundred thousand acres of waste land in Nova Scotia, New Brunswick and Prince Edward Island, and to make preparation for the reception of about ten thousand souls. He was to proceed to these places without delay, to confer with the lieutenant-governors of these provinces, to inspect, personally, the land, and, above all, he was to keep in mind the advantage to be derived from placing new settlements as near to inhabited parts of the country as possible. One

HISTORICAL SURVEY: 1815-1912

month's provisions were actually to be stored at each settlement previous to the arrival of the emigrants. There was one proviso added to these plans. All was to be ready, were the assisted people to proceed, but should their exodus be deferred or abandoned, Colonel Cockburn was to cancel his arrangements.

The projects were abandoned, and Colonel Cockburn was called upon to nullify the arrangements on which he had spent so much labour. The reasons for this change of policy were threefold. Suitable land could not be found of the requisite quantities in the provinces mentioned; coin of the realm was so scarce that it was felt that the emigrants would not be able to repay their indebtedness with anything but produce, which the Government could not undertake to accept, and, finally, there were fears that a man might leave his homestead and journey into the United States and so shirk his liability.

Although the loan was refused by the Treasury on this occasion, grants in aid of emigration were made by Parliament in 1819,[1] 1821, 1823, 1825, and 1827 amounting to £50,000, £68,760, £15,000, £30,000 and £20,480 respectively. In 1834, an Act was passed enabling parishes to mortgage their rates and to spend a sum not exceeding £10 a head on emigration. In the same year emigration agents were placed at various ports of the United Kingdom, and from that time until 1878 sums varying in amount up to £25,000 were voted annually by Parliament for purposes of promoting the removal of indigent people from this country. The money, however, was mostly spent on directing the flow of human beings to Australia.

---

[1] Page 327 of the Report on Agricultural Settlements says that the grant of 1819 does not seem to have been spent. There is, however, ample evidence to show that a sum of £50,000 was spent on the Albany settlers in the year in question. Of this there is abundant though perhaps not official testimony. Surely this expenditure is the grant of 1819.

In 1830, a searching enquiry into the state of the Irish Poor was undertaken by the House of Commons, and the report,[1] which was subsequently communicated to the House of Lords, said, " Emigration, as a remedial measure, is more applicable to Ireland than to any other part of the Empire. The main cause which produces the influx of Irish labourers into Britain is undoubtedly the higher rate of wages which prevails in one island than in the other. Emigration from Great Britain, if effectual as a remedy, must tend to raise the rate of wages in the latter country, and thus to increase the temptation of the immigration (i.e. into England and Scotland) of the Irish labourer. Colonisation from Ireland, on the contrary, by raising the rate of wages in the latter country, diminishes this inducement and lessens the number of Irish labourers in the British market."

From about the year 1830, the views put forward by Mr. E. G. Wakefield[2] grew in popularity. His efforts were directed to the discovery of means whereby capital and labour might be introduced into a colony in such a manner and in such proportions as to lead to its more stable development. He disapproved not only of the form of emigration which was then in vogue, but also of the system of making free grants of colonial lands. Land, he held, should not be given gratuitously, but should be sold and the proceeds used in conveying other emigrants to the colony. The basis of all successful colonization, he once wrote,[3] lies in keeping a certain ratio between the amount of alienated land and the amount of labour available in any colony. If land be given away lavishly, the ratio immediately breaks down, for labourers speedily become landowners and capitalists suffer from an urgent want of labour. When, however, tracts are

---

[1] Report of the Committee appointed to enquire into the state of the Poorer Classes in Ireland and the best means of improving their condition.
[2] Vide *The Art of Colonisation*.   [3] In *The Art of Colonisation*.

sold and the money so obtained is used in conveying further batches of emigrants to the colony, the ratio holds good, for the more the sales, the more the labour which can be introduced by the proceeds of the sales and the more the labour which can find remunerative employment. Obviously, his system demanded that the selling price of real property should be carefully adjusted, from time to time, with the amount of available labour.

The views of Wakefield were carried out in a few of the settlements of the Australian Colonies, and some effect was given to them by the South Australian Act and the Australian Land Act of 1842. But Gibbon Wakefield did more than theorise on questions affecting real property. Before he studied the question of emigration, people had looked upon life in the colonies as socially degrading, and having much in common with penal transportation, but with the spreading of his teachings they grew to consider it a means whereby individuals might improve their position as well as a factor which would strengthen the Empire by the foundation of overseas-dominions.[1]

In 1831, a Government Commission on Emigration was formed and, in the same year, the Commissioners reported that from an annual average of about nine thousand during the first ten years after the Peace, the inflow to Canada had increased in the five years ending with 1831 to an annual average of more than twenty thousand, also that these great multitudes of people had mostly gone out by their own means and disposed of themselves through their own efforts without any serious or lasting inconvenience. The Commissioners did not propose, therefore, to interfere by a direct grant of money with a practice which appeared to thrive so well spontaneously. They recognised, probably, how vast an outlay would be

---
[1] Report of the Committee on Agricultural Settlements in British Colonies, vol. I, 1906, p. 2.

necessary to carry on the business to a corresponding extent through public funds, while it must always have remained to be seen whether any immediate interposition of the Government could have provided for such multifarious bodies so well as individual judgment and energy, stimulated by the sense of self-dependence.

The Commissioners, therefore, contented themselves, in regard to the North American Colonies, with collecting, publishing and diffusing, as widely as possible, correct accounts of prices and wages, and with pointing out the impositions against which emigrants should be most on their guard. This body was dissolved, however, in 1832 and the practical working of its recommendations entrusted to the Colonial Department.[1]

In 1838, Lord Durham held an enquiry into the unrest then existing in Upper and Lower Canada; his observations, together with the views of Gibbon Wakefield and Charles Buller,[2] appeared as a Blue Book in January, 1839. After discussing the differences which gave rise to friction between the French and British inhabitants, the report dealt somewhat fully with the evils encompassing the lot of the emigrant, the want of administration which characterised the action of the Colonial authorities, and the unsatisfactory systems then in vogue of granting land. Durham advised that self-government should be given to Canada, but, in addition to this important recommendation, suggested that emigration to these areas should be made more attractive,[3] that the lands

---

[1] Report to the Secretary of State for the Colonies from the Agent-General for Emigration, April 28, 1838, No. 388, p. 3.

[2] Vide Sir Charles Lucas—Lord Durham's Report, vol. 3, p. 336, etc., and especially page 351, for account of Durham's mission.

[3] " All the gentlemen whose evidence I have last quoted are warm advocates of systematic emigration. I object, along with them, only to such emigration as now takes place without forethought, preparation, method, or system of any kind."—Lord Durham's Report on the Affairs of British North America, vol. 1, p. 189.

should be efficiently surveyed, and that a judicious system of colonisation should be introduced.

Buller complained that though emigration to Canada was more or less unsatisfactory yet people were content to allow the system to continue unchallenged. "This misconception is undoubtedly attributable, in a great degree," he said, " to the circumstance that all evidence obtained on the subject was collected in the country from which the emigrants departed, instead of that at which they arrived. Had the position of the enquiries been reversed, they must have arrived at very different conclusions, and have discovered that no emigration so imperatively demanded the regulating interposition of the Legislature as that for which they specially refused to provide."[1] Buller then went on to point out the trials which beset the emigrant on landing in Canada.[2] It was the duty of the Government, he affirmed, to organise the outflow to North America just as much as that to Australia. There may be a difference in the character and circumstances of the movement to the two regions, he argued, but none so great as to free the former from all interference, while the latter was to a great extent officially regulated.

Buller summarised his views as follows :[3] "The measures which Government have adopted are deplorably defective. They have left untouched some of the chief evils of emigration, and have very incompletely remedied those even against which they were specially directed. Although the safeguards for the emigrant during the passage are increased, and, in many places, enforced, yet there is still no check of any sort whatever over a large proportion of the emigrant vessels.[4] The provisions for the reception

---
[1] Report, p. 225.
[2] Vide Chapter VII. "The Reception of Immigrants."
[3] Report, p. 227.
[4] i.e. those carrying fewer passengers than constitute an emigrants' ship.

of emigrants at Quebec, so far as the Government is concerned, are of the most inefficient and unsatisfactory character : and the poorer classes would have to find their way as they best might to the Upper Provinces, or to the United States, were it not for the operation of societies whose main object is not the advantage of emigrants, but to free the cities of Quebec and Montreal from the intolerable nuisance of a crowd of unemployed, miserable and, too often, diseased persons. The Government agent at Quebec has no power; he has not even any rules for his guidance. At Montreal there has not been any agent for the last two years. The whole extent, therefore, of the Government interference has been to establish in England agents to superintend the enforcement of the provisions of the Passengers' Acts, in respect of the emigrants from some ports, and to maintain an agent in the Province of Lower Canada to observe rather than regulate the emigration into that province.

"I would recommend, therefore, that a specified portion of the produce of the wild-land tax and of the future sales of land and timber should be applied in providing for emigration : a part in furnishing free passage to emigrants of the most desirable age, as far as may be of both sexes in equal numbers, and part in defraying any expenses occasioned by the superintendence of the emigration of those to whom, in conformity with this rule, or from other circumstances, a free passage cannot be offered.

"The whole emigration from the United Kingdom should be so far placed under the superintendence of Government that emigrants conveyed at the public expense should necessarily proceed in vessels chartered and regulated by the Government, and that all persons willing to pay for their own passage should be entitled to proceed in vessels so chartered and regulated at a cost for the passage not exceeding the charge in private vessels. Proper means of shelter and transport should

HISTORICAL SURVEY: 1815-1912

be provided at the different ports in the Colonies to which emigrants proceed; and they should be forwarded to the place where they can obtain employment under the direction of responsible agents acting under central authority."

When, in 1845, the Great Famine overtook Ireland with such disastrous results, a Select Committee was appointed to consider the means by which colonisation might be employed to alleviate the sufferings which were then existing in that country. After examining the causes which had brought about the crisis, the Committee directed its attentions to an enquiry into the following matters:

1. The capacity which certain Colonies possessed for absorbing European labour.
2. The extent to which a supply of labour might be safely introduced into the various Colonies.
3. The effect of an increased supply of emigrant labour on the productiveness and value of Colonial land.
4. The effect which colonisation would probably produce on the investment of British capital within the colony to which such colonisation might be directed.
5. The effect which might be anticipated by the promotion or encouragement of works of undisputed usefulness, such as the railroads projected in British North America.
6. The effect of an augmented population in the British Colonies, not only in increasing their wealth, their agricultural, mineral and commercial resources, but in adding to their strength and means of defence and thus consolidating and securing the power of the Empire.

Unfortunately, little or no good came of the enquiry. Charitable societies continued to do their utmost to alleviate the sufferings of the afflicted people, but governmental action was in no wise accelerated as a result of the enquiry.

In consequence of the representations made by Lord Durham, the Colonial Land and Emigration Department was founded in 1840. The principal functions of this body were to collect and diffuse statistical information pertaining to the Colonies, to effect sales of colonial lands in Australia, to promote by the proceeds of such sales emigration to the Colonies in which the sales had occurred, to superintend, generally, all emigration movements connected with this country and its dependencies, and, lastly, to carry into execution the Passengers' Acts.[1]

The operations of the Board were fluctuating, but between 1847 and 1869 they sent out 339,338 emigrants at a cost of £4,864,000 of which £532,000 was provided by those taking part in the exodus or their friends, and the rest by colonial funds. The arrangements were mostly concerned with Australia.

In their thirty-third report, under the date of April 30th, 1873, the Chief Commissioner wrote: "My Lord, We have the honour to submit to your Lordship our Report on Emigration for the year 1872. As the administration of the Passengers' Act has been entrusted by the Act of last session (35 and 36 Vict. c. 73) to the Board of Trade, this is the last report we shall have to make to the Secretary of State on emigration from this country." Other functions which they performed had been gradually taken from them as the Colonies, one by one, became self-governing. After the Act of 1872 their sole duties consisted in controlling the movement of coolie labour, and, when each commissioner retired, his post was allowed to lapse. The last commissioner withdrew in 1878. Between 1873 and 1877 a Colonisation Circular was published annually.

---

[1] Lord John Russell's instructions to the Emigration Commissioners, January 14th, 1840 (Govmt. paper, No. 35) :—

" In your capacity of a General Board for the sale of lands and for promoting emigration, your duties may be conveniently arranged under the four following heads : First, the collection and diffusion of accurate statistical knowledge ; secondly, the sale in this country of waste-lands in the colonies ; thirdly, the application of the proceeds of such sales towards the removal of emigrants ; and, fourthly, the rendering of periodical accounts, both pecuniary and statistical, of your administration of this trust."

HISTORICAL SURVEY: 1815-1912

In 1880, the Canadian authorities approached the Home Government with a colonisation scheme by which the latter should advance moneys, about £80 per family, for meeting expenses incurred in transporting and settling poor families from Ireland on plots situated in the North-West Provinces. The Canadian Government was to give each settler 160 acres of land, upon which the advance was to be secured by a first charge, but they were to undertake no guarantee for the repayment of such advance. It was intended to carry out the scheme through a commission or association. These proposals were submitted to the Irish authorities, who took no action in the matter.[1] The reasons for allowing the proposal to lapse were never definitely stated, but it may be conjectured that the home authorities were dissatisfied, first, with the guarantees, and, secondly, with the refusal of the Canadian officials to undertake the task of collecting the repayments.

In 1883, the North-West Land Company of Canada empowered Sir George Stephen to place another proposal before the Imperial Parliament. The basis of this scheme was as follows : the Government was to lend the company a million pounds for ten years, free of interest, and in consideration of this loan the company would undertake to remove ten thousand families, say fifty thousand people, from the west of Ireland and settle them in the north-west of Canada.

In the ordinary way the Canadian Government was prepared to give each head of a family 160 acres of land, and the Company proposed to supply him with a house, a cow, implements and everything necessary to ensure a fair start, even to providing sufficient ploughing and seeding for the first year's crop. The Company also agreed to meet all expenditure incidental to the removal and settlement of the emigrants. It was thus submitted that the cost to

---
[1] Report on Colonisation, 1891, Appendix, p. 45, para. 1.

the Home Government would only be the interest on £100 for ten years, say, at the rate of 2½ per cent, £25 per family. The emigrants themselves, however, were to be called upon to pay certain moderate charges to the Company. This scheme received the warm support of the Colonial Office and the Irish Government, though the latter made two requests which were approved by the Treasury, viz. (*a*) that the emigrants should be drawn in entire families from the congested districts only, and (*b*) that the holding of each emigrating family should be consolidated with a neighbouring holding.

The proposal, it must be added, was abandoned because the Treasury thought it necessary to stipulate that the Dominion Government should make itself responsible for recovering the advances from the settlers, both principal and interest, a burden which the Canadian authorities declined to undertake on political grounds.[1] Other schemes of emigration were suggested from time to time, but all suffered rejection, as the Home Government was temporarily averse to considering any which returned less than 3⅛ per cent interest on the capital involved, and in which they were not relieved of all financial liability.

The prolonged depression amongst the working classes which lasted between 1884 and 1886, however, forced the Government to change its views, and Mr. Rathbone[2] wrote:[3] "In the autumn of 1887 Lord Lothian asked the land companies if they would renew their proposals; but they declined to do so, stating that the circumstances had altered (though in what way did not appear) and the scheme which was eventually agreed upon was far less favourable to the Government, in that there was no guarantee by the companies for repayment even of the capital."

---

[1] Report on Colonisation, 1891, Appendix, p. 45, para. 2.
[2] A member of the Colonisation Committee of 1891.
[3] Report on Colonisation, 1891, Appendix, p. 46, para. 3.

HISTORICAL SURVEY: 1815–1912

The scheme to which Mr. Rathbone referred was the Crofters' Colonisation Scheme of 1888 and 1889.

As a result of numerous representations made to the Government by philanthropists who viewed emigration with favour, the Emigrants' Information Office was opened in October, 1886. From its inception this Institution has been placed under the control of the Colonial Office. It is subsidised by Government but managed by a voluntary unpaid committee.[1] The committee included Members of Parliament, philanthropists and representatives of the working classes. The Secretary of State for the Colonies is nominally President of the committee, but does not actually preside. He nominates the members of the committee, and all points on which any serious doubt arises are referred for his decision, but the expenditure of the Parliamentary grant and the management and working of the office are left to the discretion of the committee.

The Government at the outset allowed an annual sum of £650 to cover rent of rooms and all office expenses, in addition to free printing and postage. After the report of the Colonisation Committee in 1891 the sum was raised to £1000 and the grant became subsequently increased to £1500.

Originally the scope of the office was confined to the British Colonies and to those Colonies, only, which are outside the tropics, and are thus fields of emigration in the ordinary sense. It was found necessary, however, to widen its sphere and to give information—though more limited in extent—not only as to certain tropical colonies, but also, from time to time, concerning various foreign countries; and especially it has been found necessary to issue warnings in cases where, as, for example, in the case of Brazil, it has seemed desirable to discourage emigration from the Mother Country.

---

[1] The Chairman, who is a member of the Colonial Office, is paid.

In regard to foreign countries, the Committee derives its information almost entirely through the Foreign Office and His Majesty's representatives abroad. In regard to the British Colonies, information is supplied partly by official, partly by unofficial sources.

In June and July of the year 1889 a Select Committee of the House of Commons sat to " inquire into various schemes which have been proposed to Her Majesty's Government in order to facilitate emigration from the congested districts of the United Kingdom to the British Colonies or elsewhere; to examine into the results of any schemes which have received practical trial in recent years; and to report generally whether, in their opinion, it is desirable that further facilities should be given to promote emigration; and, if so, upon the means by and the conditions under which such emigration can best be carried out, and the quarters to which it can most advantageously be directed."[1] After having examined nine witnesses the following interim report was issued towards the end of the month of July : " Your Committee are of opinion that at this late period of the Session it will not be in their power to conclude their investigations; they have therefore agreed to report the evidence, already taken, to the House, and to recommend that a committee on the same subject should be appointed early in the next Session of Parliament."[2] The Committee again sat in 1890, and for a third time in 1891. It was in the latter year that the following summary of their conclusions was issued :

(a) Your Committee have no grounds for thinking that the present condition of the United Kingdom generally calls for any general scheme of state-organised colonisation or emigration.

---

[1] Report on Colonisation, 1889, p. 111.   [2] *Ibid.*

HISTORICAL SURVEY: 1815-1912

(b) The powers in possession of local authorities should be sufficient to enable them, at no onerous risk, to assist in the colonisation or emigration of persons or families from their own localities.

(c) The congested districts of Ireland and of the Highlands and Islands of Scotland form an exceptional case and require relief by assistance to industries, to colonisation or emigration and, where suitable, to migration.

(d) The provisions proposed in the Land and Congested Districts (Ireland) Bill are ample for these purposes.

(e) Provisions similar to some of the foregoing should be made for the Crofter districts of Scotland.

(f) The Colonisation Board be continued and reconstructed for the purpose of colonisation and emigration from such districts.

(g) The power of enlarging crofters' holdings in that Act should be kept alive.

(h) Crofts vacated by emigration or migration should be added to existing holdings without power of subdivision.

(i) The experiment of colonising the crofter population in Canada should be further tried.

(j) The proposals of the Government of British Columbia[1] should be favourably entertained.

(k) The agency of companies for colonisation and emigration should be taken advantage of, both as regards the aforesaid colonisation in Canada and elsewhere.

(l) The Government grant to the Emigrants' Information Office should be increased.[2]

As a result of this report, further governmental schemes were dropped, but the grant awarded annually to the Emigrants' Information Office was augmented. From 1891 to 1905 no action seems to have been taken, but, in the latter year, the Unemployed Workmen Act,[3] which contained clauses facilitating the transference of needy workpeople, was passed.[4] In

---

[1] These proposals fell through as the Governments failed to agree on matters of finance.
[2] Report on Colonisation, 1891, p. xvi.   [3] Vide Chapter IV.
[4] " The Central Body may, if they think fit, in any case of an unemployed person referred to them by a distress committee, assist that person by aiding the emigration or removal to another area of that person and any of his dependants."—5 Ed. 7, ch. 18, sec. 5.

the following year, Sir Rider Haggard made certain suggestions for a colonisation scheme, which may be briefly summarised as follows. The authorities at home were to advance to the Salvation Army, or a similar body, a sum of money roughly equalling thirty thousand pounds, and in return the institution was to collect a vast number of distressed town-bred families and install them on farm plots in Canada. A departmental committee was appointed to give consideration to the suggestions, but this body reported unfavourably and the scheme was not attempted.[1] Since 1906 the inactivity of the central authorities has been continued, but a great expansion in the working of charitable institutions has marked the period. To-day there are considerably more than a hundred societies engaged in the emigration movement; some give their services in a general way, others confine their operations to people of certain religious denominations or to dwellers in particular localities, whilst others again deal only with women or children. The majority give financial assistance in deserving cases, though certain of them are organised merely to provide information, guidance and protection. As a general rule, the societies are doing valuable work by sending to the various colonies able-bodied people who could not otherwise join in the exodus.

In bygone years, certain of the less responsible organisations made emigration a vehicle for transferring " undesirables " from the Mother Country to the Colonies. As no such practices have been attempted for many years past, it is somewhat discouraging to note the attitude with which a few of the Colonial Governments still approach the home societies as a body. Everything which can be done to eliminate the unfit from the fit is now performed by the societies, and none but those who can undergo a severe and

---

[1] Cf. *Colonisation Schemes*, Chapter X, p. 244.

HISTORICAL SURVEY: 1815–1912

searching test are permitted to proceed. In many cases, farm colonies have been instituted within the United Kingdom and prospective settlers are required to give practical demonstrations of their fitness at one or other of them before they are passed as suitable. Not only do the societies themselves require their candidates to pass a very severe test, but the officials attached to the staffs of the various High Commissioners and Agents-General institute searching enquiries also. Authentic figures are available to prove that, of the people befriended by the East End Emigration Fund, less than 5 per cent turn out failures, only 5 per cent fail from the Church Emigration Society, never more than 4 per cent annually from the South African Colonisation Society, less than 2 per cent from Dr. Barnardo's Homes, whilst other societies can show equally satisfactory records.[1] In spite of this complex system of selection and these reassuring figures, there are still people, living in the colonies, who condemn the work of the societies in general. A writer living at Hamilton, Ontario, says :[2] " At present, among the great stream of English people whom your agencies are sending to us, are many who are the scourings from London streets— the hangers-on to Church charitable organisations— the type of men who demand work, but that is the last thing they really desire." It will be noticed that in this quotation not one shred of evidence is given to support the serious allegations made, nor does the writer seem to be aware that no man who was work-shy and studied his comforts would leave London for Hamilton ; also, it may be pointed out that such statements not only condemn the operations of our home organisations, but they presuppose a want of confidence in the colonial emigration commissioners as well.

---

[1] Official Report of the Emigration Conference convened by the Royal Colonial Institute, 1910, pp. 33, 37, 39, 43, etc.
[2] Quoted from *The Times* of May 30th, 1910.

Within recent years public opinion has gradually grown to view with considerable disfavour any form of British emigration proceeding to foreign countries. In 1907, the Imperial Conference gave expression to this feeling by passing the following resolution:

> That it is desirable to encourage British emigrants to proceed to British Colonies rather than foreign countries: that the Imperial Government be requested to co-operate with any Colonies desiring immigrants in assisting suitable persons to emigrate: that the Secretary of State for the Colonies be requested to nominate representatives of the Dominions to the committee of the Emigrants' Information Office.

In 1908, the question of emigration was discussed by the Poor Law Commission. Unfortunately, the ground necessarily covered by this enquiry was so extensive that little time could be spared for an adequate consideration of the factors governing the national exodus. The Majority Report of this Commission spoke of the value of emigration when supplemented with other reforms, but gave no hint as to the ways and means of organising such a movement. The Minority Report was more informing. Whatever provisions are made for minimising unemployment, it affirmed, there will always be a residuum of men and women who will be in want of work; for them, an emigration and immigration division will prove valuable. This division, it suggested, should develop the office now maintained by the Secretary of State for the Colonies in close communication with the responsible governments of other parts of the Empire. A Minister of Labour would direct this office, and his duties would include not only the control of aided but non-aided emigrants as well. So far as they go, the suggestions made by the Minority Commissioners are valuable, but, from such an authoritative body, a complete sketch of the machinery

HISTORICAL SURVEY: 1815–1912   35

required· to control both the emigration from home and the immigration to the Colonies would have proved welcome.

Finally, the subject of emigration was considered by the recent Imperial Conference of 1911. Mr. Burns, as President of the Local Government Board, said that since the last Conference the object of the resolution passed in 1907[1] had been, to a great extent, secured. In 1906, the total number of emigrants from the Mother Country was 194,671, of whom the different parts of the Empire took 105,178 or 54 per cent. In 1910, the numbers were 233,944 and 159,000 respectively, showing 68 per cent to the Empire. For the first four months of the year 1911 there was an increase over the corresponding period of 1910 of 23,000 or 29 per cent, and the Empire had taken the whole of that increase. Australia and New Zealand had received ten thousand more people in the first four months of 1911 than in the similar period of 1910, or 133 per cent increase. If the rate of increase for the first four months were continued for the whole of 1911, the total emigrants for Great Britain to all countries would amount, he said, to three hundred thousand, of whom, it was estimated, 230,000, or nearly 80 per cent, would go to different parts of the Empire, a generous contribution in quantity and quality from the Mother Country. In 1900, the percentage absorbed by the Empire of the total emigration from the United Kingdom was only 33 per cent. The increase from 33 per cent to 80 per cent was a justification of the excellent and increasing work in the right direction carried on by the now admirably organised Emigrants' Information Office at home. Moreover, it was generally admitted that the quality of the emigrants had also improved. The total estimated emigration of 300,000 for 1911 represented 60 per cent of the

---

[1] Vide *supra*.

natural increase of the population of the United Kingdom as compared with 48 per cent in 1910 and 50 per cent in 1907. But for the saving in life represented by a lower death-rate, and a much lower infant mortality, this emigration would be a very heavy drain on the United Kingdom. In ten years Scotland and Ireland combined had increased their population by 210,000, or less than the total emigration from Great Britain for the one year 1910. With a diminishing birth-rate the Mother Country could not safely go beyond 300,000 a year, and if 80 per cent of these went to different parts of the Empire, the Conference would probably agree that this was as much as they could reasonably require. The Dominions were entitled to have the surplus, but they must not diminish the seed plot. They could absorb the overflow, but they must not empty the tank.

In reviewing emigration generally, Mr. Burns said that the business of the Emigrants' Information Office had more than doubled since 1907, and that its machinery was being kept up to modern requirements. Over-organisation, or attempts to do more than was now being done, would probably check many of the voluntary non-political and benevolent associations connected with the work, which filled a place that no State organisation could possibly occupy. Information was disseminated through one thousand public libraries and municipal buildings in addition to many post offices. Six hundred and fifty Boards of Guardians sent all their emigrated children to the Dominions. In twenty-one years 9300 Poor Law children had been emigrated at a cost to the rates of £109,000. The quality of these children was indicated by the fact that out of 12,790 children from the Poor Law Schools of London, only 62 had been returned by their employers in consequence of natural defects, incompatibility of temper or disposition. One hundred and thirty Distress Committees had sent 16,000 emigrants to different parts of the Empire in five years at a cost of £127,000. Lastly, before 1907, army reservists were not allowed to leave this country and to continue to draw their reserve pay. This regulation had been modified, with the result that since 1907, 8000 reservists had been allowed to reside abroad, of whom only 329 were not under the British flag.

CHAPTER III

THE CAUSES OF EMIGRATION

FROM the year 1815 to the present day, the British emigrants leaving the United Kingdom for various parts of North America may be fairly estimated as totalling slightly more than twelve million souls.[1] This vast exodus of people has been brought about by the interplay of a variety of forces, the principal no doubt among these being the phenomenal increase of population which overtook the nation in the early years of last century. Various authorities roughly estimate the inhabitants of the three kingdoms in 1700 as being eight millions, nearly fifteen millions in 1801, and over twenty-seven millions in 1851.[2] From these figures, it is evident that the population increased in the first half of the nineteenth century twice as rapidly as it did between 1701 and 1801. During these years of expansion, we find that the amount of emigration also grew by leaps and bounds. At the end of the first decade of the century, when the people of the United Kingdom roughly equalled sixteen millions,[3] emigration stood at twenty thousand; in the second decade there were twenty millions[4] of people against one hundred and twenty-one thousand emigrants; in the third decade, the figures were twenty-three millions[5]

---

[1] Actual figures, 1815–1910: To United States, 9,798,934; to British North America, 2,918,328.

[2] *Journal of the Royal Statistical Society*, vol. 15, p. 256, 1852. The earlier figures are based on various authorities; the later are those given by the Census Returns.

[3] [4] [5] Estimated from the Census Returns. The period between 1801 and 1810, before a Census was taken in Ireland, is computed from data given in the *Journal of the Royal Statistical Society*, vol. 1, p. 259.

THE CAUSES OF EMIGRATION 39

and six hundred and twenty-one thousand; and in the fifth decade they rose to twenty-seven millions[1] and one million five hundred and seventeen thousand. From the foregoing data we may note that, as the population grew during this period of fifty years, so the exodus became more extensive.

After 1851, when in a single year 309,962 people left our shores,[2] the volume of emigration declined in spite of the fact that the population of England and Scotland continued to increase. The reason for this was that Ireland, the country which had furnished the greater portion of the emigrants, was gradually declining in population. In 1791, its people numbered 4,206,602;[3] in 1841, they had increased to 8,175,124;[4] but in 1851 there was a shrinkage to six and a half millions.[5] These statements may be summarised, therefore, by saying that during the first half of the nineteenth century emigration increased because of the enormous increase of population in the whole of the United Kingdom, but declined soon after 1850 owing to a contraction in the number of people in Ireland.

Beyond these general and more or less gradual waves of increase and decrease of population, we find that certain definite areas have at times become overcrowded and so given an impetus to local emigration. The Select Committee, which sat in 1826-7, reported that the Kingdom contained many districts where the amount of available labour was considerably in excess of the quantity that could find employment; but emigration, it added, was being resorted to as a successful palliative. A case in point was furnished by Rum in the Hebrides.[6] The proprietor of this island found,

---

[1] Census Returns.
[2] For British North America and the United States.
[3] *Journal of the Royal Statistical Society*, vol. 1, p. 259.
[4,5] Census of Ireland, 1901, Table 44.
[6] Report of Committee on Emigration—Scotland, 1841. Vol. VI, p. 98.

in 1825, that his rents were £300 in arrears. A visit to the locality conclusively showed him that the indebtedness of the people was not due to any lack of industry on their part, but that the overcrowded numbers precluded any of them from gaining an adequate livelihood. Recognising that matters would never improve of themselves, he cancelled their debts, shared a sum of £600 amongst them, gave them cattle, and paid their passage out to Canada. Later on, it is recorded that this proprietor had repeopled his island on a less crowded basis and was deriving £800 per annum as rent from it.

By no means did Rum furnish an isolated instance of local congestion which found relief in emigration. In 1823 the districts of Fermoy, Mallow, and Newmarket in county Cork, being over-populated, experienced a copious outflow; in 1826, the northern areas of the Hebrides, as well as the islands of Tiree, Coll, and Mull, resorted to emigration on account of the overcrowded condition of these lands; in 1838, the counties of Armagh, Monaghan, sections of Cavan, Fermanagh, Antrim, and Down, as well as Tipperary, Limerick, Cork, and Waterford also became congested and found relief in an extensive exodus. Similar conditions prevailed three years later in Argyllshire, Inverness, Ross, Mull, Tiree, Coll, Skye, and the chain of islands from the Butt of Lewis to Barra Head, whilst, in more recent times, we may point to the misery and wretchedness which was relieved by a recourse to emigration, some twenty odd years ago, within the islands of Lewis, Harris, North Uist, and Benbecula.

Not only have areas of over-dense population been recorded in remote parts of Ireland and Scotland, but England has also suffered. During the early part of the nineteenth century much distress occurred in the southern counties from this cause. Many of the parishes in Sussex, Hampshire, Surrey, and Wiltshire

THE CAUSES OF EMIGRATION

found that their population was increasing as much as 15 per cent in ten years, and this without any new or reinforced industry coming forward to absorb the surplus labour. The people naturally became very demoralised, wages were reduced to a minimum, parish relief was accepted as a matter of course, and many of the inhabitants were compelled to emigrate.[1]

In England, this overcrowded condition seems to have arisen largely owing to the machinery of the poor-law. Until 2-3 Will. IV, 96, sec. 4 was enacted in 1832, it was the practice[2] of the parish authorities to level up the wages of the labourers with money derived from the rates. It was, therefore, to the advantage of the overlords that their estates should be cleared of all people likely to seek relief. As a consequence, thousands of tenants were ejected from their homes, and their houses razed to the ground.[3] Those who were cast adrift gradually found their way into the neighbouring "open villages," and it was in these settlements that the congestion took place.

The type of man who suffered most under this inequitable system of levelling up wages with parish funds was the small farmer, whose land and residence came within the jurisdiction of one of these overcrowded "open villages." Though perhaps he employed no labour, and so gained nothing from the hire of men whose services were partly paid for by the local authorities, yet he was called upon to contribute lavishly towards the poor-rates, which were unduly high owing to the presence, in his district, of crowds of underpaid labourers who had been ejected from neighbouring parishes. At the best of times, the income of such a farmer was seldom sufficient for his

---

[1] See Third Report of Select Committee on Emigration from United Kingdom, pp. 11, 84, 138, 142.

[2] By the interpretation of Gilbert's Act. 22 Geo. III, c. 83, sec. 32, and 36 Geo. III, c. 23.

[3] Cf. Report on the Poor Laws, 1834, p. 72; also *Edinburgh Review*, Vol. XLV, 1826-7, pp. 72-3.

frugal needs, but when he became tortured with an ever-increasing rate, life grew impossible and emigration helped to solve his troubles. The reports issued by the Select Committee on Emigration from the United Kingdom, published in 1826 and 1827, refer to scores of men of this type who fled to America in order to escape this burdensome taxation.[1]

In Scotland, the suffering was chiefly caused by the common practice of subdividing crofts on the marriage of the crofters' children, a plan which speedily reduced the land into divisions too small for the support of a family.[2]

In Ireland the crowded conditions arose in the villages which received the farmers who had been evicted as a result of the spread of the consolidation movement of farm-holdings. Moritz Bonn states that in the short period intervening between 1849 and 1856,[3] no less than fifty thousand men had been turned adrift from their farm plots to satisfy this desire for linking up the small holdings.[4] The policy grew so destructive, from a popular standpoint, that a governmental Commission was appointed in 1843 to enquire into the matter.[5] The report, which was afterwards published, stated that the majority of the landowners were heartless and cared little for the misery which their actions caused to the ejected tenants. When a lease for a small plot fell in, the farmer was cast out and no opportunity was given him to renew it, even at a higher rental. In contrast to the action of these landowners, we read that certain of the landed gentry compensated their tenants when they evicted them. Colonel Wyndham, for instance, issued a statement to the effect that after

---

[1] See pp. 84, 105, 106, etc., of the Second Report, 1827.
[2] Report of the Commissioners of Scotland and Emigration, 1840, Vol. VI.
[3] *Modern Ireland and her Agrarian Problem*, p. 67.
[4] In his book *Modern Ireland*.
[5] Commission to enquire into the law and practice in respect to the occupation of land in Ireland.

THE CAUSES OF EMIGRATION 43

a certain date he would renew no leases for less than twenty acres. Instead, he would either compensate his ejected tenants at the rate of two pounds for each acre they held or would pay all expenses connected with their emigration to Canada. It is not known how many of his tenants selected the emigration benefit, for the report only states that " some two hundred people preferred the money, and a lesser number desired emigration."[1] Wyndham was by no means the only landlord who helped his ejected farmers to start life afresh on the less crowded side of the Atlantic. Lord Midleton spent several hundred pounds on emigration ;[2] the Marquess of Clanricarde disbursed £551 between 1841 and 1842 for a similar purpose ;[3] Lord Stanley provided passages to Quebec for his tenantry ;[4] the Lord of Castlecomer sent no less than 1050 people from his estate, paying two guineas for each adult and one guinea for each child,[5] whilst the Hon. Colonel Stratford contributed two pounds towards the emigration of each of the dispossessed tenants on his lands.[6] Numbers of additional instances might be cited, but we have quoted sufficiently to show that an important stream of emigration was occasioned by the consolidating movement in Ireland,[7] and that, in numerous cases, the landowners provided the necessary assistance.

The process of amalgamating small farms was not confined to Ireland. In England there was a tendency in the early part of the nineteenth century to increase

---

[1] Report on Law and Practice in respect to occupation of Land in Ireland, paras. 1–10.
[2] Ibid., para. 32.
[3] Report on Law and Practice in respect to occupation of Land in Ireland, paras. 13–15.
[4] Ibid., paras. 15, 16.   [5] Ibid., para. 31.   [6] Ibid., para. 80.
[7] Mulhall, in *The Dictionary of Statistics*, states that between 1849 and 1860 there were 1,865,000 evicted tenants, whilst emigration stood at 551,000 ; between 1861 and 1870 there were 236,000 evicted tenants, whilst emigration stood at 867,000 ; between 1871 and 1882 there were 311 000 evicted tenants, whilst emigration stood at 712,000.

the amount of corn-growing lands, for the population was multiplying with unusual rapidity and needed large supplies of wheat, barley, and oats. Foreign corn could only be imported when prices stood at over 63s. per quarter, according to a statute enacted in 1804, so that the home produce received definite encouragement. But corn was found to be most profitable when produced on large farms; thus in both England and Ireland, the trend was for the large farmer to absorb many small men. Beyond the question of grain producing, we find there was every reason, at this time, for the disappearance of the small-holding as, in many ways, it was less economical to manage than the large one. This economy, however, meant not only economy of money and implements, but also of labour, with the result that figures concerning emigration quickly indicated the change.

A further practice which helped to swell the exodus for American shores was that of changing arable into pasture land.[1] An early report referring to the north-western districts of Scotland says:[2] "The most powerful cause of emigration is that of converting large districts of the country into extensive sheep-walks. This not only requires much fewer people to manage the same tract of country, but, in general, an entirely new people are brought from the south." The same report mentions that in one year alone, 1801, three thousand people, who formerly practised tilling were forced to give up their lands and sail for America.

With such apprehension was emigration viewed, in the early part of the nineteenth century, that the Commission of 1802 was asked to suggest a means whereby its flow might be stemmed. The emigration, it reported, was due to the landowners changing the "Œconomy of their Estates," and a law should be

---

[1] It will be remembered that the Glengarries were largely affected by this change.
[2] Report of the Coast of Scotland and Naval Enquiry, 1802-3, p. 15.

THE CAUSES OF EMIGRATION

enacted forbidding the lairds from lessening the people on their lands below a given proportion.

It is needless to say that the suggestion never obtained legal support, and fresh districts were constantly being cleared. In Perthshire, the population was given at 142,166 in 1831; 127,768 in 1871; and 129,007 in 1881, or a decrease of 13,000 in fifty years. In Argyleshire, it was estimated at 100,973 in 1831, and 76,468 in 1881; a decrease of 24,000 within the same period. In Inverness-shire it stood at 94,799 in 1831, and, after slightly rising in 1841, fell to 90,454 in 1881. One estate, that of Strathconan, comprising 71,900 acres, reduced its thousand inhabitants of 1829 to 508 by 1849.[1] As emigration was proceeding rapidly from these areas, we may reasonably infer that a large percentage of it was due to unemployment, consequent on the change from arable to pasture land.

The profits, which the large farmer reaped from his increased harvest of grain, or the higher prices obtained for meat, were, of course, shared by the landowner, who advanced the rents whenever an opportunity occurred. It is to be believed, however, that a corresponding reduction was not made when produce fell in value. During seasons of prosperity, the increased rents were met easily enough, but as soon as a lean year overtook the agriculturalist, and, through lack of knowledge, these unfavourable times recurred somewhat frequently, it became necessary to curtail expenses. Instead of successfully agitating for a reduction in the charges made by the landlord, most employers used less labour and paid lower wages. Mr. Bowley[2] gives the average weekly wage of the agricultural labourer as 11s. in 1800; 11s. 5d. in 1805; 14s. 6d. in 1813;[3] but 12s. in 1818, and 10s. in 1823.

---

[1] *Report on Colonisation*, 1890. See Mr. A. Mackenzie's evidence on p. 284 *et seq.*; also Mr. Gerald Balfour's reply, p. 410 *et seq.*
[2] *Wages in the United Kingdom*, p. 34.
[3] It must be remembered that food-prices were high at this time.

From the foregoing, then, there is ample evidence to show that as the early years of the nineteenth century progressed, so the lot of the farm-hand grew less and less attractive. In the first year or so, his right of keeping a cow and a few fowls and geese upon the common lands was taken from him by the gradual spread of enclosures; when the Poor Law was amended in 1834, his earnings were no longer supplemented by parochial assistance;[1] with the amalgamation of farms and the introduction of such agricultural implements as the threshing machine, there came less chance of employment and when landlords raised the rentals, the farmer lowered his wages. These conditions culminated in a great agricultural depression which lasted, with varying severity, from 1816 to 1822. During these years, no less than 475 petitions were presented to the House of Commons,[2] complaining of the uneasy state in agricultural circles, with the result that a Royal Commission was appointed in the latter year to investigate the situation.

This Commission recorded its belief that the crisis was due to the fall in prices, consequent on the cessation of the Napoleonic Wars and to the more settled state of Europe. Taking wheat as a standard indication of the cost of foods, we find that in 1793-4 this commodity stood at 50s. per quarter. From this time, it rose quickly, until in 1801 it had reached 120s. It then occasionally increased, but fell sharply at the end of 1813 to 39s. $5\frac{1}{2}$d.[3] A Corn Law which put a duty on foreign wheat whenever prices were below 80s.[4] was enacted in 1815 in order to protect the position of the home-farmer, but Tooke says

---

[1] The magistrates of Cottesloe, Buckinghamshire, allowed, in 1828, 6s. per week to a man and wife with one child under ten; 7s. for two children; 8s. for three; 9s. for four; and 10s. for five.—Poor Law Report, 1828, Vol. IV, p. 38.

[2] Report of Committee on Agriculture, 1822, p. 67.

[3] Bowley, *Wages in the United Kingdom*, p. 31.

[4] 55 Geo. III, c. 26.

THE CAUSES OF EMIGRATION

that it only served to make the market extremely sensitive to the slightest variations in the yield of the crops, and, as a result, ruined many of the very men it was framed to assist. Tooke's statement is merely offered as the expression of an opinion, but his figures may be accepted as reliable. In January, 1816, he quotes wheat at 52s. 6d.,[1] but says that owing to a shortage in the 1816 crops it temporarily rose to 117s. in June, 1817. From these facts, it is clear that the farmer could never gauge the value of his produce, and many gave up their occupation in disgust and emigrated.

Another agricultural depression overtook the country at the beginning of the thirties, and a Commission sat in 1833 to enquire into its causes. After examining a number of farm-witnesses, representing a variety of localities within the three kingdoms, this body decided that "the want of a sufficient margin between the value of the produce of the soil and the cost of it "[2] was the cause of the evil. A more practical explanation of the situation would have mentioned first the excessive rainfall which had visited the country during the three or four previous seasons; second, the lamentable ignorance which even large farmers displayed in these times when confronted with exceptional difficulties; and third, the scarcity of gold.

As a result of these depressing conditions, a continuous stream of agricultural workers crossed the Atlantic Ocean and settled in the United States and Canada. In 1830 emigration from the United Kingdom stood at 55,461; in 1831 the volume increased to 71,485; whilst in 1832 it had grown to 99,211. These figures, it will be seen, are significantly high when it is remembered that during the previous ten years the exodus had not risen above an annual average of

---

[1] Tooke's *Prices*, vol. 2, pp. 4, 18.
[2] Report of Committee on Agriculture, 1833, p. 204.

twenty thousand. Kent, Cheshire, Derbyshire, Hampshire, Somersetshire and Surrey furnished the greatest numbers sailing from England, but the depression must be considered general throughout Ireland and the north of Scotland.[1]

The report dealing with these agricultural disturbances tells us that some thousands of small farmers, possessing a little capital, took part in the outflow from England, and that a large percentage of them continued to farm when they had settled down in their new homes. We can but wonder what was the ultimate fate of these men, and what measure of success attended their later efforts, knowing, as we do, that their failure in the United Kingdom resulted largely from lack of personal reliability and initiative, qualities highly necessary for the pioneer settler.

As a direct result of this emigration, many local bodies reported a substantial decrease in the amount of relief which they were called upon to provide. The parish of Benenden in Kent, for instance, was able to lower its poor rate from 18s. to 10s., after the local unemployed were assisted to leave the country,[2] whilst the parish of Headcorn near Maidstone sent out twenty-three paupers at a cost of £179, and its expenditure for relief fell in three years from £2308 11s. 3d. to £1919 16s.[3]

In the north of Scotland, the distress in agricultural circles was felt acutely, as the people were still suffering from the collapse of the kelp industry. For many years, salt, which was a rival to kelp, had been subjected to heavy duties but, in 1822, the levy on it was reduced from 15s. to 2s. per bushel

---

[1] Report of Committee on Agriculture, 1833: various references.
[2] *Ibid.*, p. 248.
[3] Report of Select Committee on Emigration from United Kingdom, Vol. II, pp. 144-5.

THE CAUSES OF EMIGRATION 49

and then abolished altogether.[1] As a consequence, the demand for salt and barilla rose appreciably, whilst kelp fell in value from £10 to £2 or £3 per ton. In the profitable days of this industry, the manufacturers did all in their power to attract people to settle along the northern sea-coast, knowing, first, that the quantity of kelp produced depended on the number of people engaged in its collection, and, second, that its market was practically unlimited.[2] When the fall came, many of the merchants were ruined, whilst many more closed down their premises. As a consequence, hundreds of men and women were thrown out of work; some of them fell back on the already over-stocked industry of agriculture, but others preferred to embark for North America.

A further period of agricultural uneasiness occurred in 1836, and many farmers in Yorkshire, Buckinghamshire, Huntingdonshire and other localities where the soil was of clay, and at that time undrained, found that owing to the excessive rainfall they could not continue to employ profitably the usual complement of labour. Many of the workers who were turned adrift owing to this decision had to be assisted to emigrate. On this occasion the landowners seem to have proved unusually generous, for many of them granted free passages to those who wished to leave the Mother Country. They properly argued that it was better to give such support voluntarily than to allow the people to burden the rates. In connection with those who did receive local assistance, an interesting decision was given by the Assistant Commissioner of Emigration. Certain families who desired to proceed from Yapton, in Sussex, applied to the parish officers for partial passage assistance. When on the point of granting it, in accordance with the provisions of the Poor Law

---

[1] Report of Committee on Agriculture, 1833, p. 248.
[2] Extract from a letter sent by the proprietor of the Island of Harris to Lord Glenelg, April 10th, 1829.

Amendment Act, the authorities were informed by the Assistant Commissioner, that such aid could only be extended to people whose destination was one or other of the colonies. As most of the Yapton emigrants had intended to join friends in the United States, much dissatisfaction arose, and many refused to proceed.[1] This is probably the first occasion on which it was decided that local finances could not be used for furthering emigration to a foreign state.[2]

The potato famine of 1847, which spread throughout Ireland, carrying death and misery in its train, was probably the most potent factor which has ever influenced the flow of emigration. To appreciate the extent of this disaster, we must remember that the population of the country had reached a point of unusual density, being just over eight millions, and also that the peasants depended on the potato as their staple article of food. The state of the country, even prior to the failure of the crop, was none too satisfactory, for poverty had risen to such a degree that all attempts to cope with it had seemed to be of no avail. The famine, however, solved the problem, sweeping away thousands by starvation and death, and causing a still greater number to leave their country owing to the fear of sharing in a like fate.

An exodus unparalleled in the history of emigration then commenced. Between January 1st, 1847, and December 31st, 1854, no less than 1,656,044 people left Ireland for North America, more than 1,300,000 of whom made the United States their new home. For the year 1852 alone, the exodus is recorded as numbering 190,322,[3] whereas to-day it is no more than 32,457.[4] Of all the vast num-

---

[1] Evidence given before the Select Committee on Agricultural Distress, 1836, p. 194.   [2] This decision was afterwards rescinded.

[3] This is the earliest year for which trustworthy figures are available for Ireland.

[4] Figures given for 1910 on page 4 of *Emigration Statistics of Ireland*, 1911.

THE CAUSES OF EMIGRATION 51

bers which crowded on to the embarking stages and clamoured for berths in the outgoing vessels, we can only trace a few who owed their passage to governmental assistance. In 1848, 234, and in 1849, 922 people were sent to Canada under the provisions of the Irish Poor Relief Extension Act.[1]

Though a great deal of apparent apathy seems to have characterised the action of the Government, whose policy was *laissez-faire* in general, the same cannot be said of private enterprise. The major section of this Irish emigration depended, it is true, upon individual effort,[2] but charitable institutions put forth their utmost efforts to alleviate the distress. Amongst these, the Society of Friends may be given a premier position as having rendered signal aid both in providing for the immediate wants of the sufferers and also in shipping off to America many who were too poor to assist themselves.[3] Whilst dealing with unofficial assistance, it is necessary to mention that the cash remittances sent back to the old country from North America by former emigrants rose considerably during this period of want. In 1848 the money received in the whole of the United Kingdom from this source was £460,000; in 1849 it grew to £540,000; in 1850 to £957,000; in 1851 to £990,000; whilst in 1852 it reached a total of £1,404,000.[4] Unfortunately there are no statistics available to show the exact sums received in Ireland alone as apart from the United Kingdom in general. These, however, may be roughly estimated. For the year 1848 we shall be ascribing too little, probably, to our Irish neighbours if we apportion them a third of the £460,000 mentioned above;

---

[1] 10 Vict. c. 31.
[2] Report of the Committee of Poor Law (Irish), Vol. XVI, 1849, paras. 1851, 1852.
[3] See Transactions of the Central Relief Committee of the Society of Friends, during the Famine in Ireland in 1846 and 1847.
[4] Figures obtained from the Annual Reports of the Colonial Land and Emigration Commissioners.

most likely the correct amount is a trifle short of £130,000.[1] For each of the years 1849, 1850, 1851, and 1852 we may safely take the one hundred and thirty thousand pounds estimated for 1848 and add to it the increase between the total for the individual year and the total for the year 1848. Thus, in 1852, the Irish received approximately a million pounds as remittances from North America.

The five years following the famine may be described as a period during which the inflow to America was excessively high; people were departing, others were preparing to depart, and thousands more contemplating a similar move as soon as the opportunity presented itself. After 1853 a certain measure of prosperity returned to the country and both agriculture and commerce became more settled, with the consequence that the exodus grew gradually less. In 1853 the outgoings numbered 173,148, but by 1856 they had shrunk to 90,781.[2]

Ever since 1847 the figures at our disposal show that there is some important relation between the value of the potato crops and Irish emigration. To substantiate this statement, we may instance the years 1863, 1880, 1883, and 1887 as periods during which the outflow to America has been above the normal. The Registrar-General for Ireland[3] estimated the potato crop in thousands of tons as 1814·4 in 1861; 2137·8 in 1862; 1095·9 in 1879; 2011·2 in 1882; and 2640·0 in 1887; whilst the mean between 1847 and 1890 stood at 3352·8. Thus it will be seen that prior to each of the years of accelerated Irish emigration there was a contracted crop of potatoes. Conversely, we find that the yields were especially good in 1853, 1855, 1858, 1864,

---

[1] The Irish have always been more ready to send home remittances than the Scotch or English.

[2] Emigration Statistics of Ireland. See Report of 1912.

[3] *Facts and Figures about Ireland*, by T. W. Grimshaw, Registrar-General for Ireland.

THE CAUSES OF EMIGRATION

1870, 1876, and 1883. Of these seven years, no less than five were followed by seasons of contracted emigration.

During the latter part of the nineteenth century, the position of the agricultural labourer gradually improved. His average wages rose from £33 16s. per annum in 1866 to £37 in 1870, and £40 in 1891;[1] while the price of food-stuffs, during the period of 1866–91, materially fell. Some years were naturally less prosperous than others, as for instance, those of 1873 and 1883; but, generally speaking, the need for quitting the Mother Land has never been so pressing since as it was in the early days of the last century.

Not only has emigration from Britain been prompted by a series of agricultural depressions, but it has also derived much of its velocity from industrial disturbances. In discussing this latter factor as an exciting cause, it is necessary to go back to the era of important inventions, when, in the space of a few years, the spinning jenny, the water-frame, the " mule," and the power-loom revolutionised the work of both the hand-spinner and the hand-weaver. As may be expected, these labour-saving devices had a disastrous effect on the employees who practised the old systems, and, though many of them learnt the new methods, the contracted demand for hands necessarily gave rise to considerable unemployment, with the consequence that much of the surplus labour was transferred to North America. The report of the Select Committee on Emigration of 1826–7[2] states, with reference to the hand-loom weavers : " For some time, the advance in the cotton trade was so rapid as nearly, if not altogether, to absorb, in the more productive system, the hands thus thrown out of employment. But difficulties, arising from a temporary check in trade, shortly fell upon the weavers, with the double pressure

---
[1] Bowley, *Wages of the United Kingdom*, p. 35.
[2] *Op. cit.*, p. 3, second report.

of these two combined causes, a diminished demand for the produce of their industry and an increased facility of production." To this twofold reason, we may add a third. The Irish, who were at this time passing through a period of acute depression, crossed the channel separating them from Great Britain in large numbers and flooded the newer industries with their cheaper labour. As a consequence, wages in the Lanark district fell nearly fifty per cent in eight years, being 21s. per week in 1805, and 11s. in 1813.[1] In Glasgow the skilled operator averaged a pound a week between 1810 and 1816; 18s. between 1816 and 1820; 12s. 6d. in 1826; 10s. 6d. in 1832 and 1833; and only 9s. 6d. in 1838.[2] Thus in twenty-eight years the wages of this type of worker were reduced to less than one half of their original amount. A witness, giving evidence before the Hand-loom Weavers' Commission[3] of 1835, quoted figures showing the relation existing between the earning power of the weaver and the cost of food. From 1797 to 1804, he said, an operator could earn enough money each week to buy either 100 lbs. of flour, 142 lbs. of oatmeal, 826 lbs. of potatoes or 55 lbs. of butcher's meat, which, it may be added, would allow him an average of 280 lbs. of food if he bought of each kind. But between 1804 and 1811, his wages would only purchase an average of 238 lbs.; between 1811 and 1818, 131 lbs.; between 1818 and 1825, 108 lbs.; and, lastly, between 1825 and 1834 only 83 lbs. From these figures, we see that his food supply was reduced by nearly 200 lbs. weekly in the course of some thirty odd years.

The records of the unemployed weavers were most disquieting. In 1826 Yorkshire reported that fifteen thousand of its people were out of work; in Lancashire the total was greater, being ninety thousand; in

---

[1] Report on Hand-Loom Weavers, Vol. XLII, 1839, p. 527, etc.
[2] Bowley, *Wages of the United Kingdom*, p. 111.
[3] Report on Hand-Loom Weavers, Vol. XIII, 1835.

THE CAUSES OF EMIGRATION 55

Blackburn alone there were 10,682, whilst Oldham estimated that half of its population was deprived of the means of gaining an adequate livelihood. Areas of Cheshire and Cumberland in England, and Renfrewshire in Scotland were also in this distressing plight.[1]

In spite of the widespread misery which overtook the weavers, and the great amount of emigration which must have followed as a consequence, we can only point to a few references which directly speak of this exodus. Our chief source of information lies in the local north country gazettes, which were constantly recording the departure, at this period, of little bands of workers from various localities. Though such records are enlightening, their spasmodic appearance and unconnected character enable us to form no accurate conception of the extent nor of the real origin of this departing stream of humanity. We do know that the weavers had formed many emigration societies amongst themselves,[2] also that it was a frequent occurrence, about this time, for ships to sail from unfrequented bays and creeks without reporting their departure, in order that the customs regulations might be avoided. This would naturally prevent a record being kept of the class of people crossing the Atlantic on these irregular vessels. We also have mentions of settlers in Canada who claimed to have been employed in weaving before they left the Mother Country.[3] Beyond such evidence the figures dealing with emigration in general show a considerable increase during the years this occupation was declining. They rose from 1889 in 1815 to 55,461 in 1830. It seems but[4] reasonable, therefore, to ascribe

---

[1] Report of Select Committee of Emigration from United Kingdom, 1826–7, Second Report, p. 4 and p. 245.
[2] Accounts and Papers, Vol. XXXI, 1842, p. 6.
[3] Report of Hand-Loom Weavers' Commission, Vol. XXIII, 1840, p. 715.
[4] Quoted from the Annual Reports of the Colonial Land and Emigration Commissioners.

some portion of this increase to the exodus of the men and women belonging to this trade.[1]

Another industrial factor which contributed extensively to the exodus of British labour was the introduction of steam-power. Prior to the use of this new motive force workshops were spread about the country in places where running water was plentiful. After 1785,[2] when the steam-engine was introduced, the factory system began to assert itself and the need for water was no longer so important as supplies of cheap coal and plenty of labour. As a consequence, the old sites situated on river banks, perhaps amidst rural surroundings, were given up in favour of urban situations, where labour could be obtained and where coal was plentiful. This meant that numbers of industries gradually left the localities in which they had long been quartered and reappeared in some northern or midland town. As a rule, the new conditions called for a new set of workers and the old hands were left behind to battle vainly in keeping alive their decaying occupations. This, we know, happened in Devizes, Bradford-on-Avon, and Warminster, where the serge trade had been formerly carried on; in Stroud and Taunton, the old centres of the cloth trade; in Norwich, once noted for crêpes and bombazines, as well as in many other southern and eastern districts. Not only were numbers of employees ousted in this manner, when steam was introduced, but much of the work now became of a mechanical nature and boys

---

[1] Whilst dealing with weavers, the following quotation from the *Daily News* of March 15th, 1910, is interesting :—

"Having received an offer of £5 per week for the first month and £6 per week afterwards, a number of young hand framework knitters from various Notts villages are, this week, leaving for the United States. They will take with them their own machines, and will thereby introduce a new industry into America—that of making high-class silk and lace ties, motor-scarves, shawls and veilings, all of which are now imported."

[2] James Watt took out his patent for the steam-engine in 1769, but it was not until 1785 that steam-power was used for cotton spinning.

THE CAUSES OF EMIGRATION 57

and girls were employed instead of skilled men. Under such conditions there is little wonder that poverty increased, and in order to escape misery and starvation many people looked to emigration as an only hope.

A further outburst of unemployment overshadowed many trades between 1836 and 1845, occasioned, in the main, so it was alleged, by the growth of foreign competition. It must be remembered that on the cessation of the Napoleonic Wars the United Kingdom gained an enormous lead in the industrial world from her numerous patents and inventions; her lands also, it is well to add, had not been harassed by the actual presence of warfare, as had been the case with almost every other European power. When, however, a more settled condition prevailed throughout the world, attempts were made by foreign manufacturers to develop along British lines. The Act of Parliament which forbade the exportation of machinery[1] and the statutes which prohibited artisans from emigrating[2] were both ineffectual in preserving the secrecy of these inventions. Artisans, we know, did emigrate in considerable numbers, whilst much contraband machinery also left the country. We have definite records of several vessels sailing in 1825 and 1826 from Liverpool with Yorkshire and Lancashire operatives on board who were going to take up engagements in the American calico printing trade, whilst a witness, giving evidence before the Royal Commission which sat to consider the question of the exportation of machinery,[3]

---

[1] 7 and 8 Will. III, c. 20, § 8. Refer also to the Proclamation forbidding the exportation of machinery (January 15th, 1666). It must be pointed out that much of the force of this Act disappeared when the practice was made of granting licences to exporters of machinery, tools, etc. Such licences were not granted at this period, however, in cases of machinery and tools relating to the processes of spinning and weaving. See Second Report on Exportation of Machinery, 1841, p. iv.

[2] 5 Geo. I, c. 27, and 23 Geo. III, c, 14.

[3] First Report on Exportation of Machinery, Vol. VII, 1841.

described[1] to this committee how he spent his whole time collecting and despatching the best workmen he could engage in this country. These men, it appears, were easily persuaded to leave their Mother Country by the offer of very advanced wages, but the remuneration was always reduced to a normal level when once their system of working had been grasped by others.[2] In short, the report leaves no doubt that during some fifteen years an organised campaign was afoot to entice British workmen with their machinery into foreign countries, especially into the United States.

The sequel to these practices came with a decreased home trade and an augmentation of American exports between 1836 and 1845. As a consequence, the field for labour in Great Britain was somewhat narrowed, and many work-people found it advantageous to transfer their services to the United States, where business was flourishing. Stockport, a town which seems to have been seriously affected by this growth of foreign competition, reported that it had 1058 horse-power of machinery lying idle in 1843. This amount of power, it said, would give employment to no less than 5290 operatives. What became of these workless people we cannot definitely tell, but it is known that when the destitution was at its height, an office was opened in the town for the sale of emigrant passage tickets. It is only fair to add that the business was by no means lucrative, for, in the first season, the broker sold but ten passages for Canada and forty-seven for Australia. He, however, supplied such a quantity of emigrant literature and entered into such an amount of correspondence as to lead one to suppose that the Stockport residents were really interested in emigration and went to him for advice, but purchased their tickets elsewhere, say in Liverpool or Manchester, in order to obscure their movements. It may be mentioned that

---

[1] *Ibid.*, paras. 1104, 1105.   [2] *Ibid.*, para. 1774.

THE CAUSES OF EMIGRATION 59

it was a common practice with lower-class emigrants for them to make all arrangements affecting their departure in some town where they were not known, in order that their home liabilities might be shirked.

Another centre which suffered considerably from foreign competition was Paisley. Between June, 1841, and February, 1843, the number of people who accepted monetary aid from the weekly parochial doles was never less than 2180 above the average number of cases assisted in ordinary times. In one week, the excess even reached 14,791 cases. Paisley's distress was met, however, by a national subscription, and, with the money collected in this manner, many people emigrated,[1] but there is some conflict of evidence regarding the number of people who were assisted and the sums of money expended in this direction.

Later on, in the early sixties, we find that foreign competition seriously affected the occupation of the ribbon weavers who lived in and around Coventry. So great was their distress that an Emigration Fund Committee was appointed in January, 1862, to collect money with which to enable the destitute members of this trade to emigrate. £1304 was subscribed in three months, and was spent in sending out 257 people from Coventry and certain surrounding parishes, including Coleshill and Nuneaton, to Canada and other colonies.[2] A further party of one hundred men and women from Coventry was despatched to Canada in 1863, at the expense of the late Baroness Burdett Coutts.[3] In all, it is estimated that at least eleven hundred ribbon weavers, who selected North America as their destination, left the district between 1860 and 1863.

After having stood at a low level for some consider-

---

[1] Report of Select Committee on Destitute Inhabitants of Paisley, p. vii, 1843.
[2] *Coventry Standard*, May 2nd, 1862.
[3] *Ibid.*, February 13th, 1863.

able while, the figures governing the human outflow rose significantly in the year 1886. At this time, trade and industry were so depressed that a Royal Commission was appointed to enquire into the home situation. The report[1] which was afterwards published said: " As regards the causes which have contributed to bring about the depressed state of things, there was, as might be expected, less unanimity of opinion among the commissioners; but the following enumeration will, we think, include all those to which any importance was attached: (1) over-production; (2) a continuous fall of prices caused by an appreciation of the standard of value; (3) the effect of foreign tariffs and bounties, and the restrictive commercial policy of foreign countries in limiting our markets; (4) foreign competition, which we are beginning to feel both in our own and neutral markets; (5) an increase in local taxation and the burdens on industry generally; (6) cheaper rates of carriage enjoyed by our foreign competitors; (7) legislation affecting the employment of labour in industrial undertakings; and (8) superior technical education of the workmen in foreign countries."

During the last ten to fifteen years the composition of the emigration flow from the United Kingdom has undergone a material change. To-day, it may be divided broadly into two classes. The first and largest division is composed of men and women who find that the struggle for an urban existence is too keen and exacting for them; the second comprises the youth of our agricultural and industrial occupations who do not sail to evade distress, but are led to depart by the laudable intention of bettering themselves. The former division shows a tendency to contract in point of numbers owing to the increasing severity of the restrictive measures enforced across the Atlantic,

---

[1] Final Report Royal Commission on Depression of Trade and Industry, 1886, p. x.

THE CAUSES OF EMIGRATION

whilst the latter is quickly growing as a result of the propaganda carried on by colonial enterprise.

The former class is forced to emigrate, not by failing health nor by any other such disability, but through the difficulty of securing occupations in the Mother Country, a matter which grows daily more arduous, owing to the competition set up by the flocking into urban areas of agricultural workers; by the natural growth of town populations being greater than the increase of openings for employment; by the improvements in machinery, and by the slackness of particular trades.

Agricultural and industrial conditions are but little concerned with the exodus of the better class emigrants. This type of worker proceeds largely as a result of the representations made to him by organisations which are interested in the transport and reception of immigrants. Briefly, the method of these concerns is to advertise, to scatter descriptive literature, to canvass, to organise lectures, to attract attention by means of exhibits, and to persuade people to sail for America who would otherwise stay at home.

Though this induced or stimulated emigration has only assumed extensive proportions within recent times, it was nevertheless encouraged, in a small way, as far back as in 1823. Between February and May of that year the American Chamber of Commerce opened an office at 4, Coopers' Row, Liverpool, with the object of persuading men to leave their work in England in favour of a life in North America. A few years later, in 1831, His Majesty's Commissioners undertook the task of circulating facts concerning Canada, presumably with the object of accelerating the flow of people to that colony. Publicity was sought by means of leaflets which set out the ruling scales of wages, the opportunities afforded immigrants for taking up land, the cost of living, and the prices obtained for various articles of cultivation.[1] This literature was scattered broadcast not only throughout England, but in Ireland and Scotland as well, and must have exerted a good deal of influence in persuading people to try their fortunes in the new lands of North America.

From these early beginnings the work of inducing emigration has grown until to-day it has developed into a science worthy of the twentieth century. In North America, the chief agencies engaged in stimulating this flow of human lives are the Dominion Government of Canada, the various provincial governments of Canada, the Canadian Pacific Railway Company, the western railroad companies of the United States, and the wealthier land companies of the Republic, especially those having dealings in Missouri, Kansas, Colorado, Arkansas, Louisiana, Oklahoma and Texas. During the year 1910 the staff at the Dominion Offices in England advised close on thirty thousand personal callers, received and despatched a hundred thousand letters, and mailed many tons of booklets. They also distributed some thousands of school atlases dealing with Canadian territories, sent hundreds of wall maps to as many elementary schools, and furnished quantities of lantern-slides, illustrating various aspects of life in the Dominion, to a host of educational establishments.[2] The Canadian Government owns two large motor-vans, fitted with exhibits displaying the produce of its lands, which tour the agricultural districts of England during the summer months, while horse-drawn exhibition vans serve a similar purpose in the northern areas of Wales, Scotland and Ireland. The following extract from the *Toronto Globe*,[3] which embodies the substance of a speech made by Mr. Sifton, when Minister of the

---

[1] Accounts and Papers, Vol. XXXII, 1831, p. 216.
[2] *Canada To-day*, 1911, p. 37.   [3] January 5th, 1904.

THE CAUSES OF EMIGRATION 63

Interior, is interesting in so far as it reveals the methods of inducing immigration which the Dominion at present practises.

Mr. Sifton believed that an excellent class of settler could be obtained from the United States. He stationed men at convenient centres of population there, and was not discouraged because for the first year or more there seemed to be no results. Some of his agents became discouraged and sent in their resignations, but he induced them to take heart of grace and keep pegging away. Tons of information about Canada were distributed where it was hoped it would have some effect, and at length the harvest began to come in. In the first year of effort, only 792 persons from the United States were induced to adventure into the Canadian west. Last year 49,000 settlers came from there. Similar methods have been pursued in Great Britain. A special office, distinctively Canadian in every respect, had been established in the busiest part of the world's metropolis. From this, as a centre, intelligence about the promised land radiated to the four corners of Britain. No trust was put in the mere scattering of literature promiscuously. The addresses of virtually every farmer and farm labourer throughout the three kingdoms were obtained and a newspaper setting forth the attractions of the Dominion mailed to every address. The distribution of these prints surpassed the million mark. A textbook on Canada was introduced in the schools; 25,000 maps of the Dominion were hung on the school walls. Almost instantly, as a result of these and other similar efforts, letters began to pour into the London Office, and care was taken that when once a man was heard from he was kept in touch until his intentions were ascertained. The result of this methodical system was that 50,000 settlers came from Great Britain alone last year (i.e. the year 1903), whereas four years ago the number from all sources was 42,000. In 1903, the immigrants from the various countries numbered 128,000.

These operations had cost some money. Since 1897, the work in the United States had cost $701,000, but as a result of it, 123,000 settlers had come into the country, who had brought in with them stock, household goods, and farming implements to the value of $18,848,891 and $25,000,000 in cash. These were not guesses but ascertained facts. Of these 123,000 persons probably 25,000 were heads of families, and it was within the mark to say that on an average in their first full year of operation they would each extract from the soil $2000 worth of products, or a total of $50,000,000 added to the wealth of the Dominion every year. The cost of securing these settlers worked out at $3.25 per head.

The broader causes which have helped to promote the flow of emigration from the United Kingdom have now been recounted; it still remains to note briefly certain issues of lesser importance. Lord Selkirk, in his writings, mentions an instance which is worthy of record.[1] After the rebellion of 1745, Scotland, he says, was disarmed, intersected by military roads, garrisoned with soldiers, and the authority of a regular government brought into being. The local chiefs thus ceased to be petty monarchs, and the services of their followers were no longer required for defence, and were equally useless for plundering. The lands owned by these overlords, though often extensive, were seldom so vast as to supply enough agricultural labour to keep all the retainers occupied. As the military aspect of their work was taken from them, it is clear that many were deprived of their occupation, and suffered dismissal as a consequence. The distress occasioned by this change was not felt until many years after the establishment of the central authority, seeing that feudal vanity prevented the chiefs from reducing their retinue immediately. One by one these petty monarchs died, and it was their successors, as a rule, who disbanded the superabundant labour. As will be noted in another chapter, Selkirk gathered together many of the dismissed retainers, and helped them to begin life afresh on the shores of the Canadian lakes.

The exertions made by benevolent societies during

---

[1] *Edinburgh Review*, vol. 7, pp. 188, 190.

THE CAUSES OF EMIGRATION 65

periods of special stress have also materially helped to raise the number of people emigrating. In 1872, we find that the exodus from England, as separate from the United Kingdom, was heavier than that accredited to any previous year, not only because there was intense distress reigning in London at that time, but because the charitable institutions, recognising the need for action, did their utmost to remove the sufferers from their squalid surroundings. Thus the year 1872 constituted, up to that date, a record in so far as English emigration is concerned, not because there was an undue amount of distress in the country, but because the emigration societies, noting this degree of want and poverty, made an unparalleled effort to send as many necessitous people out of the land as their funds would permit.[1] During the year in question, the British and Colonial Society, alone, sent out no less than 5089 people, whilst the East End Family Emigration Fund assisted over a thousand. The efforts of the West Ham Distress Committee, which provided for the emigration of 1034 people in 1906-7,[2] is also worthy of mention under this head.

The cost of the passage is another factor which may influence the flow of men and women from our shores, though on this matter a diversity of opinion exists. The Allan Line writes with reference to this question: " An experience extending now over more than fifty years enables us to say that rate-cutting has absolutely no effect whatever on the volume of emigration business. It may happen that during the currency of specially low passage rates, intending emigrants may anticipate their arrangements by a few weeks, possibly months, but we think it may be stated as an absolute fact that no British emigrant ever made

---

[1] Thirty-first Annual Report Colonial Land and Emigration Commissioners, 1870, p. 346.
[2] See Third Annual Report West Ham Distress Committee.

up his mind to leave his native country, and try his fortunes in Canada, the United States, or any of our Colonies, because there happens to be a temporary reduction in the rates of passage money. This remark, of course, does not apply to people of the class who may be described as 'transients,' who drift about from country to country whenever a favourable opportunity may offer."[1] Somewhat contradictory to this opinion expressed by the Allan Line is the following quotation, taken from the *Canadian Labour Gazette*.[2] "In September, 1904, the immigration movement from Great Britain was stimulated by the low steerage rates offered by the Atlantic transportation companies."

Emigration from the United Kingdom has thus been promoted by a number of causes, the chief among them being the phenomenal growth of population at the commencement of last century,[3] the many agricultural depressions of the same period, the continual introduction of labour-saving devices, the famine in Ireland, the growing competition in foreign markets, and the recent immigration propaganda organised by Colonial bodies. It would be impossible, says T. W. Page,[4] to enumerate all the causes which induce men to leave old homes for new. Sometimes, it is a mere spirit of adventure, a love of change. Very often the reasons are personal; sometimes they are involved and complicated, and however strongly felt, are but vaguely understood even by those who move under their influence. Whatever weakens the ties of home—bereavement, altered

---

[1] Communicated privately. [2] Issue of October, 1904, p. 417.

[3] Chandèze argues that in no European country during the nineteenth century did the growth of population outstrip the growth of wealth. The increase of wealth, he says, did not accrue in favourable proportions to the workers, but went to benefit the moneyed classes.—*De l'intervention des pouvoirs publics dans l'émigration*, p. 54.

[4] In the *Journal of Political Economy* (Chicago University publication), No. 8, October, 1911, p. 676.

THE CAUSES OF EMIGRATION

surroundings, domestic infelicity, social or political disappointment, economic difficulties, in short, any one of many things which may darken the current of life, urges men to a change of habitation. At the present day, when the means of transportation have become cheap, quick, and secure, the motives of emigration need not be so strong as was necessary to induce men to leave for America in the first three-quarters of the nineteenth century.

Finally, it must be claimed that emigration has been affected not only by conditions, economic and otherwise, ruling in the Home Country, but has been impelled and attracted also by various factors arising in the land of reception. The rapid expansion of industry and commerce within the United States and Canada, the almost unlimited scope for labour, the certainty of constant employment for such as are industrious, the ease with which land has been and still is acquired, and the freedom of civil institutions have all combined to swell the human streams which flow westward across the Atlantic.

CHAPTER IV

UNASSISTED AND ASSISTED EMIGRATION

BRITISH emigration may, for financial purposes, be classified under two headings, (*a*) unassisted and (*b*) assisted. The former class includes the people who are able, out of their own resources, to secure their transference to North America, whilst the latter embraces the vast numbers of emigrants who look to public or charitable funds for their passage, outfit, and other necessaries. In spite of the liberal sums which a generous nation has expended in this direction, it may be said that the former class is by far the greater.[1] The unassisted exodus is ever going on, month by month, year by year, never at any time unduly extensive, but formidable from its constancy. The assisted, on the other hand, is often subjected to greater measures of restriction, is more influenced by conditions of trade, politics, public feeling, and charity, and is therefore spasmodic.

The unassisted emigrants have left but few records behind them, preferring generally to quit their Mother Country as unostentatiously as possible. Nevertheless, there is sufficient information available to say that they disappear in a fairly constant stream, often taking with them considerable sums of money. No actual figures can be given of their numbers, but a rough estimate may be obtained by subtracting those who are known to have been assisted in any year from the total exodus. As an example, we may take the case of Ireland in the year 1888. The total Irish emigration

---

[1] See Report on Colonisation, 1889, p. 131, § 2466.

UNASSISTED & ASSISTED EMIGRATION 69

for this period was 79,000. Major Ruttledge Fair, giving evidence before one of the Select Committees on Colonisation,[1] estimated the cases assisted by the Poor Law as numbering 720,[2] whilst other cases receiving assistance were very few, being almost nil. Thus we may consider unassisted Irish emigration in 1888 roughly totalled 78,000 as against about 1000 assisted.

During the first fifteen odd years of the nineteenth century there was but little assistance available, so that the deductions necessary to give the unassisted exodus during this period are negligible.[3] It is true that some dispossessed farmers were helped by their overlords to sail to America, but this practice had not yet become general, and the numbers that left in this way were small. Lord Selkirk[4] may be mentioned as one who gave valuable aid to many Highland farmers, but the numbers he helped were infinitesimal when compared with those that actually sailed. Further evidence showing the popularity of unaided emigration may be gained indirectly from random quotations. The Report of the Coast of Scotland and Naval Enquiry,[5] tells that three thousand people emigrated from the Highlands in 1801 at their own expense. The Report of the Select Committee on Emigration of 1826, mentions the case of three hundred Scotchmen who sailed for Cape Breton Island in 1824, their passages being paid individually. The same report explains the system adopted by canvassers who travelled through the country persuading the people to buy ocean passages, naturally without any public assistance. In more recent times, we have records of the Barr

---

[1] The Select Committee on Colonisation, July 16, 1889.
[2] *Ibid.*, Report, p. 131.
[3] The figures of assisted emigration may be found in such annual publications as the Land and Emigration Commissioners' Reports, the Poor Law Reports, and the Local Government Board Reports.
[4] *Observations on the Present State of the Highlands*, by Selkirk, 1805.
[5] *Op. cit.*, p. 16.

Colony, a party of two thousand people who also went to Canada after providing for the journey themselves. Certain sources of shipping intelligence are also informing. In 1802 four vessels sailed from the west of Scotland, having on board fourteen hundred souls, who took a total of £100,000 sterling with them. Elsewhere, we read of three ships which chanced to leave Cork, in one day, bound for Canada and laden with emigrants who paid their own fares. The note casually mentions that one of the passengers on board cashed a cheque for £750 at the Provincial Bank of Ireland, a few hours before embarking, a fact which shows that one, at least, of the travellers was in possession of ample funds. At the present time, the volume of assisted emigration is considerably less than that of the unassisted,[1] a condition which, in some measure, arises from the restrictive policy adopted by the United States and Canada, which discourages the introduction of people unable to finance themselves.

Another form of emigration which has sometimes been classified as " semi-assisted " is that which springs from the remittances sent home by prosperous and grateful settlers in the New World. In this way, husbands are constantly sending for their wives and children, brothers for sisters, sons and daughters for parents, and friends for friends. This disposition to assist people in the Old Country is found to exist much more strongly among the Irish than the Scotch and English,[2] and obtains more frequently in the United States than in Canada. Some twenty years ago it was estimated that no less than 70 per cent of the passengers to the United States had their fares paid by friends already settled there, but with Canada the figures have never exceeded 5 per cent of the total.[3]

---

[1] Found by computing the known assisted emigration and subtracting it from the total exodus.

[2] Report on State of Irish Poor in Great Britain, p. 33, 1835.

[3] Canadian Sessional Papers, Vol. XXVIII., No. 9, p. 15, 1895.

Assistance of this nature is usually provided in the form of prepaid passage tickets, supplemented with small sums of money. A regular business is done in the sale of these tickets in the United States. The Inman Steamship Company engages 3400 agents to traffic in " advanced passages," and estimates that 33 per cent of its outward steerage passengers travel with them. The Anchor Line has 2500 agents, and 50 per cent of its steerage are provided with these tickets, while the percentage of prepaid people on the Cunard is fifteen and the Red Star Line, ten.[1] Large sums of actual money are also sent back annually to the Mother Country. For many years the Land and Emigration Commissioners, and afterwards the Board of Trade, gave estimates of these sums in their yearly reports, but as they could never correctly gauge the amounts forwarded privately, and as bankers grew more and more unwilling to publish returns indicating the moneys transmitted to them, it was considered useless to continue their publication. The annual assessments varied considerably; the maximum sum was credited to the year 1852, when £1,404,000 reached the United Kingdom from America; the minimum was recorded for the year 1864, when the sum forwarded was £332,172.[2] Between 1848 and 1878, a period of thirty years, the total amount remitted exceeded £21,000,000[3] a sum sufficient to emigrate comfortably an army of no less than two million people.

One of the earliest forms of assisted emigration of which we have any authentic record was that provided by certain captains who gratuitously carried destitute passengers to North America conditionally that, on landing, they should have the right to hire them to agricultural farmers for an arranged period of years.[4]

---

[1] Above figures given in evidence before the Ford Immigration Committee. See Report, pp. 1–56.
[2] Cf. Annual Reports of Land and Emigration Commissioners.
[3] Ibid.   [4] *Gentleman's Magazine*, vol. 65, 1795, p. 760.

This iniquitous system was one that imposed indescribable hardships on the redemptioners, as the employees were called. The employer had but one interest, that of exacting the fullest amount of work from his unfortunate charges before their period of slavery ceased, generally caring nothing for their condition when the term of bondage expired. It may be added that this arrangement was constantly practised in both the United States and Canada until about 1805.

The most important form of assisted emigration is that provided by philanthropic individuals and societies. We have already mentioned, in a previous chapter, the case of the proprietor of the Island of Rum who, in 1825, shared £600 amongst his tenants in order that they might escape from their crowded homes in Scotland. His action may be taken as typical of numbers of other instances. We have also spoken of the assistance afforded by Irish landlords who, between 1845 and 1856, dispossessed many of their smaller tenants. Further, we know that at the time of the Irish Famine, in order that sufferers might emigrate, considerable sums were privately raised to supplement the inadequate Government contributions. We may add to these examples the grants made during periods of agricultural depression by landlords who felt that it would be more satisfactory to subscribe voluntarily towards emigrating unemployed local labour than to be called upon to pay heavy parochial charges.

So far, the instances given go to show that assistance was of a spasmodic and disorganised nature, often emanating from people who benefited financially by the departure of those whom they helped. The year 1869, however, saw the commencement of an era of private enterprise which had, as its basis, charitable as distinct from commercial motives. As a pioneer in this sympathetic movement, the Baroness Burdett Coutts may be mentioned, for in this year she lent a considerable sum of money to a number of Ayrshire weavers in order that they might be enabled to emigrate.[1] The money so provided, it may be said, was not given outright, but merely tendered in the form of loans. Though we know that these weavers prospered and even sent back considerable sums to their friends, they never attempted to repay a penny to the Baroness —a line of action which seems to be followed by a large number of those who receive loans to enable them to emigrate.

Another benefactor was Mr. J. H. Tuke. He came forward in 1882 to render assistance to the poorer population of the west of Ireland. In three years, 1882, 1883, and 1884, he sent to Canada and the United States no less than 9482 people.[2] In the first year the expenses were entirely borne by private contributions, which in the three years amounted to about £20,000. Towards this sum, the then Chief Secretary for Ireland personally subscribed £500, the Duchess of Marlborough collected £3606 12s. 7d.,[3] and a few people who met at a gathering held by the Duke of Bedford spontaneously gave £8000.[4] Mr. Tuke and his committee, urged by the success of their first year's work, memorialised the Government, with the result that they received £44,000 under clauses in the Arrears of Rent Act, 1882, and the Tramways Act, 1883.[5] It should be added that a very small proportion of the money for this scheme was found by the emigrants themselves.

Lady Gordon Cathcart must also be mentioned as another philanthropist who gave much assistance to the emigrant classes. In 1878, on succeeding to her estates in the Hebrides, she found that many of the tenants were existing in a state of extreme want. In order to relieve this distress she devised various schemes

---

[1] See Report on Colonisation, 1889, p. 59. [2] *Ibid.*, p. 108.
[3] *Ibid.*, p. 108.   [4] *Ibid.*, 1890, p. 202.   [5] *Ibid.*, pp. 202-3.

for providing temporary employment, such as the draining and levelling of land, but no permanent good resulted, and the poverty gradually grew more intense. As a final measure, she turned to emigration, and provided for the colonisation of ten families in 1883 and fifty-six in 1884.[1] The Dominion Land Act of 1883 came before her notice, and she availed herself of its provisions. The Act enabled a philanthropically disposed person to spend £100 on the settling of a family in Manitoba or the North-West Territories, and to recover the sum from the head of the family, together with 6 per cent interest, before the Dominion would grant the settler his patent for the land.[2] It may be said that the Act was slightly amended in 1886 and 1889, the amount of interest and the initial capital being modified.

Lady Cathcart made a loan of £100 to each of the families which sailed in 1883, and a similar amount was provided by her in conjunction with the North-West Land Company for the fifty-six families in 1884. The average sum spent on each family for passage to Winnipeg was £25, whilst an additional £10 was disbursed for outfit and other expenses on this side of the Atlantic.[3] The remainder of the loan was expended in preparing the homestead.

In return for these benefits the settlers showed but little gratitude. Many of them, after a few years' residence, claimed to be destitute though they seem to have possessed means.[4] During the ensuing twenty-three years, only one recipient refunded his loan in full, whilst most of his neighbours had not even kept up the payments of the promised interest. Some clamoured successfully for a reduction of the interest from 6 to 3 per cent, whilst others begged to be allowed to spend their savings on the purchase of additional

---

[1] Report on Colonisation, 1890, pp. 217–8.
[2] See Report on Colonisation, 1889, pp. 190–1.
[3] Ibid., 1891, p. 48, § VI.   [4] Ibid.

UNASSISTED & ASSISTED EMIGRATION

stock. Financially, Lady Gordon Cathcart fared badly over the transaction.[1]

Of a somewhat different nature was the scheme carried out by Sir J. Rankin, another philanthropist, in 1885. He contended that if a settler could only weather the first season or two while his lands were being cleared, his success would be assured. As an experiment, therefore, Sir J. Rankin secured land in 1882 at Elkhorn in Manitoba, and gradually developed it. In 1885 he selected twenty-five families, making a total of one hundred and twenty people, and put them to work on the partly prepared land. He bore all expenses incidental to passage, taxes, seeds, etc., on condition that each tenant should give him half the crops. Nothing was spared to ensure success for the scheme; £32,000 was spent in money, thousands of people were examined before the twenty-five heads of families were chosen, and only those likely to prove healthy and hardworking finally sailed. In spite of these precautions the plan proved a failure, but it is satisfactory to know that Sir J. Rankin estimated he had received a return of 2 per cent on his capital from the sale of the crops which reverted to him during the first four years, and that he suffered no pecuniary loss on selling his untenanted plots, as these had undergone some measure of improvement.[2]

During the last thirty years a number of societies have come into existence for the purpose of emigrating the needy, whilst many long-established charitable associations have added emigration departments to their various activities. All of these bodies are cramped for funds and overcrowded with applications for assistance. As a consequence, the process of selecting candidates, adopted by them, is conducted

---

[1] See Report on Agricultural Settlements in British Colonies, 1906, § 1080. Also Chapter X., "Colonisation Schemes."

[2] See Report on Colonisation, 1891, p. 48, § VII.; and also 1890, Report generally.

with much severity. In many cases the inspection or examination extends over a period of some weeks, and is always of a most searching nature. The routine of inspection is much the same whatever the society. The Charity Organisation Society and the East End Emigration Fund usually require an applicant to obtain a written promise from some friend, already settled in the Colonies, who will guarantee to provide for him between his arrival and the time when he obtains employment. In addition to this, the colonial friend is also asked to obtain a certificate from a local government official, stating that he, himself, is a fit person to undertake the guarantee. When these papers can be produced, the candidate is called upon to submit to a somewhat severe examination not only medically,[1] but also concerning his character. Emerging from this to his credit, his debts are paid for him, any articles he may have pledged are redeemed, and clothes to complete his outfit supplied. He is then conducted to the railway or steamer, and met again when landing on American soil.

In order to save working expenses, many of the societies have amalgamated their vigilance departments. The Charity Organisation Society and the East End Emigration Fund work hand in hand, the Church Army has sent numbers of people through the Self-Help Society,[2] and many smaller organisations use the machinery of the Salvation Army. In 1885 some attempt was made to link up the various agencies in London, with a view to saving routine and management fees, but though an influential body was formed consisting of such well-known men as Lord Lorne, Lord Meath, the Right Honourable W. H. Smith, Sir J. Rankin and Mr. Tuke, the federation failed,

---

[1] Some societies require no medical examination; e.g. "Self-Help."

[2] See Report on Agricultural Settlements in British Colonies, 1906, § 1260.

UNASSISTED & ASSISTED EMIGRATION

as the various societies feared that they might lose their individuality and consequently their public support.[1]

The Self-Help Emigration Society commenced work in 1884, since which date it has emigrated an average of four hundred people yearly. It usually assists those who show an inclination for agricultural occupations, and sends chiefly to Canada. Married people with two or three children are encouraged in preference to those with large families, as the latter, the Society holds, are apt to drift to the bigger towns. The Society, as its name implies, only helps those who can provide part of their own expenses. Up to 1905 it had spent £47,000, of which £37,000 came from sources other than those provided by its own funds.[2] In 1911, 465 people received assistance at a cost of £4214, of which the emigrants personally furnished £3561.[3] In cases where the head of a family wishes to go to Canada or Australia, but cannot make any contribution towards his expenses, he is referred to his local relieving officer, who, through the Board of Guardians, has power[4] to make him a grant of not more than £10, which the Self-Help Society may then supplement.

The combined forces of the East End Emigration Fund and the Charity Organisation Society sent 1138 people to Canada, 42 to the United States, 163 to Australasia, and 6 to South Africa, making a total of 1349 souls, in the year 1910–11.[5] Towards this exodus, general donations provided a sum of £3773 2s. 6d. ;

---

[1] See " Federation of Emigration Societies " in Report on Colonisation, 1890.

[2] See Report on Agricultural Settlements in British Colonies, 1906, pp. 50–3.

[3] General Handbook (Emigrants' Information Office), 1912 edition p. 105.

[4] For powers, see section of this chapter dealing with Governmen assistance.

[5] See Thirtieth Annual Report East End Emigration Fund, pp. 12–13

Local Relief Agencies, £5161 8s. 4d.; and the emigrants themselves, £1421 3s. The year was commenced with a balance in hand of £78 10s. 10d., and a sum of £571 5s. 6d. remained after all expenses had been defrayed. The joint body has sent out no less than 23,598 people during the last thirty years.

The Church Emigration Society was inaugurated in 1886 to locate emigrant members of the Church of England in places where they could be cared for by co-religionists. The system, however, has recently been reconstructed on a broader basis, and non-church people are now assisted also. Emigrants are always sent in batches under the guidance of a chaplain, who sees that each of his charges on landing is placed in the care of a supervisor, the latter promising to give every assistance in both spiritual and temporal matters. During 1911, 703 individuals were despatched by the Society, at a cost of £4792.[1]

The Church Army has been engaged in emigration work during the last twenty years. At first it began by arranging for thirty or forty people to sail each year, but the numbers grew until in 1907 the total for the season nearly reached 1500 emigrants. This Society escorts those who are able to pay their own fares, but who need guidance; it obtains situations for them, gives them introductions to local clergy, and otherwise befriends them. It also pays the passages of people who are penniless, but requires repayment in small instalments after work has been obtained. It strongly believes in some previous training before the new country is reached. With this view, a prospective candidate for emigration must serve, first, a period of apprenticeship in one of the Army labour homes, and second, a course of training in the special colony at Newdigate, Surrey.

---

[1] See Annual Report of the Society.

UNASSISTED & ASSISTED EMIGRATION 79

The Army expenditure for the season 1907 was £11,266, of which the emigrants and their friends contributed £3971.[1]

The Salvation Army first organised an emigration department some eleven years ago.[2] It was prompted to enter into this field as a result of the congested condition of its home labour bureaux. Since this time, assistance has been extended to no less than fifty thousand people, financial assistance being rendered in over eight thousand cases.[3] Where passages and money grants are provided they are not extended as gifts, but repayment is expected. In 1903, £1000 was advanced in this way, a quarter of which sum had been refunded by October, 1906.[4] The Army does exceptionally good work, in that the bulk of its followers, being town-bred people, are provided with occupations of an agricultural nature. Of five thousand emigrants cared for in 1904 and 1905, no less than 76 per cent were found work on farms.[5]

Many other philanthropic bodies have provided emigration assistance. The following are amongst the most noted: the Bristol Emigration Society, which shipped 375 people in 1911; the Central Emigration Board, which assisted 367 people in 1907, the year of its inception; the Jewish Board of Guardians and the Jewish Emigration Society, the latter of which has provided for an aggregate of no less than 11,425 members; the London Colonisation Aid Society; the Tunbridge Wells Colonisation Association; the Liverpool Self-Help Society; and the Tower Hamlets Mission Emigration and Colonisation Fund, a body which as a rule pays half the passage money to those whom it befriends.[6] In addition to

---

[1] See Annual Report of the Society.
[2] Information kindly supplied by Colonel Lamb, of the Salvation Army.   [3] *Ibid.*
[4] Report on Agricultural Settlements in British Colonies, 1906, § 770.   [5] *Ibid.*, § 908.
[6] See various Annual Reports of these societies.

the above there are societies which devote their energies solely to the care of women and children, as, for example, the British Women's Emigration Association and Dr. Barnardo's Homes.[1]

Yet another form of assisted emigration has sprung into existence owing to the provisions of the Dominion Land Act, an Act which has been mentioned already in connection with the enterprise of Lady Cathcart. Several commercial associations have been floated to provide emigrants with farm plots, seeds, implements, and money; in return they receive payments in accordance with the provisions of this Act. The chief companies which have been concerned in this business are the Commercial Colonisation Company of Manitoba, the Canada Settlers' Loan and Trust Company, the North-West Land Company, and the Manitoba and North-West Railway Company. The operations of these concerns in no wise partake of a charitable nature, but are worked on a purely commercial basis.[2]

An important source of assistance is that which must be credited to the emigration funds of various trade unions. The first intimation we have that help was being given in this quarter dates from the early forties. *The Potter's Examiner* for June 8th, 1844, contains the following advertisement :—

A HOME FOR THE POOR!

On Wednesday Evening Next, June 11th, 1844.

A Public Meeting of all branches of Operative Potters will take place in the Temperance Hall, Burslem, when the principles and rules of

The Potter's Joint Stock & Emigration Company

will be laid before the meeting and its object duly explained.

Doors open at 7. Chair at 7.30. Admission Free.

" Oh shame that bread should be so dear
and human lives so cheap."

---

[1] See Chapters XI and XII.
[2] Report on Colonisation, p. 124, § 2141, etc.

UNASSISTED & ASSISTED EMIGRATION

The joint stock company referred to above, it may be explained, had for its object the purchase of twelve thousand acres of land in the Western States, which it proposed to sell in small lots to members at cost price, the repayment being made by instalments spread over ten years. Previous to the founding of this company, the Potter's Union had been spending £60 to £70 weekly in providing assistance for its members, and it felt that this sum would be effecting a more lasting good were it diverted to an emigration fund. References in later issues of *The Examiner* show that many people within the Staffordshire district paid a fee of sixpence weekly and became members, emigrating in due course.

From this time until the early sixties, we find that the balance sheets of many of the larger unions included sums spent on providing emigration assistance.[1] At first this expenditure was incurred with the idea of clearing the particular trade of its surplus workers, and so keeping the wages at a normal level, but, after a while, it was found that the money which could be spared for this purpose was so rapidly absorbed that the benefits were imperceptible. After 1860, therefore, the expenditure of union funds for emigration purposes gradually shrank, a condition which was welcomed by Australian and American trade unions, as these bodies looked with fear upon the organised importation of labour from the Mother Country.[2]

In spite of the tendency for trade unions to cease providing emigration benefits, certain societies still offer their members assistance of this nature. The London Society of Compositors has paid the following sums in emigration benefits :—[3]

---

[1] Webb, *History of Trade Unionism*, p. 184.
[2] Mr. Burnett's evidence before Select Committee on Colonisation, 1889. See Report, p. 98, § 1863.
[3] See Jubilee Record of London Society of Compositors, 1898.

				£	s.	d.			£	s.	d.
Between	1853	and	1857	800	0	0, giving an annual average of	....	160	0	0
,,	1857	,,	1871	. (discontinued paying emigration benefits).
,,	1871	,,	1872	345	14	0, giving an average of	172	17	0
,,	1873	,,	1877	674	16	10	,,	,,	134	19	4
,,	1878	,,	1882	979	12	0	,,	,,	195	18	7
,,	1883	,,	1887	1054	0	0	,,	,,	210	16	0
,,	1888	,,	1892	1070	0	0	,,	,,	214	0	0
,,	1893	,,	1897	983	11	8	,,	,,	196	14	4

Total between 1853 and 1897, £5907 14s. 6d., giving an average of £190 11s. 5d. per annum.

Until 1890, the maximum allowance per member was £10, but afterwards it was increased to £15. The Amalgamated Society of Lithographic Printers spent the following money :—

			£
Half year ending	March, 1888	....	15
,,	,,	September, 1888	....	47
,,	,,	March, 1889	....	43
,,	,,	September, 1889	....	22
,,	,,	March, 1890	....	14
,,	,,	September, 1890	....	45
,,	,,	September, 1891	....	28
,,	,,	March, 1892	....	12
,,	,,	September, 1892	....	12

Other societies that have been known to grant emigration assistance are the Alliance Cabinet Makers' Society, which has paid £240 in nineteen years ; the Amalgamated Cabinet Makers, £262 in twelve years ; the Iron Founders, £4712 in twelve years ; the Kent and Sussex Labourers, £2094 in seventeen years ; the Cigar Makers, £1257 in seven years ; the Northumberland Miners, £1293 in four years ; the Locomotive Enginemen and Firemen, £261 in 1887, and £125 in 1888.[1]

The rules controlling emigration of the Union of Saddle and Harness Makers are both typical and informing. In their Annual Report of 1891, they state them as follows : (*a*) Members desirous of emigrating, who have joined at least twelve calendar months, benefit by £1 ; if joined at least two years, £2 ; and

---

[1] These figures are obtained from the Annual Reports of the various unions. The Reports are preserved in the " Webb Collection " at the Library of Political Science, London.

if three or more years, £3. If, however, a three years member intends travelling over five thousand miles, £4 will be paid to his shipping agent, or to him if he produces his passage warrant. (*b*) Any member who returns within two years from the date of departure, and repays two-thirds of his emigration benefit, is entitled to come on the fund at any future time if he so desires. (*c*) A member being away over two years may return and enjoy the full privileges of the society after a lapse of three months. Similar rules to (*b*) and (*c*) have been framed by most of the unions which still provide assistance of this nature, a fact which seems to suggest that emigrants sailing under the auspices of trade societies have a weakness for returning to their Mother Country.

Co-operation is a feature which, from earliest times, marked the growth of trade union assistance. As far back as 1858, we hear of neighbouring societies putting their emigration money into common funds, for, as they rightly argued, the departure of a workman from a certain trade not only relieved his own society, but helped to prevent the over-stocking of his particular trade. One of the first cases of this form of co-operation was furnished by the Scottish Typographical Union, which undertook the emigration business of the printing unions of Glasgow, Edinburgh, and other Scotch towns.[1] At its inaugural meeting in 1858 a speaker said :—

> The object of our emigration fund is to lessen the pressure on the labour market generally, and I am of opinion that the members of other societies are equally benefited, and therefore the burden of those leaving the country should be borne by the whole branches throughout Scotland.

The speaker went on to urge as a second reason for co-operation, the abuses which often arose in small local societies.

---

[1] See Circular published by Scottish Typographical Union, March, 1858, p. 64.

Beyond this, I must refer to the local influence which is brought to bear when a person is going away. It must be obvious to the delegates that a person applying for aid could bring as many friends to the meeting at which his case was to be considered as would vote a sum of money far too large: some members had received as much as £7 10s. when leaving. The *modus operandi* proposed is this: Instead of a person applying for aid to the local society, all the circumstances should be communicated to and decided upon by the Board.

Of late years, trade union funds have been devoted almost solely to benefiting members who have become marked men,[1] or "victims," as the societies term them. These people have usually taken an active part in some trade dispute, and, in consequence, have brought personal disrepute upon themselves. The Cotton Spinners' Society, which now only assists such members, has a rule as follows: "In the event of any member of this association being in receipt of the Society's funds as a victim and being wishful to emigrate to some foreign country, he shall be allowed to do so, and to receive one-half the pay he is entitled to at the time he wishes to emigrate. Any member who is in receipt of Dispute pay shall be allowed nine weeks full pay. Victim pay is 12s. a week for twenty weeks, and Dispute pay is 10s. a week for the same length of time."[2]

As a general rule, the unions make no stipulation that a person is to settle in any special country when accepting their assistance. They feel that an emigrant should be allowed a free hand to go where he pleases, in spite of the fact that he may be taking his skilled labour into a country possessing a tariff hostile to British interests. In modification of this principle, it may be well to mention a regulation framed by the Amalgamated Society of Engineers, which says that

---

[1] See Report on Colonisation, 1889, p. 92, § 1784.
[2] See Rules of Society.
[3] See Report on Colonisation, 1889, §§ 1833, 1838.

UNASSISTED & ASSISTED EMIGRATION

the members are only allowed to settle in districts where less than 7½ per cent of the local members are unemployed.

So far, this enquiry into assisted emigration has dealt only with that section of the movement which has arisen out of such organisations as have been promoted by charitably disposed persons or bodies. The State, however, has also played some part in this national undertaking, having promoted emigration both with central and local funds.

The first Government grant consisted of a sum of £50,000, given by the House of Commons in 1819, to assist emigration to the Cape of Good Hope.[1] Subsequent grants in aid were voted and spent on settling distressed agricultural workers in Canada and the Cape. These amounted to £68,760 in 1821; £15,000 in 1823; and £30,000 in 1825.[2] In 1827 a further grant of £20,480 was made for emigration purposes generally, £10,000 of which was to be reserved, however, for surveys and enquiries in Canada.[3]

The first appearance of an emigration establishment on the Imperial vote was in 1834, when £1457 was provided for seven half-pay lieutenants who were appointed emigration agents at Liverpool, Bristol, Dublin, Belfast, Cork, Limerick and Greenock respectively, with a salary of £208 5s. each. This grant was the nucleus of a vote which grew rapidly, reaching at one time £25,000 per annum, and which continued to appear in Class 5, year by year, between 1834 and 1878 inclusive.[4] In later years, an annual grant of various amounts has been made for the maintenance of the Emigrants' Information Office.

---

[1] Report on Agricultural Settlements in British Colonies, 1906, p. 327; also cf. Chapter II.
[2] *Ibid.*   [3] *Ibid.*   [4] *Ibid.*

Isolated grants were made at various times. In 1836-7 a sum of £70,000 was collected, towards which the Government contributed freely, to alleviate the distress in Scotch agricultural circles. In 1845 the Imperial Parliament made a temporary annual vote of £2000 to assist indigent emigrants on landing in Canada. This sum was increased to £10,000 during the Irish Famine. Lastly, in 1888-9, a grant of £10,000 was made on behalf of the Crofters' Colonisation Scheme.[1]

Not only has the Government, in the past, made direct grants of money towards the furtherance of the emigration movement, but it has also invested certain local bodies with statutory powers in order that they may spend money for a like purpose. Up till 1834 English parishes could grant moneys for assisting emigration, but they had no special instructions in the matter. The Report of the Select Committee on Emigration of 1826 mentions, *inter alia*, the case of certain Kentish labourers who were provided from Poor Law funds with sums of £13 each in order to enable them to sail for New York.

The first statutory provision which directly dealt with English and Welsh emigration was the Poor Law Amendment Act of 1834,[2] an Act which was suggested by the Poor Law Commission of 1832. Its aim was to enable ratepayers and owners of property to raise money on the security of the rates in order to meet the expenses incurred in emigrating poor people having settlements in the parish. Any ratepayer could request the overseer of his parish to convene a meeting to consider the need of emigrating people who were chargeable to the rates. If the meeting were favourably inclined to the proposal, the Commissioners were to be approached and they would supply the necessary moneys from the Treasury on condition that the parish

---

[1] Vide Chapter X, "Colonisation Schemes," p. 240.
[2] 4 and 5 Will. c. 76, sec. 62.

UNASSISTED & ASSISTED EMIGRATION

made the repayments in certain stated instalments. The parish had then to levy an emigration rate twice a year, on March 25th and September 29th, and the debt was to be cleared in ten years. No greater sum than half the average yearly rate for the three preceeding years, it may be said, could be spent for this purpose.

This Act of 1834 was frequently amended. In 1844, 7 and 8 Vict. c. 101, sec. 29, provided that the emigration fund should be applied by the Guardians of a union instead of by the churchwardens and overseers of a parish as was previously the case. In 1848 the Poor Law Relief Act[1] empowered the Guardians, with consent from the Poor Law Board, to assist in procuring the emigration of poor people who were chargeable and irremovable by virtue of 9 and 10 Vict. c. 66. The cost of this relief was to be borne by the several parishes of the union in proportion to their rateable value. Later, in 1849, by 12 and 13 Vict. c. 103, sec. 20, the Guardians could expend limited sums without calling a previous meeting of ratepayers as required by the Act of 1834. Section 14 of this same statute set out financial measures for the temporary housing, in workhouses belonging to unions other than their own, of people awaiting the departure of their vessels. This was enacted in order to facilitate matters of transit, to escape overcrowding, and to avoid contagion in times of epidemics.

With a view to curtailing still further the direct power of ratepayers and owners of property and increasing that of the Guardians, the Union Chargeability Act of 1865[2] removed emigration expenses from the list of parish charges and placed them among those of the union. 29 and 30 Vict. c. 113, sec. 9, directed that money raised for emigration and not spent for this purpose should be used either in reducing emigra-

---

[1] 11 and 12 Vict. c. 110, sec. 5.
[2] 28 and 29 Vict. c. 79.

tion loans or should be applied to aid the current rate. A further Act[1] in 1871 established the present Local Government Board and vested in it, *inter alia*, all the powers hitherto entrusted to the Poor Law Commissioners, and subsequently the Poor Law Board. No Board of Guardians, therefore, can now assist any person to emigrate out of the rates, unless in each case the sanction of the Local Government Board is first obtained.

At the present moment, the Guardians of a union or of any separate parish may expend, subject to the rules of the Local Government Board, but not otherwise, any sum of money not exceeding £10 for each person, in emigrating poor people having settlements in or being irremovable from such union or parish.[2] This power may be exercised whether the person is in receipt of relief or not, but no money may be utilised in transferring people to the United States.

At this point, it is well to see how these various statutes have assisted in the cause of emigration. From June, 1835, to June, 1836, 5141 adults were given emigration relief by the English and Welsh Boards of Guardians at a cost of £28,414 7s.[3] During the following twelve months, 1836 to 1837, the numbers fell to 982, and the expenditure to £7531.[4] In the four succeeding years, the people numbered 752, 829, 963, and 675; whilst the cost incurred on their behalf was £3478 19s. 5½d., £3069 4s. 2½d., £2700 4s. 1d., and £5918 3s. 2d. respectively.[5]

It is interesting to note how these figures were spread over the country. The Second Report of the Poor Law Commissioners gives the following details:—

---

[1] 34 and 35 Vict. c. 70.
[2] Provided by 11 and 12 Vict. c. 110, sec. 5, and 12 and 13 Vict. c. 103, sec. 20.
[3] Second Poor Law Commissioners' Report, p. 574.
[4] Third Poor Law Commissioners' Report, p. 126.
[5] 4th, 5th, 6th, and 7th Poor Law Comm. Reports.

UNASSISTED & ASSISTED EMIGRATION

					£	s.	d.
Bradford emigrated	18 people.	Raised emigration fund of	215	0	0
Buckingham	,,	25	,,	,,	100	0	0
Berks	,,	30	,,	,,	150	0	0
Cambridge	,,	39	,,	,,	201	0	0
Huntingdon	,,	27	,,	,,	200	0	0
Hants	,,	182	,,	,,	1068	14	0
Kent	,,	320	,,	,,	1823	9	3
Lincoln	,,	17	,,	,,	100	0	0
Middlesex	,,	88	,,	,,	860	0	0
Northampton	,,	23	,,	,,	135	0	0
Norfolk	,,	3068	,,	,,	15,198	10	0
Oxford	,,	11	,,	,,	40	0	0
Somerset	,,	11	,,	,,	50	0	0
Sussex	,,	248	,,	,,	2032	7	4
Suffolk	,,	787	,,	,,	4198	0	0
Wilts	,,	347	,,	,.	2042	0	0

During the years 1836-46 the Poor Law Commissioners provided assistance for 14,000 people in England and Wales, a sum of £80,000 to £90,000 being awarded by the parishes for this purpose.[1] The exodus leaving under the auspices of the various Boards of Guardians averaged 1400 annually during these ten years, quite a small number when we remember that the mean annual emigration for this period amounted to 18,000. Kent, Somerset, and Sussex provided the highest figures, whilst Buckinghamshire took fourth place. As a rule, the people accepting assistance were directed to Canada, but a few were allowed to sail for Australia, and a much smaller number had special permission to join friends in the United States.

An examination of the Annual Reports of the Poor Law Commissioners and the Poor Law Board shows that Parish assistance gradually waned until in 1864-5 a total throughout the country of only thirty-six people received its benefits, the cost in this case being £387 15s.[2] After the appointment of the Local Government Board in 1871, a certain measure of popularity seems to have returned temporarily to

---

[1] Mr. Lumley's evidence on " Parish Assistance " before Select Committee of House of Lords, 1847.
[2] See Seventeenth Annual Report Poor Law Board, 1864-5.

parochially assisted emigration. The following figures, taken from the Board's Annual Reports, serve not only to record local activity, but also to trace, somewhat indirectly, the rising and falling prosperity of the working classes since 1871.

Year.	Sums expended.			People emigrated locally.[1]	Page of reference in Annual Report for the year mentioned.
1871	7451	16	0	893	490
1872	5106	0	0	718	XXXVII
1873	2234	0	0	369	See Eighth Report
1874	1799	0	0	302	XXXII
1875	378	0	0	108	XXXV
1876	245	0	0	70	XXXIX
1877	97	0	0	27	XLII
1878	104	0	0	23	XLIX
1879	122	0	0	34	XXXVIII
1880	248	0	0	52	XXXVII
1881	593	0	0	173	XLIV
1882	781	4	6	220	XLII
1883	525	0	0	296	XLIX
1884	925	19	0	196	XXXV
1885	716	1	2	133	XXXVI
1886	730	0	0	223	LIII
1887	1121	0	0	369	LXIV
1888	663	14	2	268	XCVII
1889	473	14	6	130	XCII
1890	271	10	0	72	XCIII
1891	274	15	1	43	LXXXIV
1892	209	10	0	59	LXXXVIII
1893	197	0	0	38	XCV
1894	301	0	0	45	CIV
1895	237	0	0	46	LXXXVIII
1896	146	0	0	21	XCIII
1897	128	0	0	14	LXXVII
1898	115	0	0	12	LXXXVIII
1899	111	0	0	21	XCII
1900	168	0	0	17	XCI
1901	188	0	0	21	CI
1902	308	0	0	47	CXIII
1903	445	0	0	66	CVIII
1904	652	0	0	77	CXIX
1905	2512	0	0	317	CXXXV
1906	3236	0	0	498	CXXVIII
1907	5897	0	0	867	CXXX
1908	1062[2]	0	0	196	p. 152 Appendix
1909	1421	0	0	213	39th Report, 1909–10, Part I

[1] Not including children emigrated under Special Childrens' Act.
[2] Decrease due to the severe restrictive policy of the Dominion of Canada.

UNASSISTED & ASSISTED EMIGRATION

With reference to Ireland, the first Act which gave emigration powers to Boards of Guardians was the Poor Law Relief Act of 1838.[1] This enabled the Poor Law Commissioners, upon the application of the Guardians, to direct a meeting of ratepayers to be called. When the majority, in value, of such ratepayers agreed to the levying of an emigration rate, the Commissioners could direct the Guardians to raise sums for this purpose not exceeding a shilling in the pound upon the net value of the rateable property of such division. The further Amendment Act of 1843[2] required no preliminary meeting of the ratepayers, and limited the levy to sixpence instead of a shilling in the pound. The Poor Relief Act of 1847,[3] empowered the Guardians to spend money on destitute people who were not inmates of workhouses. It also gave facilities for assisting landlords who encouraged their destitute tenants to emigrate. The section[4] of the Act which allowed these privileges ran as follows :—

"If it shall be proved to the satisfaction of the Board of Guardians at any time that any occupier of land within such union rated at a net annual value not exceeding five pounds shall be willing to give up to his landlord his right and title to the actual possession of the said land, whether held under lease or as tenant at will and to emigrate, together with all persons who may be dependent upon him for their support and maintenance, and that such occupier shall have been approved by Her Majesty's Principal Secretary of State for the Colonies, or such person as he may appoint for that purpose, as a fit and proper person to be admitted as an emigrant ; and that the immediate lessor of such occupier is willing, upon the emigration of such occupier and his family, and upon the surrender of the land occupied by him, to forego any claim for rent which he may have upon the said occupier, and also to provide two-thirds of such fair and reasonable sum as shall be required for the emigration of such occupier and his family, then and in such cases it shall be lawful for the Board of Guar-

---

[1] 1 and 2 Vict. c. 56, sec. 51.
[3] 10 and 11 Vict. c. 31.
[2] 6 and 7 Vict. c. 92, sec. 18.
[4] Section 13.

dians of such union, if they shall think fit, upon payment to them of such last-mentioned sum, to charge upon the rates and to pay in addition to such sum, in such manner as shall be directed by the Poor Law Commissioners, in aid of such occupier and his family, any sum not exceeding one-half of the sum contributed and paid by such immediate lessors as aforesaid, notwithstanding that such occupier and his family may not be nor have been inmates of the workhouse of such union.

The Further Amending Act of 1849[1] enabled Guardians to assist the progress of emigration with moneys arising out of any rate, and not as in former cases with moneys collected for this purpose alone; it allowed them to raise loans for furthering emigration, and cancelled the order which required them to depend solely on local levies; it also allowed assistance to be given when the destination was outside the Queen's Dominions. These extreme measures were necessitated by the famine which was devastating the country at that time. No further changes affecting Irish emigration were enacted until the Arrears of Rent Act[2] became law in 1882. This Act had much in common with its predecessor of 1849, the chief points of difference being concerned with the matter of advances. These, the new Act said, may be made by the Commissioners of Public Works out of moneys granted to them for the purpose of loans instead of by the Public Works Loans Commissioners, who had hitherto undertaken such transactions. Every such advance was to bear interest at 3½ per cent per annum, and was to be repaid within a period, to be decided by the Treasury, of not less than fifteen nor more than thirty years. Powers were also given, by this Act, to the Lord-Lieutenant for the proper conduct of emigration.

Turning now to the figures which resulted from these legislative measures, we find that the data affecting

---

[1] 12 and 13 Vict. c. 104, secs. 26–8.
[2] 45 and 46 Vict. c. 47, secs. 18–19.

UNASSISTED & ASSISTED EMIGRATION

the early years are somewhat untrustworthy,[1] and on this account are of little value. The audited, and therefore reliable, accounts for the six months ending September 29th, 1846, however, state that £797 was expended during this period by Irish Boards of Guardians, and the letterpress explanations, accompanying the figures, convey the impression that this sum is well in advance of any earlier ones. More definite information has been preserved in connection with later enterprise. During the famine of 1847–9 money was provided in accordance with the provisions of the Poor Relief Extension Act of 1847 to provide for the following numbers, numbers which are absurdly small when compared with the distress then prevailing.[2]

Union of	Kilrush	1848	124 people
,,	,,	1849	149 ,,
,,	Tipperary	1848	35 ,,
,,	Larne	1848	6 ,,
,,	Londonderry	1848	8 ,,
,,	Ennis	1848	24 ,,
,,	Loughrea	1848	8 ,,
,,	Listowel	1848	22 ,,
,,	Manorhamilton	1848	7 ,,
,,	,,	1849	90 ,,
,,	Baltinglase	1849	442 ,,
,,	Ballycastle	1849	30 ,,
,,	Coleraine	1849	59 ,,
,,	Naas	1849	3 ,,

Under the Act of 1849, and the modifying Act of 1882, 44,860 people were assisted to emigrate up to March 31st, 1909, at a total expense of £161,725. Of these emigrants 5840 were men, 20,929 were women, and 18,081 were children under fifteen years of age. The annual figures are much the largest for the twelve months ending March 25th, 1852, 1853, 1854, and 1855, when 4386, 3825, 2601, and 3794 people left, respectively. The only subsequent years in which the exodus exceeded a thousand were those ending March 25th, 1866, 1881, 1882, 1883, and 1884, the

---

[1] See 'Major Ruttledge Fair's Memorandum A on p. 200, Report on Colonisation, 1889.

[2] Report of Committee operating Irish Poor Laws, 1849, Vol. XVI., p.63.

number in this latter year being 2161. In the year ending March, 1911, the Irish Boards of Guardians only provided for twenty-six people, the expenditure incurred being £176.[1]

From the foregoing, it will be seen that the powers vested in the English, Welsh, and Irish Boards are of an important and comprehensive nature. In spite of this, these bodies have never provided emigration assistance on an adequate scale. The reasons are perhaps twofold. The emigrants themselves are often very loath to set out burdened with the cloak of pauperism; and, secondly, the class of people who do apply for parochial help are largely composed of those whom the various American Immigration Laws are framed to shut out. On this point, the Secretary of the Local Government Board said, when giving evidence before the Select Committee on Colonisation in 1889.[2] "The number of people who actually become chargeable to the rates and who are in any way fit for emigration, is very small. A comparatively small number of men apply for relief on the ground of being out of work, a certain proportion of whom might perhaps be fit to emigrate, but the Guardians know very well that these men are only likely to remain a charge on the rates for short periods, and they do not think it necessary to assist in the emigration of persons of that class."

Emigration powers have also been entrusted to County Councils and certain Borough Councils.[3] By the English and Welsh Local Government Act of 1888,[4] these bodies may, with the consent of the Local Government Board, borrow money for the purpose of making advances to any person in their area who is desirous and fit to emigrate or colonise. Sums so

---

[1] Report of Local Government Board (Ireland).
[2] Pages 154–5 of the Report.
[3] Those which had either a population of over 50,000 on June 1st, 1888, or are referred to in the Act as county boroughs.
[4] 51 and 52 Vict. c. 41, sec. 69.

UNASSISTED & ASSISTED EMIGRATION   95

borrowed must be repaid within thirty years in amounts as directed by the Local Loans Act of 1875.[1] So far, no Council has ever made use of these powers, probably owing to an almost prohibitive clause which requires a local authority to stand as guarantee for such repayments. Referring to this matter, the Report on Colonisation of 1891 says :[2] " With respect to the guarantee, almost the only local authority that can be expected to give it is a Poor Law Authority, and the intervention of such an authority in a scheme of emigration or colonisation is not likely to render it more acceptable to the Government either of a colony or of a foreign country. There seems also to be great practical difficulty in a County or Borough Council obtaining a guarantee directly from the Government of a colony."

Almost similar powers were conferred on County Councils in Scotland by the Local Government (Scotland) Act of 1889, section 67, but up to the present day they also have not been utilised.

From time to time, various responsible bodies in the United Kingdom, other than Boards of Guardians and County Councils, have been granted parliamentary powers with the object of furthering the cause of emigration. In Ireland, the Land Law Act of 1881[3] enabled the Land Commissioners to advance loans for this purpose to an amount not exceeding £200,000. The Arrears of Rent Act, already mentioned in connection with Boards of Guardians, empowered the Commissioners of Public Works to make grants to certain poor unions or persons in aid of emigration, but the aggregate payments, which were to be made a charge on the Irish Church Temporalities Fund, were limited to £100,000, whilst the award per person was never to exceed £5. These amounts were, however,

---

[1] 38 and 39 Vict. c. 83. [2] *Op. cit.*, p. vi.
[3] 44 and 45 Vict. c. 49, sec. 32.

increased to £200,000 and £8 respectively by the Tramways and Public Companies Act of 1883.[1] It is necessary to mention that this legislation of 1881, 1882, and 1883 did not apply to the whole of Ireland, but to certain distressed areas in Galway and Mayo which were known as the " Scheduled Districts."[2] They comprised a tract of 4,454,969 acres and affected 839,704 souls.[3]

As to the value of these Acts, it may be said that no loans were ever made according to the provisions of the Land Law Act, but that 24,329 people received assistance up to March, 1889, at a cost of £131,400 under the statutes enacted in 1882 and 1883.[4]

In order to assist the Congested Districts Board in its work of amalgamating holdings that were unduly small, the Purchase of Land Act (Ireland) of 1891 provided funds for emigrating tenants who were willing to abandon all interests in their own lands. In 1889, 257 people were assisted in this way at a cost of £1672 1s. 3d. ; in the following year, the numbers fell to ten and the cost to £56 16s. 4d. ; in 1891 nobody was emigrated, and in 1892 the Act was repealed.[5]

Until the County Councils were vested, in 1889, with authority to provide emigration assistance, Scotland had only two Acts which dealt with this matter. These[6] were the statutes of 1851 and 1856, which authorised the Inclosure Commissioners for England and Wales to lend money to Scotch landowners who were anxious to defray the emigration expenses of

---

[1] 46 Vict. c. 43 was an Act entitled " An Act for promoting the extension of Tramway Communication in Ireland and for assisting Emigration and for extending certain provisions of the Land Law (Ireland) Act, 1881, and the case of Public Companies." Part II dealt with " Emigration and Purchase of Lands by Public Companies."

[2] They were scheduled under the 12th section of the Tramways and Public Works Act.

[3] Report on Colonisation, 1889, p. 136.

[4] See various Reports of Local Government Board.

[5] Local Government Board Reports, 1891, 1892.

[6] 14 and 15 Vict. c. 91, secs. 1, 2 ; and 19 and 20 Vict. c. 9.

UNASSISTED & ASSISTED EMIGRATION

their poor tenants. The total amount advanced by these Commissioners under the provisions of 14 and 15 Vict. c. 91 was £5249 11s., in the years 1853 and 1854; seven landowners being the recipients.[1] Further statistics are unavailable.

The Unemployed Workmen Act of 1905[2] is the only legislative measure which has applied to adult emigration for the whole of the United Kingdom. This Act authorises the establishment of distress committees throughout the British Isles. In London, a local committee has been appointed for each metropolitan borough, and its work is supervised by a central body. Funds are provided by voluntary contributions and by a borough rate not exceeding ½d. in the pound, or 1d. under exceptional circumstances. People receiving assistance must satisfy the Central Body that they are fit to undertake work of an agricultural nature, also that they have resided in a given district at least twelve months, a condition which involves great hardships on those whose occupation has necessitated a constant change of domicile. The Act, when first introduced, disqualified people who had received recent parish relief, but the clause was deleted in 1906. The acceptance of assistance under these provisions is possible without loss of self-respect, as the statute provides that help of this character shall not disentitle a man to be registered nor to vote as a parliamentary, county, or parochial elector.

In 1911, 2775 persons were assisted by the Central (Unemployed) Body and by twenty-two Provincial Distress Committees, as compared with 1702 persons in 1909–10; 634 men, with 657 dependents were despatched from London, and 699 men, with 785 dependents, were similarly assisted by committees outside London. Among the latter may be noticed the

---

[1] From information supplied by the Land Office, now the Board of Agriculture.   [2] 5 Edw. c. 18.

emigration of 608 persons from West Ham, and 265 from Norwich.[1]

In Ireland the Act has remained inoperative. The only distress committees in Scotland which assisted persons to emigrate in the year ending May 15th, 1911, were those of Edinburgh and Leith. Forty-seven people were assisted by these bodies, the cost being £142.[2]

The many and varied sources providing financial emigration assistance within the United Kingdom have now been discussed at length, and wonder may be aroused at the subordinate part which the Government has played in the matter. In times of special stress it has done but little. This apparent inertia, however, cannot be ascribed to a want of sympathy in the movement. Every obstacle has crossed its path; petitions denouncing the depopulating effects of emigration have been sent from Scotland; Irish bishops have proclaimed from the pulpits that these departures robbed men of their religion; trade unions beyond the seas have grown to look with disfavour upon the arrival of our surplus workmen, and the Colonies have partly shut their doors to those receiving State aid.

The Land and Emigration Commissioners discussed the question of governmental aid somewhat fully in 1840.[3] They decided that such assistance was only justifiable when helping to alleviate national depression, and on this account should not be given in cases of distress affecting individual trades. As the majority of people who emigrated, at that time, were forced to proceed out of the country through the overstocking or decaying of definite occupations, it is clear that by giving this decision the Commissioners were debarring a large number of deserving cases from receiving the

---

[1] Cf. Return of the Distress Committees, 1912.
[2] Report of Local Government Board (Scotland) Distress Committees, Cd. 5912, 1911.
[3] Accounts and Papers, Vol. XXXIII, p. 128.

UNASSISTED & ASSISTED EMIGRATION

State assistance which might have been otherwise accorded them.

Beyond these disabilities, there was the important question of private charity. Would Government aid arrest the flow of charitable subscriptions ? The Commissioners in 1850[1] gave it as their opinion that it would. They also argued that even if a parliamentary grant were applied in good faith to emigrating the hopelessly destitute, it is not certain that the result would be a desirable one. The aged, the infirm, the incorrigibly idle and vicious might be bribed by the offer of a free passage to take themselves to America, a state of things which would entail a wastage of public funds and the enforcement, sooner or later, of a stricter code of immigration laws in the countries of arrival.

The cost of the emigration movement, it must be finally added, has not been wholly borne by home sources. Both the Dominion of Canada and the United States spend considerable sums annually on welcoming British and other immigrants and on financing the immigration section of the Departments of the Interior. Such expenditure, during the last forty years, has averaged, in Canada alone, over $328,000.[2]

[1] Annual Report Colonial Land and Emigration Commissioners, 1850, Vol. XXIII, p. 62.

[2] Public Accounts, Table CXXXII, p. 365, *Canada Year Book*, 1908. Annual Expenditure given as follows :—

1868 = $36,050	1882 = $215,339	1896 = $120,199
1869 = 26,952	1883 = 373,958	1897 = 127,438
1870 = 55,966	1884 = 511,209	1898 = 261,195
1871 = 54,004	1885 = 423,861	1899 = 255,879
1872 = 109,954	1886 = 257,355	1900 = 434,563
1873 = 265,718	1887 = 341,236	1901 = 444,730
1874 = 291,297	1888 = 244,789	1902 = 494,842
1875 = 278,777	1889 = 202,499	1903 = 642,914
1876 = 338,179	1890 = 110,092	1904 = 744,788
1877 = 309,353	1891 = 181,045	1905 = 972,357
1878 = 154,351	1892 = 177,605	1906 = 842,668
1879 = 186,403	1893 = 180,677	1907 = 611,201
1880 = 161,213	1894 = 202,236	(nine months)
1881 = 214,251	1895 = 195,653	1908 = 1,074,697

Total for 40 years 9 months : $13,127,493.

Thus the cost of maintaining the human exodus which flows from the United Kingdom to North America is borne by a multitude of sources. The individual, the Mother Country, the local bodies, the charitable societies, and the receiving states, all play a part in sharing the somewhat heavy burden.

CHAPTER V

THE TRANSPORT OF EMIGRANTS

PREVIOUS to the year 1803 there was no legislation which restricted the carriage of emigrants from the United Kingdom to America. Until the close of the eighteenth century efficiency of service had been maintained by the spirit of competition and rivalry which existed among shipowners.[1] Early in the nineteenth century, however, a great impetus was given to emigration by the conditions of distress at home So overwhelming were the streams of people who desired to proceed across the Atlantic that one master no longer competed with another for passengers, no longer was there any need to tempt men and women by low fares and comfortable quarters. If competition still existed, it existed among the would-be emigrants in their frenzy to secure berths, and not among the captains in an endeavour to obtain full complements of passengers. Such a state of things naturally led to an independent spirit among shipowners; unseaworthy boats were pressed into service, overcrowding became a constant source of danger, whilst the provisions and comforts afforded the unfortunate travellers were of the worst possible nature. Instances of extreme suffering on the part of the emigrants were so frequent that a committee sat in 1802-3, which enquired into the abuses then affecting the transport trade. The report,[2] which was subsequently published, clearly demonstrated the

---

[1] Vide *Edinburgh Review*, December, 1826, p. 61.
[2] Report of Coast of Scotland and Naval Inquiry, 1802-3.

need for immediate legislation. Ships, it was found, seldom reached the American shores without sustaining one or more losses by death; the supplies of water, which were frequently polluted, and the system of sleeping passengers in relays, having much to answer for in this matter.

To check such obvious abuses should have been simple enough, but we must remember that private interests were extremely powerful in those early years. On the one hand, the landowners were anxious to clear the surplus people off their estates as speedily as possible, and any step which might indirectly raise the cost of passages was strongly denounced by them; on the other hand, the Highland Society and many minor bodies holding similar views exerted their full strength to stifle emigration on the grounds that it was perniciously denuding the land of its population. The real issue, that is to say the question as to whether the passengers were receiving proper treatment, seems to have been of secondary importance. It was only with much difficulty, then, that Parliament could be made to give its consent to the first Passengers' Act; this it did in 1803.[1] This Act required that every vessel bound for Canada and the United States should carry sufficient food to last at least twelve weeks. Every person was to have a half-pound of meat, one and a half pounds of biscuits or oatmeal, a half-pound of molasses and one gallon of water, daily. A ship was also restricted as to the number of people it could carry; one person being the utmost for every two tons of its unladen capacity. There were other regulations which dealt with cleanliness, the carrying of a surgeon, and the accurate keeping of a log book. Finally, the Act decreed that all shipowners, captains, and surgeons should henceforth be required to enter into a bond of £100 each, as a

---

[1] 43 Geo. 3, c. 56 (1803).

THE TRANSPORT OF EMIGRANTS 103

guarantee that they would faithfully perform their several duties.

Unfortunately, the restrictions of the first Passengers' Act were often avoided. Instead of sailing from a recognised port, it was a daily occurrence for boats to proceed from unfrequented bays and creeks, and thus to escape the inspection of the customs officials who were the enforcers of the Act. Such vessels neither carried surgeons nor provided the regulation diet, and the captains and owners were in no wise restricted by guarantees. In parenthesis, it may be mentioned that the figures relating to emigration in these early years are of little value, as they take no account of these surreptitious sailings. To check this practice, the Acts of 1823 and 1825 were framed;[1] they required every ship carrying more than one person for each five tons burden, the crew were included, to have the letter " P "[2] painted in white, at least three feet in height, on some conspicuous part of the hulk or canvas. The officers of Government vessels were then instructed to board and inspect ships they met on the high seas with this distinguishing letter, and to report instances of cruelty or overcrowding. The same Acts made it illegal for people to embark at any but recognised ports, and altered the owner's bond, guaranteeing seaworthiness to twenty pounds per passenger. The provision allowance was also increased. These Acts were to be worked, it was decided, by the Commissioners of Customs at home, the local authorities in the Colonies, the officers of the navy on the high seas, and the consuls abroad.

Though some form of legislation was undoubtedly necessary to check the abuses which had sprung up in the Atlantic transport trade, it was generally felt that the first Passengers' Act imposed unnecessary

---

[1] 4 Geo. 4, c. 83 (1823), and 6 Geo. 4, c. 116 (1825).
[2] " P " denoted the presence of passengers.

hardships on the shipowners, and consequently on the emigrants themselves. The sudden edict which went forth requiring all ships to carry a qualified doctor, created such a demand for men of this profession that a dearth quickly arose, and many vessels were compelled to postpone their departure until a qualified man could be secured. The regulations concerning the provisions were also unnecessarily severe. We must remember that an important section of the emigrants of this time were of Irish nationality, whose usual diet consisted largely of milk, potatoes, and herrings. In spite of this, the Government decreed that, *inter alia*, the passengers were to be provided with half a pound of meat daily. In practice, the meat usually consisted of salt pork. Thus, not only were the people supplied with provisions unsuited to their requirements, but they were given them at a time when they were restricted in their movements and deprived of exercise. The effect which this improper feeding produced on the general health of the passengers may be best imagined. As may be expected, such oppressive regulations were the subject of violent controversies in the Press ; the *Edinburgh Review*, for instance, published a succession of caustic comments upon the Act.[1] When, as a result of agitation, the Lords of the Treasury removed certain of the restrictions imposed on Irish vessels, an uproar arose in England and Scotland, and every shipowner demanded why Ireland alone was favoured.

The swing of the pendulum came in 1827, for in that year the Emigration Commission advised Parliament to repeal the offending Act, which it did without delay.[2] For a little over six months the shipping trade was left unhampered by any form of legislation, but such freedom was quickly abused. The

---

[1] See, *inter alia*, issue of December, 1826, pp. 61–3.
[2] 7 and 8 Geo. 4, c. 19 (1826–7).

home authorities witnessed hundreds of cases of overcrowding, but were powerless to interfere. Letters soon reached England from the authorities in the Colonies and the consuls in the United States, complaining of the terrible conditions to which British passengers were being subjected. One of the worst cases was reported by Sir James Kempt, the Lieutenant-Governor of Nova Scotia. "The *James*," he wrote, " has arrived from Ireland with a hundred and sixty emigrants on board. Five have died during the passage, thirty-five were left at Newfoundland as they were too ill to proceed, and one hundred and twenty were suffering from typhus."[1] Not a single passenger escaped from the ravages of disease in some form or other! A new Act was therefore deemed necessary in 1828.[2] The stipulations as to food were once more enforced, whilst new clauses were framed to insure passengers against being crowded together, and against being landed at any other than at the port for which they had contracted.

Seven years later, in 1835, the Act of 5 and 6 Will. 4, c. 56, repealed all former legislation and re-enacted almost identical provisions, but with the following additions : (*a*) The journey to North America could henceforth be reckoned as taking not twelve but ten weeks, and supplies might be proportionately reduced ; (*b*) each ship was to be surveyed before it could be considered seaworthy ; (*c*) a surgeon was only necessary when a hundred or more people were on board ; (*d*) the quantity of spirits carried for sale among the passengers was to be restricted ; (*e*) lists were to be handed to the chief officer of customs before sailing, giving every passenger's name, age, and occupation ; (*f*) emigrants finding their ship not ready to leave on

---

[1] Hansard, Second Series, vol. 18, p. 962.
[2] 9 Geo. 4, c. 21. It affected B.N.A. only.

the appointed day were to be victualled free or allowed a shilling a day in lieu; and (*g*) everyone who desired was to be permitted to remain on board for a period of forty-eight hours after the vessel had reached its destination. This Act, it may be added, only applied to ships sailing from ports in Great Britain, and not to those journeying in an opposite direction, nor to those plying between one colony and another.

Enough has already been said to show that the aim of British legislation was to secure better treatment and more comfortable travelling for the people sailing from the Mother Country. In the United States, however, a different goal was aimed at. There we find that the restrictions imposed on the passenger traffic were usually devised with a view to protecting the American citizen, or to making the movement provide the money which was required to regulate it. The first American Act came into force in 1819, but no one seriously observed its provisions. Five years later, in 1824, the Legislature of New York, noticing, with concern, the heavy burden which immigrants were becoming to the local rates, decreed that every shipmaster bringing alien passengers should enter into a bond with the mayor to the extent of not more than $300 for each person landed by him.[1] The city could thus recoup itself out of these levies whenever a passenger became a public charge. Later on, when it was found that disease and contagion were spread by the fresh arrivals, the city authorities framed laws to regulate the amount of space and provisions supplied to passengers during the voyage. It is thus obvious that a ship sailing from, say, Liverpool to New York was bound not only by British but also by American statutes. As there were wide differences between these two codes of legislation, we find that

---

[1] Cf. Chapter V.

THE TRANSPORT OF EMIGRANTS 107

the British regulations were honoured at the port of clearing, and the New York code was observed when entering American waters. We may add that, in a number of cases, no code at all was observed when on the high seas.

In his report of 1839, Lord Durham pointed to the want of control which then characterised the Atlantic passenger movement.[1] Ships, he said, were inadequately examined at the embarkation ports, a matter which gave masters the opportunity of exceeding their numbers; insufficient supplies of water were carried and leaky casks often employed; incapable surgeons[2] were engaged, whilst the returns issued by these officers were frequently fraudulent; false decks were used in many vessels in order that the cubic space required by law might be reduced; passengers were persuaded to return their ages at less than they actually were, and thus assist in defrauding the collectors of the head-tax, and captains made it a practice of inducing their passengers to bring on board less provisions than were really required so that supplies might be sold to them at exorbitant prices. The two following passages, quoted from Lord Durham's report,[3] give a valuable insight into the transport conditions as then ruling. The first was evidence given by Dr. Morrin, Inspecting Physician of the Port of Quebec; the second, by Dr. Skey, Deputy Inspector-General of Hospitals (Canada).

I am almost at a loss for words to describe the state in which the emigrants frequently arrived: with a few exceptions, the state of the ships was quite abominable: so much so, that the harbour-master's boatmen had no difficulty, at the distance of gunshot, either when the wind was favourable or in a dead calm, in distinguishing by the odour alone a crowded emigrant

---

[1] Under the Act of 1835.

[2] Lord Durham quoted the case of a surgeon who reported that the captain had fractured both the tibia and fibula of his arm. These, of course, are bones in the leg. *Op. cit.*, p. 90.

[3] *Op. cit.*, p. 87.

ship. I have known as many as from thirty to forty deaths to have taken place, in the course of a voyage, from typhus fever on board of a ship containing from 500 to 600 passengers.

Upon the arrival of emigrants in the river, a great number of sick have landed. A regular importation of contagious diseases into this country has annually taken place; that disease originated on board ship, and was occasioned, I should say, by bad management in consequence of the ships being ill-found, ill-provisioned, over-crowded, and ill-ventilated. I should say that the mortality during the voyage has been dreadful; to such an extent that, in 1834, the inhabitants of Quebec, taking alarm at the number of shipwrecks, at the mortality of the passengers, and the fatal diseases which accumulated at the Quarantine Establishment at Grosse Isle, and the Emigrant Hospital of this city, involving the inhabitants of Quebec in the calamity, called upon the Emigrants' Society to take the subject into consideration, and make representations to the Government thereon.

Commenting on the above, Lord Durham wrote in his report :

From this and other evidence, it will appear that the Amended Passengers' Act of 1835 alone, as it has been hitherto administered, would have afforded no efficient remedy of the dreadful evils described by Dr. Morrin and Dr. Skey. Those evils have, however, been greatly mitigated by two measures of the Provincial Government: first, the application of a tax upon passengers from the United Kingdom, to providing shelter, medical attendance, and the means of further transport to destitute emigrants; secondly, the establishment of the Quarantine Station at Grosse Isle, a desert island some miles below Quebec, where all vessels arriving with cases of contagious disease are detained; the diseased persons are removed to an hospital, and emigrants not affected with disease are landed, and subjected to some discipline for the purposes of cleanliness, the ship also being cleaned while they remain on shore. By these arrangements, the accumulation of wretched paupers at Quebec, and the spread of contagious disease, are prevented. An arrangement made only in 1837, whereby the quarantine physician at Grosse Isle decides whether or not an emigrant ship shall be detained there or proceed on its voyage

THE TRANSPORT OF EMIGRANTS 109

has, to use the words of Dr. Poole, " operated as a premium to care and attention on the part of the captain, and has had a salutary effect on the comfort of the emigrants."

I cordially rejoice in these improvements, but would observe that the chief means by which the good has been accomplished indicates the greatness of the evil that remains. The necessity of a Quarantine Establishment for preventing the importation of contagious disease from Britain to her Colonies, as if the emigrants had departed from one of those Eastern countries which are the home of the plague, shows beyond a doubt either that our very system of emigration is most defective or that it is most carelessly administered.[1]

On the appointment of the Colonial Land and Emigration Commissioners in 1840, the subject of the passenger movement received more organised attention than had hitherto been possible. It must be remembered that up to that time the various Passengers' Acts had been drafted by different people who were actuated by ideals and motives of a widely diversified nature; little wonder then that the benefits accruing from one set of statutes were often swept away by a subsequent enactment. These Commissioners set to work with definite aims before them which they summarised as follows :—[2]

1. To regulate the number of emigrants conveyed in the different vessels and to provide for their proper accommodation.
2. To ensure a proper supply of provisions and water.
3. To provide for the seaworthiness of the vessels.
4. To afford the poorer classes of emigrants protection from the numerous frauds practised upon them before they leave the country; to provide for their being carried to their stipulated destination and to secure them a reasonable time for making arrangements before they are landed from the ship.[3]

---

[1] *Op. cit.*, p. 88–9.
[2] Report of Land and Emigration Commissioners on Passenger Acts, 1842, p. 3.
[3] See letter by Lord John Russell to the three Commissioners, quoted on page 2, Accounts and Papers, 1840, Vol. XXXIII.
The following is an extract: " In your capacity of a General Board for the sale of lands and for promoting emigration, your duties may be

A HISTORY OF EMIGRATION

The original Commissioners proved a capable and conscientious body of men. In every possible way they studied the various questions which their duties involved, and their rulings were invariably based on sound judgment. Under their care, the Atlantic crossings were made much more comfortable and healthy, as the following figures help to show. In the year of their appointment the death-rate on British ships sailing for Canada was 1·005 per cent. In the next year, 1841, it fell to ·69, in 1842 it was ·6, and in 1843 it was as low as ·29.[1]

The following regulations reprinted from an abstract of " the Queen's Orders in Council for preserving order and cleanliness," and drawn up by the Emigration Commissioners, are interesting in that they help us to form a vivid mental picture of the daily life of an emigrant passenger of over sixty years ago :[2]

1. Every passenger to rise at 7 a.m. unless otherwise permitted by the surgeon, or if no surgeon by the master.
2. Breakfast from 8 to 9 a.m., dinner at 1 p.m., supper at 6 p.m.
3. The passengers to be in their beds by 10 p.m.
4. Fires to be lighted by the passengers' cook at 7 a.m. and kept alight by him till 7 p.m., then to be extinguished unless otherwise directed by the master, or required for the use of the sick.
5. Three safety lamps to be lit at dusk; one to be kept burning all the night at the main hatchway, the two others may be extinguished at 10 p.m.
6. No naked light to be allowed at any time or on any account.

---

conveniently arranged under the four following heads : first, the collection and diffusion of accurate statistical knowledge ; secondly, the sale in this country of waste lands in the colonies ; thirdly, the application of the proceeds of such sales towards the removal of emigrants ; and fourthly, the rendering of periodical accounts, both pecuniary and statistical, of your administration of this trust."

[1] Figures taken from the Annual Reports of the Commissioners.
[2] Colonial Land and Emigration Commissioners' Annual Report, 1848.

THE TRANSPORT OF EMIGRANTS

7. The passengers, when dressed, to roll up their beds, to sweep the decks, including the space under the bottom of the berths, and to throw the dirt overboard.

8. Breakfast not to commence till this is done.

9. The sweepers for the day to be taken in rotation from the males above 14, in the proportion of 5 for every 100 passengers.

10. Duties of the sweepers to be to clean the ladders, hospitals and round houses, to sweep the decks after every meal, and to dry, holystone, and scrape them after breakfast.

11. The occupant of every berth to see that his own berth is well brushed out.

12. The beds to be well shaken and aired on the deck and the bottom boards, if not fixtures, to be removed and dry-scrubbed and taken on deck, at least twice a week.

13. Two days in the week to be appointed by the master as washing days, but no clothes to be washed or dried between decks.

14. The coppers and cooking vessels to be cleaned every day.

15. The scuttles and stern ports, if any, to be kept open (weather permitting) from 7 a.m. to 10 p.m., and the hatches at all hours.

16. Hospitals to be established with an area, in ships carrying a hundred passengers, of not less than 48 superficial feet, with two or four bed-berths and, in ships carrying 200 passengers, of not less than 120 superficial feet, with six bed-berths.

17. On Sundays, the passengers to be mustered at 10 a.m. when they will be expected to appear in clean and decent apparel. The day to be observed as religiously as circumstances will admit.

18. No spirits or gunpowder to be taken on board by any passenger. Any that may be discovered to be taken into custody of the master till the expiration of the voyage.

19. No smoking to be allowed between decks.

20. All fighting, gambling, riotous or quarrelsome behaviour, swearing, and violent language to be at once put a stop to. Swords and other offensive weapons, as soon as passengers embark, to be placed in the custody of the master.

21. No sailor to remain on the passengers' deck among the passengers except when on duty.

22. No passenger to go to the ship's cook-house without special permission of the master.

The Commissioners directed much care and thought to the various methods of provisioning emigrants during the Atlantic voyage. It is evident, from the reports which they issued, that they were personally in favour of each individual providing his own supplies, but they were convinced that such a plan was impracticable. Many people, they said, could beg from neighbours and friends sufficient food to last them the journey, but, at the same time, could not afford to pay the shipowners in money for being victualled during the passage. On the other hand, experience showed that when each person brought his own supply, there was much waste, much went bad, many had insufficient to last the journey, and all living-rooms were more or less polluted by the presence of a multitude of parcels containing food. The Commissioners decided, then, that provisions should be supplied by the shipowners, and that the cost be included in the price of the passage ticket.

To prevent overcrowding a law was framed in 1842,[1] which required each person to be provided with ten superficial feet as bed space, whilst stipulation was also made that the height between decks was to be at least six feet. Little attention need be attached to the actual figures, for they were changed almost yearly; they are given here merely to show the spirit of the Act, and to point out the methods adopted by the Commissioners to ensure healthy passages. Dangerous and offensive cargoes such as gunpowder, vitriol, and green hides, were no longer to be carried on emigrant ships, whilst heavy freight, such as iron rails and bars, were to be stowed where they would cause the least amount of rolling. As shipwrecks were frequent at this time, the Act of 1842 also

---

[1] 5 and 6 Vict. c. 107

THE TRANSPORT OF EMIGRANTS 113

required every vessel, sailing with passengers, to carry small boats, two if the ship were between 150 and 250 tons, three if between 250 and 500, and four if over this tonnage. Though these small boats proved hopelessly inadequate in times of total wrecks, their requisition by law indicated progress in a desirable direction.

The Commissioners also directed their efforts towards checking the many forms of fraud which unscrupulous people practised daily on emigrants sailing for America. The selling of passage tickets for non-existing vessels, and also for vessels that had already sailed were the most common ruses perpetrated by crimps,[1] who infested the embarking stages of many ports. In order to put a stop to such evil practices, 5 and 6 Vict. c. 107 enacted that no person, not being the master of a ship, was to sell passage tickets to North American stations, or otherwise conduct the business of a broker unless he had previously obtained a licence from justices assembled at Petty or Quarter Sessions, and had had his name placed on the list of brokers kept at the offices of the Emigration Commissioners. Unfortunately, the authorities were far too busy to enforce this and similar Acts with the necessary firmness, and, though corruption continued to flourish, prosecutions were seldom instituted. In 1843, when fraud and deception were probably at their height, the Commissioners only instituted seven prosecutions in the Mother Country. The first resulted in the master of the bark *John Francis*, of Cork, being fined £20 for issuing unwholesome provisions. The second concerned the brig *Mary Ann*, of Bideford. In this case the master was fined £15. The third dealt with the brig *Coxon*, from Cork. This ship had sailed from an irregular

---

[1] A crimp was the name technically given to a man who frequented the embarking stages with the set purpose of defrauding departing emigrants.

port in order to avoid the usual customs inspection, and the master was fined £20. In the fourth case, the master of the Plymouth bark *Florence* had neglected to issue proper allowances of water. For so serious an offence he was called upon to pay the nominal fine of £5. The fifth case dealt with the bark *Constitution*, of Belfast. The master issued unwholesome bread and short supplies of water. He was fined £50. In the sixth instance, the master of the *Jane Duffies*, from Glasgow, was fined £40 for carrying an excess of eight passengers. No record is available of the seventh prosecution.[1]

In 1851 the entire business connected with the carriage of emigrants had become so corrupt that a Royal Commission was appointed to enquire into the matter. The Commission directed its attention more particularly to the conditions which prevailed on voyages to North America rather than to other parts of the world; first, because this quarter of the globe attracted the largest number[2] of British emigrants, and, secondly, because the people who journeyed there were " ignorant, helpless, an easy prey to fraud, and least able to obtain redress." The emigrants as a class were uneducated and lacking in mental training, and therefore were easily imposed upon. They arrived at the port of embarkation with various bundles which unmistakably proclaimed their mission. Here dishonest porters and crimps seized upon them, more by force than persuasion, and took them to boarding-houses kept by equally dishonest landlords. As lights were prohibited on board ships that were lying in dock, no one was allowed to embark until within a few hours of the sailing time. The interval between the moment of setting foot in the port and the time for weighing anchor was thus necessarily

---

[1] Data collected from 1844 Report of the Commissioners.
[2] In 1850, 257,663 people sailed to North America and 16,037 to Australia and New Zealand.

THE TRANSPORT OF EMIGRANTS 115

spent in the clutches of the evil boarding-house keepers. These latter used every device for extorting money from their guests. Affecting the rôle of a friendly adviser, they would provide the gullible traveller with all sorts of useless utensils at exorbitant prices, telling him that they were necessary articles for the voyage. They would change English into American money, and, needless to say, " dollared " their victim, as frauds connected with money changing were technically termed. Passage tickets were also pressed on to the bewildered emigrant, but naturally at an enhanced figure. In some cases, even, the landlords drugged their lodgers, and took from them the savings with which they had intended to start life afresh in the New World. No form of theft or extortion seemed too mean to be undertaken by these rapacious people.

Unfortunately, acts of dishonesty were not confined to the keepers of boarding-houses. Once out at sea, the harassed traveller found that the ship's captain was no more dependable than the crimps and the runners on shore. The rations which he distributed were inferior in quality and less in quantity than those stipulated by the Government regulations, and frequently they were unfit for consumption. Overcrowding was usual, and, more often than not, the passengers were bullied and ill-treated by the crew. It must not be thought that proper food and humane treatment were unobtainable; they were procurable by those who cared to pay handsomely for them. Extortion was as rife aboard as on shore, and few dared to complain, as it was common knowledge that the working of the law was slow and costly.

Though the home officials worked strenuously to ensure the shipment of the proper kind and the necessary quantities of food, it was a simple matter for a captain to evade the vigilance of these men, were he so minded. Stores of an unsound nature were freely shipped with the knowledge that, though feeding passengers on decayed food was an offence at law, no penalty could be imposed for merely shipping unsound supplies. Were the nature of the food to be detected by the authorities, the only punishment was that incurred by a waste of time and labour in providing a fresh cargo. For many years it was a frequent practice for certain captains to put into one of the many obscure ports on the coast of Ireland, and there to exchange good barrels of oatmeal for unsound ones. Their log-books recorded a halt at such and such a port owing to stress of weather. Captains who wished to sail with short supplies, complained that their ships when fully laden were unable to ride over the sill of the dock. A clearance was then given them on condition that they took aboard whatever supplies they lacked when the exterior of the harbour was reached. On reaching a point without the harbour, they were met by small boats carrying the necessary provisions, but these were left unshipped.

Once out on the open sea, the lot of the emigrant was usually a terrible one. Mr. Vere Foster, a philanthropist who sent, at different times, no less than sixteen thousand women to Canada at his own expense, embarked in 1850 on the *Washington* as a steerage passenger. His identity he kept a secret, wishing to obtain a true insight into the treatment of the poorer classes who travelled across the Atlantic. In a letter written[1] to a friend, he said, the medical examination consisted of What's your name? Are you well? Hold out your tongue. All right. It was all said in one breath, and lasted one or two seconds. On the first day, the nine hundred people mustered on deck for their water. While it was being pumped into their cans, the mates cursed, abused, cuffed and kicked the people without any provocation, and only served

---

[1] Quoted from Accounts and Paper, Vol. XL, 1851.

THE TRANSPORT OF EMIGRANTS 117

thirty of them; the others having to go without. In spite of what the contract promised, no provisions were served on that or on the following day, and, as many people were almost starving, a letter of complaint was written to the captain. The man who composed it was knocked down by a blow in the face from the first mate. The next day half rations were served. Supplies were always given out raw; to get near the cooking fires many people bribed the sailors; those who were too poor to offer them money only managed their turn once in two or three days. Several serious injuries were wantonly inflicted on the passengers by the mates. Twelve children died from dysentery or, more truthfully, from want of nourishing food. From this letter, we may picture, not the life experienced on board an isolated ship managed by an exceptionally brutal master, but the existence endured by hundreds and thousands of people, many of them ill, underfed and wretched, who left Britain for North America during the first half of the nineteenth century. It is interesting to know that, on reaching the United States, Mr. Vere Foster took legal proceedings against the defaulting captain, but withdrew them when he discovered how much time and money they would entail if pursued. We can but conclude that the law was in a very useless state if Mr. Foster, a wealthy man, felt himself beyond its protection.

On landing in America, the emigrant was required to face yet further troubles. Awaiting him on the quays were gangs of porters known as runners, who pestered him with even more audacity than was displayed by the crimps of the old country. Seizing his baggage, they led him to a lodging-house kept by a confederate, and there began over again the extortion which was practised at the port of embarkation. Not until he had purchased a transportation ticket to some distant inland town, probably at a fabulous price, was he rid of the terrors inseparable from an Atlantic passage.

In 1850 the staff of emigration officials at Liverpool consisted of an officer with a salary of £150 per annum, two assistant officers with salaries of £100, a clerk at £80, and three medical inspectors who were paid on a *per capita* basis, but whose pay averaged between £400 and £500 annually. In the year stated, this staff was called upon to superintend the departure of 174,188 people, and to examine as many as 568 ships. Little wonder then that the Commission of 1851 emphasised the need for a stronger body of inspectors at the most frequented ports. When these were appointed, a stricter interpretation of the various Acts was made possible, and the Atlantic journey became more comfortable in consequence.

Almost contemporary with these improvements was the opening of Castle Garden, a landing dock for emigrant ships, adjoining the city of New York. Within this dockyard were appointed a convenient set of shops and offices wherein the fresh arrival could obtain whatever rail tickets or information he needed for the further pursuit of his journey. On the quays of Castle Garden were to be found none but licensed porters, licensed passage brokers, licensed lodging-house keepers, and the various governmental officials. The immigrant was thus able to land and see to his numerous wants free from the attentions of the undesirable people[1] who had hitherto molested him.

In addition to providing comfortable landing arrangements, the New York authorities were determined that the people arriving at their port should also receive comfortable treatment during the voyage. With this object in view, they legislated in 1855[2]

---

[1] Kapp. *Immigration and the Commissioners of Emigration of the State of New York*, Chapter IV. Also various notes in the Annual Reports of the Colonial Land and Emigration Commissioners.

[2] Colonial Land and Emigration Commissioners, Seventeenth Report, 1854, p. 106.

to the effect that a more ample diet should be provided on all passenger ships, that better ventilation should be arranged, whilst they also increased the regulation space allotted to each individual. In order that the captains might take, at least, a pecuniary interest in the health of their living freight, it was decided to impose a fine of ten dollars in respect of every death which occurred whilst at sea.

In 1852, a member of the House of Commons asked for a statement to be prepared which would give an idea as to the frequency with which shipwrecks occurred among vessels carrying passengers. In reply to this question, it was stated that during the five years ending December 31st, 1851, 7129 emigrant ships were given a clearance, of which 44 were wrecked, involving a loss of 1043 lives. The statement proceeded to say that of every hundred people who took passage in emigrant ships during this period ·06 were drowned.[1] The wrecks were reported as being due to unsound ships, to inadequate crews, and to improper stowing of the cargo. As a result of this enquiry, Parliament passed the three following Acts, 15 and 16 Vict. c. 44 (1852), 16 and 17 Vict. c. 84 (1853), and 18 and 19 Vict. c. 119 (1855). By these, the Secretary of State at home, the Governors in the Colonies, and the Consuls in foreign countries were allowed to defray the cost of the passages back to the United Kingdom of all shipwrecked emigrants who applied to them for assistance. The Acts empowered the home authorities to recover any such expenditure from the shipowners, but such sums were not to exceed the fares paid by the emigrants for their passage. In practice, the return passages usually amounted to far more than the sum recoverable; when this was the case, the difference was met with Government funds. Long before these Acts were passed the Colonial

---

[1] Colonial Land and Emigration Commissioners, Seventeenth Report, 1854.

Land and Emigration Commissioners had expended money on relieving shipwrecked emigrants, but such expenditure was not recoverable. A typical instance of the succour which they provided in this manner was furnished by the ship *Robert Isaacs*, which sailed from Liverpool in 1845. After being at sea for six weeks, the vessel had to put back to the Azores, and was there condemned as unseaworthy. Her distressed passengers, most of them were extremely poor, were brought to Southampton by the West Indian Mail steamer *Forth*. The Commissioners were speedily acquainted with the fact, and immediately despatched a responsible inspector to provide whatever comforts and necessaries the unfortunate travellers lacked. Clothes and food were distributed without delay, whilst rail-tickets were duly supplied in order that all might return to their starting-point. As this occurred prior to the legislation of 1852, it is clear that the Commissioners could not recover their expenditure from the shipowners, and these, it may be added, saw no occasion to tender it voluntarily.

A revolution in the passenger services was experienced when the old sailing vessels gave way to the fast-going steamships.[1] It is claimed that the *Royal William* was the first steamer to cross the Atlantic, but it was not until the Cunard Company put their four liners on the ocean service in 1840, that emigrants were given the benefit of steam-propelled passages; it may be even suggested that they did not benefit, to any appreciable extent, by the

---

[1] An interesting inscription has been placed on the wall of the entrance to the Parliamentary Library at Ottawa. It runs: " In honour of the men by whose enterprise, courage, and skill, the *Royal William*, the first vessel to cross the Atlantic by steam power, was wholly constructed in Canada and navigated to England in 1833." It was launched April, 1831: started from Pictow, August 18th, 1833, and reached Gravesend, September 12th, 1833. The first Cunard steamboat left on July 4th, 1840. The first screw-propelled vessel, the *Globe*, sailed on December 11th, 1850. The *Globe* did much to divert the emigrant passengers from the sailing to steam vessels.

THE TRANSPORT OF EMIGRANTS

new method of locomotion until the year 1848. The change, from sail to steam, was extremely rapid. So successful were the Cunard boats, that other vessels, similarly propelled, were quickly pressed into the service, and within a period of a dozen years, almost the whole of the traffic passed into the hands of the steamship companies. The Emigration Commissioners in their annual report for 1861 stated that during the year 1860 a total of 7836 emigrants journeyed up the St. Lawrence, of which no less than 6932 travelled by steam. Thus in a dozen years the newer vessels had captured six-sevenths of the trade. These figures by no means refer to an exceptional destination, but may be taken as typical for all ports situated on the Atlantic seaboard.

The introduction of steam brought many changes in its train. The old sailing boats were largely owned by individuals and private companies, whilst the new vessels, being of a much costlier type, were beyond the reach of all except rich and comparatively influential companies. The small owners were thus squeezed out of the trade, but their disappearance was not to be regretted, as most of the fraud and deception which had flourished on the high seas was due to their ingenuity. Sailings became more regular, for the journey depended far less on weather conditions than heretofore, and the ships were controlled more centrally. As a result of this improved organisation, emigrants were not kept waiting at the embarkation ports during extended periods; they could arrange to make their arrival at the port coincide with the advertised time of sailing, and thus were able to escape much of the undesirable attention of crimps and boarding-house keepers. The introduction of steam also helped temporarily to modify the existing passenger routes from the Continent to America. People who could afford to pay slightly enhanced fares, and who wished to secure quicker and more comfortable journeys, came from their continental homes to England and took steamer from Liverpool. Much of this trade was only diverted through the home country during the time steam was being introduced to European ports, though an appreciable amount has remained with us to the present time. Whilst speaking of this deviation of route, it is well to point out that the Emigration Commissioners, at this period, took no steps to differentiate between British and Continental emigrants embarking at ports within their jurisdiction. The figures issued by them for the years 1850 onwards are, therefore, somewhat misleading, as many of the people set out as British were really of foreign origin.

As may be expected, the mortality arising on the high seas quickly dropped when the journey was shortened by the use of steam-power. The annual reports of the Emigration Commissioners showed that in 1840, the passengers sailing to Canada suffered a death-rate of 1·005 per cent, but in 1863, when steam carried six-sevenths of the people, the rate had fallen to ·19 per cent; no more, in fact, than would have occurred among the passengers had they remained at home. Not only did the death-rate fall, but the number of prosecutions arising out of Atlantic passages declined also. At Quebec, New York, and Liverpool, the reports showed that complaints were comparatively rare after steam had ousted the sailing vessel. The agent at Quebec wrote, in 1854, to the Emigration Commissioners, and said, " It is only very rarely that I now have to proceed against masters for breaches of the Act. There is now an honourable class of shipowner who is catering for the trade."[1]

By 1860 the Atlantic passenger trade had lost its old terrors and discomforts, most of the rapacious and dishonest captains had left the service, and the

---

[1] Vide Annual Report, 1854–5.

THE TRANSPORT OF EMIGRANTS 123

journey was no longer fraught with disease and suffering.[1] As a consequence of these ameliorated conditions, no changes of material importance were introduced until 1894. In this year the Merchant Shipping Act[2] repealed all former Acts concerning the passage of emigrants, and enforced a comprehensive code of statutes to take their place. As much doubt had existed in the past as to what exactly constituted an emigrant ship, a cabin passenger, and a steerage passenger, the Act commenced by defining these. An emigrant ship, it said, was every sea-going vessel whether British or foreign, and, whether or not taking mails, carrying more than fifty steerage passengers or a greater number of such people, if a sailing vessel, than one adult for each thirty-three tons of registered tonnage, and one adult for every twenty tons when propelled by steam. A cabin passenger was defined as one having at least thirty-six clear superficial feet allotted to his exclusive use, having meals throughout the journey at the same table as the master or first officer, and paying no less than thirty shillings per week while the voyage lasted, if the destination were south of the Equator, and twenty shillings if north of it. A steerage passenger was a person not fulfilling the conditions required of the cabin passengers.

To ensure seaworthiness and proper equipment every emigrant ship was to be inspected prior to each sailing by two or more competent surveyors appointed by the Board of Trade or the Commissioners of Customs. The inspection was to be made before any part of the cargo had been taken on board, and even the ballast was to be shifted from place to place, in order to view every part of the ship's frame, if the surveyors deemed it necessary. Each vessel was to be provided with three steering compasses, one azimuth

---

[1] Cf. R. L. Stevenson, "The Amateur Emigrant," in *Essays of Travel*. [2] 57 and 58 Vict. c. 60.

compass, one or two chronometers according to whether proceeding to ports north or south of the Equator, an adequate fire-engine, three bower anchors, signal apparatus and, if a foreign vessel, with four properly fitted lifebuoys. A sufficient supply of water and food together with medicines, medical instruments, and disinfectants were also necessary. In order to minimise risks of accidents and disease, certain goods were not to be carried. Amongst those scheduled were vitriol, lucifer matches, guano, green hides, articles coming within the meaning of the Explosives Act of 1875, and any other cargo which from its size or composition might endanger personal safety.[1]

The Act gave directions for the staffing of emigrant ships. When more than thirty steerage or a total of three hundred people, including the crew and officers, were on board, a medical practitioner was to be carried. A steward and a cook were likewise to form part of the crew when the steerage contained one hundred or more people, whilst foreign vessels, having no officers who could speak the English language intelligibly, needed an interpreter when two hundred and fifty British subjects were carried.

No emigrant ship was to proceed until the crew and every steerage passenger had been medically examined and certified as being free from disease. If, on examination, a person suffering from some contagious complaint were found to have already been aboard, the examining officer could, at his discretion, require all the other passengers to be detained and placed under observation, but passage money was to be refunded to any person who was landed for medical reasons. In order that temporary measures might be immediately enforced in times of necessity, the Act said that Her Majesty could, by Orders in Council, make regulations for preserving order, pro-

---

[1] Captains must now satisfy the Board of Trade that they have sufficient small boats to hold passengers and crew.

THE TRANSPORT OF EMIGRANTS 125

moting health, and securing cleanliness and ventilation on board ships. In a similar way, emigration could be temporarily prohibited from ports where epidemics were known to prevail.

A bond of two thousand pounds was required from the master and owner of each emigrant ship, a sum which was advanced to five thousand pounds when the owner of a vessel resided beyond the limits of the British Isles. In the latter case, owners had to give an undertaking to indemnify the Crown if expenses were incurred in rescuing, maintaining, or forwarding passengers who had not been carried to their proper destination.

Before a ship sailing with steerage passengers could leave for ports beyond Europe, other than those in the Mediterranean Sea, a list of all passengers had to be handed to the emigration officers. Failure to comply with this regulation could entail seizure and forfeiture of the vessel by the Crown.

In order that the poorer classes of emigrants might not suffer through the non-sailing of a boat on which they had booked passages, the Act required that when a ship, from any cause, was rendered unfit to proceed on its journey, the master was to hand immediately to the local emigration official a written undertaking that the steerage people would be conveyed to their destination within six weeks. In the interval between the advertised and the actual sailing, he was to provide them with board and lodgings of a nature similar to that which was allotted them aboard the vessel. In cases where such responsibility was shirked, the governor, consul, or other official in authority was empowered to send on the stranded passengers to their destination, whilst the Crown would take proceedings to recover the expenditure from the defaulting owner, charterer, or master.

Profiting by the experience of the past, the framers of the Act decided that all people should be placed under control who had commercial connections with the emigration traffic. A passage broker was compelled to obtain a licence and enter into a bond of one thousand pounds with the Crown. He obtained the licence, if residing in London, from the Justices of the Peace sitting at petty sessions; if living elsewhere in England, from the county borough or county district council. The licensing authority in Scotland was the local sheriff; in Ireland, the justices at petty sessions. Emigrant runners were also placed under restriction, for the Act determined that every person, other than a broker and his bona-fide clerk, who within five miles of any port solicited, influenced or recommended an intending emigrant on behalf of a broker, vessel, lodging-house, tavern, money-changer, etc., in preparation for an impending passage, was to be deemed a runner and be registered and licensed in a way similar to that stated for brokers, but, in addition, was required to wear a distinguishing badge.

To-day, the journey from the Mother Country to North America is comfortable,[1] healthy, and free from the impositions which characterised it three-quarters of a century ago. The Merchant Shipping Act of 1894, with its slight amendments[2] of 1906, controls the traffic, whilst the Board of Trade at home, the governors in the British possessions, and the consuls in foreign countries are entrusted with the actual fulfilment of the various statutes. Both the Dominion of Canada and the United States have drawn up certain enactments which affect the Atlantic passage, but all their important legislation is of a restrictive nature and, on that account, is dealt with elsewhere in this book.

The chief embarkation ports are London, Liverpool, Glasgow, Southampton, Queenstown, and Lon-

---

[1] This statement does not necessarily apply to sailings between continental Europe and North America. Vide ' A Bord des Transatlantiques," *Le Monde*, October, 1911, p. 679.

[2] The amendments of 1906 were only slight in so far as they controlled the traffic of passengers.

THE TRANSPORT OF EMIGRANTS 127

donderry, whilst the most frequented American ports on the Atlantic seaboard are New York, Boston, Portland (Maine) and Philadelphia in the United States, and Quebec, Montreal, Halifax, and St. John (New Brunswick) in Canada. The fares vary slightly from time to time, but steerage rates average from £5 10s. to £6 15s.,[1] whilst second cabin costs from £8 upwards. A great number of steamship companies are engaged in the trade; the most important are the Allan Line, the American Line, the Anchor Line, the Atlantic Steamship Lines (Canadian Pacific Railway Company's steamers), the Cunard Line, the Hamburg-Amerika Line, the Norddeutscher Lloyd Line, and the White Star Line. The two German companies, it should be noted, do not carry steerage passengers from the United Kingdom, and are thus subject to Board of Trade regulations only as far as their saloon and second-class passengers are concerned.[2]

No matter what the destination and the ship

---

[1] A search through various Blue Books shows that the cost of steerage passages has varied but little during the last hundred and ten years. The following are a few quotations selected at random:

(a) The approximate expense of emigrating to Canada in 1820 and 1821 was £6.—Report on Emigration, 1826-7, Vol. V, p. 51.

(b) In 1820 a vessel was chartered for £700, which was at the rate of £4 5s. per passenger, including provisions; the journey being from Scotland to Canada.—Report on Emigration, 1826-7, Vol. V, p. 90.

(c) Fare to Nova Scotia or New Brunswick, with twelve weeks' provisions, £4 14s. 6d.—*Ibid.*, p. 291.

(d) Fare from Liverpool to Quebec, £3 5s.; to New York, £3 10s.; from London to Quebec, £4; to New York, £4 10s.—Tenth Report, Colonial Land and Emigration Commissioners, 1850, Vol. XXIII, p. 59.

(e) Fare to Prince Edward Island or Cape Breton, including food, £4 per head. Extra cost for conveyance to Upper Canada, £1 5s. One man went from Aberdeen to Toronto for £5 10s.—First Report of the Select Committee on Emigration from Scotland, 1841, Vol. VI, p. 139.

(f) Owing to keen competition, the fare at one period of the 1848 season from Liverpool to New York was £2 15s.—Ninth Report of the Colonial Land and Emigration Commissioners, 1849, Vol. XXII, p. 8.

(g) Cost of sending an emigrant to Canada or the United States is £4 10s.—*Ibid.*, Ninth Report, p. 4.

(h) In the year 1855, the whole expense of emigrating Irish people averaged £5 10s. per head.—*Ibid.*, Sixteenth Report, 1856, Vol. XXIV, p. 334.

[2] For additional information on this subject see "How to get to Canada," p. 147, in *Canada, To-day*, 1911.

selected for the journey, the routine of an Atlantic steerage passage to-day is much the same. Arrived at the port of embarkation, the emigrant calls at the transport company's quay-side office and there obtains a ticket indicating the number of his berth, together with other final instructions. No choice is allowed in the matter of selecting the berth; they are allocated in strict rotation in order to eliminate any thought of partiality. Provided with this ticket, the emigrant proceeds to the ship and crosses the gangway. Once aboard he is met by two doctors, the ship's doctor and the shore surgeon, who scrutinise him. Long years of experience enable these men to detect physical defects almost at a glance, and it is a rare occurrence for a sufferer to get beyond them unchallenged. A little later the Board of Trade doctor appears and institutes a more thorough examination. This official does not confine his inspection to the steerage people, but requires first and second-class passengers together with the whole crew to submit to the ordeal.

The steerage sleeping quarters are no longer arranged in dormitory fashion, but are composed of a number of small cabins, each holding a few berths. The bed itself is usually made of a spring wire mattress provided with an overlay which is filled with a fresh supply of straw at the commencement of each journey. Ample deck space is available for exercise, whilst smoke-rooms, sitting-rooms, saloons, and other quarters provide comforts which usually surpass expectation. Probably the most irksome part of the journey is the regularity with which life aboard needs to be conducted. With a complement of some hundreds of passengers, often over a thousand, method and system must be expected to govern the daily programme.

Each morning a tour of inspection is made of the steerage quarters by the captain and chief officers, whilst notices hang in prominent places stating that on these occasions the staff is prepared to investigate

THE TRANSPORT OF EMIGRANTS 129

complaints which dissatisfied passengers may feel disposed to make. As each immigrant must satisfy the quarantine officers on landing, that he has either been vaccinated or has had small-pox, the ship's doctor is at all times prepared to vaccinate those who are unable to display the necessary proofs.

On nearing land, the customs and quarantine officials board the vessel and turn their attention, in the first place, to the saloon and second-class passengers. This plan enables the more wealthy travellers to proceed on their land journey without delay, but the steerage people are often kept at the emigration sheds during the best part of a day. At Quebec,[1] this wait is notoriously protracted, although the appointment of a few more officers and the enlargement of the shed accommodation would tend to save much valuable time. When entering the United States, the inspection is carried out with greater despatch, though it is hard to appreciate the necessity for two separate medical examinations taking place one after the other, the first being conducted by the doctor belonging to the Federal Government's staff and the second under the direction of the doctor appointed by the State Legislature. There remain to be considered the involved conditions which regulate the landing of emigrants; these, however, are reserved for the following chapter.

Before concluding, it may be well to touch briefly on a matter which has caused much needless harm and anxiety. We refer to a certain section of the Press which seems to delight in distorting facts connected with the transport of emigrants. A favourite plan of these periodicals is to discover some obscure case of overcrowding, cruelty, or, better still, immorality, and to publish it broadcast as though it were an incident

---

[1] All third-class passengers entering Canada are required to land at Quebec during the summer months. The winter ports are Halifax and St. John.

happening every day on the high seas. As a matter of fact, people who are in a position to express an authoritative opinion, have constantly stated that the conduct of British emigrants during the passage is exemplary, whilst the treatment meted out to them by the steamship companies is usually better than that required by the Board of Trade. When a case, cited by these journals has permitted of investigation, and it may be added that but few of them are ever reported with sufficient detail to allow of this, the impression gained from the enquiry has been that the whole matter was distorted and exaggerated for the sake of journalistic sensation.

CHAPTER VI

IMMIGRATION RESTRICTIONS

DURING the hundred and fifty years with which this survey is concerned, the reception of immigrants arriving in North American ports has undergone remarkable changes. In the earliest times, no legislation of any kind dealt with the entrance of people arriving from British shores; the condition of the labour markets was then such that all who arrived were speedily provided with work; in fact, the demand for able-bodied men and women was in excess of the supply. When necessitous or ailing people were landed, either the charitable residents took pity on them and attended to their wants or prospective employers gave them succour in the hope of subsequently securing their labours. The system permitted few people to become a public burden, and thus there was little or no reason for State interference.

With the increased flow of emigration, which commenced about 1820, an altered condition of circumstances arose. No longer was there the same dearth of labour; work, it is true, was still plentiful, but men took longer to become settled as their occupations led them further afield. Also, the overcrowded and unsanitary condition of the transport vessels caused an increase in the number of invalids who were landed at the various Atlantic ports. These altered conditions made immigrants, as a class, far more dependent than they had hitherto been, and considerable numbers of them became burdensome. With a growing tide of destitute humanity, the presence of which meant an increasing charge upon the local finances, it is little wonder that the city of New York sought means to protect itself. This it was able to do, though only partially, by promoting the first of all American restrictive measures.

From this early beginning, a complicated code of prohibitory measures has been gradually evolved by both the United States and the Canadian Governments, a code which has grown more stringent whenever the inflow of European visitors has quickened. To-day, the restrictions are such that they shut out the diseased, the criminal, the vicious, the person unable to support himself, and in some cases the contract labourer. They involve strict examinations, concerning both health and finances, and often necessitate quarantine and other forms of detention.

Until the second decade of the nineteenth century, the two North American powers welcomed all comers as long as they were able-bodied and industrious. Later on, we find that only those who knew a trade, or were willing to work on the land, received this welcome,[1] whilst to-day the economic demands of labour and politics have, in certain cases, closed the door to all but agricultural hands and female domestic servants.[2] Thus it will be seen that in the last ninety years a complex system of restriction has sprung up having for its object the exclusion of people who might prove a burden or dangerous, people whose habits and natures would prevent them from associating with their neighbours ; and lastly, people in such numbers as to cause an economic disturbance in the country of reception.

As we have said, the first North American restrictive measure was imposed in the United States.[3] It

---

[1] Vide Report of Emigration, 1826-7.

[2] i.e. in the case of Canada, when the emigrant receives charitable or public assistance.

[3] An Act was passed by the Legislature of New York in 1819, but its provisions were never regarded seriously.

was enforced in 1824 and required the master of every ship, landing aliens at the port of New York, to enter into a bond with the mayor, the sum of which was never to exceed three hundred dollars per passenger. In cases where sick or destitute people were landed, the city provided for their wants and subtracted the cost from the bond money. This enactment, it must be added, partook of the nature of a local by-law and only affected New York City.

To appreciate the need for this legislation, we must remember that the burden of providing hospital and other treatment for the necessitous arrivals fell entirely on the city funds. The city, however, obtained no return for its outlay, as the people, as soon as they were fit to travel, passed on into the interior and were lost for ever to New York itself.

The law led to serious abuses. A regular trade immediately sprang up in insuring the captains against their new liability. Certain financiers made it a regular business to contract with the masters to act as their guarantors. These took charge of all unfortunate passengers who happened to require either medical treatment or other support, and lodged them in private boarding-houses where only the harshest of treatment and the meanest of accommodation were available. In this way the destitute people did not become a public charge, and no liabilities were entered against the guarantors by the city. It is almost superfluous to add that the expense incurred per person in these boarding establishments never reached a tithe of the sum which the authorities would have disbursed had they taken charge of the sick and needy.

The enactment of 1824 continued in force, with some few unimportant modifications, until 1832, when it was withdrawn in favour of a new regulation which marked a second step in the history of restriction. The earlier legislation only levied a toll in cases where expense had been incurred by the city, but the latter Act allowed a master to escape the execution of the usual bond on payment of a tax of one dollar for every alien who disembarked from his ship.[1] The money so collected was reserved for assisting cases of temporary want or illness and in providing a more or less adequate staff to superintend the arrangements incidental to landing.

In the same year, on February 25th, the province of Lower Canada legalised a head tax.[2] In this case it amounted to five shillings currency or about four shillings and two pence sterling for each adult. Two children between the ages of seven and seventeen, or three between one and seven years were, for this purpose, reckoned as an adult, whilst babies of less than twelve months of age were passed in untaxed. The money derived in this manner was used partly in providing indigent people with passages to Upper Canada, an action which Lord Durham denounced in his report of 1839,[3] and partly in financing the Emigration Hospital, Quebec, the General Hospital, Montreal, the Quebec Emigration Society, and the Montreal Emigration Society. The sums handed to these bodies, it may be said, were considerable, amounting to £6605 9s. 2d. in 1832, £4775 19s. 2d. in 1833, and £2449 6s. 8d. in 1835.[4]

One drawback to the legislation of this period was that it lacked uniformity. Not only were there wide differences between the decrees of the United States and those of Canada, but each province of the British

---

[1] *Immigration, and the Commissioners of Emigration of the State of New York*, by F. Kapp, p. 45, 1870.
[2] Accounts and Papers, Vol. XXXII, 1831.
[3] Similar Acts were introduced by Nova Scotia and New Brunswick. Lord Durham wrote: " To tax the whole body of emigrants for the purpose of providing a remedy for evils which no adequate means have been adopted to prevent, and thus to compel the most prudent of that class to bear the burden of imprudence and negligence in others, is surely a measure of very doubtful justice."—Report, p. 227.
[4] Accounts and Papers, Vol. XL, 1836, p. 484.

IMMIGRATION RESTRICTIONS 135

territories imposed its own code of laws, all, presumably, to effect the same end. In some cases, the smaller provinces seem to have legislated without full consideration of the consequent issues, with the result that ambiguous and impracticable enactments sometimes followed. A case in point was provided by New Brunswick.[1] In 1842, a decree was in force which levied a tax on fresh arrivals to assist their indigent fellow-travellers. The sums so received were to be paid into the provincial treasury, whilst the monies expended on giving relief could only be obtained by applying to the Legislature. Curiously enough this latter body never met until the immigration season was over; thus the money was collected for an object for which it could never be spent. In practice the needy people were either subjected to unnecessary want or were assisted by the Commissioners of the Poor and consequently received the taint of pauperism.

A further stage in the development of restriction dates from the appointment of the first Board of Immigration Commissioners of the State of New York.[2] The initial business of this body was to enquire into the abuses which then affected the regulations governing the landing of immigrants. At that time, captains bringing alien passengers had the option of entering into a bond or of paying a head-tax for each person who disembarked. This system was unsatisfactory, for ship-masters, as a rule, exacted the toll of one dollar from each immigrant under the pretext of paying the head-tax, but negotiated with insurance brokers for the reception, at a low figure, in private almshouses of any who might become a public charge. Friedrich Kapp mentions in his work, *Immigration and the Commissioners of Emigration*,[3] that

---
[1] Accounts and Papers, Vol. XXXIV, p. 47, 1843.
[2] Appointed May 5th, 1847.
[3] Published in New York in 1870. Vide p. 50.

in the three years 1839-1841 there were 181,615 people who entered the city of New York, most of whom were called upon by their respective captains to pay the dollar head-tax. As a set-off against this, he states that the city only received $41,392 in head money, thus inferring that the sum of, presumably, $140,223 had been shared between the ship-masters and insurance brokers.

The first decree of this newly constituted immigration board required all aliens entering the city to pay a tax of one dollar, a sum which was soon raised to two and then to two and a half dollars, whilst the bond, which had hitherto been optional, was abolished. So far, the various restrictions had only been directed against people who were unable to support themselves either through temporary ill-health or lack of employment, but the Commissioners looked with growing disfavour upon those who arrived with mental troubles as well as the deaf, the dumb, and the infirm. In order to discourage captains from bringing such people as these, it was required that when deficient persons were landed without a parent or guardian to watch over them, the ship-master was to find two people who resided in the State to act as their sureties. These had to defray all expenses, to the extent of three hundred dollars, which the authorities might incur on behalf of each afflicted immigrant, but a period of five years was mentioned as the time during which the liability existed.

In the following year, 1848, what was then looked upon as a novel experiment was tried by the Canadian Legislature. In order that people might be induced to reach the Atlantic shores during the summer months, when outdoor work was plentiful, an immigrant tax on a sliding scale was introduced. Between March and August the levy was one of ten shillings, during September it was raised to twenty shillings, but from October, through the winter months, it stood at thirty shillings.¹ Apparently the experiment did not give satisfaction, for we find that no such increased scale of charges was made on winter and autumn arrivals during the following year, 1849, though the system, in a modified form, has once again been resorted to in recent times.

Hardly a twelve-month passed in these early years but the head-tax in Canada was altered, sometimes even considerably. In 1832, it was five shillings currency: on March 23rd, 1848,² it had risen to ten shillings, whilst in 1849, we find that it fell to seven and sixpence. The spirit of the tax, however, remained the same, which was to provide money for supporting the immigration department in its work of caring for the needy and sick on arrival. After 1856, the expenses incurred by the quarantine department were also met by the head-tax fund.³

No further changes of importance were made in the restrictive laws of either Canada or the United States until 1869, when a Canadian Act gave the Governor in Council power to issue, at any time, a proclamation prohibiting the landing of any immigrant who did not possess sufficient money to enable him to reach his destination.⁴ Though the enactment was made in 1869 effect was not given to its provisions until January, 1880. The reason for this non-enforcement is not far to seek. The object of the law was to prevent people from landing at certain points and so causing congestion. But whilst over-population was causing embarrassment at the ports of entry, great hinterlands were at a standstill for the want of additional labour. Rather than enforce a law, which seems to have been introduced at an inopportune moment,

---

¹ Appendix K to Minutes of Evidence, House of Lords Select Committee on the operation of Irish Poor Laws, 1849.
² *Ibid.*   ³ Accounts and Papers, Vol. X, 1857, p. 908.
⁴ Debate in the House of Commons, Dominion of Canada, 1880, Vol. 1, p. 199.

and so prevent useful people from entering the country the Dominion agreed to transfer suitable but destitute immigrants from the overstocked maritime areas to various inland points within Ontario. The central legislature arranged to bear one-third of the expense whilst the provincial government undertook to furnish the remaining two-thirds. For some time this arrangement gave much satisfaction, but in 1879–1880 Ontario petitioned for the supply of labour to be checked as its requirements at the moment were more than supplied. It was then that the provisions of 1869, so long kept in abeyance, were put into effect and the non-self-supporting element refused an entry. Amongst the provisions, every immigrant person who landed was required to be in possession of a sum of twenty dollars. This was the first occasion on which a show of money as distinct from a levy was made a condition of admission to Canada.

In 1876, the Supreme Court of the United States declared that the Commissioners of the State of New York were pursuing an illegal course in demanding head-money from immigrants. The reason given for this decision was that the exaction interfered with commerce, and was therefore a matter upon which an individual state could not legislate. Complications immediately arose; the steamship companies naturally ceased to continue their payments, whilst one of their number, the Inman Steamship Company, sued the Commissioners for a return of all the moneys they had paid during a number of previous years. Not wishing to involve the State in financial embarrassment, Congress legalised the past actions of the Commissioners by framing a special Act in 1878, which briefly said that the decision was not to have a retrospective interpretation. In spite of this ruling, the position of the Commissioners was still an unenviable one. Deprived of their main source of revenue, they had to depend on inadequate grants voted by the local treasury with which to carry on their work of controlling the streams of immigrants then flowing through the port of New York. Intended as a way out of the difficulty, a State Act was hurriedly passed in 1881 which levied a tax of one dollar on every new arrival, ostensibly to cover the cost of medical inspection. This enactment was immediately contested by the Compagnie Générale Transatlantique and also declared illegal by the high courts.

The State of New York then argued with much force that it was unreasonable for its local treasury to be saddled with the major part of the cost of organising and marshalling the inflow of aliens. Were all the crowds of humanity which entered its ports to remain in the territory under its control the burden was rightly one for it to bear. But it was well known that New York was a gateway to the West and that thousands of people merely partook of the hospitality provided by the city whilst they were preparing to proceed to other parts of the Union. Obviously, as the whole Union gained by the inflow of population, so also should the whole Union contribute to the immigration expenditure incurred by New York State. Either, it said, the work should be undertaken by the United States as a nation, or the national treasury should provide the money for its proper conduct. Matters were finally arranged in 1882, for in that year, Congress enacted that no unfit people should be allowed to enter the Republic and at the same time ordered a head-tax of fifty cents to be levied on each immigrant coming by sea. The money was collected under the supervision of the Secretary of the Treasury and he contracted with the Commissioners of New York for the work to be carried out by them as heretofore.

Since immigration into the United States has been controlled by the central legislature, many additions have been made to the restrictive measures already existing. At the present time the following comprehensive list describes the various classes of aliens who are debarred from entering the country.[1]

Persons who have had two or more attacks of insanity at any time previously.
Paupers.
Persons likely to become a public charge.
Professional beggars.
Persons afflicted with tuberculosis or with a loathsome or dangerous contagious disease.
Persons otherwise morally or physically defective in a way which may affect their ability to earn a living.
Persons who have been convicted of a felony or other crime or misdemeanour involving moral turpitude.
Polygamists, anarchists, or persons who believe in or advocate the overthrow by force or violence of the Government of the United States, or of all Governments, or of all forms of law, or the assassination of public officials.
Certain people of immoral intent.
Persons called contract labourers, who have been induced or solicited to migrate to the States by offers or promises of employment, or in consequence of agreements, oral, written, or printed, expressed or implied, to perform labour in the States, of any kind, skilled or unskilled.
Persons, who have been, within one year from the date of the application for admission to the United States, deported as having been induced or solicited to migrate as above described; and also
Any person whose ticket or passage is paid for with the money of another, or who is assisted by others to come, unless it is affirmatively and satisfactorily shown that such person does not belong to the foregoing excluded classes: and that the said ticket or passage was not paid for by any corporation, association, society, municipality, or foreign Government, either directly or indirectly.
All children under sixteen years of age, unaccompanied by one or both of their parents, at the discretion of the Secretary

---

[1] Sec. 2 of the Act " To regulate the immigration of aliens into the United States," 1907.

IMMIGRATION RESTRICTIONS

of Commerce and Labour, or under such regulations as he may from time to time prescribe.

Provided that nothing in this Act shall exclude, if otherwise admissible, persons convicted of an offence purely political not involving moral turpitude.

Provided further, that the provisions of this section relating to the payments for tickets or passage by any corporation, association, society, municipality, or foreign Government, shall not apply to the tickets of passage of aliens in immediate and continuous transit through the United States to foreign contiguous territory.

Provided further that skilled labour may be imported, if labour of like kind unemployed cannot be found in the United States; and

Provided further that the provisions of this law applicable to contract labour shall not be held to exclude professional actors, artists, lecturers, singers, ministers of any religious denomination, professors for colleges, or seminaries, persons belonging to any recognised learned profession, or persons employed strictly as personal or domestic servants.

All idiots, imbeciles, feeble-minded persons, epileptics, insane persons, and persons who have been insane within five years previous.

The following information has recently been drawn up by the Commissioner of Immigration at Ellis Island for the proper conduct of immigration into the United States :—

1. The immigration authorities decline to determine whether or not an immigrant is qualified to land until after he has arrived and submitted himself for inspection.

2. The immigration laws apply to all aliens, whether they have previously resided in the United States or not. Alien residents who go abroad, though with the intention of returning, are upon their return nevertheless subject to inspection, and the $4 head-tax is payable on their account. A person who has not yet obtained final citizenship papers, though he may have declared his intention of becoming a citizen, is still an alien.

3. The immigration laws apply to all aliens, irrespective of

whether they travel in cabin quarters or in the steerage. All steerage aliens are brought to Ellis Island for inspection as a matter of course. Cabin aliens are usually inspected on board between quarantine and the pier, and those only brought to Ellis Island whose right to land is not clear.

4. The law provides that every alien who does not appear to the examining inspector to be "clearly and beyond a doubt" entitled to land shall be detained for "special enquiry." Such enquiry occurs before boards composed of three officials with power to admit or exclude.

5. Immigrants should come here qualified to land and not expect to qualify after arrival through gifts of money from persons under no legal obligation to make them. The Government considers that they have but little bearing on the question of admissibility, even after the immigrant has been placed in possession thereof, especially when made after detention or exclusion.

6. The Government is under no obligation to receive or deliver to detained immigrants remittances sent them in its care. It does so only as a matter of convenience, at the sender's risk and to the extent of its ability to transact this business without interference with official work. Often, through the pressure of official work, delay in delivering is unavoidable.

7. In determining whether or not an immigrant is a pauper or likely to become a public charge, the immigration authorities consider among other matters his occupation, his proficiency in the same (including where relevant his physical ability to pursue it, and his mental aptitude therefore), the number of persons who may be dependent upon him for support either here or abroad, his chances of securing and holding employment, and the amount in his possession.

8. In the absence of a statutory provision, no hard and fast rule can be laid down as to the amount of money an immigrant must bring with him. In most cases, however, it will be unsafe for him to arrive with less than $25, besides ticket to destination, while often he should have more. In any event he must have enough to provide for his reasonable wants until such time as he is likely to find employment.

9. Some of the physical defects considered in connection with the provision excluding persons suffering from any

IMMIGRATION RESTRICTIONS 143

physical defect which may effect their ability to earn a living are : Ankylosis of various joints, arterio-sclerosis, atrophy of extremities, chronic progressive diseases of central nervous system, chronic inflammation of lymph glands of neck, dislocation of hip joints with shortening and lameness, double hernia, goitre, poor physical development, locomotor ataxia, psoriasis and lupus (chronic skin diseases), valvular disease of heart, and well-marked varicose veins. Such physical defects are not *per se* ground for exclusion (as are idiocy, insanity, and loathsome or dangerous contagious diseases), but when present in aggravated form, they usually affect the immigrant's ability to earn a living—in fact they frequently render him incapable to do so—and thus operate to exclude him, irrespective of whether in addition he is a person likely to become a public charge.

10. Children under sixteen unaccompanied by either parent may be excluded at the discretion of the Secretary of Commerce and Labour. Where admission is to occur, the minimum requirements are that the children shall enjoy good health, shall be going to close relatives who are able and willing to support and properly care for them, shall be sent to school until sixteen, and shall not be put at work unsuited to their years. Frequently a bond is required as a condition of admission. Where it is claimed that the parents of such children are in the United States, the latter will usually be held until the parents have been heard from.

11. All detention expenses at Ellis Island are payable by the steamship company concerned, irrespective of whether the immigrant is subsequently admitted or deported, except in the few instances covered by the provisos of Section 19, or by Section 37 of the Immigration Law, and where deportation is stayed at the request of a relative or friend.

12. Immigrants suffering from what are known as " quarantinable diseases " are removed from the vessel by the quarantine authorities of the State of New York and remain in their custody (usually at Hoffman and Swinburne islands) until cure has been effected, when they are sent to Ellis Island for inspection. Requests for information concerning such immigrants must be addressed to " Health Officer of the Port, Quarantine Station, Staten Island, N.Y." Quarantinable diseases at the port of New York now include not only cholera, yellow fever, small-pox, typhus fever, leprosy, and plague, but also such

acute contagious and infectious diseases as measles, scarlet fever, diphtheria, erysipelas, etc.

13. An alien may be deported at any time within three years of his arrival in cases either (1) he entered the United States in violation of law, or (2) he entered without inspection, or (3) he has become a public charge from a cause existing prior to landing. An alien has entered the United States in violation of law if in fact he belonged to one of the excluded classes, although such fact may at the time of entry have escaped attention. Usual instances in which an alien becomes a public charge are where he enters a public almshouse or a hospital, or is sent to jail. What may be a " cause existing prior to landing " depends somewhat on the circumstances of the case. Where the alien is found in a public almshouse or a hospital, the proof usually required to show that his presence there is due to a " cause existing prior to landing," is a medical certificate establishing the existence of some mental or physical disability prior to the time when he entered the country.

Contract labourers were first refused admission in the year 1885. Their exclusion was due to the agitation of the associates of the Independent Labour Party, but chiefly those living in the mining regions of Pennsylvania and the factory cities of the Eastern States. The party viewed this form of labour with much disfavour, as contract men had frequently been drawn into the United States by manufacturers to fill the place of strikers and in various other ways to lower the standard of wages. The Act forbidding contract labour says : " It shall be a misdemeanour for any person, company, partnership or corporation, in any manner whatsoever, to prepay the transportation, or in any way to assist or encourage the importation or migration of any contract labourer into the United States, unless he is exempt under the two provisos of Section 2." [1]

These provisos did not form part of the original Act, but were added at a later date in order to put an

---

[1] i.e. unless he is an actor, artist, singer, etc. See note above.

end to much senseless litigation. We must remember that the authorities, recognising their inability to work the enactment without private assistance, called upon individuals to report cases coming under their notice where the law had been transgressed. This appeal placed power into the hands of unscrupulous people, as the following incident shows : In 1885-6 the Rev. E. Walpole Warren of Lambeth, London, was asked by the Church of Holy Trinity in New York to fill the vacancy of pastor. After due consideration he accepted the offer, sailed for America and took up his duties in New York. Just at this time, a certain Scotch society with quarters in New York had had a considerable number of its members sent back to Scotland, a judge ruling that they were contract labourers. Aggravated by the decision, the society attempted to ridicule the legislation by drawing up an indictment against the English pastor, in which he, also, was accused of being a contract worker. Though the proceedings were fought by the ablest counsels, the Church authorities were found guilty of introducing illegal labour and fined a thousand dollars. The provisos mentioned above have therefore been added to the original Act, to prevent a repetition of such frivolous actions as the foregoing.

At the present time the law is entrusted to labour inspectors who, by boarding all incoming vessels and mixing with immigrants both before and after landing, obtain information which enables them to pick out the contract men. So skilled are these inspectors in their work, that comparatively few people can evade their clutches. The following case helps to show their astuteness. In November, 1892, the glass-blowers of Pittsburgh went on strike. The disagreement between masters and men lasted a considerable while, and, as a last resource, the former secretly invited Belgian glass-blowers to come and fill the vacancies. This action had been anticipated on the part of the inspectors, and when the Belgians arrived on board the *Friesland* they challenged every one of them, and all were detained at Ellis Island. It transpired afterwards that the inspectors looked at the mouths of the passengers and selected as glass-blowers those who had corns or skin excresences on their lips, a condition which comes through constant glass-blowing.[1]

Notwithstanding so formidable an array of restrictive measures as is listed above, it is due to the immigration commissioners to say that for many years they judged cases more on their individual merits than by following the strict letter of the law. Many instances could be brought forward to corroborate this statement, but it will prove sufficient to detail a single case. For a considerable while, nobody in authority seemed to know just what constituted a pauper, though the statute plainly said that such a person was to be forbidden an entrance. Obviously, a man was a pauper if he had been an inmate of a workhouse, but could this term apply to him if he had never accepted relief until the Guardians assisted him to emigrate ? While the question remained unanswered the English Poor Law authority happened to send a party of seven hundred and twenty people to the United States, and none were refused admission.[2] In every case, these people were judged according to their individual merits which, proving satisfactory, gained for them an entrance into the new country, in spite of the ban which had been placed on the introduction of paupers.

As much misunderstanding arose, at various times, from an insufficient knowledge of the views taken by Congress on the subject of State-aided emigration, Sir Lionel West wrote to Mr. Bayard asking for enlightenment

---

[1] See article, " American Immigration Laws," in *Annual of the Co-operative Wholesale Society*, 1894, p. 185.

[2] Report on Colonisation, 1889, p. 131-2.

on this important question. He received the following reply: "The economic and political conditions of the United States have always led the Government to favour immigration, and all persons seeking a new field of effort, and coming hither with a view to the improvement of their condition by the free exercise of their faculties, have been cordially received. The same conditions have caused other kinds of immigration to be regarded as undesirable and led to the adoption by Congress of laws to prevent the coming of paupers, contract labourers, criminals, and certain other enumerated classes. Such immigration, the economic and political conditions of the United States render particularly unacceptable. In view of this policy and these laws, this Government could not fail to look with disfavour and concern upon the sending to this country, by foreign governmental agencies, and at the public cost, of persons not only unlikely to develop qualities of thrift and self-support, but sent here because it is assumed that they have 'friends' in this country able to 'help and support' them. The mere fact of poverty has never been regarded as an objection to an immigrant, and a large part of those who have come to our shores have been persons who relied for support solely upon the exercise of thrift and manual industry; and to such persons, it may be said, the development of the country has in a large degree been due. But persons whose only escape from immediately becoming and remaining a charge upon the community is the expected, but entirely contingent, voluntary help and support of friends, are not a desirable accession to our population, and their exportation hither by a foreign Government in order to get rid of the burden of their support could scarcely be regarded as a friendly act, or in harmony with existing laws."[1] As an outcome of this and correspondence of a similar

---

[1] Quoted from p. 151, Report on Colonisation, 1889.

nature, the Local Government Board, in 1888, refused to sanction expenditure of any kind in connection with emigration directed to the United States.

In spite of the fact that probably no country in the world possesses a more advanced code of restrictive laws than the United States, yet the popular opinion ruling in the New England states is that these measures require still further strengthening; such at least is the impression to be gained from an acquaintance with such publications as the *North American Review*, the *American Law Review*, the *Political Science Quarterly*, and the *Outlook*.[1]

In the first place, the people of the United States find fault with the medical inspections on the ground that they are somewhat casual and wanting in thoroughness. The aliens on reaching Ellis Island are required to file in hundreds along a narrow fenced-in passage. At intervals, surgeons are stationed; one watches for physical deformities, another for mental weaknesses, a third for eye-diseases, whilst others search for still further defects. Should an abnormal person be discovered, he is sent to a consulting-room for an extended examination and is then styled " off the line." When this more thorough scrutiny corroborates the earlier suspicion of unfitness, the alien is handed a certificate of disability and returned to the steamship company which landed him. Even now he has one chance left of resisting deportation, and that is to appeal to the special Board of Enquiry.

From the foregoing, it will be seen that the alien suffering from a specific complaint is no menace to the country; his fate is swiftly determined. It is, however, the person of poor physique who presents a real danger. In cases where no signs of active disease are shown, he is usually admitted if someone will guarantee that he will not become a public charge. Needless to add, such guarantees are usually worthless,

---

[1] See also Report on Colonisation, 1889, p. 96.

IMMIGRATION RESTRICTIONS 149

although they may have been reduced to writing. That this form of evil is real and not imaginary is plainly shown by the fact that during the year ending June 30th, 1906, 5747 aliens were certified by the surgeons of Ellis Island as being of poor physique, of which number only 1117 were deported. In addition to this, 26,424 cases were certified as having minor physical defects, but not one person amongst them suffered deportation.[1]

Having noted that people of more or less poor physique are admitted into the United States, it is interesting to trace their ultimate fate. In the year 1905, 26,839 patients found admission to seven of the largest hospitals in the City of New York. Of this number 12,550, or 46·6 per cent, were native born, whilst 14,289, or 54·4 per cent, were foreign born.[2] If we remember that the foreign-born element of New York is only 36·5 per cent of the whole, we see that the figures are more alarming than they appear at first sight.

Not only is the health of the city jeopardised by the acceptance of such people, but its finances are also affected. Bellevue and its allied hospitals treated, in 1905, a total of 35,199 patients; of these 19,146, or 54·4 per cent, were foreign born. As these hospitals cost the city authorities a sum of $648,480.76, it will be seen that the amount expended on the alien population was $352,773.54. During the same period, the City and Metropolitan hospitals received 17,461 patients, and of this number 10,533, or 60·3 per cent, were foreign born. These institutions cost the Department of Public Charities $2,027,480.16, so that 60 per cent of this amount may be reckoned as the sum disbursed on alien assistance.[3] If we turn to almost any

---

[1] "The Medico-Economic Aspect of the Immigration Problem" *North American Review*, vol. 183, 1906, pp. 1262-71.
[2] *Ibid.* [3] *Ibid.*

specific malady we still find that the alien is the chief sufferer. In 1902, 5724 people died of tuberculosis in New York City. Of this number 637 were of native maternal parentage, whilst 5087 were of foreign maternal parentage.[1] Lastly, we may refer to the report of the New York State Lunacy Commission, issued in March, 1904. Figures given therein show that when the publication was issued, 60 per cent of the insane patients under treatment in the city of New York were of foreign birth.

From the above statements, we see that the immigrant population of the Atlantic states is largely composed of an undesirable element. On this account the admission laws, in all probability, will be shortly made more difficult of fulfilment, especially those statutes which deal with the illiterate, the alien of poor physique, and the alien with some minor defect.

Though the prohibition laws of the United States are of a highly stringent nature, those controlling Canadian immigrants are, perhaps, equally severe. Various Acts have been drawn up in 1886, 1902, 1906, 1907, 1908, 1909, and 1910, and each has afforded greater protection to the Dominion than its predecessor. The statutes which are at present in force are of an involved and lengthy description, but the spirit of them may be gained from the following extracts :—

No immigrant, passenger, or other person, unless he is a Canadian citizen, or has a Canadian domicile, shall be permitted to land in Canada, or in case of having landed in or entered Canada shall be permitted to remain therein, who belongs to any of the following classes, hereinafter called " prohibited classes " :

(*a*) Idiots, imbeciles, feeble-minded persons, epileptics, insane persons, and persons who have been insane within five years previous.

---

[1] "The Medico-Economic Aspect of the Immigration Problem," *North American Review*, vol. 183, 1906, pp. 1262-71.

(b) Persons afflicted with any loathsome disease, or with a disease which is contagious or infectious, or which may become dangerous to the public health, whether such persons intend to settle in Canada or only to pass through Canada in transit to some other country : provided that if such disease is one which is curable within a reasonably short time, such persons may, subject to the regulations in that behalf, if any, be permitted to remain on board ship if hospital facilities do not exist on shore, or to leave ship for medical treatment.

(c) Immigrants who are dumb, blind, or otherwise physically defective, unless in the opinion of a Board of Inquiry, or officer acting as such, they have sufficient money, or have such profession, occupation, trade, employment, or other legitimate mode of earning a living that they are not liable to become a public charge or unless they belong to a family accompanying them or already in Canada and which gives security satisfactory to the Minister against such immigrants becoming a public charge.

(d) Persons who have been convicted of any crime involving moral turpitude.

(e) Certain persons of immoral intent.

(f) Professional beggars or vagrants, or persons likely to become a public charge.

(g) Immigrants to whom money has been given or loaned by any charitable organisation for the purpose of enabling them to qualify for landing in Canada under this Act, or whose passage to Canada has been paid wholly or in part by any charitable organisation, or out of public moneys, unless it is shown that the authority in writing of the Superintendent of Immigration, or in case of persons coming from Europe, the authority in writing of the Assistant-Superintendent of Immigration for Canada, in London, has been obtained for the landing in Canada of such persons, and that such authority has been acted upon within a period of sixty days thereafter.

Every passenger or other person seeking to land in Canada shall first appear before an immigration officer, and shall be forthwith examined as required under this Act, either on shipboard·or on train or at some other place designated for that purpose.

Every passenger or other person, as to whose right to land the examining officer has any doubt, shall be detained for further examination by the officer in charge, or by the Board of Inquiry, and such examination shall be forthwith conducted separate and apart from the public, and upon the conclusion thereof such passenger or other person shall be either immediately landed or shall be rejected and kept in custody pending his deportation.

An order for deportation by a Board of Inquiry or officer in charge may be made in the form B in the schedule to this Act, and a copy of the said order shall forthwith be delivered to such passenger or other person, and a copy of the said order shall at the same time be served upon the master or owner of the ship or upon the local agent or other official of the transportation company by which such person was brought to Canada; and such person shall thereupon be deported by such company subject to any appeal which may have been entered on his behalf under Section 19 of this Act.

Any transportation company or person knowingly and wilfully landing, or assisting to land or attempting to land in Canada, any prohibited immigrant or person whose entry into Canada has been forbidden under this Act, shall be guilty of an offence and shall be liable on conviction to a fine of not more than five hundred and not less than fifty dollars for each prohibited immigrant or other person so landed in Canada, or whose landing in Canada was so attempted.

Regulations made by the Governor in Council under this Act may provide as a condition to permission to land in Canada that immigrants and tourists shall possess in their own right money to a prescribed minimum amount, which amount may vary according to the race, occupation, or destination of such immigrant or tourist, and otherwise according to the circumstances; and may also provide that all persons coming to Canada directly or indirectly from countries which issue passports or penal certificates to persons leaving such countries shall produce such passports or penal certificates on demand of the immigration officer in charge before being allowed to land in Canada.

The Governor in Council may, by proclamation or order,[1] whenever he deems it necessary or expedient :—

(*a*) Prohibit the landing in Canada or at any specified port

---

[1] A Regulation to this effect was passed on May 9th, 1910.

IMMIGRATION RESTRICTIONS

of entry in Canada of any immigrant who has come to Canada otherwise than by continuous journey from the country of which he is a native or naturalised citizen, and upon a through ticket purchased in that country, or prepaid in Canada;

(b) prohibit the landing in Canada of passengers brought to Canada by any transportation company which refuses or neglects to comply with the provisions of this Act.

(c) Prohibit for a stated period, or permanently, the landing in Canada, or the landing at any specified port of entry in Canada, of immigrants belonging to any race deemed unsuited to the climate or requirements of Canada, or of immigrants of any specified class, occupation or character.

Whenever any person, other than a Canadian citizen, within three years after landing in Canada has been convicted of a criminal offence in Canada, or has been guilty of certain immoral conduct, or has become a professional beggar or a public charge, or an inmate of a penitentiary, gaol, reformatory, prison, hospital, insane asylum or public charitable institution, or enters or remains in Canada contrary to any provision of this Act, it shall be the duty of any officer cognisant thereof, and the duty of the clerk, secretary, or other official of any municipality in Canada wherein such person may be, to forthwith send a written complaint thereof to the Minister or Superintendent of Immigration, giving full particulars.

Whenever any person, other than a Canadian citizen advocates in Canada the overthrow by force or violence of the Government of Great Britain, or Canada, or other British dominion, colony, possession or dependency, or the overthrow by force or violence of constituted law and authority, or the assassination of any official of the Government of Great Britain or Canada or other British dominion, colony, possession or dependency, or of any foreign Government, or shall by word or act create or attempt to create riot or public disorder in Canada, or shall by common repute belong to or be suspected of belonging to any secret society or organisation which extorts money from, or in any way attempts to control, any resident of Canada by force or threat of bodily harm, or by blackmail; such person for the purposes of this Act shall be considered and classed as an undesirable immigrant, and it shall be the duty of any officer becoming cognisant thereof, and the duty of the clerk, secretary, or other official of any municipality in Canada wherein such person may be, to forthwith send a written complaint thereof to the Minister or Superintendent of Immigration, giving full particulars.

Upon receiving a complaint from any officer, or from any clerk or secretary or other official of a municipality, whether directly or through the Superintendent of Immigration, against any person alleged to belong to any prohibited or undesirable class, the Minister may order such person to be taken into custody and detained at an immigrant station for examination and an investigation of the facts alleged in the said complaint to be made by a Board of Inquiry or by an officer acting as such. Such Board of Inquiry or officer shall have the same powers and privileges, and shall follow the same procedure, as if the person against whom complaint is made were being examined before landing as provided in Section 33 of the Act of 1910; and similarly the person against whom complaint is made shall have the same rights and privileges as he would have if seeking to land in Canada.

If upon investigation of the facts such Board of Inquiry or examining officer is satisfied that such person belongs to any of the prohibited or undesirable classes mentioned in Sections 40 and 41 of the above Act, such person shall be deported forthwith, as provided for in Section 33, subject, however, to such right of appeal as he may have to the Minister.

The Governor in Council may, at any time, order any such person found by a Board of Inquiry or examining officer to belong to any of the undesirable classes referred to in Section 41 to leave Canada within a specified period. Such order may be in the form D in the schedule to the Act, and shall be in force as soon as it is served upon such persons, or is left for him by any officer at the last known place of abode or address of such person.

Any person rejected or deported under the Act of 1910 who enters or remains in or returns to Canada after such rejection or deportation without a permit under this Act or other lawful excuse, or who refuses or neglects to leave Canada when ordered so to do by the Governor in Council as provided for in this section, shall be guilty of an offence against this Act, and may forthwith be arrested by any officer and be deported on an order from the Minister or the Superintendent of Immigration, or may be prosecuted for such offence, and shall be liable,

IMMIGRATION RESTRICTIONS 155

on conviction to two years imprisonment, and immediately after expiry of any sentence imposed for such offence may be again deported or ordered to leave Canada under this section.

In any case[1] where deportation of the head of a family is ordered, all dependent members of the family may be deported at the same time. And in any case where deportation of a dependent member of a family is ordered on account of having become a public charge, and in the opinion of the Minister such circumstance is due to wilful neglect or non-support by the head or other members of the family morally bound to support such dependent members, then all members of the family may be deported at the same time. Such deportation shall be at the cost of the persons so deported; and if that be not possible then the cost of such deportation shall be paid by the Department of the Interior.

Every immigrant, passenger, stowaway, or other person brought to Canada by a transportation company and rejected by the Board of Inquiry or officer in charge, shall, if practicable, be sent back to the place whence he came, on the vessel, railway train, or other vehicle by which he was brought to Canada. The cost of his maintenance, while being detained at any immigrant station after having been rejected, as well as the cost of his return, shall be paid by such transportation company.

Every person who causes or procures the publication or circulation, by advertisement or otherwise, in a country outside of Canada, of false representations as to the opportunities for employment in Canada, or as to the state of the labour market in Canada, intended or adapted to encourage or induce, or to deter or prevent, the immigration into Canada of persons resident in such outside country, or who does anything in Canada for the purpose of causing or procuring the communication to any resident of such country of any such representations which are thereafter so published, circulated or communicated, shall be guilty of an offence against the Act, and liable, on summary conviction before two justices of the peace to a fine of not more than five hundred dollars, or to imprisonment for a term not exceeding six months, or to both fine and imprisonment.

---

[1] 3149 immigrants were deported during the years 1902-9, of whom 2303 were British or Irish.

To assist the immigration of foreigners under contract to perform labour in Canada is prohibited by ch. 97, of Revised Statutes 1906. But this Act does not apply to skilled workmen in new industries, if such labour cannot be otherwise obtained, nor to actors, artists, lecturers or singers, nor personal or domestic servants, nor to relatives intending to settle, nor to any foreign country at all, unless it has applied to Canada a law similar to this Act. This secton has therefore no force in the United Kingdom.

Other restrictive enactments exist beyond these mentioned above. A complete code of measures has been drawn up to regulate the entrance of children, but these will be discussed in a later chapter. Also, it may be added, that certain provincial legislatures have introduced Acts to meet local contingencies, e.g. British Columbia has enforced an education test.

Until within the last two or three years the restrictive measures formulated by the Dominion were interpreted with a spirit of toleration and elasticity such as was not to be found across the frontier in the United States. Each Canadian official, dealing with the inspection of immigrants was given a memorandum from which the following is an extract: " Inspectors appointed to enforce the provisions of the Immigration Act and the regulations made thereunder in respect to immigrants arriving in Canada by railway or other means are expected to use fair discretion in carrying out their duties, bearing in mind that the policy of the Department is not one of exclusion of immigrants, excepting in cases where their admission is directly provided against in the Act."[1] To-day, however, there is little to choose between the treatment meted out to British subjects entering either the immigration sheds at New York or those stationed at Quebec. The Dominion, it is true, will accept contract labourers coming from the United Kingdom,

---

[1] *Canadian Labour Gazette*, August, 1908.

which the Republic will not, and will also allow, under
certain specific conditions, the entry of people aided
by benevolent institutions and local authorities who
are absolutely prohibited a landing in the United
States. On the other hand, the regulations framed
by the United States are seldom varied, with the result
that their force and nature are understood throughout
the length and breadth of Europe. In Canada, unfortunately, the measures restricting immigration are
modified and recast frequently, so that much unnecessary misunderstanding often arises.

As to the course which restrictive emigration will
take in the near future, we may expect to see, owing
to the growing power of labour, a gradual tightening
of all the various prohibitions. As time elapses, we
shall probably find that the examination of immigrants
will take place more and more in the country of departure and correspondingly less in that of arrival.
In the former place, reliable information concerning
character, health, and finance is always obtainable, but
at the ports of arrival such evidence is often a matter
of conjecture, and therefore likely to be inaccurate
Immigrants sailing to Canada will probably be inspected and reported on by the Assistant-Superintendent of Immigration or some other officer on much
the same lines as now holds for people assisted by charitable and local authorities. For United States-bound
immigrants, the consular service may undertake the
examination ; such, at least, is the suggestion which
has been made by Mr. George Catlin, the United
States Consul at Zurich.[1]

---

[1] See *Political Science Quarterly*, Vol. IV, p. 490.

CHAPTER VII

THE RECEPTION OF IMMIGRANTS

THE information available to-day concerning the reception of immigrants in Canada and the United States prior to the year 1820 is of a very meagre character. What knowledge we possess with regard to Canada is largely furnished by the reports of the Emigration Commissioners, issued in 1826 and 1827, whilst the works of Friedrich Kapp[1] give reliable information pertaining to the United States. Beyond these sources, many contributions touching on the life and treatment of immigrants in their new homes appeared in various contemporary reviews and magazines, but as their writers often held views narrowed by prejudice, such testimony as they offered must be accepted with caution.[2]

We do know, however, that the demand for labour in America was in excess of the supply, a matter which caused employers to compete one with another when hiring fresh arrivals. As may be expected, such a procedure favoured the immigrant and secured comforts for him which would not have been extended otherwise. We also know that at one time the Provincial Government of Canada provided pecuniary aid, as well as gifts of provisions and tools.[3] Even in these early years, a society had been instituted at York on Lake Ontario for the relief of strangers in

---

[1] See *Immigration and the Commissioners of Emigration of the State of New York*, by Friedrich Kapp, 1870.

[2] As an instance, we may mention that writers in the *Edinburgh Review* often gave prominence to the discomforts of emigration in order to arrest the outflow of population which they held would, in time, deplete Scotland of the most valuable section of its community.

[3] Accounts and Papers, Vol. XXXII, 1831, p. 216.

THE RECEPTION OF IMMIGRANTS 159

distress. In many instances, the immigrants proceeded in large parties and went to settlements which had been already prepared for their reception. The reasons are many, then, for assuming that when once the journey had been overcome, the lot of the immigrant was by no means such as should excite undue sympathy.

After 1820, when the exodus from the Mother Country became more of an organised undertaking, circumstances quickly changed. The annual outflow of immigrants to Canada and the United States grew considerably, with the consequence that work was harder to find, and many cases of acute suffering were reported. The horrors of the Atlantic crossing often remained with the people after they had landed; thousands fell victims to the deprivations which at that date seemed inseparable from the journey, whilst shipload after shipload of humanity became a prey to the ravages of contagious diseases. As a result of these terrible conditions, British labour fell into ill-favour, and for a time was shunned by the settled population of both Canada and the United States.[1]

In Canada the care of the diseased and suffering immigrants was entrusted, for many years, to charitable bodies organised by religious communities[2] of the Roman Catholic faith, but, in 1823, the statute of 3 Geo. IV, c. 7 authorised the Governor of Lower Canada to expend through the medium of the justices of the peace a sum of £750 currency for the relief of indigent sick immigrants. With part of this money an immigrant hospital was established.

In the following year, by 4 Geo. IV. c. 32, £600 currency was granted for assisting in the work of caring for "indigent sick, labouring under contagious diseases." £700 was granted in 1825, £950 in 1826, and over a £1000 in each of the years 1827–30. In this

---

[1] Accounts and Papers, 1835. Volume on emigration, p. 280.
[2] These bodies were controlled by trustees and every colonist and community of Lower Canada was bound to contribute annually to the funds.—P. 428, Lord Durham's Report.

latter year, a temporary fever hospital was erected at Point Levi, on the south bank of the St. Lawrence, opposite Quebec.¹

In the month of December, 1831, a serious outbreak of Asiatic cholera devastated the north of England. Hoping to keep Lower Canada free from the pestilence, the Executive Government established a second quarantine hospital, at Grosse Isle. In spite of these precautionary measures, the old French capital was not spared from a visitation of this dreaded complaint. Perhaps the following narrative, quoted verbatim from an Appendix to Lord Durham's Report,² will help to reveal the manner in which the infection was disseminated.

I have been informed by a shipmaster that, on one occasion, he came up the St. Lawrence with upwards of thirty cases of fever among the passengers, many of whom were in a state of delirium. Fearing that on his arrival in port he should get into trouble he quietly landed fourteen of the most violent of his poor wretches on the island of Orleans to shift for themselves. The harbour-master boarded him on his arrival, but he persuaded the other passengers who were not ill to come on deck and get up a fight in the noise and hubbub of which the screams and cries of the sick never reached the ears of the officer who was glad to escape from the scene of uproar. When night came on he landed the remainder with their luggage in the usual way.

The epidemic of 1831–2 clearly showed that quarantine and hospital quarters for immigrants were a necessity.³ We find, therefore, that the temporary

---

¹ By 10 and 11 Geo. 4, c. 18.   ² *Op. cit.*, p. 280.
³ The following table compiled from figures given in Lord Durham's Report indicates the number of cases received at Grosse Isle during the early years of its inception:—

	Total number of passengers arriving.	Became Patients at the Quarantine, Grosse Isle,				Died in Hospital.
		with Cholera.	with Fever.	with Smallpox.	with other diseases.	
1833	22062	—	159	34	46	27
1834	30982	290	404	12	138	264
1835	11580	—	24	48	54	10
1836	27986	—	338	50	66	58
1837	31894	—	481	104	13	57
1838	2918	—	21	16	16	5

structure at Grosse Isle was made permanent and constantly enlarged and improved. By 1850, the whole island had been cleared of its private dwellings and agricultural settlements and divided into three sections; the eastern end contained the hospital proper, the middle was given over to the military and quarantine officers, whilst the western end constituted an isolation station. In this latter division, people were housed whilst they were undergoing surveillance or during the time that their ship was being fumigated.[1]

In 1902 the Minister of the Interior authorised the immigration authorities to purchase a plot of three acres in the neighbourhood of Quebec. On this site, two buildings, each having a ground plan of 150 by 50 feet, were erected; the former serves as a detention hospital, and the latter provides a home for housing relatives and dependents of those detained in the adjacent building.[2] Thus, after some seventy odd years of service, the arrangements at Grosse Isle have been recently superseded.

The Quebec isolation station has proved so satisfactory, that others at St. John, Halifax, Montreal, Vancouver, and Victoria have since been erected. Their maintenance is provided for by the Dominion Acts of 1902 and 1904. The first of these legislative measures required the steamship companies to pay a sum of 50 cents daily for each person landed by them who needed treatment. As this rate of payment was found insufficient to make the institutions self-supporting, the daily charge was raised to 75 cents for each patient, and 50 cents per person detained on account of the patient. Curiously enough, the original Act omitted to impose a similar toll on the railway companies which brought people into the Dominion from the States, with the result that these corporations resisted, until lately, all attempts that were made to

---
[1] Accounts and Papers, Vol. XL, 1850, p. 25.
[2] *Canadian Labour Gazette*, April, 1904, p. 1025.

bring them into line with the steamship companies.¹

Since the Canadian Department of the Interior undertook the work of treating immigrants suffering from curable complaints, much good has been effected. Before the system was adopted, the suffering immigrant was either returned to his native land, which constituted an economic loss of man-power to the Dominion, or he was allowed to mix with and so become a menace to his neighbours. The importance of these curative establishments may be gauged from the fact that between July, 1904, and June, 1905, the first year during which the higher scale of charges was exacted, no less than 2559 patients were detained in the four depots, Quebec, Halifax, St. John, and Montreal, and they aggregated a total of 34,414 days of detention. Of this number of patients, as many as 2291 were isolated on account of eye complaints.² In the year 1906-7 the six hospitals, that is the four above mentioned, together with those at Vancouver and Victoria, provided 55,868 days of accommodation at a cost of $38,872·98. Here again, the reports state that eye diseases—trachoma and conjunctivitis—supplied the majority of the cases.³

Hospitals for the reception of immigrants have also been provided in the United States. The Commissioners erected a building for detention treatment on Ward's Island, New York, in 1847. At first, they were bound to give treatment at this establishment not only to new-comers but also to invalid immigrants who had been in the State less than five years; the period, however, was reduced to twelve months in 1882. At the present time, medical examinations are conducted at Ellis Island,⁴ whilst quarantine accommodation is provided at Hoffman and Swinburne Islands.

---

[1] Canadian Sessional Papers, Vol. XLI, No. 10, 1906-7, p. 119.
[2] Canadian Sessional Papers, Vol. XL, p. 124.
[3] Canadian Sessional Papers, Vol. XLI, No. 10, 1906-7, p. 119.
[4] See " In the Gateway of Nations," *Century Magazine*, March, 1903, p. 674.

THE RECEPTION OF IMMIGRANTS

Though the United States have throughout all these years provided a certain amount of medical treatment, the arrangements have only within recent times equalled those of the Dominion of Canada. We must remember that until 1882, the State of New York was heavily handicapped in having to bear the major portion of the cost attached to immigration connected with the whole of the Eastern and Central States. It could not afford, therefore, to carry out such hospital arrangements as it knew to be necessary. Even when Congress decided to relieve it of its embarrassment, the situation was not satisfactorily adjusted, as the Secretary for the Treasury declined to accept the responsibility of paying the rent and repairs of the buildings at Ward's Island, with the consequence that these soon fell into an unsatisfactory condition. Of late years, since Congress has undertaken the entire management of the immigration traffic, the restrictive measures have been so severe that the type of immigrant has been largely shut out to whom hospital treatment would appeal.

Mention must be made, at this point, of the valuable work done by the Bureau of Industries and Immigration which the State Department of Labour in New York opened on October 3rd, 1910. The Bureau provides first, a tribunal where any immigrant may bring his troubles, whether he has been exploited, defrauded, intimidated, misinformed or is in search of advice, or information which will help him to improve his prospects. The State, the Bureau tells us in its leaflets, wants to know what the difficulties and problems of its law-abiding immigrants are, why they fail and also why they succeed, and to make them, if possible, helpful to the next stranger that arrives.

The Bureau does not furnish employment, but directs men to reliable agencies, investigates the need and demand for labour throughout the State, and facilitates the location of industries outside the cities.

It is also in a position to advise on matters of education, civics, and land opportunities within the State.

In its broadest sense, the Bureau has been established to understand and deal intelligently with the conditions of immigrants, to bring to their aid the laws that exist for their protection, and to help them to become useful and successful citizens. It has already helped immigrants who have been defrauded by employment agents, commissaries, or padroni, contractors, private bankers, notaries public, immigrant homes and boarding houses, steamship ticket agents, loan and land companies, medical companies, etc.

The Bureau does not furnish relief or financial aid, but directs those in need to such existing agencies. All of its services are without charge and communications or complaints are dwelt with in any language.

This body has also duties of a State-advisory nature. From time to time, it is required to offer suggestions on existing laws concerning immigration, and also to recommend the enactment of further legislation where necessary. Once a year, it draws up a report which probably contains more official information concerning the popular movement than any other document published in the United States.

Whilst dealing with the reception of immigrants, some mention must be made of the conditions under which the disembarkation of these people has been effected. Between 1820 and 1840, the chief landing-stages for Canada were Quebec and Montreal, whilst New York held a similar position for the United States. At these three points, almost the whole of the immigration traffic to North America was focussed. Into these towns flocked crowds of new-comers, inexperienced, illiterate, unintelligent, and all understanding but little of the new conditions which surrounded them. As a natural sequel, we find that bands of unscrupulous people infested the quays with the set purpose of defrauding these defenceless and gullible men and women. There were dishonest porters, boarding-house keepers, ticket agents, and tradesmen who all conspired to cheat their visitors; in fact, the immigrant rubbed shoulders with hardly a single honest man whilst he tarried in the port of arrival.[1]

The Canadian authorities first took measures to overcome these scandalous practices in 1835, for in this year they engaged a staff of officials whose duty it was to meet all Atlantic vessels and assist in the transference of immigrants' effects to the river boats. The officials, it may be said, wore a distinctive dress. Thanks to these arrangements, the new arrivals from the Motherland were spared much of the imposition which designing runners endeavoured to impose on them.[2]

In the United States precautionary measures of a similar nature were instituted in 1855. In this year, an immigration dock at Castle Garden was opened. Here ships could anchor and land their passengers free from the attentions of undesirable crimps.[3]

Landing arrangements have gradually improved since 1835, until, to-day, they leave little or nothing to be desired. At all the chief immigrant ports in North America, sheds and buildings have been erected for the temporary reception of the incoming people. This form of accommodation is usually provided free, whilst food is sold at a cheap rate.

The dispersal of immigrant arrivals at the various North American ports has long been a matter which has deservedly claimed serious attention. Even during the first twenty years of last century it was recognised that some artificial stimulus was required to attract the people from the ports and adjacent towns to the

---

[1] Friedrich Kapp, *Immigration and the Commissioners of Emigration of the State of New York*, Chapter IV. Also see various contemporary Accounts and Papers.

[2] Accounts and Papers, 1835, Vol. on Emigration, p. 280.

[3] Thirtieth Report of the Land and Emigration Commissioners, Vol. XVII, 1870, p. 136. See also Chapter V.

farm lands of the interior. In Canada the problem was met by the provision of free passages from the St. Lawrence to various points on the lakes and also by organising settlement parties, such as were undertaken by Colonel Talbot and Peter Robinson. In the United States the matter was almost wholly entrusted to the railroad companies and certain charity associations which had come into being for the express purpose of befriending the alien visitor.

In addition to affording these measures of assistance, the lot of the settler in Canada was made easier by the institution of information bureaux. These were situated along the most frequented routes to the West and were controlled from the "Office of His Majesty's Chief Agent for the Superintendence of Emigration to Upper and Lower Canada."[1] This body was always prepared to advise intending colonists, it provided accommodation for those who fell sick whilst travelling up-country and published numerous pamphlets touching on matters of settlement.

Officials attached to this office were also stationed at the chief ports of arrival, where they met the incoming boats and assisted penniless passengers. In deserving cases they provided food, destination rail tickets and lodgings for one or more nights. In no instance were people expected to leave without having a definite goal in view. Usually the address of some large employer was given to the immigrants, but when none were available the officer sent them to persons who acted as labour distributers in the outlying districts.[2] In providing board and travel tickets in this manner, large sums were spent annually. Quebec, for instance, befriended 1904 people in 1841 and disbursed £311 12s. 7d. in affording them various forms of comforts.[3]

---

[1] Accounts and Papers, 1835, Vol. on Emigration, p. 280.
[2] Accounts and Papers, Vol. XXXIV, 1843, p. 26.
[3] Accounts and Papers, Vol. XXXI, 1842, p. 7.

THE RECEPTION OF IMMIGRANTS 167

The system of giving free transit tickets, though it provided so much satisfaction, had to be abandoned for a time. It was found that people who admitted to the Colonial Land and Emigration Commissioners in Great Britain that they possessed ample means, posed as penniless when they landed in Canada. In fact, a writer in the Accounts and Papers for 1872[1] states that immigrants regularly calculated on having their rail or steamboat fare paid for them, whether they were poor or not. A perhaps greater abuse of this system was that effected by numbers of people who desired to reach inland stations in the United States. These unprincipled travellers journeyed across the Atlantic to Canada and then, under the plea of poverty, obtained a gratuitous steamboat ticket to some lake port adjacent to the frontier. Reaching this point, they left the ship, carefully avoiding any official who might be awaiting them, and hastened into the United States. It was obviously a dishonest plan, which involved the Provincial Legislature in an expenditure of an unproductive character.[2]

In 1872 the distribution of free destination tickets was temporarily discontinued. Instead, a necessitous emigrant was requested to obtain a certificate of character in his Mother Country which was exchanged on arriving in Canada for a passage warrant. This latter enabled him to obtain an inland rail ticket at about two-thirds the usual cost.[3] Even this concession was disallowed after a few years when the destination was one of the older and nearer provinces. Finally, the Report on Colonisation, published in 1889, stated that, on political grounds, no financial assistance of any kind could henceforth be granted to adult immigrants.[4]

---

[1] Accounts and Papers, Vol. XLIII, 1872, p. 368–9.
[2] Report of the Colonial Land and Emigration Commissioners 1849, p. 2.
[3] Accounts and Papers, Vol. XLIII, 1872, p. 368–9.
[4] *Op. cit.*, p. 75.

It may be necessary to point out that although the Dominion has ceased to make money grants to those who visit its shores, it still encourages agents to canvass various European countries and pays them a *per capita* sum for every person they persuade to become a settler.

At the present time, the methods of dispersing the inflow of European labour varies slightly with the locality. In the United States, the railway companies are largely responsible, but there are also a number of employment bureaux[1] where masters and workmen apply for assistance. In Ontario a more complex system obtains. In this province, the Department of Crown Lands canvasses the various employers of farm labour once a year, and so obtains a knowledge of the localities where immigrants will be welcome. Possessed of this information, its officers meet all new-comers as they arrive at Toronto, and these are apprised of whatever posts are vacant. When a labourer has decided to take up one of the vacancies the railroad company provides him with a cheap settler's ticket to enable him to reach his destination.[2] A similar arrangement has been planned in Manitoba and also in the North-West Territories. This system gives much satisfaction, as it places the immigrant without loss of time, it overcomes the congestion of idle hands at the more important rail and steamship centres, and it helps to spread the people over the thinly populated areas.

The provincial legislatures of Canada do not labour single-handed in planning for the dispersal of fresh arrivals. Side by side with their enterprise the Dominion Government carries on its own system for placing farm hands and domestic servants. Since February 15th, 1907, the Department of the Interior has engaged a band of over one hundred and eighty

---

[1] Thirteen in 1904.
[2] *Canadian Labour Gazette*, September, 1904, p. 258.

THE RECEPTION OF IMMIGRANTS

canvassers whose business it is to introduce unemployed farm labourers or domestic servants to employers having vacancies.[1] When appointments ensue as a result of their efforts the canvassers are paid the sum of two pounds for each person placed, whether man, woman, or child; no remuneration, it must be added, is given for securing positions other than as farm or domestic workers. These canvassers are greatly assisted by the booking agents in the United Kingdom, who not only provide the intending emigrant with the name of the canvasser located nearest to his destination, but they also apprise this official of the approaching arrival of the emigrant.

It is the harmonious working of such systems as the above which enabled the Commissioner of Emigration for Canada to say in his evidence before the committee which sat to consider Sir H. Rider Haggard's propositions regarding agricultural settlements: "Our arrangements are such that immediately on the arrival of an emigrant, if he is looking for agricultural employment, no difficulty whatever is experienced in getting him properly placed. If he is an experienced agriculturist from the beginning he gets very good wages: if he is inexperienced then wages are much less, but these increase as his qualifications or acquaintance with the work improves."

Charitable societies have also done much to ease the lot of the immigrant. Until the advent of steam it was a frequent practice with unscrupulous captains to land their passengers at a port other than that for which they had contracted. This naturally occasioned an immigrant much inconvenience and expense, but, when it happened, the institutions often stepped in and helped him to reach his proper destination, sheltering him whilst the necessary arrangements for

---

[1] *Canadian Labour Gazette*, March, 1907, p. 1011–12.—The work of these canvassers lies wholly within the Dominion.

his despatch were being effected. Shipwrecks were also not at all uncommon in the early days. People, therefore, were being constantly landed in remote out-of-the-way places, having, as likely as not, lost all their belongings. The societies also befriended such cases as these. As a rule, the organisations neither gave nor lent money, but lodgings and outfits were provided, whilst, in some instances, food tickets which could be exchanged locally for supplies of provisions were distributed to necessitous people.

The early societies, though they did good work, were often of short-lived duration. It is on this account that the Blue Books and other sources of information of, say, fifty years ago contain a constant chain of names, few of which recur a second or third time. Perhaps the Society for the Relief of Strangers at Toronto and the Protective Emigrant Society of New York may be singled out as being of more than ordinary note.

The interval between landing and commencing work is necessarily a time of much concern for an immigrant, especially if his resources are few or if he brings a family with him. It is this anxious period which the charitable societies are now largely occupied in easing. At the present time there are a number of institutions scattered throughout the United States and Canada which work with this object. Many of them have merely a local interest whilst others are affiliated to contributory concerns in Europe. Most of them depend solely on charity for their support, but a few are subsidised by Dominion or Provincial Government grants. A typical society is the British Welcome League, which has branches throughout Ontario. Its objects, as stated on the prospectus, are " to extend to all deserving immigrants from the British Isles, irrespective of nationality or religion, a hearty welcome, and, if need be, temporary accommodation and to render such other help and advice as will

THE RECEPTION OF IMMIGRANTS 171

enable them to become worthy citizens of Canada."[1] This society was inaugurated in March, 1907, through the initiative of two periodicals, the *Toronto Globe* and the *Toronto World*. Its work during the first two years consisted in dealing with 8500 men, women, and children, 6000 of whom were, by its enterprise, placed in situations. The dormitories provided 12,500 nights' lodgings, free, whilst the free meals totalled 27,000. The Society appeals for charitable donations, but has also been the recipient of a grant of a thousand dollars from the Ontario Government. Other societies which deal with women and children exclusively, are described in later chapters.[2]

Somewhat akin to the work of these societies is the assistance provided by the American branches of the Salvation Army and the Church Army. These organisations have agents scattered throughout the whole of the New Continent who advise and assist needy immigrants. In the year 1904-5 the former agency dealt with five thousand people, 76 per cent of whom went directly to the land and 10 per cent became domestic servants.[3]

A society possessing unique aims is the Imperial Home Reunion Association of Winnipeg.[4] As its name implies, this body advances loans in order that wives and children, left behind in the Motherland, may be reunited with the breadwinner in Canada. The Society, though founded late in 1910, has already been the means of linking up many divided families. The procedure of the Society is simplicity itself. An applicant fills in a form with his name, his address,

---

[1] The Annual Report and other printed matter may be obtained from W. Chadwick, Esq., 87, Front St., Toronto.

[2] Chapters XI and XII.

[3] Report on Agricultural Settlements in British Colonies, 1906, § 908.

[4] *The Colonizer* has many references, in its monthly issues, to this Society.

the name of his employer, the nature of his work and weekly wage, the names in full and ages of his wife and children. He must certify that the persons whom he wishes to bring to Canada are not affected with apoplexy or epileptic fits, that they have not been confined in an insane asylum during the previous five years, that they are not deaf, dumb, nor blind, and have no contagious diseases of eyes or skin, and they are not deformed and are in good health. He specifies the sailing port from which he desires his family to start, the amount he wishes advanced, what sum he can pay down, and the monthly repayments he will be prepared to make. This he signs, and the first step is completed.

As soon as there are fifteen or twenty of these applications on file the secretary calls a meeting of the Advisory Board. These meetings are held at night so that the applicants who attend may not lose time from their work. Each man whose application is to come before the meeting receives a notice of the time, place, and purpose of the meeting, and is requested to be present.

This personal meeting has been found to be of great assistance in deciding cases attended by doubtful features—doubtful because it is not easy to fill out an application form so as to give exact information on all points required. A question or two by members of the board, an answer or two from the applicant, and such doubts are settled, usually in favour of the applicant, because it has been found that men who wish to bring their families to join them in Canada are of a grade too high to stoop to deception to gain their ends. In all the applications that have been filed only one has been found at variance with facts; a man stated his weekly wage at $15, whereas his employer's answer to an enquiry on this point placed the amount at $12. This application was rejected.

Sometimes an applicant, in his eagerness to send for

THE RECEPTION OF IMMIGRANTS 173

his family, is disposed to take a larger contract than he can handle. The board is composed of keen business men whose minds are free from the natural bent of an impetuous parent separated by an ocean and half a continent from those he loves. When, therefore, a man who earns $60 a month wishes to bring out a family of ten—wife and nine children—and this has happened, the members of the board act as his counsellor and guide. They point out that he will be taking on a heavy responsibility, and perhaps an embarrassing expense, by attempting to get his whole family out at once. They suggest that three grown-up children be brought out first so that they may help to earn the money to bring out the balance of the family. These children—usually over eighteen years of age—will quadruple the father's earnings and make it possible to have a good home ready for the mother and younger children a little later on.

In many ways it is apparent that Canada's great need is to make farmers of its immigrants. It is little wonder, then, that the Dominion Government has instituted a number of experimental farms in various districts where the uninitiated may obtain practical advice, where the novice may gain experience, and where the immigrant settler may turn for information, supplies of seeds, and personal help. The first of these institutions was established in 1887 on the recommendation of a parliamentary committee. Almost simultaneously, five of the experimental farms grew into being—the Central Experimental Farm near Ottawa, the branch farm for the Maritime Provinces at Nappan, that for Manitoba at Brandon, the Indian Head Farm in the North-West Territories, and the Agassiz Farm in British Columbia. In 1905, on the throwing open of some three hundred million acres of agricultural land in Saskatchewan and Alberta, additional establishments were found to be necessary. The Department of Agriculture accordingly made a branch farm at Rosthern in North Saskatchewan and two in Alberta, one south of Lethbridge and the other at Lacombe. The northern part of this province is served by a small branch station on the farm of one of the older settlers at Fort Vermilion on the Peace River. In the spring of 1910, an eleventh farm was opened near Charlottetown, Prince Edward Island, whilst a twelfth has since been inaugurated near Lake Abitibi, in Quebec Province.

The correspondence entered into by the experimental farms has grown remarkably of recent years. In 1900 the letters received at the whole of these institutions numbered 69,669. This number has increased to 100,000 in 1908, and during the year ending March, 1910, it was 102,651. Many of these letters were applications for samples of seed grain, for publications, and for advice on specific matters.[1] Postage, it may be said, is free between Dominion farmers and the farm authorities.

From experimental farms to agricultural colleges is an obvious step, and many of these useful institutions are gradually growing up within the Dominion. The Ontario Agricultural College, situated on the outskirts of the small town of Guelph, about forty miles west of Toronto, was founded in 1874. It was then realised that only a small minority of farmers were working on sound methods. Most of them at that date depended upon increased acreage for increased returns. Hence the College was established to train young men in the science and art of improved husbandry and to conduct experiments and publish the results. In 1904, through the action of Sir William Macdonald, the Macdonald Institute was erected, and the College thus enlarged its scope so as to provide courses of instruction in Home Economics, chiefly for farmers' daughters. Thus at Guelph a school

---

[1] " How Canada Helps its Farmers," in *Canada* (weekly periodical), January 21st, 1911, p. 75.

THE RECEPTION OF IMMIGRANTS 175

has been established which attacks the rural problem at three fundamental points. The State of Ontario finances and controls this institution.[1]

The Provincial Government of Nova Scotia possesses another successful college at Truro. Its management is under the direction of the Secretary for Agriculture of the Province. This establishment affords a thorough agricultural education, both theoretically and practically. No fee is charged for tuition, the only expenses to the student being his board and lodgings, which average fourteen shillings a week.[2]

Not only are the Dominion and Provincial Governments engaged in promoting a knowledge of agriculture among settlers and farm hands, but the Canadian Pacific Railway Company is also giving attention to this matter. Demonstration farms have been scattered at intervals over the irrigation tracts owned by this company east of Calgary, and, at any of these, purchasers of land may obtain advice based on local conditions.

From the foregoing, it will be seen that during the last ninety years, comprehensive schemes of a generous nature have been formulated in both Canada and the United States for providing immigrants with assistance of various kinds.

---

[1] The question of agricultural education in Canada was reported on in 1910 by a deputation which visited the Dominion in the same year. See the Report, published by University College, Reading.

[2] Vide prospectus issued by the College at Truro.

CHAPTER VIII

THE DESTINATION OF BRITISH EMIGRANTS

THE volume of British emigration which has proceeded to North America since 1815,[1] may be roughly estimated as amounting to slightly more than twelve million[2] souls. Of this total, some nine and three-quarter million people have selected the United States as their destination, whilst the Dominion of Canada has claimed not quite three millions. Until the year 1817, the United States attracted a larger annual total of these immigrants than did British North America, but from 1818 to 1831, the years 1827 and 1828 being excepted, the conditions were reversed and our American colonies welcomed the major part of the outflow. From 1832 to the year 1909,[3] the United States once more proved the home of the bulk of the British exodus, but since 1910 the lead has again been taken by Canada.[4]

The preference which British emigrants have so clearly displayed during a period of more than eighty years for the United States is due, first, to a desire, commonly shown by those who quit their native country, for settling where their relations and friends have settled before them ; and, second, to the more advanced economic conditions which have existed within the Republic. When British North America

---

[1] The year when statistical information relating to this movement was first preserved.

[2] Actual figures, 1815-1910: To United States, 9,798,934; to British North America, 2,918,328.

[3] The year 1834 excepted.

[4] Emigration and Immigration Tables, 1912, issued by the Board of Trade.

was little more than the home of fur-traders and intrepid hunters, the States were enjoying a considerable measure of commercial prosperity. Thousands of miles of turnpike roads were being planned, bridges were in course of construction, steamboats were being made for lake and river service, and trade was growing by leaps and bounds.[1] Little wonder, then, that the unskilled emigrant from the Mother Country preferred to settle in the United States, where work was plentiful, than make his home in so unattractive a colony as British North America.

In his report of 1839,[2] Lord Durham graphically contrasted these two countries. " By describing one side and reversing the picture," he said, " the other would be also described. On the American side all is activity and bustle. The forest," he continued, " has been widely cleared; every year numerous settlements are formed, and thousands of farms are created out of the waste; the country is intersected by common roads; canals and railroads are finished, or in the course of formation; the ways of communication and transport are crowded with people, and enlivened by numerous carriages and large steamboats. The observer is surprised at the number of harbours on the lakes, and the number of vessels they contain; while bridges, artificial landing-places and commodious wharves are formed in all directions as soon as required. Good houses, warehouses, mills, inns, villages, towns, and even great cities, are seen almost to spring up out of the desert. Every village has its schoolhouse and place of public worship. Every town has many of both, with its township buildings, its book stores, and probably one or two banks and newspapers; and the cities, with their fine churches, their great hotels, their exchanges, court-houses, and municipal halls, of stone

---

[1] Professor J. B. McMaster of Pennsylvania University, *Cambridge Modern History*, Vol. VII, p. 351.
[2] Sir Charles Lucas—Lord Durham's Report, vol. 2, p. 212

or marble, so new and fresh as to mark the recent existence of the forest where they now stand, would be admired in any part of the Old World. On the British side of the line, with the exception of a few favoured spots, where some approach to American prosperity is apparent, all seems waste and desolate. There is but one railroad in all British America,[1] and that, running between the St. Lawrence and Lake Champlain, is only fifteen miles long.[2] The ancient city of Montreal, which is naturally the commercial capital of the Canadas, will not bear the least comparison, in any respect, with Buffalo, which is a creation of yesterday. But it is not in the difference between the larger towns on the two sides that we shall find the strongest evidence of our own inferiority. That painful but undeniable truth is most manifest in the country districts through which the line of national separation passes for a thousand miles. There, on the side of both the Canadas, and also of New Brunswick and Nova Scotia, a widely scattered population, poor and apparently unenterprising, though hardy and industrious, without towns and markets, almost without roads, living in mean houses, drawing little more than a rude subsistence from ill-cultivated land, and seeming incapable of improving their condition, present to us the most instructive contrast to their enterprising and thriving neighbours on the American side." So primitive are the lines of communication that it is a common practice, added Lord Durham, for settlers living on the frontier of Lower Canada to cross over into the State of Vermont and make use of the roads there when they wish to reach some neighbouring town in British territory.[3]

---

[1] This was written in 1838-9.
[2] The railway ran from Laprairie on the St. Lawrence to St. John's on the Richelieu River. It was begun in 1835, opened with horses in 1836, and worked with locomotives in 1837.
[3] It is only fair to say that these remarks of Lord Durham were strongly criticised by the authorities in Upper Canada at the time of their publication.

DESTINATION OF EMIGRANTS

Not only did the United States offer to the unskilled labourer far more opportunities, in these times, than could be found in Canada, but it attracted the farmer and settler in a way which was unknown in the adjacent British colony. In the Republic, land was surveyed with reasonable accuracy. After the year 1800, it was sold at a low rate in plots of convenient shape, whilst purchase could be effected almost at any time. In Lower Canada, the French law recognised a system of land-division on the death of a parent, with the result that plots granted " en seigneurie," were inconveniently small. Usually, they were long and narrow in shape and quite unsuited to British ideas of farming.[1] In Upper Canada, much of the land was supposed to be unhealthily situated, the surveys were so inaccurate as to be the cause of constant litigation, whilst the Crown grants could only be obtained by journeying to the land council's office and attending there in person.[2] It need hardly be added that immigrants requiring homesteads, much preferred to deal with the Republican land offices than with those situated in the adjoining British territories. Lord Durham, in his report of 1839, affirmed that the unsatisfactory systems of conveying land were largely responsible for the lack of sympathy which emigrants possessed for the colony. Sixty per cent of the people who reach Canada, he said, leave for the United States, a large number of them taking up land when they arrive there. Thus, owing to the want of adequate organisation in the distribution of homesteads and small farm plots, the very people of whom the Empire stood in most need were allowed to drift into a foreign State.

So far, the question of the preference for the United States has only been treated in a broad sense. As may be judged, there were many minor issues which

---

[1] Cf. Chapter IX.

[2] Sometimes the purchasers were kept waiting as many as six weeks whilst their grants were being conveyed to them.

diverted the stream of British emigration from Canadian shores. The state of the currency, for instance, was so unsatisfactory in British North America that commerce became seriously handicapped. In the early years of the nineteenth century, transactions were seldom effected with the assistance of specie, but card money,[1] as the paper currency was then called, was used instead. English money gradually found its way into both the upper and lower provinces and the United States coinage was not unknown along the Canadian frontier, but the supplies of these were limited. As a result, people were forced to adopt a system of barter; farmers took household commodities in exchange for their produce, and labourers were given board, lodgings, and stock as a reward for their labours. The system enabled the bare necessities of life to be obtained but seriously crippled all efforts of thrift.

Whilst contrasting the progress of emigration to Canada and the United States in the opening years of the nineteenth century, it is necessary to mention that certain Acts of Parliament restricted the exodus of British people to the States and so gave a possible preference to British North America. To trace the history of these preventive Acts, it is necessary to go back to the time of Charles I. In this reign, a proclamation was issued to suppress " the disorderly transporting of His Majesty's subjects to the plantations within the parts of America."[2] Many years later, in 1718, the spirit of this enactment reappeared in 5 Geo. I, c. 27, which was " an Act to prevent the inconvenience arising from seducing artificers in the manufactures of Great Britain into foreign parts." This legislation was extended by 23 Geo. III, c. 14, which added, " that any person who shall contract

---

[1] A facsimile illustration of the Canadian card money is given in Bourinot, " The Story of Canada," p. 162.
[2] Enacted July 20th, 1635.

DESTINATION OF EMIGRANTS 181

with, entice, persuade, solicit, or seduce any manufacturer, workman or artificer in wool, mohair, cotton or silk, or in iron, steel, brass or other metal, or any clockmaker, watchmaker or other manufacturer, workman or artificer in any other of the manufactures of Great Britain or Ireland of what nature or kind soever to go out of this Kingdom into any foreign country not within the dominions of the Crown is liable to be indicted and to forfeit £500, to suffer imprisonment for twelve months and until the forfeiture is paid." This Act, framed in 1782, was still in force in the early part of the last century, during which time it may have affected emigration to the United States. Probably the restrictions which were thus imposed on the freedom of personal movement were more nominal than real, for the artificers and others whom it controlled often evaded the oppressive measures by sailing first for Canada, after which they journeyed south into the United States. Huskisson, it may be added, repealed the Act in 1824.

With so many advantages awaiting them in the United States, it may be wondered why emigrants thought of Canada at all, in these early times. No doubt, many people went without knowing the real conditions awaiting them and once they were settled in their new homes could not afford to pass on into the States. It must be remembered that those who took part in the early exodus were largely recruited from an ignorant and destitute class: to them, the matter of deciding on a suitable destination would naturally present many difficulties. The mere fact that ships sailing for Canada were less crowded and often charged a slightly lower fare would alone be the means of attracting a certain element of the exodus to that country. Also, it may be stated that when parishes gave free passages to their pauper men and women and the Government voted grants in aid of emigration, a stipulation was often made that

Canada should be the destination of those who benefited.

For the reasons here described, it is obvious then that the emigrant who understood American conditions and who had a free hand in selecting his own destination, usually elected to settle in the United States. His choice of settlement, however, not only affected his own destiny but also that of his brothers, sisters, and friends. His prosperity, we must remember, would reach the ears of those whom he had left behind in the Old Country, and if economic conditions began to squeeze them out of their employment, they too would emigrate, as likely as not, at his expense. Their new abode would be close to his, in the States, in fact; probably they would live under his roof, and, more than likely, he would have work awaiting them on their arrival. Even within the last decade, when British North America has made up for her early backwardness, the total inflow of British emigration to the United States has still proved greater than that which has proceeded to Canada.[1] One of the great factors operating to this end has, undoubtedly, been the desire of relations to settle near relations and friends close to friends.

An important period in the history of migration was the interval between 1846 and 1854. During these years, over one and three-quarter million people left the Mother Country for the United States, whilst not quite half a million others sailed to Canada.[2] This preference, shown by emigrants from the United Kingdom for institutions in the States, was largely due to the great proportion of Irish people who joined in the exodus. As is well known, these people have often been anxious, in the past, to sever their connections with British rule, a factor which enables

---

[1] It was annually greater up to and including the season 1909.
[2] See Annual Reports of the Colonial Land and Emigration Commissioners.

DESTINATION OF EMIGRANTS 183

us to assert that, generally, when Irish emigration increases, the proportion of emigrants from the three kingdoms settling in foreign countries also increases, and, conversely, the proportion of those going to colonies correspondingly decreases.[1]

Beyond this antipathy for British rule, it is usually agreed that Irish emigrants, as a body, are more suited to an urban existence where they can work in factories, assist in constructional undertakings, act as car-drivers, etc., than to a life spent on the land where farm work is entailed.[2] This being so, it is only natural that they should prefer the United States, with its network of towns and industries, to an agricultural calling in the prairie lands of Canada.

Not only did the Irish element show a preference, at this time, for a Republican destination, but the English and Scotch, in a lesser proportion, also flocked to the United States during the immigration wave of 1846–54. Trade at home was depressed, a famine was devastating Ireland, but a signal reason for so great an inflow into the States was the discovery of gold in California during the autumn of 1847.

In recent years the wheat-growing possibilities of the Dominion of Canada have gradually become known, with the result that ceaseless streams of British emigrants have poured into this colony. In 1896 some fifteen thousand people left the Mother Country for the Dominion; in 1906 their numbers had increased to one hundred and fourteen thousand; whilst in

---

[1] It seems probable that, until 1831, the Irish preferred to settle in British North America than in the United States. Cf. opening paragraph to this chapter. Referring to the year 1837, Sir Charles Lucas writes in Lord Durham's Report, Part I, p. 190, " But even in the year 1837, if the figures given in an Appendix to Elliot's Report are correct, out of 29,884 emigrants who left the United Kingdom for B.N.A., the emigrants from Irish ports numbered 22,463, against 7421 from Great Britain; while out of 36,770 who left for the U.S. they numbered only 3871, against 32,899 from Great Britain.

[2] In 1880 there were 377,334 Irish in the farming states of Ohio, Michigan, Wisconsin, Minnesota, Iowa, Illinois, and Indiana, but 1,161,648 in the industrial states of New York, Pennsylvania, New Jersey, Connecticut, Massachusetts, and Rhode Island.

1911 the huge total of one hundred and seventy-seven thousand was reached.[1] These figures refer only to the people who have emigrated from Great Britain and Ireland; to gain an adequate impression of the present popularity of the Dominion, it is necessary to examine also the figures governing immigration from the United States and from the Continent of Europe. During the year 1910, no less than 103,984 people entered Canada from the States, and roughly 36,000 from Continental Europe. These figures, it will be seen, represent an inflow of population into the colony at the rate of 380,000 per annum.[2]

It is only by reason of its vast commercial and industrial expansion that the Dominion has been able to assimilate so important an influx of men and women. Within the last thirty years the population has increased from four to seven millions, the exports have grown, within the same period, from eighty-seven to three hundred and one million dollars, the grain exports show an increase from fifteen to fifty-six million dollars, the total revenue has risen from twenty-three to one hundred and one million dollars, and the mineral production has leapt from ten to ninety-one million dollars. Thus, while the population has not quite doubled itself, exports have more than trebled in value, grain exports have increased almost fourfold, the total revenue has grown fivefold, and the mineral output has become nine times as great.

Probably the chief reason for Canada's present popularity among a section of the emigrants lies in its amazing wheat-growing powers. Owing to the extensive deposits of black alluvial soil found in the north-west, the Dominion is able to produce finer and harder grades of wheat than are harvested in the grain lands of the United States.[3] Not only are the

---

[1] See Table N., Appendix I.
[2] *Canada Year Book*, 1910, Table CXCII.
[3] Professor Saunders, " Government Experimental Farm, Ottawa " in *Canada and the Empire*, pp. 50–3.

DESTINATION OF EMIGRANTS 185

grades superior but the average yields per acre are higher in Canada than in the Republic. A summary of the statistics, bearing on this matter and extending over a period of ten years, shows that the average yield of wheat per acre in Manitoba equalled 21·7 bushels. In Iowa, the foremost of the wheat-growing States, the yield was 14·7 bushels; in Minnesota, it was 14·2 bushels; whilst in North and South Dakota, it averaged 12·7 and 10·4 bushels respectively. The same report states that the revenue per acre from wheat in Manitoba averaged 14·30 dollars; in North Dakota, it stood at 9·22 dollars; in Minnesota, it was 8 dollars, whilst South Dakota only averaged 6·75 dollars per acre.[1] From these figures, it will be readily gathered that wheat farming has every appearance of being more lucrative in Manitoba than in Minnesota or either of the two Dakotas.[2]

Not only has the Canadian farmer an advantage over his brother worker in the United States in the matter of soil, but he also leads on the question of freight charges. The rates in the Dominion are much lower than those levied in the States, as will be seen from the following data. The farmer in Winnipeg has his wheat hauled over the Canadian Pacific Railroad to Port Arthur, a matter of 427 miles, for 10 cents per hundred pounds weight; but the grain producer at Grand Forks, a station due south of Winnipeg situated in the Republic, has to pay 14 cents per hundred pounds to get his grain carried to Duluth, a distance of about three hundred miles. Thus a lower charge is made in the Dominion for a longer distance. Further instances to illustrate this point, may prove interesting. The charge from Gretna to Fort William, a distance of 496 miles, is

---

[1] Montague and Herbert, *Canada and the Empire*, pp. 51–2.
[2] See Report of the Royal Commission on the Supply of Food in the Time of War, paragraphs 5002, 5004, 5006, 5001, but cf. paragraph 4952.

12 cents, but 18 cents is levied between Souris and Duluth, which are 497 miles apart. Again, Pierson to Fort William is 634 miles and the rate is 16 cents, but from Avoca to Duluth, a matter of 615 miles, the charge is 25 cents.[1]

With better facilities for growing wheat and cheaper haulage rates, one might reasonably expect that farm lands would be dearer in Canada than in the United States, but this is by no means the case. In the Dominion there are great areas as yet uncultivated, and prices cannot attain their maximum until these have been broken up. In the United States, however, almost the only areas that are still available for settlement require irrigating and other artificial treatment. In the former the supply is greater than the demand; in the latter, the demand approximates the supply. As a result Canadian farm lands cost from $3 to $15 per acre, whilst in the Republic they command as much as from $25 to $40.

Added to the advantages already mentioned the farmers in Manitoba, Saskatchewan, and Alberta are said to enjoy a climate more suited to wheat growing than is the natural inheritance of the crop-raisers in Minnesota, Iowa, Ohio, and Dakota. In Canada, the severe winter frosts take considerable time to disappear, with the result that the subsoil is kept moist during the early stages in the growth of the wheat. Later, when the ears are ripening, the amount of daylight enjoyed in the Dominion wheat provinces is considerably greater than that registered in the State wheat areas. The Western provinces of Canada, for instance, secure two hours more daylight each day between June 15th and July 1st than are recorded in the State of Ohio.[2]

Such are the conditions which, at the present moment, are accounting for the unprecedented rush of immigrants to the Western Provinces of the Dominion.

---
[1] Montague and Herbert, *Canada and the Empire*, pp. 46–7.
[2] Montague and Herbert, *Canada and the Empire*, p. 48.

DESTINATION OF EMIGRANTS 187

Not only are the British Isles and certain Continental countries contributing lavishly to this westward movement, but the United States is also experiencing an outflow of people whose destination is the wheat belt of Alberta, Saskatchewan, and Manitoba. Among those leaving the Republic for the Dominion are numerous Scotch and English farmers[1] who for years have made their homes in the United States. The price of land allows them to sell their improved farms at high figures, and with the proceeds they are able to buy more extensive and far more fertile tracts in Canada. The shift to a new country where elbow room is plentiful has decided advantages; it enables father, son, and perhaps daughter to take up adjoining homesteads with the result that the family need not be broken up and scattered, as is necessary in the closely settled wheat lands of the Republic, when the children reach maturity. As to the extent of this British exodus from the United States to Western Canada, no actual figures can be quoted. The only official data bearing on this matter deal with the total Canadian inflow from the States. In 1900 this movement comprised no more than 17,987 souls, but by 1909 it had risen to 103,798 people, whilst in the last ten years it has been the means of 497,248 men and women crossing the frontier. British people and people of British descent, it may be stated, are known to have contributed lavishly to this outflow.

The exodus of farm workers from the Republic is largely organised by two huge commercial corporations having head-quarters in St. Paul. These concerns employ hundreds of agents who, in turn, give employment to some thousands of sub-agents. The work of this vast army of men consists in urging the Republican settler, with all the eloquence and per-

---

[1] Naturally, there are also many United States and Canadian-born settlers, as well as an alien element, who are taking part in this exodus from the States to the Dominions.

suasion at its command, to cross into the Dominion and purchase lands which the companies have for sale there. No town, village, or district situated within the United States wheat-growing area has escaped the attentions of these agents and sub-agents. Literature is scattered broadcast, lectures describing the fertile lands of Alberta and Saskatchewan are given at intervals, exhibits of produce are constantly on show, whilst homeseekers' excursions help to familiarise prospective settlers with the actual plots for sale.

The actual destination of immigrants furnishes another interesting subject for consideration. The earliest people to leave the Mother Country and settle in the United States made their homes within the strip of territory hemmed between the Alleghany Mountains and the Atlantic seaboard. With the natural growth of population and an important influx of immigrants the peopled areas grew cramped, and a setting back of the land boundary became necessary. As a consequence the inhabited plots advanced along the lines of least resistance, mainly along the drainage basins and river courses, though they sometimes struck out overland when such an action was found advantageous.[1] In 1790 the population began to spread up the Mohawk Valley, along the course of the Upper Potomac, and also over the Appalachians into Kentucky and Tennessee. By 1800 the westward stream had reached Ohio and Indiana, whilst settlements were not unknown in Michigan, Wisconsin, and Illinois. In 1818 an English writer named Birkbeth recorded that during the previous year the roads through Albany had been thronged with immigrants who were taking part in the feverish haste to the West,[2] whilst another writer, Ford, spoke of the flood of immigrants which in 1822 was pouring into Missouri and Illinois. The latter State, he mentioned, at-

---
[1] Dr. Robert Hill, *The Public Domain and Democracy*, p. 17.
[2] Birkbeth, *Letters from Illinois*, p. 11.

DESTINATION OF EMIGRANTS 189

tracted seventeen thousand people between 1820 and 1825.[1]

The Republican frontier, by 1840, extended in a fairly straight line from Lake Huron, across Lake Michigan to Prairie du Chien, from whence it zigzagged south-westerly to St. Joseph, and then ran due south to the Gulf of Mexico.[2] The next ten years saw the westward movement reach the upper courses of the Missouri River, by way of Iowa, as well as the opening up of Nebraska and Kansas. With the discovery of gold in California in 1847 an important stream of immigrants found its way into the territories of the Pacific coast, though these regions were not really settled until some quarter of a century later.

The Report of the Superintendent of the Census (United States) for December 1st, 1852, enables us to follow the progress of early settlement in greater detail.

It appears, says the Report,[3] that the immigration rests almost entirely in the free states. Of the 2,200,000 foreigners resident in the Union only 305,000 are in the slave states: and of these 127,000 are in the comparatively northern corn-growing states of Maryland, Virginia, Kentucky, and Missouri, and 66,000 in the commercial states of Louisiana.

The gradual progress of settlement forges ahead in a belt reaching from 36° or 37° N. to 43° or 44° N., including the central and southern parts of New England, the middle or north-western states, Maryland and Delaware, and the central and northern part of Virginia, Kentucky, and Missouri.

Less than one-third of the total immigration has entered the Lake Country and the Valley of the Mississippi. The proportion of foreign population in New York and in Massachusetts is greater than in any western agricultural state, except Wisconsin.

---

[1] See Dr. Robert Hill, *The Public Domain and Democracy*, p. 24; and Ford, *A History of Illinois*, pp. 59 and 229.
[2] Dr. Robert Hill, *The Public Domain and Democracy*, p. 24.
[3] Cf. *Edinburgh Review*, July, 1854, p. 242.

It consists principally of Irish, Germans, and English. Of the English nearly five-eighths are to be found in the Atlantic free states, about one-third in the states of the north-west, and nearly all the residue in the northern slave states.

Three-fourths of the Irish stay in New England and the middle states (principally in Massachusetts, New York, and Pennsylvania), where the commercial and manufacturing interests are seated: and they are found in the south and west only where there are great public works in construction. They change their soil and their allegiance, but keep their nature intact.

Of the Germans more than half their number are spread over the north-western states, Missouri and Kentucky, and more than one-third in New York and Pennsylvania. They stay, indeed, in the towns in great numbers, devoting themselves to mechanical arts and to trades: but a large proportion also are to be found in the agricultural districts.

The valley of the Mississippi and the Upper Lake Country has not only gained in an unexampled manner, but has been almost created within the half-century, 1800-1850. Where, in 1800, there were less than 40,000 persons clustered around the rude forts that protected them from the Indians, there are now nearly ten millions cultivating fifty-three million acres of improved land.

The people are somewhat nomadic in character. In the free states the general movement is due west—from New York, for instance, to Michigan and Wisconsin, and from Pennsylvania to Ohio. From Maine and New Hampshire it goes principally to Massachusetts; from the other New England states more to New York than elsewhere; but natives of all are found in the free north-west states in large numbers. The middle states are also represented there by an aggregate of 758,020, in addition to which they interchange very extensively with each other: the people of the small states, particularly, going to the great cities of their neighbours. The emigration from the northern Atlantic states into the six north-western states amounts to nearly 1,200,000. And so strong is this passion for motion that the West itself supplies a population to the still further West. Ohio sends 215,000 to the three states beyond her; Indiana attracts 120,000 from Ohio, but sends on 50,000 of her own; Illinois takes 95,000 from Ohio

DESTINATION OF EMIGRANTS 191

and Indiana, and gives 7000 to young Iowa; and that state, though not twenty years redeemed from the Indians, gains nearly 60,000 by the restlessness of the three, and, in its turn, breaks over the too feeble barriers of the Rocky Mountains to supply Utah and Oregon with 1200 natives of Iowa.

This movement pursued its career unchecked until 1890; it was then reported that only a fringe of land at the eastern base of the mountains and certain districts reserved for Indians still remained unoccupied. Much of this has since been broken up, with the result that the growing agricultural population has been compelled to cross over the frontier and take up lands in Alberta, Manitoba, and Saskatchewan, as mentioned earlier in this chapter.

Dealing sectionally with British North America, we find that the Nova Scotia area[1] was largely peopled with Acadians when the eighteenth-century migrants from our shores arrived. The earliest British settlers appeared between 1749 and 1752; they were disbanded soldiers and sailors; their influence was small, as by 1767 the original 2543 people had dwindled to 1085, and after this date they continued to decrease. The British were followed by German settlers who pitched their encampment at Lunenburg. These were closely followed by descendants of the Pilgrim Fathers; their settlement was made along the shores of Cape Sable. Between 1761 and 1771 many men arrived from Ulster. In 1764 Madam Isle, and, in 1770, Cheticamp received merchants from Jersey who set up fishery establishments. In 1767 the whole of Prince Edward Island was sold to sixty-seven proprietors, and these introduced large numbers of Scotch farmers and labourers.[2] The Isthmus of Chignecto welcomed an important group of Yorkshire Methodists in 1772-4. In 1773 many Highlanders

---

[1] This includes Cape Breton Island and Prince Edward Island.
[2] As mentioned in Chapter I.

were found to be thriving in Picton Bay. Great strides in settlement were made in 1784, when streams of Loyalist Refugees went to Sydney, Murray Bay, and Shelburne. In 1791 Antigonish was peopled by Roman Catholic Highlanders who gradually spread up the west coast of Cape Breton Island. The opening years of the nineteenth century saw the arrival of Highlanders in Sydney, along the east coast of Nova Scotia, and around the Bras d'Or Lake. Charlottetown received many new-comers after Waterloo, whilst Roman Catholic Irish settled at Mount Uniacke in 1819. Later, important agricultural and mining enterprises attracted people in large numbers. Beyond the more or less organised settlements here mentioned by name, continuous streams of individuals also came from the Mother Country, and, as a rule, made their homes side by side with those of their forerunners.

In New Brunswick a general departure of the Acadians made way for an inflow of New Englanders, chiefly of British descent. This happened in 1762 and 1763. The settlements were pitched in the salt-marshes between Moncton and Sackville, at the mouth of the St. John and at Maugersville. Shortly after this, a few Englishmen made their homes in Campobello Island under the leadership of Lieutenant Owen. Then fourteen regiments of Loyalists and Highlanders arrived and populated the districts of St. John, Gagetown, Fredericton and Woodstock. In 1804 numerous colonists from Ayrshire were found between St. John and Passamaquoddy Bay. After Waterloo the inrush of British settlers was continuous and helped to fill up the vacant lands which existed. The period 1820–30 must be mentioned as one of special activity among the many land companies which operated not only in New Brunswick, but also in Ontario.

As to Quebec this province was little favoured by emigrants who, as a rule, preferred to go on to Ontario. Of the few British settlements which sprang

DESTINATION OF EMIGRANTS 193

up within this area, mention must be made of Colonel Cockburn's township of Drummondville and the Irish inflow of 1830.

In Ontario[1] the record of arriving British immigrants is heaviest. Probably the earliest settlements were made on plots of land granted by the Government to disbanded soldiers. These were awarded as far back as 1750. In 1781-4, many Highlanders quitted New York State and took up their abode between Cornwall and Brockville. Then came numbers of Loyalists, who settled at Niagara in 1776, Oswego in 1795, and Kingston in 1789. The building of roads was the next factor which attracted people. On the road connecting Kingston and Toronto, at Dundas, Ancaster, and Port Hope many signs of civilisation were apparent by 1798, while Yonge Street was lined with farmers from Nova Scotia and Germany in 1794-9, and later by French Royalists, north of Markham, and, further west, by Pennsylvanian Quakers and Dutch Mennonites. In 1812-14 the shores of Lake Simcoe received Highlanders from Toronto. For some few years the arrivals were less numerous, but in 1816 Colonel Cockburn introduced veterans and Scotchmen to Perth, and in the same year Talbot received many additions to his colony. After the Napoleonic campaigns the War Office subsidised retired soldiers, the 99th and 100th Regiments at Richmond, near Ottawa, in 1818, and also three thousand Lanarkshire weavers under Captain Marshall at Lanark, in 1820. In 1819 there was another inflow of weavers, many of whom settled at Grenville and were assisted by a Glasgow emigration society. In 1823 Peter Robinson's famous band made their homes along the Rideau, close to Perth. Then came another great colonising factor, for in 1826 the Canada Company was established and was soon the means of introducing many

---

[1] Formerly Upper Canada.

settlers from the home country. In 1830 the Mohawks began to sell their lands, and thus a great barrier between east and west gradually broke down. In the fifties the spread of the railways proved a further factor of importance in the history of Canadian settlement.[1]

In 1811 the Selkirk colony was founded in the territory afterwards known as Manitoba, but the North-West traders did their utmost to discourage settlement on the prairie and forest lands which yielded them such a wealth of furs.[2] Accordingly it was not until the Dominion Government was established in 1867 that this region leapt into favour among agriculturists. Since the Government purchased this territory some forty years ago, the westward movement has taken thousands of farmers from Eastern Canada and located them in Manitoba, the vacancies made by their exodus being filled by new-comers from Europe.

The Canadian Pacific Railway entered the North-West Territory, that is to say, the old district of Assiniboia, in the summer of 1882, placing it for the first time in communication with the outer world. By the summer of 1884 it had traversed both Assiniboia and the prairie lands of Alberta and had reached as far as the Rockies.[3] The effect of this enterprise on the population of the " Provisional Districts " of Assiniboia, Saskatchewan, and Alberta may be seen from the following census figures, in which, it must be added, some twenty thousand Indians are not included.

	1881—immediately prior to extension of railway.	1885—immediately following railway extension.	Increase in 4½ years. Per cent.
Population	5624	28,171	401
Inhabited houses	2064	9460	358

With the further extension over the Rocky Moun-

---

[1] The authorities for the above notes respecting Canadian settlement are J. D. Rogers, *Historical Geography of the British Colonies* (Lucas), Vol. V; and Wm. Canniff, *History of the Settlement of Upper Canada*. [2] A. W. Jose, *The Growth of the Empire*, p. 358.
[3] Longstaff, *Studies in Statistics*, p. 116.

DESTINATION OF EMIGRANTS 195

tains of the Canadian Pacific Railroad in 1885 the province of British Columbia rapidly became available for European settlers. By reason of the fruit-growing, cattle-rearing, lumbering, and mining possibilities of this area great numbers of emigrants have been attracted from the Mother Country, as well as much capital and a considerable population from the regions along the Pacific slope of the United States.

In a general way it may be affirmed that the fresh-arriving immigrant is seldom the man who actually pushes westward the frontier of his adopted country. He is more prone to take up his abode as close as ever he can to the port at which he landed, for his finances are often unequal to the strain of an expensive inland journey. By so doing he assists in the economic expansion of the maritime community, providing and creating labour, but he rarely undertakes work of a pioneer nature; this he leaves to the older settler, at any rate until the time arrives when he himself may no longer be considered a new-comer.[1] Thus the immigrant settles on the seaboard provinces and pushes his forerunners inland. Later on either he or his children migrate westward to escape the pressure of those arriving after. Such is the movement set up by the inflow of a foreign population. Longstaff says,[2] "In Canada even more than in the United States, it would appear that the new regions are mainly settled by natives of the American continent, work for which they are especially adapted. Not only is there a flow of population from the Old World to the New, but in America itself the cry is still, 'Westward Ho!' The descendants of the early settlers move on to begin again the work of subduing the wilderness as their forefathers did, while the blank spaces left in the more settled districts of the east are

---

[1] Cf. *Edinburgh Review*, July, 1854, p. 243.
[2] In *Studies in Statistics*, p. 116.

filled by fresh immigrants from Europe." Describing the movement of population across the continent of North America, Professor Turner says,[1] " Western occupation advanced in a series of waves ; the Indian was sought by the fur trader ; the fur trader was followed by the frontiersman whose cattle exploited the natural grasses and the acorns of the forest ; next came the wave of primitive agriculture, followed by the more intensive farming and the city life. All the stages of social development went on under the eye of the traveller as he passed from the frontier towards the East."

---

[1] " Colonisation of the West," in the *American Historical Review*, p. 315, No. 2, vol. 1

CHAPTER IX

LAND SYSTEMS AFFECTING THE IMMIGRANT IN NORTH AMERICA

PRIOR to the last two decades of the eighteenth century, the methods by which land grants were made to immigrants and others in both Canada and the United States were of a highly unsatisfactory nature. With a recklessness which now seems incredible, extensive tracts were freely ceded to irresponsible people who, as often as not, made no serious attempt to bring them under cultivation. Even the poorest colonists, who had quitted the Mother Country through stress of circumstances, could secure as many acres as they wanted, though they might be lacking the necessary money to carry them on to their locations. As a result of this over-generous system of distribution, the genuine settlers were scattered through vast areas, a condition which deprived them of the friendship of neighbours and the privileges of accessible markets.

Beyond the personal inconvenience which such an arrangement imposed on colonists, there was also the question of national wastage to consider. Lord Durham mentioned in his report[1] that of seventeen million acres of surveyed land in Upper Canada, less than one million six hundred thousand acres remained unappropriated in 1839, whilst in Lower Canada, the surveys had embraced six million acres, and two-thirds of them had passed out of governmental control. In the United States an identical situation had prevailed at an earlier date. Within the space of five years a

---

[1] Sir Charles Lucas, Lord Durham's Report, vol. 2, p. 219.

New England corporation, known as the Ohio Company, purchased 892,000 acres in Ohio; the Miami Company obtained control of 272,540 acres situated in the Miami and Ohio river valleys, whilst under the title of The Erie Purchase the State of Pennsylvania reserved 202,187 acres for its private use.[1]

Of the two North American powers, the United States was the first to check these lavish grants of the public domain. Anxious to reduce the national debt, which had assumed somewhat alarming proportions during the war era of 1775–83, Congress decided that henceforth the unceded lands should be surveyed and sold at auction, the proceeds to be devoted to lessening the liabilities of the Confederation.[2] The arrangements, it may be said, applied only to the territories situated within the area bounded by the Alleghany Mountains, the northern lakes, and the Mississippi River.[3]

The new system gained the confidence of the people, and, almost immediately, the freshly-surveyed districts began to draw streams of settlers from the older states. So great was the rush to Kentucky and the western slopes of the Alleghanies that additional legislation in the matter of land-granting was felt to be necessary. In 1800, on the 10th of May, a second Act became law;[4] this created four land offices, having their location at Cincinnati, Chillicothe, Marietta, and Steubenville. Each of these offices was managed jointly by two officers, one a registrar and the other a receiver of public moneys. The duties of the former were concerned with apportioning and conveying plots to purchasers, whilst the latter collected and transmitted to the Treasury the sums accruing from the sales. In addition to these officials, two surveyors were appointed, one to map out the public lands

---

[1] Dr. Hill, *The Public Domain and Democracy* (Columbia University Studies, No. 100), p. 37.   [2] By the Act of May 7th, 1784.
[3] This was the extent of the States at that date.
[4] *The Public Domain* (U.S.A. House Miscellaneous), vol. 19, pp. 203–4.

north of the River Ohio, together with the territory of Louisiana,[1] and the other the Mississippi and Orleans district.

For many years lands had been granted in irregular misshapen tracts,[2] but the Act required that henceforth they were to be divided into townships, each of six geographical miles square, which in turn were to be sub-divided into thirty-six lots of one square mile. Both townships and subdivisions were to receive an indicating number to permit of identification.

When a township was marked out, the district registrar selected certain sections of 640 acres and offered them for sale at "public vendue," the starting price being $2 per acre. Unsold tracts could afterwards be negotiated privately with chance purchasers, but at never less than the starting price mentioned for public sales. In 1804 plots were split into quarter sections of 160 acres, and later on, in 1820, Congress legalised the selling of "half-quarter sections." It was not until much later that the minimum holding was reduced to forty acres.[3]

With the idea of attracting small farmers, the authorities made it a rule not to press for the whole of the purchase price at the time of effecting a sale. Payments were usually required in four equal instalments, the first within forty days of the deal and the remaining three in the second, third, and fourth succeeding years. Interest at the rate of 6 per cent was charged on overdue accounts, whilst an allowance of 8 per cent was made for cash settlements. A stringent measure ruled that plots having unpaid balances standing against them at the end of the fifth year were to be seized from the purchaser and publicly offered for sale, the upset price being not less than the arrears of the principal together with any interest that might

---

[1] Louisiana was included in the survey in 1803; i.e. the year it became part of the Confederation.

[2] Until Congress passed the Act of May 7th, 1784.

[3] Dr. Shusuke Sato, *Land in the United States*, John Hopkins University Studies, 1886, Vol. IV, p. 143.

be due. Should no buyer be found, the tracts were to become once more the property of the United States, the partial payments being forfeited.

There was one serious drawback to this system. Certain sections, owing perhaps to their unfavourable position or condition, were never purchased either publicly or privately, but remained on the hands of the registrar for years. No inducement in the shape of a reduction in price could be offered to likely purchasers, as the Land Acts clearly stated that the minimum price was to be $2 per acre.[1] On August 4th, 1854, however, this difficulty was removed by the Graduation Act, which permitted lands that had been in the market some considerable time to be sold at a reduction to actual settlers, but not to people who appeared to be speculators. When a surveyed tract had been standing for ten years, the price was to be lowered to $1 per acre; when it had been standing from fifteen to twenty years, the charge was to be 75 cents; when from twenty to twenty-five years, 50 cents; when from twenty-five to thirty years, 25 cents; and when upwards of thirty years, 12½ cents. So well did this legislation fulfil its purpose that the Government found that the inferior lands were soon cleared off its hands, and the Act was withdrawn as having no further use in June, 1862. During these eight years, a total of 25,696,419 acres were disposed of to settlers on the Graduation plan.[2]

From the earliest times, Congress recognised the value of reserving a proportion of its lands for the benefit of certain public services. As far back as 1785 an Act can be found which required definite plots to be handed over to the educational authorities, whilst an enactment of 1800 made further provisions in

---

[1] There was, of course, one exception to this rule. Land reverting to the Government owing to default in payment of instalments could be sold at less than $2 if the outstanding principal, plus interest, were together less. [2] *The Public Domain*, vol. 19, p. 291.

this matter. This statute decreed that one thirty-sixth part of all surveyed lands, or 640 acres in each township, were to be reserved and given in perpetuity for the support of local schools. Later, it was decided that seven entire townships, each containing 23,040 acres, namely, two in the State of Ohio and one in each of Michigan, Indiana, Illinois, Mississippi, and Orleans, were to be given in perpetuity for the support of the various seminaries of learning; they were to be let on lease and the proceeds employed for educational purposes. Religious and military societies, refugees from Canada, British deserters, and a thousand other bodies figured upon the list of beneficiaries of Government land reserves.[1] Salt springs and lands containing lead deposits, it may be added, were placed under the charge of the President of the United States, who sold or leased them and placed the proceeds to the credit of a variety of deserving causes.

In every case where surveys embraced tracts of land peopled by native Indians, these latter were formally driven from their homes and the lands thrown open to public settlement. It is comforting to know, however, that the system did not operate as harshly on these unfortunate men and women as would appear at first sight. In practice, an evicted tribesman presented himself at the district office of the registrar and there signed an affidavit saying that he was renouncing his tribal relations in favour of habits and pursuits of a civilised life. He then petitioned for a free grant of land, and was straightway given the plot on which he and his forefathers had so long expended their energies.

A previous chapter has spoken of the large number of small farmers, some of them possessing a little capital, who left England, and especially Scotland, during the second quarter of the nineteenth century.

---

[1] *The Public Domain*, vol. 19, p. 209.

To attract these and similar men, the United States Congress framed the Pre-Emption Act of 1832, which offered small uncleared farms of forty acres at reduced charges to colonists who would undertake to live on their plots for a certain length of time.

The first Pre-Emption Act, dating from March 3rd, 1801, had little in common with its successor of 1832[1] mentioned above. The earlier statute was of a private character, being intended to assist the people who had settled on the Symmes Purchase in Ohio. When John Cleves Symmes of the Ohio Company failed to meet his obligations with respect to the purchase of land, referred to at the commencement of this chapter, his numerous customers found their titles to be valueless. As these unfortunate settlers had already paid Symmes and had done much towards improving their holdings, Congress enacted that they should be given a preference or a pre-emption[2] right over other purchasers. By this, they were offered the option, before their lands were put to public auction, of acquiring them privately at one-third of the original cost. Pre-Emption Acts of a later date than 1832 required settlement, inhabitancy, and improvement of the land by the pre-emptor for his own use and not for speculation, nor for the benefit of another. To make his title, the settler had first to establish his residence on the land and then to file a pre-emption declaratory statement. If this were accepted by the registrar, it only remained for him to pay at the rate of $1.25 per acre and then to petition for the patent. In order that land speculators should not benefit under this Act, it was specified that no one would be accepted as a pre-emptor who held three hundred and twenty or more acres in any part of the United States.

---

[1] *The Public Domain*, vol. 19, p. 214.

[2] "Pre-emption is a premium in favour of, and condition for, making permanent settlement and a home. It is a preference for actual tilling and residing on a piece of land."—*The Public Domain*, p. 314.

To stimulate still further the westward movement, the first Homestead Act was introduced by Congress, under the Presidency of Abraham Lincoln on May 20th, 1862. The incidents which led up to the passing of this law have been described by Miss Coman in her book, *The Industrial History of the United States*.[1] She says :

> Agitation for the free distribution of the public lands had been persistent and unflagging for twenty years before the war. The Free Soil Democracy had led the movement with its proposal that the soil of our extensive domain be kept free for hardy pioneers of our own land and the oppressed and banished of other lands seeking homes of comfort and fields of enterprise in the New World. . . . In 1845 Andrew Johnson, of Tennessee, had brought forward in the House of Representatives a resolution in favour of giving every homeless citizen a portion of the national domain. Senator Stephen A. Douglas introduced a Bill to the same effect in 1849. Several times a homestead Bill passed the House of Representatives, only to be defeated in the Senate. The negative vote came largely from the southern states, which then held the balance of power in the Upper House. Finally (June 19th, 1860), after lengthy conferences, Senate and House agreed to concur in a Bill providing that any citizen of the United States, being the head of a family, might take up a quarter section of unappropriated land, settle thereon, and secure title after proved residence of five years. The Senate's contention that a cash payment of twenty-five cents an acre be required was accepted by the House with considerable demur.

President Johnson, in his annual message of 1865 to the people, said : " The homestead policy was established only after long and earnest resistance. Experience proves its wisdom. The lands in the hands of industrious settlers, whose labour creates wealth and contributes to the public resources, are worth more to the United States than if they had been reserved as a solitude for future purchasers."[2]

---

[1] *Op. cit.*, pp. 279-80. [2] *The Public Domain*, vol. 19, p. 349.

The original Homestead Act threw open the whole of the Public Domain to all who were prepared to fulfil certain settlement conditions and pay for the land in easy instalments. Subsequently the Act in an amended form allowed a locator the privilege of commuting his instalments if he preferred to buy outright. Unfortunately this concession favoured the land speculator more often than the genuine homesteader, as the settlement clauses could be no longer satisfactorily enforced.[1] In their Report of 1905 the Public Lands Commission (United States) complained that in many states 90 per cent of the commuted homesteads were transferred to speculators within three months of the acquisition of the title, women usually posing as the nominal commuters.

A discussion on the public land policy of the United States would be incomplete without the inclusion of some reference to the timber culture, timber and stone and desert land Acts, seeing that they form an integral part of this policy. Briefly the Timber Culture Act of 1873, amended in 1874 and 1878, granted treeless tracts of 160 acres to settlers for the encouragement of tree culture. This was a timber bounty Act. Ten acres of the territory entered were to be devoted to tree-growing during a period of eight years, after which time the patent was issued on payment of $18. The Stone and Timber Act of 1878 authorised the sale of timber land, unfit for cultivation, and lands primarily valuable for stone at $2.50 per acre. No one individual, however, could obtain more than 160 acres. At the same time a direct trespass law was enacted to prevent timber depredation. The Desert Land Act of 1877 was introduced in the hope that settlers would be induced to come forward and assist in reclaiming the dry and arid lands of the western

---

[1] Settlement under commuted privileges lasted a little over a year.

states. Entry was allowed on 640 acres and payments were rendered particularly easy in order that the holder might not be deterred from spending on improvements whatever money was necessary for irrigation schemes.[1]

At the present time the public lands which are still undisposed and open for settlement are of two classes; in one, the minimum price per acre is $1.25, whilst $2.50 is charged for the other. Titles to these lands may be acquired by private entry or location under the homestead, pre-emption and timber culture laws. Entries under the pre-emption laws are restricted to heads of families or citizens over twenty-one years of age. Other conditions of settlement remain as explained above. The homestead laws give the right of obtaining 160 acres of land at $1.25 an acre to any citizen or person over the age of twenty-one who applies for citizenship and who actually settles upon and cultivates the land to a reasonable extent. This privilege extends only to the surveyed lands and the title is perfected by the issue of a patent after five years' residence. Persons who are not citizens of the United States, or who have not declared their intention of becoming so, cannot obtain these homesteads.[2] The fees and commissions vary from a minimum of seven dollars to a maximum of thirty-four dollars for the whole tract entered, according to size, value, and place of record.

In dealing with the lands of the United States mention must be made of the great areas that have come under the control of the various railroad companies. A precedent was set on March 2nd, 1833, when Congress, desirous of assisting the Illinois Railroad Company in the work of linking up Illinois with

---

[1] Dr. Hill, *The Public Domain and Democracy* (Columbia University Studies), No. 100, pp. 56, 57.

[2] " Holding of Lands by Aliens."—Consular Report, Miscellaneous Series, 1901, No. 567.

the Atlantic coast, made the company a grant of 290,915 acres, part of which was absorbed in building the permanent way and part sold in small plots to immigrants. Ever since that date Congress has made a practice of voting extensive tracts of land to railroad concerns whose lines penetrate into undeveloped country. The company is usually given the land required for building the permanent way, the stations, and the workshops, together with alternate farm sections on either side of the track. The remaining plots are held by the Government. These are naturally sold to settlers and as a rule secure good prices owing to the rail advantages which they enjoy.

The following figures are interesting as they serve to show the lavish way in which land grants have been made by the United States land commissioners:—

APPROXIMATE DISPOSITION OF PUBLIC LANDS TO JULY 1ST, 1904.[1] (EXCLUDING ALASKA.)

Land sold for cash under various Acts	267,558,218 acres.
Railroad construction grants	117,550,292 ,,
Forest Reserves	114,502,528 ,,
Final Homestead entries	96,495,030 ,,
Indian lands	73,045,861 ,,
School grants to states and territories (to November 1st, 1904)	69,058,443 ,,
Swamp land grants	65,739,264 ,,
Entries pending (various, estimated)	39,525,840 ,,
Confirmed private land claims	33,440,482 ,,
Scrip and miscellaneous	32,378,421 ,,
Grants to states and territories (to November 1st, 1904)	20,587,863 ,,
Final Timber Culture entries	9,745,433 ,,
Wagon road, canal and river improvement grants	9,712,421 ,,
Land sold under Timber and Stone Act	7,596,078 ,,
Mineral lands	1,731,275 ,,
Total disposition	967,667,449 ,,
Unappropriated public lands of the United States	841,872,377 ,,

From the foregoing it will be gathered that the early settlers from the United Kingdom either bought

---

[1] Figures obtained from the Report of the Public Lands Commission (United States), 1905.

of speculators or obtained their holdings through one of the Government land offices. When the Pre-emption Acts and the Homestead Acts were introduced the settlers naturally secured the privileges which these afforded them. To-day they purchase chiefly from the railroad corporations.

Though we are strongly of the opinion that the British settler has been the best European customer the United States has had for its lands, no figures can be set down to prove this conviction. Unfortunately the Republic has preserved no data to show the nationality of the people to whom it has sold plots of the public domain, and has only in more recent times kept a check at the immigrant ports of the origin of the people visiting its shores. The returns made by the British Customs and the Board of Trade of emigrants leaving the British Isles for the United States also fall short of our needs, as they do not differentiate between the man who works for hire within the cities and his brother who takes up land; the figures, in fact, are unobtainable. We know, however, that Scotch and English farmers, dissatisfied with the conditions of life at home, have constantly sold their belongings and sailed for the United States, taking with them ample means. These men, it is only reasonable to argue, would obtain possession of land some time after arriving in the new country rather than work permanently as labourers. Actual instances of cases where this has taken place have been mentioned frequently in the Government reports dealing with emigration, several examples figuring in the reports published in 1826-7.[1]

Referring now to the systems of apportioning land in Lower Canada, we find that in the earliest times the French Government gave large tracts to seigneurs[2]

---

[1] See also Accounts and Papers, Vol. XXXII, 1831, p. 231.

[2] It is interesting to note that, after 1763, many of the seigneurs were of English origin. Lord Durham says that, at the time of his visit to Canada, fully half of the properties were in English hands.

in return for money and military service. The Report on Emigration, published in 1826, tells how the seigneur constructed roads, built mills, and in other ways opened up the country. He granted the land under his charge in small plots and took a considerable portion of his rent in the form of produce. As time went on the small plots became divided into even smaller areas, for the French law recognised a system of division on the death of a parent. The population soon became dense and as the soil was by no means rich, the comforts of life, where the land was granted, " en seigneurie," were certainly few. Lord Durham condemned the system in no measured terms. While the rural population of Lower Canada has steadily increased, the amount of cultivated land supporting this population, he wrote, has not increased in anything like the same proportion. According to an estimate made in 1826, the population of the various seigniories has more than quadrupled since the Loyalist immigration, that is to say, during the forty-two years intervening between 1784 and 1826: but in this interval the quantity of land under cultivation has only increased by about one-third.

After the Royal Proclamation of 1763, the official form of land tenure was that of free and common soccage, but the feudal tenure still survived in the districts where the English had but little penetrated. The dual system—though it suited the two classes of settlers, the French, in the seigneuries, and the British, in the townships situated on the frontier of the States,—gave rise to much confusion whenever cases had to be decided upon legal considerations. Munro[1] speaks of the uselessness of endeavouring to decide disputes between seigniors and habitants by the English code of law and procedure, especially when the presiding judges " knew little and cared less about existing conditions in the colony."

---

[1] *The Seigniorial System of Canada*, p. 195.

LAND SYSTEMS

Accordingly, Governor Murray thought fit to send out an edict permitting the French law to be temporarily reinstated in courts whenever cases could be expedited by its use. This action was approved of by the authorities at home. In 1766, Murray returned to England and then suggested that the English law should be swept away entirely in favour of the code which had been so long honoured by the French.

Governor Carleton, Murray's successor, also favoured a reversion to the French system and continually petitioned the authorities in London to recommend the King to permit further grants to be made " en seigneurie." On June 27th, 1771, the King in Council issued instructions favourable to Carleton, but still of a temporary nature.

In 1774, the Quebec Act restored certain of the French laws; consequently in 1775 the home Government directed that " all lands then or thereafter to be subject to the disposal of the Crown shall be granted in fief and seigniory, in like manner as was practised antecedent to the conquest, but omitting any reservation of judicial powers." In other words, under the Act, French civil law was restored for French Canadians, but there was no bar to making grants still on British tenure.

In 1786, Governor Carleton, who was then Lord Dorchester, ordered that certain grants should be made in favour of emigrant United Empire Loyalists, to disbanded soldiers, and especially to officers and privates of the 84th Foot Regiment. These grants were to be held under the Crown as seigniories and subject to all seigniorial duties. In 1791, the Constitutional Act was passed. Section XLIII made British tenure the law of the land in Upper Canada, and left matters as they were in Lower Canada. Later on, lands within the Eastern townships were ceded by patent to leaders of townships and their associates. This system, more than any of its forerunners, permitted of jobbery and waste. Happily General Prescott, then **Governor-General** of Lower Canada, recognised this and spared no pains in endeavouring to frustrate the plans which certain people made for accumulating vast tracts of the domain.[1] Between 1814 and 1818, few transactions in real property were effected, but in the latter year a system was enforced for granting plots under location tickets, upon specific conditions of settlement. In this arrangement is to be found the germ of the residence and improvement clauses which have grown to be so important a feature of present day colonial land Acts. The practice of requiring occupation and settlement continued until 1826 when instructions were issued by the Lords of the Treasury establishing a system of sale by auction, the purchase money being payable in four annual instalments without interest. Under these regulations only land, as selected by the Governor on the recommendation of the Commissioners of Crown Lands, could be put up for sale. In 1831, Lord Goderich made certain amendments to the land laws, the chief of which required deferred payments to be met twice yearly, with interest, but, in 1837, Lord Glenelg decided that cash payments, only, could be accepted in future.

A separate code of regulations operated in Nova Scotia. Until the year 1760, grants of land were made at the discretion of the Governor in Council, and all available records seem to infer that the distributions were judiciously made. In 1760, the home Government usurped the power hitherto held by the local authorities with disastrous results. Within thirteen years nearly eight million acres, including the whole of Prince Edward Island[2] were granted in blocks of from twenty to one hundred and fifty thousand acres to individuals

---

[1] "Prescott formed the view, rightly or wrongly, that various members of the Council were concerned in land jobbery and he held that public sale was the only real preventive of speculation."—Sir Charles Lucas in *History of Canada*, 1763-1812, p. 290.

[2] Till 1770, P. Edward Island was a part of Nova Scotia.

LAND SYSTEMS

and companies residing or formed in England. As may be expected, little and in some cases no effort was made to improve the ceded tracts, with the result that progress was materially retarded. The local Government constantly petitioned the home authorities for permission to reinvest the lands in the Crown by a process of escheat, but only received this permission when it was called upon to find homesteads for some four thousand United Loyalists. In 1790, for reasons which do not appear, all further grants of land were forbidden and this prohibition remained in force until 1808. Few people, however, were deterred by its ruling, for those who wished to settle either squatted or obtained a licence of occupation. In 1808, grants were once more given, a hundred acres to heads of families and fifty to each child, but not more than five hundred to any one family. A quit-rent payment of two shillings per hundred acres was demanded. This system remained in force and proved very successful until 1827.

Little is known of the early regulations affecting New Brunswick. Until 1784, it formed a part of Nova Scotia and shared the land policy of this province. Afterwards, grants were made under the authority of instructions issued from the home Government by the Governor in Council, but all such grants were subject to a quit-rent of two shillings per hundred acres. As in Nova Scotia, the system proved successful and remained in force until 1827. In 1839 it was reported that one-half of the granted lands were in possession of actual settlers, but that only one-twentieth were under cultivation.

When the Quebec Act of 1791 formally gave Upper Canada a separate identity of its own, efforts were made, within this area, to induce responsible individuals to undertake the settlement of whole townships, much after the system of " leaders and associates " which then obtained in the lower province.

The effort was fruitful, perhaps too fruitful, for the demand for land became so great that the plan had to be abandoned: even plots that had already been alienated were reclaimed by the Crown and their temporary owners compensated. From 1791 to 1804, small grants were made to individuals, the only payment being a moderate fee for the issue of the patent. In 1804 a sliding scale of fees was introduced, whilst in 1818 settlement duties were also required. United Loyalists and disbanded soldiers, it may be said, usually took up their homesteads without being called upon to make any payment whatever.

Though it was intended, at this date, to make the Government lands attractive, the intending settler usually preferred to deal with a jobber, who could offer homesteads with immediate possession, than to deal with the Crown which moved slowly and with tedious deliberation. Until 1820, it was necessary for those taking up plots to appear before the district land council. This often entailed travelling as many as two hundred miles, which at that date was a costly and fatiguing business. As the councils sat at irregular intervals and frequently postponed their meetings for as many as six weeks at a time, it will be seen that immigrants who were waiting to make their claims were put to considerable and often useless inconvenience. It is little wonder then that the prospective settler so frequently dealt with an agent or departed for the United States in sheer disgust.

The first step to remedy this unsatisfactory system of granting land was made by the Lieutenant-Governor in 1819, when the following notice was issued[1]:

EXECUTIVE COUNCIL OFFICE, YORK,
December 14*th,* 1819.

Whereas it is desirable to alleviate the situation of the poorer classes of settlers by an exemption from any charge on the patent deed, and also to remove all obstacles from the more

---

[1] Quoted from the *Upper Canada Gazette* of January 20th, 1820.

free accommodation of others with larger grants than have been usually made, his Excellency the Lieutenant-Governor in council has been pleased to order that the first-mentioned class of settler may receive a gratuitous grant of fifty acres under exclusion be it understood from any further grant from the Crown, but with liberty to lease the reserves.

To meet the above gratuity and increased burdens attending the purchase and distribution of lands, etc., it is ordered that the scale of demands on the grant of one hundred acres and upwards shall be regulated according to the annexed table, to take effect from the first of January, 1820.

It is further ordered, that the restriction from sale for three years be abolished and that deeds may issue on proper certificate of the performance of settling duties being produced. The grantee will be required to clear one-half of the road in front of each lot and the depth of two and one half chains from the road the whole length of every lot and erect a dwellinghouse. Upon all grants of land issuing under Orders in Council bearing a date subsequent to 1st January, 1820, the following sums will be paid by the patentee—

On grants of   50 acres .. Free.
     „   100   „   .. £12 sterling.
     „   200   „   .. 30   „
     „   300   „   .. 60   „
     „   400   „   .. 75   „
     „   500   „   .. 125   „

in three equal instalments. The first on receipt of the location ticket: the second on certificate being filed for settlement, and the third on receipt of the fiat of the patent.

No petition can be entertained unless accompanied by a written character or a satisfactory reason shown for such not being produced.   Signed. JOHN SMALL.

In order to facilitate still further the granting of settlements, a land office was established at York as explained in the following advertisement, here quoted from the issue of The *Upper Canada Gazette*, dated January 20th, 1820 :

GENERAL LAND AGENCY OFFICE, YORK, UPPER CANADA.

The subscribers have established an office at the seat of the government of Upper Canada for the purpose of transacting land agency business of every description. Emigrants and all others applying for lands from the Crown can obtain every requisite assistance and information to enable them to transact their business with the least possible loss of time and trouble. One of the subscribers having been appointed a commissioner to administer the oath of allegiance, additional facility is thereby offered in expediting the business of petitioners for grants of Crown Land.

This office will afford the easiest and most probable means of enabling persons to purchase or sell lands in any part of the province. A regular register of all lands offered for sale will be kept and persons wishing to purchase shall have access to it free of expense.

No pains will be spared to make this establishment of great utility to the public who, in their transactions with it, may depend upon meeting with the most ready attention.

Letters transmitted by post are requested to be post-paid.

B. GEALE,
J. FITZGIBBON.

During these early years, several groups of British emigrants were conducted to Upper Canada. Among the first to arrive was Colonel Talbot with a band of two thousand souls. He settled at Port Talbot, probably in the year 1813. Following him, in 1823, came a party guided by Lord Dalhousie, and, in the same year, another by Peter Robinson, whilst many lesser known bands made their homes at irregular intervals of time along the shores of Lakes Ontario and Erie. With all these settlers, the rule was to grant a plot of some seventy acres to each male between the ages of eighteen and forty-five, the site being chosen by the officers in charge. Adjoining each plot, distributed in this manner, was a smaller site of thirty acres, called a Crown Reserve, which was allowed to stand idle until a neighbouring farmer was prepared to pay a fee of ten pounds for its possession. These Crown Reserves, it may be said, were instituted by one of the presidents of the Executive Council at York who was a refugee Loyalist from the United States. He had watched,

LAND SYSTEMS

in his native country, the disputes which had arisen out of the various systems of taxation, and in these reserves he hoped to find a means of making Canada independent of all periodical levies.[1] Not only were there Crown Reserves, but Clergy Reserves also existed. These were established by the Constitutional Act of 1791 which directed that, in respect of all lands granted by the Crown a quantity equal to one-seventh so granted should be reserved for the benefit of the clergy.[2] As only six-sevenths of a township were apportioned in this way, the remaining seventh being reserved for the Crown itself, it is evident from the wording of the Act that the clergy should only have taken a seventh part of the six-sevenths. For a period of forty years, however, they secured for their own use a seventh part of each township, which was clearly a sixth and not a seventh part of the granted lands. In this way they appropriated some 300,000 acres more than the Act intended them to have, land which might be fairly estimated as worth £45,000.[3]

These reserves did not endow the province with the revenue that was expected of them, for instead of furnishing a handsome income they remained for the most part as waste land. In 1828, a select committee of the House of Commons, speaking of the Clergy Reserves, said, "These reserved lands, as they are at present distributed over the country, retard, more than any other circumstance, the growth of the colony, lying as they do in detached portions of each township and intervening between the occupations of actual settlers who have no means of cutting roads through the woods and morasses which thus separate them from their neighbours."[4]

But not only were these unoccupied lands a source

---

[1] Lord Durham's Report on Canada, 1839, p. 195–6.
[2] Sir Charles Lucas, Lord Durham's Report, vol. 2, p. 220.
[3] *Ibid.*, p. 221.
[4] Cf. W. Caniff, *The Settlement of Upper Canada*, p. 173.

of trouble geographically, they were also the cause of much dissent among political and religious parties. Members of the Church of England felt that the untenanted plots should be sold and the proceeds given to assist their church; other Protestants argued that they were intended to take a share of the profits also, whilst, to complicate matters, the Radicals, under Gourlay, pressed for a sale which was strongly opposed by their opponents, led by Governor Gore. A climax was reached when a band of Presbyterians in Niagara built a temporary church to take the place of one destroyed during the war and petitioned for a sum of one hundred pounds to be paid out of the Clergy Reserve Fund. To end these grievances, certain acts, notably the Imperial Act[1] of 1827, were passed which permitted the Government to sell these tracts, the proceeds to be applied to the improvement of the unsold reserves, or to the purposes for which the reserves were originally made.[2]

In 1826, the Canada Company was incorporated by royal charter and took over the Crown Reserves and certain plots of land in Upper Canada, paying the Government in all £104,819 10s. 11¼d.[3] John Radenhurst of the Surveyor-General's Office in Upper Canada, giving evidence before the enquiry conducted by Charles Buller, recorded the following interesting facts concerning this company:

The Company at first contracted for the purchase of 1,384,413 acres of Crown Reserves and 829,430 of Clergy Reserves at 3s. 6d. per acre. The Government were, however, unable to perform their contract so far as related to the Clergy Reserves and, as a substitute, the Company were allowed to select 1,100,000 acres in a block on the shores of Lake Huron at the same price for the whole as was to be paid for 800,000

---

[1] 7 and 8 Geo. IV, c. 62.
[2] Cf. Justin Winsor, *Narrative and Critical History of America*, p. 154
[3] Accounts and Papers, 1834, Vol. XLIV, p. 215.

acres of Clergy Reserves, making the whole of their purchase 2,484,413 acres; the purchase money was to be paid in the following annual instalments, viz.: In the year ending July, 1827, £20,000; 1828, £15,000; 1829, £15,000; 1830, £15,000; 1831, £16,000; 1832, £17,000; 1833, £18,000; 1834, £19,000; 1835, £20,000; and £50,000 a year for the next seven years. The Company was to be at liberty to expend one-third part of the purchase money of the block of 1,100,000 acres in public works and improvements within such block of land such as on canals, bridges, roads, churches, wharfs, and school-houses, etc.[1]

From a prospectus issued by the Company the following is quoted.[2]

The Canada Company has been incorporated by Royal Charter under the provisions of an Act of Parliament and has purchased Crown Reserves and other lands in the province of Upper Canada and hereby give notice, for those wishing to emigrate or arrange for others to do so, that the necessary preliminary arrangements have been made to receive people.

The Crown Reserves amount to 1,300,000 acres, in detached lots and blocks of 1,200 to 40,000 acres. The smaller lots are situated along the St. Lawrence and the lake shores, the larger plots in the remote west. The other land is a million acres between Lake Erie and Huron. £45,000 of the purchase money will be spent on making improvements, roads, etc.

The Company have agents at the British emigration ports who can show survey maps, etc., but no sale will be absolutely made in the Mother Country.

As the Company wish to get the land under cultivation quickly, no dealings with speculators will be entertained. Private people will be given every privilege and information, whilst liberal terms are offered in individual cases.

The Company will not defray any travelling expenses, but will advise those who arrive at Quebec and New York the best route to their destination.

In 1856, an Imperial Act was passed giving facilities

---

[1] Sir Charles Lucas, Lord Durham's Report on the Affairs of British North America, Vol. I, p. 170.

[2] Report on Emigration, 1826-7, vol. II, p. 461. See also p. 705.

for winding up the Company, but this was never carried into effect. A further Act, having similar scope, became law in 1881. The Company, however, is still in active operation.[1]

In 1830, Mr. J. Richards was directed by Lord Goderich to make a tour of the North American provinces, in order that he might draw up a report concerning the systems then ruling for the granting of land. His enquiry was the means of gathering together much useful information, but the dominant note of the report which he subsequently made was that land was granted with far too lavish a hand. Prior to 1804, he said, 4,500,000 acres had been alienated by Government, whilst between that date and 1830, no less than 3,800,000 acres had passed out of public control. Ungranted lands which still existed, he reported, numbered 1,537,439 acres.

Gradually, the methods of distributing lands were remodelled on the lines of those established, many years previously, in the United States. Free grants to immigrants were abolished in 1832[2] as many people, who had hitherto accepted them, had been unable to subsist on their means during the interval between the sowing and reaping of the first crop. From this date, farms were sold by auction, the commissioners[3] being empowered to fix the upset price. Four to five shillings was the average charge per acre for uncleared plots, whilst partially cleared or unusually well situated sections obtained from seven and sixpence to fifteen shillings.[4] The purchase money was either paid in cash or a deposit of one quarter of the sum was tendered at the time of the sale, the remaining instalments being met half yearly. The moneys so obtained,

---

[1] Cf. Sir Charles Lucas, Lord Durham's Report on the Affairs of British North America, Vol. I, p. 171.
[2] Accounts and Papers, Vol. XLIV, 1834, pp. 293, 299.
[3] These Commissioners were first appointed in 1827.
[4] Accounts and Papers, Vol. XLIV, 1834, p. 293.

it may be added, were used in improving roads, constructing bridges, or helping destitute immigrant labourers to reach towns where work was plentiful.

In 1838, Lord Durham made a thorough inspection of the land systems. Above all, he seems to have been struck with the lavish manner in which grants were made to various people. For many years, he tells us, every discharged soldier was entitled to a section of land, every intending settler received an order for it in proportion to his alleged capital, every leader of an immigrant party was endowed according to the number of his pretended followers; in short, almost everyone who applied obtained an order for land, until it seemed as if the Government had no other object but to divest itself as quickly as possible of all control over the unsettled portions of the province.[1]

When the public domain was so easily obtained, the petitions for grants often came from irresponsible individuals. These people would submit themselves to the district land surveyor, and, obtaining a location ticket, would cheerfully set off for their new home, possibly some hundred or more miles distant. Coming from the United Kingdom, they were usually but little prepared for so hazardous a journey. When at last they reached their destination, if indeed they ever did, the remoteness of other human habitations and the solitude of the seemingly impenetrable forests quickly dulled whatever ambitions they may have had for settlement. The impracticability of the situation would swiftly dawn upon them, and after another weary tramp they would find themselves once more in one of the centres of life and civilisation. Here the land jobbers would await their return and obtain from them their location ticket in exchange for the merest trifle. The jobbers usually allowed a few

---

[1] See various passages in Lord Durham's Report on Canada, 1839. Also Accounts and Papers, Vol. XXXIV, 1843, p. 185.

years to elapse, and then presented the tickets at the surveyor's office, requesting them to be exchanged for the patents. By falsely swearing that the settlement conditions had been fulfilled, the title-deeds were issued to them, and the particular land in question passed out of the Government's hands for ever.

In 1852 the Crown Lands Department,[1] situated at Quebec, gave notice that henceforth estates west of Durham and Victoria were to be sold at 7s. 6d. per acre, payable in ten annual instalments. Elsewhere, the prices were to range from 1s. in Gaspé and Saguenay to 4s. in Upper Canada, the payments there being spread over five years. Possession could only be gained at these prices, firstly, by promising to clear at least five acres annually for each hundred purchased, and, secondly, by erecting within a given time a dwelling-house, measuring no less than 18 by 26 feet.[2]

Other measures were introduced with a view to curtailing the powers of the land speculator. During the years 1840–1860 the monopolist was particularly active, securing additional plots in every province, and holding them to the detriment of the settler and the development of the country. As he often disguised himself as a charitably disposed person desirous of locating a large party of emigrants from the Mother Country, and obtained lands at a reduced rate under this pretext, the Crown Lands Department found it necessary to grant extensive plots only on the express condition that actual settlement should be performed within a stipulated period. This rule frustrated the plans of the professional jobber, but

---

[1] In 1840 the Colonial Land and Emigration Department was created, but its dealings with questions of land were not connected with North America.

[2] Report of the Colonial Land and Emigration Commissioners, 1852–3, Vol. XL, p. 142–3.

LAND SYSTEMS

imposed no hardship on the genuine organiser of emigrant parties.[1]

In the year 1856 the Grand Trunk Railroad was opened for traffic, and thus made accessible vast unpeopled areas of Ontario. To settle these parts with as little delay as possible, the system of granting free land was once more provisionally instituted. Three roads were cut, the Ottawa, the Addington, and the Hastings Roads, and, along these, plots of one hundred acres could be obtained by settlers of eighteen years of age and upwards on certain conditions of cultivation and residence.[2] This action was in no wise a change of land policy on the part of the Government, but merely a temporary measure instituted, more or less locally, to effect rapid settlement.

A change, however, came with the introduction of the Public Lands of the Dominion Act of 1872, when homesteads of 160 acres were offered free to all people over twenty-one years of age. The new system was the outcome of a democratic movement which claimed that the uncultivated lands should be no longer allowed to fall into the hands of the moneyed speculators, but should be placed within the reach of the rank and file.

The present system of granting homesteads in the Dominion has been based upon this policy, introduced in 1872. To-day there are some eighty million acres of fertile land which the Government offers free to settlers ;[3] they are situated in Manitoba, Saskatchewan, and Alberta.[4] These tracts are offered

---

[1] Twentieth Report of the Colonial Land and Emigration Commissioners, 1860, Vol. XXIX, p. 40.

[2] Report of the Colonial Land and Emigration Commissioners, 1857, Vol. XVI, p. 39.

[3] Estimated as eighty-five million acres in *Canada, its History, Productions, and Natural Resources*, published by the Department of Agriculture, Canada, 1906, p. 82.

[4] Similar lands are to be obtained in British Columbia, but they are under provincial control.

in quarter sections of 160 acres to men over the age of eighteen, also to men and women of any age who are the sole heads of families. By paying an office fee of $10 the settler obtains a section of land which he may cultivate to the exclusion of any other person, but the title is not vested in him or her until the Crown has issued the patent.

Settlement [1] is performed by dwelling upon the land at least six months in each of the first three years subsequent to receiving the claim. This, however, is unnecessary if the settler lives with his parents who themselves are responsible for a farm in the vicinity, or if the settler has his permanent residence upon other farm land owned by him in the same or some adjacent township. The Minister of the Interior has also relaxed the conditions of settlement in cases where parties of twenty or more families have desired to form a hamlet or village, in order to facilitate the establishment of schools, churches and other institutions. In all cases where such petitions have been received, the conditions relating to cultivation have been rigidly exacted before the patents have been issued.

The Dominion lands are now laid out in quadrilateral townships, each containing thirty-six sections of as nearly one square mile or 640 acres as the convergence of the meridians permits. The sections are numbered as follows:

31	32	33	34	35	36
30	29	28	27	26	25
19	20	21	22	23	24
18	17	16	15	14	13
7	8	9	10	11	12
6	5	4	3	2	1

---

[1] See Report on Colonisation, 1891, Appendix No. 4, p. 68.

LAND SYSTEMS

Each section of a township is divided into quarter sections of 160 acres, which are styled according to their positions, north-west, north-east, south-west and south-east quarter sections.

In regard to the disposal of the lands in Manitoba, Saskatchewan, and Alberta, the sections are divided into two classes, the even numbered and the odd numbered tracts. The former, with the exception of those numbered 8 and 26, which are allotted to the Hudson Bay Company, are open for homestead entries, while the latter are held either for sale or as grants in aid of the construction of railroads. The proceeds from the sales of plots numbered eleven and twenty-nine are held for educational purposes; the money which they realise being invested in Dominion securities for the endowment of schools, colleges, universities, etc. In townships which consist partly of prairie and partly of timber lands the latter are divided into wood lots of between ten and twenty acres, and these are available to settlers who do not already possess timber on their own homesteads.

In addition to the lands of Manitoba, Saskatchewan, and Alberta, which belong to the people of Canada, and are administered by the Federal Government, Ontario, Quebec, New Brunswick, British Columbia and Nova Scotia also offer homesteads to settlers, but these are controlled by the respective provincial legislatures. Ontario grants free sections on much the same lines as those adopted by the Dominion, though the plots vary from 160 to 200 acres in extent. The better situated tracts are sold at prices ranging from 50 cents to $10 an acre, whilst improved farms are marketable at $20 to $50 per acre.[1] In Quebec there are no free homesteads, but the province has surveyed some seven million acres, which it sells on

---

[1] *Canada, its History, Productions, and Natural Resources*, published by the Department of Agriculture, Canada, 1906, p. 88.

the instalment plan at 35 to 60 cents an acre.[1] New Brunswick has seven million acres of ungranted land.[2] These it offers in hundred acre farms to any man who, not owning land already, pays either $20 in cash or performs work on the public highways valued at $10 per annum for three successive years. Nova Scotia has a considerable quantity of vacant land, but much of it is unsuited to cultivation. When offered to settlers, it is at the rate of $40 for every hundred acres.[3] Yet other conditions prevail in British Columbia. Here the settler from Britain, who is over eighteen years of age, may pre-empt a tract not exceeding 160 acres, if the homestead is situated west of the Cascade Range, or twice this acreage when located east of the mountains. It may be added that the usual conditions of settlement are also required in most of the above-mentioned provinces.

A further Act which has done much to influence the land policy of Canada is the Dominion Lands Act of 1886.[4] This statute enables a person who finances a necessitous settler to cover his risk by holding a lien upon the settlement until the debt is repaid. Under this legislation a sum of £100 [5] may be lent to an immigrant, which he must repay, with 6 [6] per cent interest, in yearly instalments. The amount of the loan and the rate of interest have at times been altered under various amendments, but the spirit of the Act has remained unchanged throughout. In cases where the conditions of settlement are not performed and the homesteader leaves his plot, the person who made the loan is required to instal a second settler within two years or to sell the land to anyone desirous of buying it at a reasonable price.

---

[1] *Canada, its History, Productions, and Natural Resources*, 1906, p. 88.
[2] Ibid., p. 89.   [3] Ibid., p. 89.
[4] And its later amendments.   [5] Afterwards increased to £120.
[6] Afterwards increased to 8 per cent.

The patent for the fee simple, it may be added, is not issued until all debts have been liquidated or the financier has signified his satisfaction.[1] Many British emigrants have received assistance from their home landlords under this enactment, but the records which have been kept of their issue go to prove that the results have been somewhat disappointing.[2]

An outcome of this Act has been the birth of numerous land companies having head-quarters in various prairie regions of Canada. The object of all these concerns is to obtain financial gain by lending settlers the necessary money required for taking up and stocking homesteads. The risks incurred by the lenders are covered by the provisions of the said Act. The Commercial Colonisation Company of Manitoba may be counted a pioneer in this business. It was floated in 1887 with a capital of £200,000, of which only £20,000 was ever paid up.[3] It settled many crofters and others coming from the Orkney Islands and the north of Scotland, but fared badly at their hands. Within two years the Company was absorbed by the Canadian Settlers' Loan and Trust Company, a Glasgow concern which worked in conjunction with the Manitoba and North Western Railway. Another concern was the Canadian Agricultural, Coal and Colonisation Company. This body purchased large tracts of land situated along the route of the Canadian Pacific Railway in the neighbourhood of Regina, Saskatchewan, and divided them into homesteads, which it cleared, ploughed, and prepared ready for the reception of settlers. Only people who were skilled in farming and had at least one hundred pounds capital after paying all expenses incidental to the passage were allowed to take up sections.

---

[1] The text of the Act is to be found in the Report on Colonisation, 1889, Appendix 4, p. 190.
[2] Cf. the experiences of Lady Gordon Cathcart.
[3] Report on Colonisation, 1890, p. 124.

226 A HISTORY OF EMIGRATION

In conclusion, the following table is given to show the growing demand which exists for Canadian real property. The figures refer only to sales, etc., effected by the Government and not to those due to commercial enterprise :—[1]

Homestead Fees :

1904	1905	1906	1907	1908	1909	1910
$	$	$	$	$	$	$
255,772	304,806	417,834	215,450	301,694	389,039	415,232

Homestead Entries :

26,073	30,819	41,869	21,647	30,424	39,081	41,568

Cash Sales :

$	$	$	$	$	$	$
196,750	154,128	442,589	494,117	656,303	951,442	1,239,037

Net Revenue of all land transactions :

1,645,103	1,313,595	1,675,897	1,455,386	1,979,499	2,175,214	2,901,015

[1] *Canada Year Book*, 1910, Table CXC.

CHAPTER X

COLONISATION SCHEMES [1] [2]

SINCE the year 1815[3] many hundreds of colonisation schemes have been evolved, some under the ægis of the Home and Colonial Governments, others under the patronage of charitable bodies, whilst yet a third group owe their origin to commercial enterprise. Most of them have long been abandoned and forgotten, but the more typical of those of which we can still find records are described in the following pages.

The first scheme of note was that undertaken by Lieutenant-Colonel Cockburn at the instance of the War Office. On the termination of hostilities with the United States, in 1816, a number of British soldiers,[4] whose period of service expired whilst they were garrisoned in Canada, were persuaded to take up land in a settlement between the St. Lawrence and Ottawa

---

[1] For the sake of continuity and comparison, it has been deemed inexpedient in this chapter to confine the subject-matter to the North American Continent.

[2] Emigration differs from colonisation in that the former suggests a movement from one land to another of people who intend to make their permanent homes in the country of reception, whilst the latter infers not only the idea of movement to a new country, but also settlement on the land, usually in considerable numbers within a circumscribed area (cf. Chapter XIV).

[3] Colonisation schemes of a date prior to 1815 are dealt with in Chapter I.

[4] " Ex-soldier emigrants were numerous, but they were no new feature. Hitherto, however, they had had Provincial experience or were Gaels. Now some of them came direct from all parts of the United Kingdom into the primeval forest, where they not unnaturally proved less deft than their American brethren-in-arms. Nevertheless, many of these despised ex-soldiers were skilled sappers, miners, and engineers, many proved apt pupils, and even the most useless as a rule drew pensions, or had commuted pensions, and brought useful coin into districts where money had never yet passed."—J. D. Rogers, " Historical Geography," *Canada* (Lucas), Part V, p. 166.

rivers. It was felt that their presence in this district would prove of value should further disagreement arise at any time with the Republican states. Each man was given rations and a plot, the size of which depended upon his rank.[1] Unfortunately the settlers were ill-fitted to surmount the difficulties which confronted them, and had not additional supplies been forthcoming many would have undoubtedly perished.

In 1820 the military colonists were joined by one hundred and sixty-seven families from Lanarkshire, N.B.[2] who received rations and land in accordance with the arrangements drawn up for the disbanded soldiers. Though everything was done to make the settlement fruitful, the military and much of the civilian element drifted away, and in the year 1823 hardly a man was still to be found on his original plot.

Dissatisfied with the progress which the colonisation movement was making in Canada, the Home Government turned its attention to the Cape of Good Hope. In July, 1819, Mr. Vansittart, the then Chancellor of the Exchequer, proposed a vote of fifty thousand pounds towards emigrating certain unemployed poor.[3] The country at this time was suffering acutely from the inactivity which followed on the Napoleonic wars, and was anxious for some such assistance as emigration might afford. In response to the Government's announcement no less than ninety thousand applicants clamoured to be taken to South Africa with their families; the records at our disposal, however, state that 3,659 people embarked in twenty-six ships, and all of them arrived at the Cape between March and October, 1820. Of the 3,659 souls, 1,020 were men, 607 women, and 2,032 children.

---

[1] Privates received plots of one hundred acres ; field officers were granted twelve hundred acres.

[2] Report on Emigration, 1826, p. 217.

[3] Arnold White, "Experiments in Colonisation," *The Contemporary Review*, pp. 656–7, November, 1890.

COLONISATION SCHEMES

The callings of the settlers were various : with doctors, artists, printers, wine-dealers, rope makers, bakers, and woodcutters were mixed a few agricultural labourers. As a body they were above the average in intelligence, courage, and respectability, but the community as a whole was ill-suited to grapple with the dangers and difficulties associated with uncultivated land overrun by Kafirs. On landing at Port Elizabeth a few necessaries were served out and a general exodus followed. After days of trekking each family was located on a hundred-acre allotment forming part of the Albany Settlement. Wheat, maize, and vegetables were sown, but the prospects of a good harvest were destroyed by drought and the appearance of rust and blight. So great were the hardships which the settlers endured at the outset that the English Government increased its original grant to two hundred thousand pounds, and charitable people at home subscribed to a relief fund. After surmounting difficulties and misfortunes in a manner seldom displayed by emigrants success attended their efforts and many were eventually found to be in possession of large grazing farms. A list of the original settlers with their wives and children is still preserved at Grahamstown[1] and many family names, well known to-day in South Africa, are included in it.

In 1823,[2] the Home Government once more attempted a colonisation scheme in Canada ; this time in order to ease the condition of certain farm hands in the south of Ireland. The arrangements were carried out by Mr. Peter Robinson, a Canadian, who appears to have discharged the arduous duties committed to his charge with zeal and judgment. He selected his own followers and personally visited the disturbed areas of Fermoy, Ballyhooly, and Mallow,

---

[1] *The Story of the Settlement*, written and published by T. Sheffield, High Street, Grahamstown, contains a copy of this roll.
[2] Hansard, Second Series, vol. 18, col. 940.

convening meetings to explain to the people his projects. So acute was the suffering in these districts that the priests, who usually opposed emigration, looked with favour on Robinson's undertaking and rendered him assistance by eulogising his work from the pulpits. Besides being conveyed free of all cost, the settlers received, on arriving at the place of their destination, a supply of twelve months' provisions, seed-corn and potatoes for planting, the utensils necessary to enable them to commence clearing and cultivating the ground, and assistance in the erection of their houses, whilst a herd of 182 cattle was placed at their disposal.

Seventy acres of land were given to each head of a family on condition that he paid a small annual quit-rent, but no charge was to be levied during the first five years of the tenancy. At any time, the freehold could be obtained by paying a sum equal to the quit-rent for twenty years, but few availed themselves of this privilege.

Under the same leadership a second party journeyed to Canada in 1825. Robinson recorded the following figures concerning his 1823 party. There were 182 male heads of families, 143 women, 57 boys between the ages of fourteen and eighteen, and 186 children under fourteen. His followers thus comprised a body of 568 people. On these he spent £12,593 3s., which averaged £22 1s. 6d. per head, or about £88 6s. for each family. The voyage cost £7 per person, and the outfit with other necessaries, in most cases, amounted to £15. In addition to this expenditure, he paid £819 for cows, £230 for farming utensils, £450 for assistance in building, £150 for guides, £364 for seed corn and seed potatoes, £100 for medical outfits, and £150 for shoes and flannel.[1]

---

[1] Lieutenant-Colonel Cockburn's evidence. Report on Emigration, 1826, various pages. See also *Edinburgh Review*, December, 1826, p. 60.

COLONISATION SCHEMES

As to the success of Robinson's earlier scheme, the evidence which is available at the present time appears somewhat conflicting. Three years after the party had settled on the land it was reported that of the 182 heads of families, 120 were still on their farms, 8 had died and their plots become vacant, 44 had given up possession, but were working in other parts of Canada, 9 had gone to the United States, and 1 had returned to Ireland.[1] From this information, the record seems satisfactory enough, especially as only nine heads of families had fallen victims to the desire, which in those days was unusually strong, of going over the frontier into the United States. The testimony which Dr. Strahan, the Archdeacon of York (Upper Canada), gave before the Emigration Commissioners of 1826 was also satisfactory. The views of Lieutenant-Colonel Cockburn, a shrewd official who had had much experience in colonisation matters, were, however, less assuring. The impression in his mind, he said,[2] was that the emigrants were not doing well, and that the neighbouring settlers were so annoyed at their conduct that they wished for no more to be sent out under similar conditions. The real test as to whether Robinson's followers were successful or the reverse seems to depend not on an expression of opinion, but (*a*) on an examination of the figures which indicate the manner in which the people met their quit-rent payments, (*b*) on data showing the eagerness with which the land-patents were taken up, and (*c*) information which registers, over a long period of years, the number of heads of families who remained on their land. If Robinson's scheme be judged by these means, it cannot be considered successful. On the expiry of the five years of free tenancy many settlers left their homesteads and

---

[1] Various passages in the Report on Emigration, 1826.
[2] When giving evidence before the Emigration Commission of 1826–7.

crossed into the United States, arguing, probably, that if rent had to be paid at all it might as well be paid for land which they preferred in a more settled country. Not only were many plots vacated, but numbers of settlers who did remain on their farms gave trouble either by falling into arrears with the rent or by refusing absolutely to make any payment, however small. Only a few of them ever took out the patent for their lands, so that the Home Government sustained a substantial loss by this particular scheme.

Peter Robinson was on the point of organising a third party of emigrants when Parliament refused to vote him the necessary funds. The House very properly considered that before additional money was spent on so vital a matter, a committee of investigation should be appointed. The Emigration Commission of 1826–1827 was the outcome of this decision.[1]

For two years the question of further emigration was held in abeyance, but in 1829 a party of three hundred colonists was despatched to the Swan River, in Western Australia, partly to meet the demand experienced at home for over-seas settlement and partly owing to a desire to forestall the French, who were once again seeking territories suitable for colonial enterprise.[2] The leader, Mr. Thomas Peel, selected his followers from various parts of the country, giving preference to those who were already acquainted with farm work. The Government placed 500,000 acres of land under his control. Peel met all expenses incidental to the voyage, and agreed to pay good wages on condition that his men signed a contract to work for him for a definite period of years.[3] On arriving, however, the men found that land could be obtained easily, and, thinking

---

[1] Hansard, Second Series, vol. 18, p. 940.
[2] G. W. Rusden, *History of Australia*, vol. 1, p. 584 *et seq*.
[3] Henry C. Morris, *History of Colonisation*, vol. 2, p. 128.

COLONISATION SCHEMES

they would profit by being their own masters, broke the conditions of their bond and deserted him. Peel was thus left with a vast tract of land and few or no people to work it. The defaulters soon found that it was more difficult to gain subsistence than they had supposed, and returned to their leader, in the hope of being re-engaged. By that time, however, Peel had lost his money; his cattle had perished, and he was entirely without resources. Not being willing nor able to accept their services, the men grew threatening, and endeavoured to hang him. Finally some of his party returned to England, but the majority of them went on to Van Diemen's Land.

Contemporary with this failure was the inception of the Colonisation Society under the leadership of Edward Gibbon Wakefield,[1] a reformer who gathered around him many young men destined afterwards to become famous. The primary object of this body was to draw public attention to the causes which had led to the downfall of so many colonists in Australia and to formulate schemes for their avoidance in the future. The theories of Wakefield were warmly received by a certain section of the thinking public, and the South Australian Act of 1834 owed its origin to the widespread interest which he evoked. By this enactment a governor and a council endowed with both executive and legislative power were appointed to take over the land surveyed by Sturt and Captain Barker.[2] The chief difference between the South Australian colony and other British colonies was that land within this area was to be sold at a substantial price and never ceded gratuitously. On this experimental basis the new colony became a complete failure. The

---

[1] Wakefield, it may be repeated, formulated the theories concerning land distribution which Lord Durham suggested in his famous report
[2] A. W. Jose, *The Growth of the Empire*, p. 255.

emigrant capitalists were the first to arrive, but were quickly disheartened by the absence of labour and the hardships attending the life of pioneers. Preferring an urban existence, they gravitated to Adelaide, where they spent their capital speculating in town lots. In one day, owing to this practice, ground sites in Adelaide rose from three to thirty dollars an acre, and in 1839 many sections secured from five to ten thousand dollars an acre.[1] By defaulting, the moneyed emigrants not only ruined their own chances of success but the labourers, when they reached the colony, found no one to employ them. Deprived of the opportunity of working for hire, they applied for free grants of land, in the hope of becoming their own masters, but the fundamental law of the Constitution forbade this, and their requests had to be refused. Happily the gravity of the situation was speedily placed before the British Cabinet, and a sum sufficient to meet the temporary needs of the emigrants was voted.

Although Wakefield's scheme signally failed on this occasion, it is due to him to mention that the Colonial Land and Emigration Commissioners emigrated no less than 339,000 people between 1847 and 1869 much on the lines which he suggested. None of these people, however, settled in North America, as the lands of Canada did not come under the control of the Commissioners.

Probably the only really successful colonisation scheme of the nineteenth century was that carried out in 1873-4 by the Emigrant and Colonist Aid Corporation, in conjunction with the New Zealand Government. This Company purchased a block of 100,000 acres of Government land on terms which included the settlement of 1500 adults within a period of four years. The Company built the necessary

---

[1] H. Merivale, *Lectures on Colonisation and Colonies*, pp. 454-5.

COLONISATION SCHEMES 235

dwelling-houses, parcelled out the land, and made so many other preparations that, as a witness said before the Colonisation Committee of 1891, the emigrants on arrival " had nothing to do but hang their hats up." [1] Not only did the settlers remain on their land and work contentedly, but they met their liabilities honourably, and the Company was able to declare an average yearly dividend of 5¼ per cent. Fielding's scheme, as this was called, embraced many features which made for success. An out-of-the-way situation was selected for the colony, so that the settler had not the opportunity of escaping readily to the ordinary labour markets; the plots given to each man were small, absorbing only a portion of his time, other labour in the form of road-making for the Corporation and railway constructing for the Government was available, which enabled each male worker to earn ready money from the moment of his arrival, and much of the preliminary work of clearing the plots, which proves so disheartening to the average fresh arrival, had been effected before the colonist reached his destination. It should be added that the New Zealand Government defrayed the ocean passage expenses, and thus relieved the Company of much of the financial burden inseparable from such a scheme.

In 1880 and 1882 two attempts were made to settle poor families from the West of Ireland on farms in Minnesota. They were started under favourable circumstances, being conducted by members of the Roman Catholic faith, who were interested in their distressed Irish co-religionists, yet both were failures, and neither succeeded in ultimately settling the emigrants on the land. The former was superintended by Father Nugent, of Liverpool, who received assistance from Bishop Ireland, of Minnesota. On the

---

[1] Page 48 of the Report.

expiration of two years after their arrival only five families were still to be found on their plots. It must be admitted, however, that those who had elected to leave their settlements were reported to be doing favourably as labourers in the neighbouring towns. The second of the two schemes was promoted by Mr. Sweetman, a wealthy and benevolent Irishman. Beginning work in 1881, it took him but a year to be convinced of the failure of his project, which was mainly an experimental attempt at placing penniless labourers on the land.[1]

An interesting colonisation scheme was that devised by Lady Gordon Cathcart, of Cluny Castle, in 1883.[2] As has been mentioned earlier, ten families were selected from her distressed tenants and sent to Canada. Each was assisted with a loan of £100, which was made a charge on the homestead, in accordance with the provisions of the Dominion Land Act. Every necessary convenience was afforded the party by her representative, and also by the Canadian Government's agent at Brandon. No houses were built for them, however, but they lodged for a time in tents, and ultimately erected some turf and log houses for themselves, much after the style of those they quitted in Scotland. They raised a large crop of potatoes during their first season, and so satisfactory was their initial progress that in 1884 a further party of fifty-six families was sent to join them. An addition of ten families was also made in 1886.

As with so many other schemes, the earlier reports were extremely gratifying. The settlers seemed industrious, they appeared cheerful — a necessary factor for success—and their belongings were estimated as being worth £260 on an average. A different condition of affairs arose, however, when, on the

---

[1] Report on Colonisation, 1891, p. 48.
[2] See Chapter IV, " Unassisted and Assisted Emigration."

COLONISATION SCHEMES 237

expiry of the second year of tenancy, the initial repayment fell due. Instead of speaking of their ease and comfort, the party complained of poverty and want, but to what extent this condition of need actually existed is somewhat doubtful.[1] When heard of twenty-three years later the settlers were hopelessly in arrears, only one amongst them having paid both capital and interest in full. Financially the scheme has been an undoubted failure, but as the people have improved their conditions of life, and as the majority of them have kept to their plots, some measure of success must be credited to Lady Cathcart's efforts. The recent condition of these men and women is described in the following letter sent by a former Canadian Commissioner of Immigration to Mr. J. Murray Gibbon, and quoted from his book *Scots in Canada*.[2]

WINNIPEG, MANITOBA,
Nov. 7th, 1907.

SIR,
　　Your letter of the 27th ultimo was duly received, in which you state that Lady Gordon Cathcart was anxious to know how the colony of crofters between Moosomin and Wapella was succeeding.

Realising that Lady Gordon Cathcart would desire the information to be up to date I have had to delay this matter until one of our inspectors could make the trip.

I beg to report as follows :—

. . . .

The first ten or twelve years were a struggle, but the young men grew up able to earn money, and the settlement to-day is all right and the people doing well. They have good buildings, good horses and cattle, good machinery and equipment, and the schools and churches are very good. The English language

---

[1] There seems to exist some grounds for alleging that the settlers could have repaid their loans, but did not feel inclined to do so. One man rather resented the idea that he ought to repay it; he thought he had quite done his duty in going out—that he was, in fact, more a creditor than a debtor.—*Agricultural Settlements in British Colonies,* vol. 2, para. 1080.　　　　[2] Pages 149–51.

is spoken exclusively by the younger people, but the older ones, although they speak English, prefer the mother tongue. The average cultivation of land for each settler would be about one hundred and fifty acres.

The Inspector reports that the Lady Cathcart settlements in St. Andrews, Red Jacket, and Wapella districts are wealthy communities and independent notwithstanding the early struggle in getting established.

They also have good buildings, plenty of stock and implements. All that wanted to work succeeded well. They have good schools and churches, and the English language is generally spoken in the settlements.

The settlers in question have retained gratifying memories of Lady Gordon Cathcart, and she will be pleased to know that the people in whom she was personally interested now rank amongst our best settlers and are successful in every respect.

Your obedient servant,
J. OBED SMITH (Commissioner).

Another important movement was that directed by Sir J. Rankin, a former Member of Parliament. In the first four years of the working of his scheme [1] the return to him was 2 per cent on his capital outlay, but, of 120 persons whom he befriended, only about half a dozen families or thirty souls were still on their land in 1891. Sir J. Rankin complained somewhat bitterly of the treatment extended to him by certain of his followers. After having defrayed all expenses incidental to their journey to Canada, quite a number of them deserted him as soon as they reached a point where such labour as they could perform was in demand.[2]

In 1886 Cape Colony once more became the destination of a party of colonists. In this year twenty-four families were sent to the Wolseley settlement, situated about seventeen miles from King William's Town. The cost of this undertaking was borne by

---

[1] Vide *supra*, " Unassisted and Assisted Emigration," p. 75.
[2] Report on Colonisation, 1891, p. 48, VIII.

COLONISATION SCHEMES 239

Lady Ossington, while the management was placed in the hands of a capable committee guided by Mr. H. H. Baker. " Never in the history of colonisation," said Mr. Arnold White, a member of the committee, " did a body of settlers begin their new life under easier conditions or with more auspicious prospects." [1] The families were selected with much deliberation from a large number of applicants, all of whose characters were supported by testimonials pointing to a blameless, temperate, and industrious life. On arrival the people found many comforts awaiting them, for huts were built and furnished, implements were at hand and rations duly served. In spite of all these preparations, the settlement proved unsuccessful, and was closed within two and a half years from its inauguration.

To the issue of a monthly dole of rations may be attributed one of the chief, if not the principal, causes of this failure.[2] When these were provided there was no moral compulsion to work, and many men, knowing that their supplies did not depend on their energies, neglected their plots and spent the time in drinking and agitating. Some settlers arranged for kaffirs to manage their farms, so great had grown their distaste for work. On one occasion it was found that no less than a hundred coloured persons were employed in this way. It may be added that these Englishmen showed no apparent tendencies to idleness when they were examined prior to their departure ; the habits were, in fact, developed amidst the new surroundings. Another factor which assisted in the downfall of the settlement was brought about by a political move on the part of certain local newspapers. Knowing that under Cape rule an Englishman acquires the franchise after a year's residence,

---

[1] Arnold White, " Experiments in Colonisation," the *Contemporary Review*, November, 1890, p. 664.   [2] *Ibid.*, p. 665.

the representatives of these publications visited the settlers, and, in order to secure their political support, persuaded them that they were suffering all manner of hardships which their party alone could right for them. The discontent which was manufactured in this way was considerable. Yet another reason for failure grew out of the irresistible attraction which the Transvaal goldfields proved to some of the settlers. Thinking that life as an agriculturist was too slow and irksome, many of the Wolseley settlers quitted their houses in the middle of the night and fled across the frontier.

In June, 1888, twenty-five families, mostly from Hampshire, sailed from Southampton for the Tennyson settlement in the Stormberg district of South Africa. Extensive preparations were made for their reception, and precautions were taken to avoid, if possible, the evils which led to the downfall of the Wolseley colonists. The settlement, however, proved unsuccessful, for the chosen district was neither suited to agriculture nor were markets available for the disposal of produce. The members promised to refund the cost of their passage, rations, etc., together with 5 per cent on the capital expended; they also contracted to pay a nominal rent for their land. As had happened on so many previous occasions, the party soon became dissatisfied and broke up, ten tenants quitting their location within a year.[1]

Considerable importance attaches to the Crofters' Colonisation Scheme of 1888–9. In the former of these two years the Home Government advanced a sum of £10,000 towards emigrating certain Scotch agricultural workers, on condition that private sources should subscribe a further £2000, a sum which was speedily forthcoming. In the first season the fund

[1] Report on Agricultural Settlements, 1906, p. 45, and Arnold White in *Contemporary Review*, November, 1890, p. 670.

COLONISATION SCHEMES

was administered by the Scotch Office, but in 1889 a Colonisation Board was appointed to expend the moneys. This Board consisted of four Commissioners representing (1) the Imperial Government, (2) the Canadian Government, (3) the private subscribers, and (4) three important land companies, whose gratuitous co-operation and assistance were promised in planning the actual settlement. Family advances amounted to £100, but in some cases these were afterwards increased to £150, whilst repayment, with interest, was demanded in eight annual instalments,[1] the first of which fell due in the fifth year of residence. The Board hoped to secure this liability by holding a mortgage on the 160 acres of free grant land and also a chattel mortgage on the settlers' goods and household possessions.

On May 18th, 1888, the first batch of eighteen families sailed for the Killarney settlement in the Pelican Lake district of Southern Manitoba. These were followed on June 2nd by a further party of twelve families. All the settlers suffered some hardships on arrival, as the season was too far advanced for them to begin farming in earnest. Profiting by the experience gained in 1888, the second year's settlers, numbering forty-nine families, left home in good time, and were located on the Saltcoats settlement, two hundred miles to the north-west of the first settlers. The men, who were included among these three parties, had been previously occupied as crofters and cottars in Scotland,[2] but long periods of agricultural depression had robbed them of their chief means of subsistence. In every case where a crofter was removed the Government authorities stipulated that the land vacated by him should be handed over

---

[1] When the full grant was advanced, the annual repayment amounted to £20 17s. 8d.

[2] The first two parties were selected from Lewis and Harris, and the third from Stornaway, Harris, Barvas, and Uist.

to some neighbouring farmer, so that those who stayed at home might also benefit by the exodus. The Killarney settlers enjoyed some measure of success. Immediately on arriving they put up houses of a rough type, they did a little ploughing, and sowed small patches of ground. Afterwards they tramped to neighbouring farms and worked for hire, the men in this way earning an average of £6 and the women £3 per month.[1] When the spring came they turned to their own lands in earnest, and worked so industriously that the Government loans and the interest due upon them were quickly paid off. The Saltcoats settlers shaped somewhat differently.[2] On arrival it was decided to cast lots for the various sections, but though this method of distribution was generally approved at the outset, there were only twelve families who were willing to take the areas that fell to them. Even when the timber for their houses arrived, they refused to haul it the short distance which separated them from the railway siding. Temporary work on the railroad was offered them, but they turned from it, arguing that they had come to Canada as farmers, and not as unskilled labourers. Rather than do honest work, they wrote letters to the local papers in Scotland, and magnified their troubles, which were really those inseparable from a settler's life. In every respect the men were a failure, some left their lands almost as soon as they reached them, and only one remained to meet fully the obligations which were due to the Government.

Fifteen reports have been issued by the Commissioners appointed to carry out the Crofters' scheme of colonisation. The last report says :[3] " In the early

---

[1] Report on Colonisation, 1889, p. 8.

[2] No sufficient reason can be given for the difference of spirit displayed by the two parties. Probably a few discontented men spread their views amongst the party and so manufactured imaginary grievances.

[3] Crofter's Colonisation, issued August, 1906, Fifteenth Report, p. 3.

years of the settlement at Killarney, i.e. the migrators of 1888, the sums advanced were not repaid in accordance with the agreements entered into by the settlers. Difficulties occurred, arising from inexperience on the part of the crofters and their want of knowledge of agriculture and also of the climate of the country. Various other disturbing influences also tended to delay the satisfactory progress of the settlement. These difficulties, however, passed away and the settlers became more contented and prosperous. The instalments were paid with greater regularity, and it is now our duty to report that they have repaid the entire balance remaining to their debit of the sums originally advanced to them."

As to the Saltcoats settlement of 1889, which had been a failure from the first, the Commission reported that the vacated land was sold after much negotiation at a price sufficient to cover the indebtedness upon it, exclusive of interest.[1]

This final report of the 1888-9 Crofters' Colonisation recorded that a sum of £8611 had been repaid to the Exchequer, that the Commission then had possession of £2452, and that a balance of £5650 would soon be paid by the purchasers of the Saltcoats territory, making a total reimbursement of £16,713 as against the initial Government outlay of £13,120— a return which, from a financial though not a settlement point of view, may be regarded as satisfactory.

Another important attempt at colonisation was that made by two Canadian clergymen, Archdeacon Lloyd and the Rev. I. M. Barr. To these two organisers the Canadian Government granted a number of small plots of land adjoining which American and Canadian farmers were already settled. Nearly two thousand people from the United Kingdom went out under the ægis of the promoters in 1903; they were mostly townspeople in fair circumstances who were

---

[1] Crofters' Colonisation, issued August, 1906, Fifteenth Report, p. 3.

able to pay their own expenses.¹ The Canadian Government spared no pains nor expense in its efforts to promote the success of the colony; it prepared tents and a supply of hay and wood before the arrival of the colonists and, after they had reached their destination, made arrangements for their location on the homesteads, sent trained men to instruct them in the elements of farming, and lent oats and potatoes for seed.² Without doubt some of the settlers have done well and are thoroughly satisfied with their position, but, on the other hand, it must be recorded that only a quarter of the people were still on their land in 1905, and desertions have been continuous ever since. The Report on Agricultural Settlements³ says that the men were so ignorant of farm life that they ill-treated their live stock, with the consequence that much of it died. When this became known to the Canadian authorities, officials were despatched to instruct the settlers, but they quarrelled with these instructors, who soon left. Failure in the instance of the Barr scheme might have been avoided had a number of successful colonists, with a thorough practical knowledge of local conditions, been intermixed with the raw settlers, and secondly, had the colony been situated nearer the recognised lines of communication.

In 1906 a departmental committee, with the Right Hon. Lord Tennyson as chairman, sat to consider a colonisation scheme submitted to the Government by Sir H. Rider Haggard.⁴ The report which the committee afterwards issued summarised the general outlines of the scheme as follows:⁵

---

[1] The *Canadian Labour Gazette* states that they took with them over two million dollars in money.

[2] *Canadian Labour Gazette*, May, 1903, pp. 897-8. Also June, 1903, p. 1009; and February, 1904, p. 801.

[3] Page 5, and also page 283, Minutes of the Evidence.

[4] See p. 32.

[5] Report on Agricultural Settlements in British Colonies, p. 8, Cd. 2978.

COLONISATION SCHEMES 245

A large loan to be raised, the repayment being guaranteed by the Imperial Government, certain Colonial Governments possibly joining in the guarantee and the Municipal and Poor Laws Authorities in the large cities of Great Britain being asked to contribute. An Imperial officer to be appointed, known as the "Superintendent of Land Settlements" (perhaps assisted by a Board which would include the Agents-General of the Colonies and others) who would take charge of the funds and reside in England, but pay periodical visits to any colonies that might be established. The expense of his salary and office to be a charge upon the loan.

The Salvation Army, or other approved organisation, to undertake the selection of persons suitable—physically, mentally, and otherwise—in the cities of Great Britain: their conveyance to settlements to be established at places chosen within the borders of the British Empire: the building of their houses and barns, the advance of cash to them for the purchase of stock, seed, agricultural implements, and other necessaries: their instruction by trained persons in the arts of husbandry: the collection from them of the amounts due annually to satisfy the sums advanced and interest thereon: and their permanent care until everything was paid off, and they could be left masters of their business to pursue their own destinies free of debt.

No settlement to consist of less than one hundred families, in order that persons going from cities may have plenty of society.

The capital to be repaid by the settlers somewhat according to the lines laid down by the New Zealand Advances to Settlers Act, in annual instalments of £6 per cent, of which £5 would represent interest and expenses of management, and £1 sinking fund.

Unfortunately Sir Rider Haggard's scheme was open to so many objections that it could never be put into practice. In the first place it was suggested "That the poor law authorities in the large cities of Great Britain should be approached in order to ascertain whether they would be prepared to make a *per capita* contribution for every selected family of which the burden was taken off the rates."[1] As a matter of fact,

---

[1] Report on Agricultural Settlements in British Colonies, p. 14, § 422.

the Canadian Immigration Act of 1891 empowered the Governor-General to forbid the admission of pauper emigrants, which he did by proclamation in April, 1900. In spite of this enactment, it may be said that a certain number of paupers do find their way into the Dominion every year, but popular feeling would greatly resent their arrival in any such numbers as suggested by Sir Rider Haggard. The scheme also suggested that " the interest of a loan or loans should be guaranteed by the Imperial Government, or by the Imperial and certain Colonial Governments jointly." Canada is, however, quite unwilling to entertain such a scheme. It has only lent money once—to the Mennonites in 1876—and then its loan was secured by mortgages on valuable farm land.[1] Sir Rider Haggard also suggested that an official should be appointed by the Imperial Government, to be known as the Superintendent of Land Settlements. The appointment of any such officer would undoubtedly cause friction, sooner or later, between the Mother Country and the Dominion. Fourthly, Sir Rider Haggard's scheme deputed to the Salvation Army, or some other charitable or religious organisation, the work of managing the settlement. Not only did the Departmental Committee think that a religious body would be unsuitable for organising a settlement of this magnitude, but it felt that religious bodies of other denominations would have legitimate cause for complaint if the Salvation Army were selected to take over the scheme. Lastly, Sir Rider Haggard's scheme offered little or no security for the repayment of the loans. " Suppose," says the report, " that at the end of three or four months a settler were to obtain some more congenial occupation elsewhere—and evidence shows that townsmen, though placed on land in the colonies, have a tendency to gravitate towards the

---

[1] Report on Agricultural Settlements in British Colonies, p. 13, § 420.

COLONISATION SCHEMES

towns—or for any other reason were to abandon his holding, or to die, how could the money expended in sending him out and placing him on the land be recovered ? Sir Rider Haggard would say, ' By the sale of his holding.' But the answer to this reply is that his holding would only be the same as any other unimproved homestead block ; and, as they are to be had free, no one would pay money for this. The land laws of Canada would prevent the land being kept unoccupied indefinitely in the hope of selling it at an increased price as settlement advanced ; the money would therefore be lost."[1] For these and many minor reasons Sir Rider Haggard's colonisation plans failed to receive support.

To Sir Thomas Shaughnessy is due the most recent colonisation scheme with which we have to deal. On Canadian Pacific Railway land, fringing the Bow River near Calgary, farms have been planned, made, and irrigated. Settlers are now invited to take up homesteads on condition that they will repay all the expenses incurred on their behalf, in ten annual instalments. It is a stipulation that each settler shall be in possession of two hundred pounds on arriving, in order that he may have the means of tiding over the initial period of no returns. The people who have, so far, availed themselves of the offer are of a class much above the average ; they include amongst others, a veterinary surgeon, a coal merchant, two engineers, a Scotch gardener with a large family, a retired Indian Civil Servant, a first mate of the merchant service, a piano tuner, a Norfolk farmer, and a Cambridge M.A.[2] As the land is well irrigated, most of the colonists are attempting mixed and extensive farming ; they are not confining their attentions to grain but are making preparations for poultry and dairy farming, pig-raising, and market gardening. At

---

[1] Extract from p. 11 of the Report.
[2] Letter published in the *Daily News*, October 27th, 1910.

the time of writing the scheme is a little more than
three years old. Its issue is therefore as yet undecided.[1]

The chief colonisation settlements of the nineteenth
century have thus been located in Canada, South
Africa, Australia, New Zealand, and the United
States. As a land for colonising experiments, Canada
has obvious advantages. The sea journey is less than
three thousand miles in length, and the ocean fare is
cheaper than that to any other colony, Newfoundland
excepted. The population in the centres which are
now open to settlers is mainly of Anglo-Saxon origin,
so that the native question does not exist here as it
does in South Africa. The climate has no deteriorat-
ing influences, either on present or subsequent
generations of colonists, and the soil is usually of a
fertile nature. The long winter is, however, a drawback; outdoor work being hampered for five months
of the year.

South Africa, being farther from the Motherland
than Canada, has attracted fewer colonists, and here
the British-born are brought into contact with the
Dutch. The climate is extremely good and the soil
is capable of producing most of the products of Australia. The situation of the continent is such that
settlers cannot easily throw off their obligations and
escape from British rule, but it is open to them to
quit farming for one of the many forms of mining.
Cape Colony has few lands at present which it can
offer for colonisation purposes, but it has recently
appointed an irrigation inspector, under whose direction it is hoped that areas will soon be watered and
made available for settlement. The British South
Africa Company has suitable lands for disposal, and

---

[1] During the last two years, many schemes similar to that promoted
by Sir Thomas Shaughnessy have been planned. So far, none of them
have had time to emerge from the initial stages and are consequently
omitted from this description.

it is willing to give financial assistance to those undertaking extensive settlements.[1]

The question of colonisation in Australia is faced with various difficulties. The distance from the Mother Country is great, and much of the land is unsuited to the requirements of settlers. Mr. Arnold White, writing in the *Contemporary Review* on the subject of " Colonisation in Australia," says that the attitude of the labouring men of Australia to those of their own class at home is expressed by a resolute refusal to receive either Chinese or English if by so doing the assurance of their own comfortable lot is risked or impaired.[2] However this may be, the Agents-General in England are endeavouring, with much success, to attract farmers with capital, farm labourers, workers on cattle stations, female domestic servants, and certain kinds of mechanics.[3] New South Wales and Western Australia both offer assisted and nominated passages.[4] Victoria offers nominated passages and Queensland offers free passages.

New Zealand ranks high among the areas suitable for colonisation purposes. Its climate is like that of Great Britain, only warmer and more equable, while the periodic droughts to which the Australian states are subjected are unknown. Farming, including the keeping of live-stock, is the most important industry, but large supplies of fruit, wheat, oats, and wool are exported annually. New Zealand contains no immense undeveloped tracts of land as are to be found in Australia, Canada, Rhodesia, etc., but the land

---

[1] Report on Agricultural Settlements in British Colonies, p. 299.
[2] *Op. cit.*, p. 662, November, 1890.
[3] See the circulars on Australasia issued by the Emigrants' Information Office.
[4] Any person, domiciled in one of these states and having a friend who wishes to emigrate into the state, may submit his name to the immigration department of the colony. If considered a suitable emigrant the department provides him with a passage ticket at a specially low rate and collects payment from the nominator. This is called a nominated passage.

laws are such that small areas may be obtained at very low rates. Farms can be had on a 999 years' lease at a quit rent of 4 per cent on their cash value. Most of the unimproved land requires clearing, which is both expensive and laborious. The racial question presents no difficulty, and the great distance which separates the Dominion from the Mother Country is mitigated by the reduced passages which the former offers to certain classes of settlers.

It is generally admitted that where colonisation schemes are concerned, British enterprise should confine its endeavours to settlements situated within the King's dominions. On this account the United States is considered a less suitable destination for settlers from the Mother Country. In support of this contention, it has been stated that each inhabitant of Australia consumes £8 worth of British manufactures annually : the people of Cape Colony take £3 worth : £2 worth go to each person in British North America, but the people in the United States only require 9s. 7d. worth of our goods.[1] The Englishman proceeding to the United States thus becomes not only a numerical but a commercial loss as far as his native land is concerned.

A rough summary of the chief colonisation schemes which have been attempted during the last ninety-five years proves interesting. Of the sixteen cases recorded in this chapter, only four rank as successes, two, those of Robinson and Barr, may be classified as partial failures, whilst the suggestions of Sir Rider Haggard were not attempted, and the Shaughnessy scheme is still in its infancy. The British Government has financed five of these schemes ; the Canadian Government gave partial assistance in one instance, and all the others have depended on charity or the efforts of the individual settlers. The Home Govern-

---

[1] Arnold White's " Experiments in Colonisation," the *Contemporary Review*, November, 1890, p. 662.

COLONISATION SCHEMES

ment, it may be added, has only been associated with two successful ventures.

Of present-day colonisers, the British are undoubtedly in the foremost rank, yet, in spite of this enviable position, the colonisation schemes which we have just detailed are little more than a long succession of failures. This situation results from a multitude of causes. First, we may point out that the schemes have usually been devised to help people who could not help themselves. Now the successful coloniser is a man who needs unbounded resource, his isolated life makes it imperative that he should have initiative and be independent. To attempt to make a man of this stamp from a man who needs the assistance of a colonisation scheme is certainly a dangerous undertaking. It is argued, with a good deal of truth, that fresh surroundings, a healthier climate, and the thought of standing on the threshold of a new existence may endow a man with whatever qualities he needs in order to make a successful coloniser. Certainly, at times, the altered conditions do effect this reclaiming process, but they are far more likely to influence the emigrant than the coloniser. Secondly, we may affirm that colonisation schemes in the past have been too often planned for people who had degenerated to such an extent that they were unable to profit by a fresh start in life. Peter Robinson's followers, we know, had suffered all manner of deprivations before he took them to Canada; whilst Lady Gordon Cathcart's tenants were in a similar plight when they were shipped to America. Had they been settled on their respective locations before degeneracy of character had overtaken them, the issue would probably have been of a less unsatisfactory nature. Yet another reason for the want of success in these undertakings results from an attempt at pressing townsmen into colonisation schemes. The average urban dweller is totally unsuited to a settler's life, as was clearly demonstrated in the case of the Barr colonists. These people, it will be remembered, were quite unable to undertake the most common agricultural functions.[1] They knew nothing of farming, they watched their cattle die, and the disgust which they evinced at their own failure was so intense that they refused to accept professional advice. Some good could naturally be effected by judiciously intermixing pace-setters with the raw colonists, but this plan is expensive, and has, so far, proved unsuccessful from the moment the instructors left their posts. Training farms in both the home country and the colony would naturally fill a useful purpose if every prospective settler were required to serve an apprenticeship in one or other of them, but they are costly and add considerably to the expense of colonisation.

Many schemes owe their want of success to the position of the land chosen for the colony. In order that colonists shall not gravitate to the towns, it is usually agreed that a location should be situated at some considerable distance from the nearest urban centre, but at the same time a railway is needed, in order that produce may be sent to market. The close proximity of an important constructional undertaking, such as the building of a railroad or the cutting of a canal, is sometimes beneficial, in that it gives the colonists an opportunity of filling in their spare time profitably.

Great objections have frequently been raised to the massing together of many inexperienced settlers, but it seems impossible to carry out any scheme of magnitude without groups of this nature. It has often been suggested that fresh people should be placed on the land in well-settled districts among other farmers from whom they could learn the ways of the country. But the land sandwiched between improved farms in

---

[1] Report on Agricultural Settlements in British Colonies, p. 16, § 449.

COLONISATION SCHEMES

this manner commands an enhanced price, and is therefore out of the reach of colonisation schemes. Even were such scattered plots available for distribution, the cost of handling the settlers, of taking them and their goods to the location and of inspecting them, would be so great as to be prohibitive.

A certain number of failures have been due to the amount of assistance which has been provided for the settlers. In some instances the quantity has been excessive, as was the case with the Wolseley party, but more often the proffered help has proved inadequate. Additional sums were necessary to finance the followers of Lieutenant-Colonel Cockburn in 1816, the Grahamstown party in 1819, Lady Gordon Cathcart's tenants in 1883, and the Saltcoats crofters in more recent times. Some assistance must naturally be at hand to carry the settler over the unproductive period, but this should cease directly the productive stage is reached. Not only is financial help required, but experience seems to suggest that every man should have a small plot of land broken and sown for him before his arrival. In this way a crop will be available during the first season, and he will therefore have enough grain to take him through the winter period.

Mr. J. G. Colmer, C.M.G., who for twenty-three years was secretary to the High Commissioner of Canada, claims that successful colonisation depends on a proper observance of the following rules : [1]

(1) The families should be properly related, no parents above fifty years of age, and no additions of friends to a family, who only leave it, and leave it burdened with the cost of their passage.

(2) Greater care must be taken as to the clothing: the families should be made to provide enough for themselves before starting.

(3) The land should be selected beforehand for the people:

---

[1] Report on Colonisation, 1891, p. 49.

some of the land broken up for them the previous June, which would enable them to raise crops their first season : and a house might be erected, or partially erected for them.

(4) This, however, would necessitate that, as a condition of the money being lent, the people should undertake to settle upon the land allotted to them.

(5) On the other hand, the settlers should be allowed to choose their own stock and implements after arrival, subject to the agent being there to see that they were not cheated, otherwise, if anything goes wrong with what has been bought for them, they throw the responsibility on the agent.

(6) That instead of doling out provisions, a definite sum should be placed to the settler's credit with the storekeeper. If they know their supplies are thus limited it creates a spirit of independence, and they are more likely to go and work.

(7) Not more than forty or fifty families should be settled in one district, as it will get them mixed up with other people : and one good agent might do for two or three such groups.

(8) There is not work to be had in every district, and an attempt should be made to settle them where work is to be found, as near railway works.

From the foregoing it may be concluded that colonisation schemes are no longer of use where waste humanity is concerned. The general trend indicates, with ample certainty, that the schemes of the future will be confined to assisting the lower elements of the middle classes, elements which suffer silently and keenly from the increasing competition of commerce and industry.

CHAPTER XI

THE EMIGRATION OF WOMEN

OF women emigrants there may be said to exist two well-defined classes. The first embraces those who journey to the new country in company with their husbands, fathers or brothers, whilst the second consists of such as proceed individually from the Motherland. No special arrangements beyond those made for emigrants in general are required by the members of the former class, as their male escorts furnish them with whatever protection is necessary on the voyage and during the period of early settlement. Women of the latter class, however, are very differently situated. They require constant protection both throughout the journey and until they have found friends and occupation in their adopted country. In order that such help and guidance may be provided for this latter section, many benevolent agencies have come into existence during the last sixty years.

The first of these institutions, of which we have any record, was the London Female Emigration Society. This organisation commenced work in the spring of 1850, when eighteen women were conducted to Toronto under its ægis.[1] The initial party, consisting of working-class Londoners, sailed on board the *Elspeth*, and was received at its destination by a specially formed committee of gentlewomen. The expenses incidental to the passage, it may be said, were defrayed by the Society. The party, though small, gave much satisfaction, for all the members speedily found work,

---

[1] Accounts and Papers, Vol. XL, 1851, p. 316.

and prospered more than would have been possible had the Metropolis continued to claim their services. Encouraged by this success, the institution sent many subsequent batches of women to various points in Canada.

Closely allied to the work of these benevolent agencies were the arrangements made by certain poor-law unions in Ireland. During the early fifties many of these bodies found that they were suffering from a plethora of female paupers, a condition which they ascribed to the previous emigration of a large section of the male population. Accordingly a number of unions decided to use the powers given them by the Poor Law Relief Act of 1847 and the Further Amending Act of 1849, which allowed them to spend money on emigrating necessitous poor. With funds so obtained many parties of women, each totalling over a hundred souls, were conducted to Canada. The arrangements gave much satisfaction; paid servants of the Guardians escorted the emigrants to the port of embarkation, matrons were appointed to watch over the needs of these travellers during the passage, and Canadian immigration agents took charge of them from the moment of landing.[1] No difficulty seems to have been experienced in speedily finding employment, as domestic servants and farm helps, for all who were despatched, a matter which encouraged the unions to continue in their efforts for some years.

In this work of accelerating the stream of women emigrants the local authorities were supported by the Colonial Land and Emigration Commissioners. In 1856 this body wrote:[2] "Obvious as it is, it is not always kept in mind that for the permanent growth of a colonial population every single man who is sent out in excess of the number of single women is abso-

---

[1] Accounts and Papers, Vol. LXVIII, 1852-3, p. 479.
[2] In the Annual Report of 1856, Vol. XXIV.

THE EMIGRATION OF WOMEN 257

lutely useless. He is a mere sojourner, furnishing a temporary convenience to his employers and increasing the annual produce of the colony while he lives, but leaving nothing to replace him when he dies." Holding this view, and recognising that men emigrated readily enough of their own accord whilst individual women had few opportunities of joining in the exodus, the Commissioners, for a number of years, made a practice of sending to the Colonies two females for every male who received assistance from them.

In 1859 a further step was made towards providing comforts for women emigrants. In this year the British Ladies Emigration Society was formed with the object of maintaining a staff of matrons whose duty it was to travel to America and Australia on board ships not already provided with stewardesses. They only sailed on vessels, it may be added, which counted unmarried women and girls among their passengers.[1] In 1861 the Female Middle Class Emigration Society was formed by Miss Rye and Miss Jane Lewis, and was the means of transporting many gentlewomen needing remunerative employment to the various correspondents of the Society in the Colonies.

Amongst the many charitably disposed people who expended time and money in befriending the penniless female emigrant must be mentioned Mr. Vere Foster. Travelling through the distressed areas of Ireland in the seventies, he gave assistance to an aggregate of no less than fifteen thousand women. With private funds he provided these people with outfits, he bought them passage tickets, and despatched them to various destinations in North America, chiefly, however, to stations in the United States. The men who partook of his assistance were few, for he contended that they seldom suffered as acutely as their women-

---

[1] Colonial Land and Emigration Commissioners' Report, 1859, p. 15.

folk. Though most of the people whom he assisted were single, and had no one to depend on them, and though success came to most as a result of their efforts, it is disappointing to note that not a single penny was repaid to Mr. Foster by these women although each signed a statement to the effect that they would return a certain fraction of the loan when their savings permitted such a course.[1]

In the early eighties the subject of women's emigration began to attract more systematic attention than had hitherto been the case. Until the year 1880 assistance, as far as women and girls were concerned, had been provided spasmodically, and depended more on the enterprise of individuals than on regular organisations. At this time, however, a number of institutions came into being, notably the Women's Emigration Society, and its offshoot the Colonial Emigration Society. Of existing organisations situated within the Motherland, probably none have rendered greater services than the British Women's Emigration Association. Established in 1884 by Miss Louisa M. Hubbard, under the title of the United English Women's Emigration Association, this Society has gradually extended its operations, until to-day it is supported in the United Kingdom by a band of no less than one hundred and sixty-three workers, whilst its expenditure for the year 1910 almost reached fourteen thousand pounds. The Society pledges itself (*a*) to emigrate only such women and girls as are of good capacity and character, (*b*) to select only such men and families as are suited to the requirements of the Colony receiving them, (*c*) to secure for these people proper protection on the voyage and adequate reception on arrival, (*d*) to keep, as far as possible, in friendly touch with these people, and (*e*) to raise a loan fund for necessitous cases.

---

[1] Report on Colonisation,, 1890, p. 211.

THE EMIGRATION OF WOMEN 259

During the year 1910 this Association emigrated a total of 1057 people, of whom 878 were of English origin, 34 were Irish, 76 were Scotch, and 9 were Welsh. The destinations of these emigrants were as follows : to Canada 927, to New Zealand 92, to New South Wales 4, to Western Australia 3, to Queensland 4, to South Australia 3, to Victoria 1, and to the United States 23. Of the nine hundred odd assisted emigrants received by Canada twenty-two were men.[1]

More important than the actual volume of emigration is the status of the people forming part of this exodus. The Association reported that their emigrants sailing for Canada during the year 1910 were composed as follows : 50 industrial workers, 12 dressmakers and milliners, 145 servants, 74 middle-class women, mostly in business, 26 widows and children accompanying them, 2 laundresses, 52 wives, with children, going to their husbands, 18 escorts going to be married, 175 escorts going to friends, 53 escorts going to situations, 3 married couples (6 souls), 6 families (46 souls), 9 individual men, 20 children going to parents, 1 tailoress, 10 nurses, 24 teachers, 60 educated women, and 144 members of the Girls' Friendly Society. From this data it will be seen that the association befriends not only the servant girl and the factory hand, but also the distressed gentlewoman as well as the middle-class worker in search of a wider sphere of labour.

As a contrast to the lamentable way in which Mr. Vere Foster's female emigrants neglected to repay the loans which he advanced to them, it is pleasing to note the figures governing the Loan Fund organised by the British Women's Emigration Association. In 1906 this Society reported that its loans between the years 1900 and 1904 had amounted to £1452 12s. 10d.,

---

[1] British Women's Emigration Association Report, 1910, pp. 16–17.

whilst the repayments between 1901 and 1905 stood at £1047 16s. 2d.[1] Thus over 72 per cent of the borrowed money was repaid promptly. In 1908 the advances were £286, and all but £16 was repaid within four years. In 1909 a sum of £389 was loaned, and £251 returned within three years. In 1910 £1288 was lent, and within the space of a few months the repayments amounted to £550.[2] Probably no emigration loan fund can show a better record than this.

Prior to departing the women and girls who receive financial assistance from the British Women's Emigration Association are required to put their signatures to a loan-bond, which they are expected to re-sign on arriving in the Dominion.[3] With this doubly signed document the Association can enforce repayment, should occasion arise, in either the home or Canadian courts. The money lent to these emigrants goes to pay for the ocean passage, the inland rail ticket, and the food necessary for the inland journey; the sum therefore varies according to the destination of the individual. Clothes towards the necessary outfit are provided gratuitously when required. Honorary collectors in the Colonies gather in the repayments, and the Association reports that the return of the loans depends largely on the vigour of these officers.[4] Fifteen shillings a month is the average return per individual, though many pay more and a few less than this amount. Typical cases receiving assistance from this source are mentioned in the Society's Annual Report. Amongst others they include (a) a widow with two sons, who journeyed to Mimico, in Ontario, to open a boarding-house; (b) two girls, one a machinist, the other a mill-hand from Rochdale, both

---

[1] Report on Agricultural Settlements in British Colonies, 1906, p. 296.
[2] British Women's Emigration Association Report, 1910, p. 24.
[3] Report on Agricultural Settlements in British Colonies, 1906, p. 84. [4] *Ibid.*, p. 80.

of whom required lifting out of their miserable home conditions; and (c) a young French shop-assistant who wanted to join friends in British Columbia.

The machinery employed by this Association for selecting and placing women emigrants may be put forward as exemplary. Throughout the United Kingdom is scattered a staff of honorary workers, each of whose duty it is to examine and report upon every woman who desires to emigrate from her locality. This ordeal being complete, the case is referred to head-quarters, where it is again carefully considered. Proving suitable, the candidate prepares herself for the journey; should she be in want, clothes are provided gratuitously and part of the cost of the passage lent her; should, however, she be able to afford a short course of training, she is recommended to proceed to the Stoke Prior Colonial Training College for Educated Women, where a three months' stay does much towards making her an efficient "Home-Help." The day previous to sailing the prospective emigrant proceeds to the Wortley Hostel in London, or its sister counterpart in Liverpool, and there in company with those who are shortly to become her travelling companions spends her last evening in England. Throughout the journey matrons accompany the parties. The Honourable Mrs. Joyce, the honorary president of the society, says: "We take a compartment in the ship, or as near an approach to a compartment as the particular arrangements of the ship will permit. The matrons are with the girls throughout the day and throughout the night, and they have their written orders. Every woman is consigned to some particular place, and the matron has a book in which that consignment is entered; the women are received by the secretaries at Montreal, Toronto, Winnipeg, Regina, Calgary, Vancouver, or at whatever particular place we consign them to. One matron travels to the west coast, whilst another goes to the Province of Ontario. We provide them with their food on the railway, they making a contribution of half a crown a day." [1] Canadian secretaries, it must be mentioned, are stationed throughout the length of the Dominion, and upon these devolves the task of securing employment for the women on their arrival. For many years the Society was periodically informed by the Canadian Manufacturers' Association of cases coming to its knowledge where female factory labour was needed, and many girls obtained situations through the medium of these intimations. Since the Dominion requires all factory hands arriving during the winter months to be in possession of the sum of ten pounds, the British Women's Emigration Association states that its work in assisting this type of emigrant is now seriously and needlessly curtailed. Needlessly, it may be argued, because by this regulation the Dominion hampers the entry of a class of woman of which it stands in pressing need.

The British Women's Emigration Association is not alone in its efforts to promote the interests of female emigrants. Other British societies which are devoted to assisting women and girls are (a) The Girls' Friendly Society, (b) The Travellers' Aid Society for Girls and Women, (c) The Aberdeen Union of Women Workers, (d) The Scottish Colonisation Society, (e) The Salisbury Diocesan Ladies' Association for the Care of Friendless Girls, whilst the Country and Colonial Training School for Ladies, at Arlesley House, near Hitchin, the Stoke Prior Colonial Training College, near Bromsgrove, and the Women's Horticultural College, Swanley, train women of the middle classes who are contemplating a practical career in one or other of the overseas possessions.

Within the Dominion a vast network of agencies has also sprung into being. The National Council of

---

[1] Report on Agricultural Settlements in British Colonies, 1906, p. 80.

THE EMIGRATION OF WOMEN 263

Women of Canada has no less than twenty-one branch immigration committees scattered throughout the most populated areas of British North America; the Young Women's Christian Association of Canada has twenty-five bureaux where it boards, lodges and finds employment for female immigrants; the Girls' Friendly Society of Canada, a branch of the parent society in England, has twenty-two local secretaries, whilst the Girls' Home of Welcome, Winnipeg, the Women's Hostel, Calgary, and the Women's Hostel, Toronto, are homes of rest for women travellers. Each of these institutions, it may be said, receives an annual subvention from the Dominion and Provincial Departments. Another organisation receiving Government assistance is The Women's National Immigration Society of Montreal. Established twenty-nine years ago, this Society has rendered valuable assistance in protecting and providing for women as they arrive from the United Kingdom. Among the rules framed by this institution we note that " All women and children landing for the first time in Canada are entitled to twenty-four hours' full board and lodging, after which a charge of 50 cents a day or 3 dollars a week is made." During the year 1910, 736 people passed through the home, 524 of their number being English, 114 Scotch, 74 Irish, 7 Welsh, and 17 of various other nationalities. Towards the maintenance of these visitors the Dominion Government voted a grant of $1500, whilst the Provincial Government of Quebec provided an additional $500. Private donations amounted to $365.[1]

From the foregoing it will be seen that a complex organisation has gradually become evolved, having for its object the promotion, the protection and the employment of female emigrants. Thanks to the various institutions labouring in this sphere, women

---

[1] Annual Report of the Society, 1911, pp. 7–11 and 13.

desirous of joining in the exodus to Canada may now receive adequate protection and suitable companionship during the journey, the provision of an escort on landing in the Dominion, the offer of employment with people of reputable character, whilst loans are freely tendered to such as require financial assistance, and respectable and economical housing is available for those who are awaiting situations.

Of assisted women and girls who cross the Atlantic in search of work, by far the greater number become domestic servants.[1] This statement is borne out by the testimony of all the most influential aid societies in Canada, as well as the British Women's Emigration Association in England.[2] So great is the demand for this type of worker that the Canadian housewives frequently forward sufficient money for a girl's passage to one of the better known emigrant societies in England, with the request that a suitable servant be sent out to them. Other housewives entrust the passage money to lady organisers, who come to England and personally choose as many domestics as they require. Mrs. Helen Sanford, a worker connected with the Girls' Home of Welcome at Winnipeg, has been provided with as much as a thousand pounds in a single year for advanced passages. *The Standard of Empire,* in its issue of June 9th, 1911, stated that a party of two hundred British domestic servants arrived at Winnipeg during the week ending June 2nd, and all of them were placed in the district west of the city in a single forenoon; such is the demand for domestic labour.

Another type of female worker who is recruited largely from the ranks of the British emigrant is the " home-help." This term signifies a thoroughly

---

[1] For the twelve months ending June 30th, 1904, 1905, 1906, and 1907, the number of domestic servants arriving in Canada from the British Isles was 2523, 3889, 4467 and 5245 respectively.

[2] Information communicated privately by the various secretaries.

domesticated woman who is a capable and careful housemaid, willing to do her best at the washtub, the mangle, and the ironing-board, also able to make and bake bread and cook the three more or less simple meals of the daily fare.[1] The work of a home-help is perhaps a little arduous and requiring of resource, but it has many compensations. A girl who fills such a post is treated much as one of the family ; she sits at the same table for meals as the master and mistress, and joins in the social activities which attract them. There is always a large demand for such workers, as their ranks are constantly being thinned by those who leave to be married.

The wages obtained by female domestic servants are stated by the Emigrants' Information Office[2] to average from ten to twelve dollars per month in Prince Edward Island ; ten to fifteen dollars in Nova Scotia, New Brunswick, Quebec, and Ontario; fifteen to twenty-five dollars in Manitoba and the North-West, and fifteen to thirty dollars upwards in British Columbia. Cooks' wages are at least two or three dollars a month higher than those of general servants, and in some towns in the North-West they rise as high as twenty to twenty-five dollars. In British Columbia, where personal service is scarce, cooks receive from twenty to thirty dollars a month in private families, and as much as forty dollars upwards in boarding-houses and hotels. The wages of home-helps are everywhere slightly less than those of domestic servants. Farm-helps who are expected to work not only upon the land but also to give assistance indoors, receive five to ten dollars a month in the Eastern Provinces, seven to twelve dollars in Manitoba and the North-West, and from twelve to eighteen dollars in British Columbia. The official

---

[1] Georgina Binnie-Clark in *The Quiver*.
[2] See circular on the Emigration of Women, published by the Emigrants' Information Office.

returns [1] for 1908 state the average wage of female farm-helps to be 130 dollars per annum throughout the Dominion. The lowest rate is found in Prince Edward Island, where it stands at eighty-six dollars; the highest is in British Columbia, the average rate of pay for such labour in this province being 180 dollars. In every case mentioned above, board and lodgings are provided in addition to the wages stated.

Milliners and dressmakers are in demand in most of the larger centres. Needle-women in Ontario earn six dollars and upwards a week; in New Brunswick tailoresses receive one and a quarter dollars a day, and dressmakers from two and a half to seven dollars per dress. In Winnipeg tailoresses, milliners, and dressmakers average a dollar per day; at Edmonton, Alberta, their pay is twenty dollars per month with board; in British Columbia, where the demand for such workers is far in excess of the supply, dressmakers go to work in private houses, and receive from one to two dollars per day, with food. The demand for female factory hands of all classes is gradually improving, but as the wages are low compared with those paid in other occupations and no board is provided, such service is often considered insufficiently attractive by the British emigrant.

The openings for better class women are shared between home-helps, nurses and teachers. Trained nurses are urgently needed in the North-West both for hospital and private practice, but especially for maternity work. Each province has its own regulations, but a nurse from the Mother Country must invariably obtain a permit from the district medical board before she can follow her occupation. Certificates granted in the United Kingdom are recognised after being endorsed by a medical man who can testify to the capabilities of the possessor. The Royal Victoria

---

[1] *Canada Year Book*, 1908, p. xxx.

THE EMIGRATION OF WOMEN 267

Order of Nurses, the headquarters of which are at Ottawa, has a system for the employment of qualified nurses in country districts.

The opportunities awaiting the immigrant teacher are more numerous. With a rapidly growing population, embracing a large proportion of children, it is little wonder that many areas within the Dominion are confronted with a dearth of instructors. In Saskatchewan it is on record that six hundred school districts were without staffs during 1909; which means that, while buildings existed and children were needing education, no classes were held in these particular neighbourhoods owing to the lack of teachers. Speaking in the Saskatchewan Cabinet recently, the Minister of Education said : " The lack of English-speaking teachers is the greatest question before the people of the province." [1] The speed with which educational establishments are increasing in number may be seen from the official figures here quoted. In 1905 Saskatchewan possessed 896 school districts, in which there were 887 public schools and nine "separate" schools.[2] Four years later, there were 1988 or more than twice as many school districts, whilst the public schools had increased to 1963, the " separate " schools to fourteen, and there was a new entry of eleven high schools. In Alberta equally rapid progress has been recorded. At the end of 1907 the school districts numbered 902; the following year they increased to 1070. The school population for 1908 was 50,000; in 1909 it grew to 60,000.[3] Little wonder then that Alberta alone can absorb an inflow of three to four hundred teachers each year, divided roughly in the proportion of two women to one man.

---

[1] *Canada To-day*, 1911, p. 60.
[2] A public school is the Canadian parallel of an English board or council school, and a " separate " school is what would be described under the English Education Act as a non-provided school.
[3] *Canada To-day*, 1911, p. 60.

The regulations which control the appointment of immigrant teachers with qualifications gained in the United Kingdom vary with each province. The Governments of Prince Edward Island, New Brunswick, Nova Scotia, and British Columbia possess their own normal colleges, and appoint none but those who have undergone a course of training in one or other of these institutions. In Ontario teachers from the Mother Country are granted provisional certificates, which they are expected subsequently to replace by those obtained within the province. In Manitoba, Saskatchewan, and Alberta the English instructor has greater opportunities, as his or her standing is regulated according to the qualifications obtained in the United Kingdom. The salaries paid to teachers in Canada depend largely on the particular district and the local cost of living. In Quebec and Ontario the pay varies from £65 to £105 per annum; in Manitoba the highest salary granted in rural schools is £160; in Saskatchewan and Alberta it ranges from £108 to £156 in rural districts, and in city, town, and village districts, from £120 to £144 for junior, and £144 to £300 for senior departments.[1] Other appointments at higher salaries than those mentioned here are occasionally made, but they are few and unimportant from an immigrant's point of view.

The positive and negative value of emigration in general will be discussed at length in a later chapter; here it is merely proposed to speak of the conditions as they particularly affect women. Primarily, the benefits which accrue from a female exodus spring from the disparity in numbers of the sexes which exists both at home and in the overseas dominions. The latest census returns for England and Wales state

---

[1] Official Circular, "Information for British Teachers Regarding School-work in Canada." Issued by the British Women's Emigration Association.

THE EMIGRATION OF WOMEN 269

that the males number 17,448,476 and the females 18,626,793; the balance in favour of the latter class is thus 1,178,317. On the other hand, the latest figures for Canada show that the males are in the majority, totalling 2,751,708, as against 2,619,607 females.[1] From these figures we may conclude that an exodus of women from the home country is attended with beneficial results, as its tendency is to equalise the sexes both in the country of departure and that of arrival. An inflow of women into the land of reception where men predominate must eventually mean an increased marriage rate, probably followed by an increased birth rate. The population will therefore rise and the settlement of the country proceed at a speedier rate than would otherwise be the case.

As to the results which attend the efforts of the women who emigrate to Canada, there is ample evidence to prove that as a body they prosper and lead contented lives. Unemployment, as far as they are concerned, is practically non-existing, whilst class distinctions, being less marked, allow women to rise to the level for which their capacities most fit them. In the home country many consider it degrading to turn their hands to remunerative work, and distress often overtakes them as a result of this notion. No such evil effects arise, however, in the Dominion, for the conditions of life are so arranged that the woman who shuns work is not tolerated. It must not be forgotten also that the high marriage rate of women acts as a constant drain on the supplies of female labour, with the consequence that the demand is always considerable.

On comparing the wages commanded by female labour at home with those obtained in the Dominion, the advantages of emigration become less evident. If the case of women school-teachers be taken, it will

---

[1] Figures of 1901, Census, quoted from *Canada Year Book*.

be found that only the lowest grades of the profession earn less than £50 per annum in England, yet the average yearly wage of all schoolmistresses in Canada works out at $246·76, or £51 4s.[1] After making some deduction for the increased cost of living, it will be seen that Canadian teachers are by no means well paid. Unfortunately these remarks apply with certain modifications to other fields of labour; the female factory worker's earnings average just under £39 a year; the female agricultural worker obtains less than £30,[2] but usually her board is found, and must therefore be added to this sum, whilst milliners, tailoresses and dressmakers earn approximately the same as in England, though almost every article they buy, other than food-stuffs, is more expensive. The domestic servant is, comparatively speaking, the best-paid woman worker in Canada. Her wages average $137·5 a year, whilst few of this class earn less than £2 per month. Undoubtedly, the remuneration given for such work as she performs is higher in the Dominion than in the Motherland, but the task allotted to her is both harder and more exacting. The facility with which these domestic workers obtain colonial husbands and resign their employment is, of course, an attractive feature of the service which must not be overlooked. Before concluding these remarks it may be well to point out that being a new country Canada offers opportunities for personal advancement such as are unknown in the homeland; it is, therefore, somewhat misleading to compare salary averages in the two countries without making due allowance for the greater chances of progression which await the worker in the Dominion.

It will be noted that little or no mention has been made in this chapter of the women who set out for

---

[1] *Canada Year Book*, 1908, p. 160, Table LXXIII.
[2] *Canada Year Book*, p. 159. Table LXX.

THE EMIGRATION OF WOMEN

the United States. This arises from the fact that practically the whole of the arrangements which have been made for the protection of individual women and girls encourages them to proceed to a British colony as opposed to a foreign state. Those who do select the United States as their destination are usually accompanied and protected by relations or intimate friends, and therefore require no special organisation to safeguard their welfare.

CHAPTER XII

THE EMIGRATION OF CHILDREN

DURING the early years of the nineteenth century it was a common practice among overseers of the poor to apprentice their juvenile charges to mill-owners and other employers of factory labour. The system was one that gave much satisfaction, first to the parish authorities, as it cleared the unions of boys and girls who would otherwise need the support of the rates; and second to the manufacturers, as it enabled them to obtain labour in the cheapest possible manner. The practice, however, was one that imposed terrible hardships on the children; their working hours were long, they received no wages, they were fed and clothed improperly, they slept in relays, in filthy beds, and some, who attempted to run away, were fettered with chains. As a result of these disgraceful conditions an Act was passed in 1802 " for the preservation of the health and morals of apprentices and others employed in cotton and other mills." Though this early enactment proved a step in the right direction, we know that the iniquitous system continued for many years in a more or less modified form. In 1811 a committee sat to consider the position of the parish apprentice, and the report, which was published subsequently, gave a most distressing account of his treatment at the hands of factory superintendents.[1] A second committee sat in 1815, and, on the recommendations of this body, an Act was legalised which

---

[1] Refer to this report; Report on Parish Apprentices, 1811, for fuller account of the situation given here.

THE EMIGRATION OF CHILDREN

forbade the directors of the poor to send union children a distance of more than fifty miles from their parish.[1]

From these statements it is evident that from 1815 onwards the overseers were debarred in a large measure from driving the boys and girls under their charge into the factories. As this profitable channel of employment was closed to them, they cast about for other means of ridding themselves of their youthful burdens. The means they eventually adopted were those provided by a recourse to emigration.

Not only was the workhouse child forced to become an unwilling emigrant, but many other children were sent out of the country as well. We must remember that at this period the population of the three kingdoms was increasing rapidly; as a consequence there was much unemployment among children, and juvenile crime grew by leaps and bounds. In the House of Correction at Brixton Hill there were 60 youthful prisoners in 1820, but 541 in 1825, whilst in the prison at Cold Bath Fields the figures relating to the same period rose from 1129 to 1599.[2] Instead of adopting educational and disciplinary measures to overcome this wave of unemployment and crime, the authorities conceived the plan of shipping across the Atlantic as many boys and girls as they could persuade to go. Mr. R. J. Chambers, a Metropolitan police magistrate, expressed an opinion, which was then general. " I conceive," he said, " that London has become too full of children. There has been a great increase of juvenile offences, which I attribute to want of employment for people between the ages of twelve and twenty. I therefore suggest emigration as a remedy."[3]

Emigration certainly was a remedy in so far as it

---

[1] 56 Geo. 3, c. 139.
[2] Report on Emigration from the United Kingdom, 1826, pp. 83, 91.
[3] *Ibid.*

lightened the work of magistrates or lessened the expenses of parish directors; it was little or no remedy, however, as far as the children themselves were concerned. Taken from their squalid homes, they were herded together in insanitary ships and subjected to the tyranny of sea-captains for some five to twelve weeks. On landing their condition was such that many of them died, whilst others required hospital treatment before they could take up work. Altogether the system reflected the greatest discredit on those who allowed it to proceed.

For many years the directors of the poor continued with this inhuman business, but were careful to cloak their operations, firstly because they were none too proud of them, and secondly because, had it become generally known that they were sending children out of the country, they might have been overwhelmed by inhuman parents, who would have been glad to disembarrass themselves of their own offspring at the expense of the country.

Children were first openly emigrated in 1830. In this year the "Society for the Suppression of Juvenile Vagrancy"[1] was established, having for its object the promotion of emigration among destitute but non-criminal children. The Society gathered together a number of youthful vagrants, and gave them short periods of training in their two homes, the Brenton Juvenile Asylum at Hackney, and the Royal Victoria Asylum at Chiswick; the former for boys and the latter for girls. All children sent to the Colonies by this body were bound in apprenticeship to respectable persons, and carefully watched over. The Cape was the colony almost exclusively selected at first, but the " luxurious habits " of the colonists and the large " admixture of races " appeared to the Society less favourable to the moral well-being of their protégés than the hardier life and simpler habits of the farmers

---
[1] Subsequently called the Children's Friendly Society.

THE EMIGRATION OF CHILDREN 275

of Canada, and accordingly destinations in British North America were, after a short time, more generally selected.[1]

The next to receive emigration assistance were orphan girls, 4175 in number, selected from 118 Irish unions, and forwarded to New South Wales and South Australia in 1848-50. These girls, it may be said, were also given adequate protection. The Unions provided outfits costing £5 per head, and paid rail and steamer fares to Plymouth, whilst the Colonial Land and Emigration Commissioners defrayed all other expenses with money derived from land sales in Australia. On arrival at their destination agents met them and found them suitable occupations.[2]

Though by no means the pioneers of organised juvenile emigration, the London Ragged Schools were the first to send out children in large parties. In 1848 this body began by sending out 150 boys and girls to Australia,[3] a somewhat similar number proceeding each year until the early sixties. The children, for the most part, were recruited from the reformatory schools of the country, and proceeded, as a rule, to South Australia and New South Wales; their fares were paid by the Colonial Land and Emigration Commissioners.

During what may be termed the second period of juvenile emigration, that is to say, between 1848 and 1869, the colonial authorities seem to have been most anxious to welcome children from the United Kingdom. Appeals from various legislative bodies in both Australia and North America were constantly received in the Mother Country,[4] but though the

---
[1] E. M. Hance, *Reformatories and Industrial Schools*, p. 9.
[2] Report on Colonisation, 1890, p. 351.
[3] Tenth Report on the Operation of the Poor Law in Ireland, Vol. XVI, 1849.
[4] Land and Emigration Commissioners Report, Vol. XL, 1852-3, p. 47.

Boards of Guardians would have gladly shipped off numbers of their apprentices, the central authorities viewed child emigration with disfavour and discouraged it in every possible way. Many unions, however, were so eager to rid themselves of those placed under their care that they either wilfully or negligently acted contrary to the legislation formulated for their guidance. The Directors of the St. Pancras Union, for instance, sent three and probably more parties of children to Bermuda in the years 1850 and 1851, in direct contravention of 4 and 5 Will. 4, c. 76, sec. 62, and 7 and 8 Vict. c. 101, sec. 29, statutes which only permitted emigration after the sanction of the Poor Law Board had been obtained.[1] As many of the boys and girls who formed these parties were under sixteen years of age, it is clear that the guardians also violated 13 and 14 Vict. c. 101, sec. 4, which required that orphans, deserted children, and others deprived of parental care, when giving their consent to being emigrated, should do so in petty sessions before two Justices of the Peace. The Poor Law Board discovered the illegal practices of the St. Pancras Guardians, and only allowed them to be passed over after finding on enquiry that the particular children in question had not suffered through their transference to Bermuda.

The accompanying extract from the *Morning Chronicle*, dated January 18th, 1851, is interesting in that it throws much light on the methods at one time employed for clearing the home country of its friendless children. This extract seems to imply that various London Boards of Guardians made it a practice of contracting with certain unscrupulous sea-captains for the removal, to nowhere in particular, of the girls and boys who had become chargeable to the rates. It will be seen that the few shillings which the

---

[1] Accounts and Papers, Vol. XL, 1851, pp. 19, 20.

THE EMIGRATION OF CHILDREN

Guardians paid per head were quite insufficient to defray the passage; the inference, therefore, is that the captains found a profitable overseas market for their charges. They carried on, in fact, a species of slave trade.

MARYLEBONE BOARD OF GUARDIANS

At the weekly meeting of the Guardians yesterday, Mr. Mechie in the Chair, and after the disposal of the usual routine business, Captain Burrows, of the brig *James*, sent in a written application for boys and girls from the workhouse, to be conveyed by him to Bermuda as emigrants.

The following questions were put to the captain:—

Question.—What must be the ages of the children?

Answer.—Between twelve and fourteen.

Q.—What do you do with them when you get them to Bermuda?

A.—I apprentice them as domestic servants until they are eighteen.

Q.—On what conditions do you take them?

A.—I charge six shillings passage money, for which I find them bed, bedding, and board. The parish provides their outfit.

Q.—After they serve their apprenticeship what becomes of them?

A.—Why, they get other situations.

Q.—Are there any funds to assist them in getting situations or returning home, if they desire it, after their apprenticeship?

A.—No, sir. I have taken out sixty children from St. Pancras Workhouse.

Q.—Are they steerage passengers?

A.—No, I put them in the cabin.

Q.—Have you a female to attend them on board?

A.—The last time I went out there was in the cabin a female passenger aged nineteen.

Q.—That was accidental?

A.—Yes, sir.

Q.—Suppose you can't get situations for them when they reach Bermuda, what do you do?

A.—I engage to provide them with situations; I have places for them all.

278 A HISTORY OF EMIGRATION

Q.—Don't tell me so, for I know Bermuda well. Have you any premiums on these children ?
A.—No.
Q.—Have you any letters to testify that the children are comfortably placed in Bermuda ?
A.—Mr. Eaton, Master of St. Pancras Workhouse, has written a letter recommending me. Here is a copy of my agreement with the authorities of St. Pancras.
Mr. Thom, the clerk, read the document, which ran as follows :—
" I, Thomas W. B. Burrows, master of the brig *James*, do hereby agree with the Directors and Guardians of the Poor of St. Pancras to take under my charge the under-mentioned boys and girls for the purpose of conveying them to Bermuda. I hereby agree with the said Directors to see that the said children are placed under the care and charge of persons of good repute in the same island and as near to the name of the person set opposite each boy and girl as possible."
(Then followed the names of the children.)
Q.—You have stated that you have had sent you from the sixty children from St. Pancras original letters in which they speak highly of their comforts. Surely you can produce thirty of these letters ?
A.—They are with the master of St. Pancras Workhouse.
Q.—When do you sail ?
A.—On the 25th.[1]
Q.—How many children will you take ?
A.—As many as you please. (Laughter.)
The petition of Captain Burrows was refused.

For many years juvenile emigration was prohibited by the central authorities and shunned by private enterprise. In 1869, however, owing to the zeal of Miss Rye and Miss Macpherson, a third period in the history of this movement commenced. These two lady philanthropists conceived the idea of establishing receiving and distributing houses for their young recruits in both the country of departure and reception ; they thus did much towards putting juvenile emigration on an organised basis. In the year under

---

[1] That is to say, he sailed eight days after the date of the meeting.

THE EMIGRATION OF CHILDREN 279

question they escorted seventy-three workhouse and other children, principally girls, to their depot at Niagara, and quickly found places for them all. The arrangements acted so well that in 1870 the Poor Law Board, recognising the good work of these gentlewomen, permitted a further party of 149 children to sail for Canada, and yet a third of 451 children in 1871.

So far the Rye-Macpherson plans had been laid with the utmost care, but from the year 1871 onwards a lower standard of organisation seems to have characterised the undertaking. Apparently Miss Rye allowed a number of workhouse girls to join her parties who were between the ages of eighteen and twenty. This factor, coupled with Miss Rye's boast of having "no set plans, no rules, no sharply defined policy about overlooking the children in Canada," [1] readily explains the ease with which many of the girls fell into the worst form of evil.

A governmental enquiry was instituted, under the direction of Mr. Andrew Doyle, and his report mentions many cases of neglect, hardship and even cruelty arising from Miss Rye's management. Numerous instances are given in the report of children who were placed with unknown foster-parents in remote country districts, and never subsequently inspected nor visited. The case of Mary Ford is typical of many others. This girl was entrusted to Miss Rye by the Guardians of Merthyr Tydvil Union in 1873, and she placed her in service at Hamilton. For purposes relating to his enquiry Doyle went to the town in order to find the girl. Reaching the street in which she lived, and asking a passer-by, a coloured man, for the house, and naming Mary Ford, the man said, "Oh, I am glad anybody has come to look after her. I have seen that child flogged worse than a slave, but," he added cautiously, "don't mention me as telling you, for I do all the white washing of the

---

[1] Report of Doyle v. Rye, LXXI, 1877, pp. 3, 4.

house." On questioning the mistress, she admitted the infliction of frequent punishments, but excused herself by referring to the bad character of the girl. Doyle then asked why Miss Rye had not been acquainted with these facts, whereupon the woman replied that she had written more than once for her to come and take away the child, but no notice had been taken of the letters.[1]

In summarising his condemnation of Miss Rye's management, Doyle said : " There is a total absence of efficient supervision, and consequently children are exposed to suffering and wrong, for which they get neither relief nor redress. The sudden transition from an English workhouse to Canadian domestic service, the habits and conditions of which are essentially different from those to which they have been accustomed, is attended with very unsatisfactory results.[2] Further," he said, "the conditions under which they are placed in service are far too unfavourable to the children themselves. In no other way can one account for the eagerness of Canadian employers to get them, and the unwillingness of the working people of Canada to send their own children into service upon the same terms."

So far, we entirely agree with the remarks of Mr. Doyle, but admittedly there are two sides to even this question. Miss Rye, we must remember, was a pioneer in emigrating children, and had to face obstacles and prejudices which have now disappeared, perhaps, largely through her own efforts. Doyle infers that her financial transactions were not all that could be desired. He tells us in his report that Boards of Guardians at home always allowed her £8 for each child, and that she received a sum of £1 4s. per head from the Government of Ontario. Against this total of £9 4s. she disbursed £3 15s. for the Atlantic passage, and £1 might be estimated for the expenses incurred at the receiving home. Thus there was a profit of

---

[1] Report of Doyle v. Rye, LXXI, 1877, pp. 8, 9.   [2] Ibid, p. 1.

THE EMIGRATION OF CHILDREN

£4 9s. on each child taken under her charge.[1] As a reply to this statement, we may point out that the expenditure is much underestimated, seeing that no allowance is made for lease, rates, and management of the various depots nor for the costly rail fares of the children.

Doyle's report was instrumental in causing the Local Government Board to prohibit afresh the emigration of Poor Law Children, but Miss Rye continued in her work, confining her attentions largely to boys and girls who had either severed their connections with the Unions or who had never received parochial assistance.

The question of juvenile emigration was one that interested parish authorities too keenly for it to remain unconsidered long. We therefore find that in 1883 the Local Government Board, after much discussion, once more sanctioned expenditure for this purpose. A memorandum, which it issued in 1883, stated that money taken from local funds could be spent in providing outfits, passages, residence in both receiving and distributing homes, and also in providing a staff of officials necessary to carry on the work with satisfaction. That such permission has been appreciated may be seen from the following annual returns:—[2]

Pauper Children emigrated to Canada. (Under conditions specified by various memoranda issued by the Local Government Board):—

Year	Number			£	Year	Number			£
1883	133	at a cost of		1329	1897	85	at a cost of		1019
1884	301	,,	,,	3053	1898	78	,,	,,	1054
1885	75	,,	,,	744	1899	143	,,	,,	1962
1886	164	,,	,,	1606	1900	173	,,	,,	2471
1887	411	,,	,,	4193	1901	174	,,	,,	2601
1888	596	,,	,,	6415	1902	141	,,	,,	2038
1889	428	,,	,,	4792	1903	398	,,	,,	5826
1890	375	,,	,,	4191	1904	374	,,	,,	5581
1891	296	,,	,,	3450	1905	491	,,	,,	7571
1892	322	,,	,,	3825	1906	441	,,	,,	6742
1893	360	,,	,,	4339	1907	397	,,	,,	6242
1894	299	,,	,,	3578	1908	391	,,	,,	6092
1895	246	,,	,,	2917	1909	422	,,	,,	6531
1896	207	,,	,,	2616					

[1] Report of Doyle v. Rye, LXXI, 1877, final paragraph of report.
[2] These figures are quoted from the Annual Reports of the Local Government Board.

In 1888 the Board secured the interest and co-operation of the Canadian Government in the matter of juvenile emigration, and the two bodies jointly drew up a code of regulations which has virtually remained unchanged until the present day. The chief provisions affecting the emigration of pauper children may be stated as follows :—

(a) The Guardians shall in each case obtain an undertaking in writing from any person[1] entrusted by them with the care of taking children to Canada, and of placing them in homes; that immediately after a child is placed out the Department of the Interior[2] at Ottawa shall be furnished with a report containing the name and age of the child, and the name and address of the person[3] with whom the child is placed, and that a report containing similar information shall be furnished to the Guardians of the Union from which the child is taken.

(b) The Guardians on receipt of such report shall cause a copy of it to be furnished to the Local Government Board.

(c) The person proposed to be entrusted by the Guardians with the emigration of a child shall have notice from the Guardians whether the child is a Protestant or a Roman Catholic, and he shall give an undertaking to place it with a family of its own faith.

(d) A child before being sent to Canada shall have been under previous instruction for at least six months—

I.—In a workhouse or separate school under the Guardians, or a district school : or at a public elementary school at the cost of the Guardians : or

II.—In a school certified by the Board under 25.26. Vic., Ch. 43.[4]

---

[1] Such person must be licensed by the Lieutenant-Governor, vide Immigrant Acts of Ontario, 1897; Manitoba, 1897; and Quebec, 1899.

[2] When these measures were first drawn up, notification had to be made to the Canadian Department of Agriculture.

[3] It is required that the name of the nearest post office, the name of the lot, the concession, and the name of the township should form part of the address.

[4] About 270 industrial and training schools have been certified under this Act. A school wishing to be certified by the L.G.B. is inspected, as set forth in the *Emigration Statutes and General Handbook*, 1910, p. 17. Emigrants' Information Office Publication.

THE EMIGRATION OF CHILDREN 283

It is not required that such period of training shall immediately precede the emigration.

(*e*) The Guardians shall instruct one of their medical officers personally to examine each child proposed to be sent to Canada, and to report in writing as to his or her health, both of body and mind, and to certify whether, in his opinion, the child is in all respects a suitable subject for emigration to that country.

(*f*) The Guardians must have such evidence as they deem satisfactory that the person taking out the children has a reasonable prospect of finding suitable homes for them in Canada.

(*g*) The Board considers that, as a general rule girls should not be sent out above the age of ten, and, in no case, except under very exceptional circumstances, above the age of twelve.[1]

Until the year 1898 it was the practice of the Dominion authorities to make one report only to the Local Government Board on each child received. This latter body rightly felt that, in the interests of the youthful emigrants, an inspection and report should become a half-yearly feature. This view was communicated to the Canadian Government, and the inspectors have now arranged to visit and report on each child twice a year [2] until it reaches the age of sixteen. The Dominion bears the cost of the initial inspection, but the cost of subsequent visits is met by the Guardians or agency who send out the children. The following table gives the sums which must be borne by the local or other authorities on this account :—[3]

---

[1] The above seven clauses are extracted from various L.G.B. memoranda. They are also printed with additional matter on pp. 15, 16 of *Emigration Statutes and General Handbook*, 1910.

[2] Between 1898 and 1906 the Reports were made annually.

[3] Local Government Board circular of April 20th, 1898.

					£	s.	d.
For each child of	14	and under	15	…………	1	4	8
,,	,,	13	,,	14 …………	2	8	4
,,	,,	12	,,	13 …………	3	10	11
,,	,,	11	,,	12 …………	4	12	6
,,	,,	10	,,	11 …………	5	3	0
,,	,,	9	,,	10 …………	6	12	6
,,	,,	8	,,	9 …………	7	11	0
,,	,,	7	,,	8 …………	8	8	6
,,	,,	6	,,	7 …………	9	4	11
,,	,,	5	,,	6 …………	10	0	4
,,	,,	4	,,	5 …………	10	14	9

In 1891 an Act [1] was passed which facilitated the emigration of children who were placed out on licence from certified reformatory or industrial schools in England and Scotland. At first the privilege was used freely, but of late years, owing to a strong objection which the Dominion has shown for such boys and girls, the numbers have considerably fallen. In 1906, of a total of 1407 reformatory discharges, only 48 boys and 5 girls were emigrated, whilst no more than 163 boys and 34 girls, from a total of 3727 children, were sent to Canada from industrial schools.[2]

Many societies have sprung into existence in the Mother Country with the object of promoting juvenile emigration. Most of them appeal to the charitable public for funds, but some derive a considerable portion of their revenue from moneys paid to them by Boards of Guardians. In consideration of these payments, the societies train Poor Law children in farming and domestic occupations, and prepare them generally for a colonial life. As a certain stigma clings to boys and girls who are emigrated direct from parochial institutions, this period of training is almost imperative.

Dr. Barnardo's Homes, probably the foremost of these institutions, commenced work as far back as 1867,

---

[1] The Reformatory and Industrial Schools Act, 1891, 54 and 55 Vict. c. 24.

[2] Report of the Inspector of Reformatories and Industrial Schools, 1906, part 2.

THE EMIGRATION OF CHILDREN 285

since when it has helped, at an average cost of £10,[1] over twenty-two thousand children to seek a colonial life in North America. The detailed figures relating to the emigration work of this institution are as follows :—

	Boys.	Girls.	Totals.		Boys.	Girls.	Totals.
1867–87	1585	865	2450	1899	446	201	647
1887	371	41	412	1900	592	339	931
1888	395	94	489	1901	698	315	1013
1889	396	107	503	1902	684	369	1053
1890	291	—	291	1903	836	401	1237
1891	417	5	422	1904	863	403	1266
1892	596	131	727	1905	981	333	1314
1893	758	76	834	1906	728	443	1171
1894	635	89	724	1907	742	340	1082
1895	578	155	733	1908	630	313	943
1896	490	188	678	1909	632	335	967
1897	438	226	662	1910	630	332	962
1898	371	242	613				

Not only have Dr. Barnardo's Homes sent a total of 22,126 boys and girls to Canada, but they have also placed 488 young people in Australia, New Zealand, and South Africa. The contribution to the emigration outflow from this source has thus exceeded twenty-two and a half thousand souls.[2]

In the case of this institution it may be said that the children are not always put to work immediately on reaching Canada. Many of these juvenile emigrants are transferred to the colonies when quite young, that is to say, when less than ten years of age, and are then boarded out in private families, where they are well cared for and trained. The management make these arrangements because they consider that the earlier such children are acclimatised to the Dominion, the better citizens they ultimately become.

With such a carefully planned organisation as this institution possesses it is little wonder that about 98 per cent of its youthful emigrants prove successful

---

[1] Information supplied privately by the Secretary.
[2] Vide *For God and Country*, being the Forty-fifth Annual Report of the Homes, p. 30.

in after life, and that the Dominion Immigrant Inspectors invariably report well of them.

A number of other societies are engaged in this work. The Children's Emigration Homes at Birmingham were opened in 1872, and have sent 3797 boys and girls to Canada; the Sheltering Home at Liverpool has forwarded over five thousand within thirty-five years; the National Children's Home and Orphanage have placed more than two thousand in the Dominion since 1869, and the Annie Macpherson Home of Industry has 7526 cases to its credit.[1]

On arriving in Canada the children are required to submit to the usual medical examination which confronts all emigrants. Passing this with satisfaction, they are drafted on to special homes which have been established for their reception. No trouble is experienced by the organisations in finding work for all their young charges; the difficulty is rather to obtain sufficient boys and girls to meet the demands of eager employers.

An interesting article printed in one of the Canadian Sessional Papers [2] states that a large proportion of the people who require this juvenile labour are young farmers, recently married, who are as yet unable to afford the expense of hiring an adult, elderly couples whose children have grown up and left them to settle elsewhere on their own account, and large farmers who keep a number of men, but who require one or two boys to do odd work.

Before an applicant is entrusted with the care of an immigrant child he is subjected to a personal examination. In the first place he must supply the following information : (*a*) the condition under which he wishes to take the child ; (*b*) the nature of the work to be per-

---

[1] Fuller particulars of these homes with a list of others, not mentioned here, may be found in the Annual Charities Register and Digest. See also Annual Reports of these societies.
[2] *Op. cit.*, Vol. XL, No. 11, 1906, p. 135.

THE EMIGRATION OF CHILDREN 287

formed; (*c*) the wages offered; and (*d*) his religious denomination. Afterwards he must furnish a certificate testifying to his good character and general standing in his community, credentials which should usually bear the signature of a Justice of the Peace and also a priest in holy orders. Many of the distributing homes [1] have drawn up regulations additional to those imposed by the Government, and only entrust the children to farmers and others who bind themselves to observe the extra conditions.

Until he reaches his twenty-first birthday a child is never completely cut adrift from the agency which has befriended him. Should his master die, become bankrupt, or leave the country, his receiving home must always be prepared to welcome him. If he is dissatisfied with his employer or his employer with him, the home must again take him until some other work can be found. Should any unfortunate occurrence arise of whatever nature, the home must be ready to tide him over his troubles.[2] In this way the Dominion protects not only itself, but the children entrusted to it by the Mother Couutry.

The movements of all juvenile emigrants are carefully recorded by the inspectors of British Immigrant children whose duty it is to see that none are overworked nor treated with harshness. Surprise visits are paid to the homes of employers at odd times, though never less than half-yearly, until a boy or girl reaches the age of eighteen or sixteen, according to the province of residence. After this age the Dominion agencies voluntarily continue the inspections for a

---

[1] e.g. Ontario Children's Aid Society. The additional regulations refer to wages, food, clothing, education, etc., Vide *Canadian Labour Gazette*, March, 1905, vol. 5, p. 1001.

[2] By the Ontario Immigration Act of 1897, a home must be prepared to receive back its juvenile immigrants at any time until they reach the age of eighteen; *idem.* by the Quebec Immigration Act of 1899; until they reach the age of sixteen, by the Manitoba Immigration Act of 1897. In practice, all homes are prepared to receive them back until they become of age.

period of three or five years. Every six months a report is made on each child by the Canadian Government, and forwarded to the organisation in the United Kingdom responsible for his or her emigration. The reports referring to the Poor Law children are frequently reprinted in the annual Local Government Reports, and usually appear to be of a highly satisfactory character. Commenting on these Canadian reports, the Local Government Board wrote in 1892 :[1]

> The children are reported to be generally contented and well cared for, and the greater number of their homes to be free from objection. Though in many cases reference is made to the faults in the character, disposition, or habits of the children, there appear to be comparatively few instances where the foster-parents have expressed an intention to part with them in consequence. The reports show that in some of the cases the children and their foster-parents have become greatly attached to each other : and that in others the foster-parents take an unselfish and parental interest in the present and future welfare of the children committed to their keeping. There are somewhat fewer cases than formerly in which children are said to have been adopted, but it is apparent, both from the present and former reports, that the system of adoption does not in Canada necessarily imply that the foster-parent accepts once for all the care of a child as his own. With regard to five homes only the reports are not favourable, and, in two of these the children are stated to have been " not well used," and " not well treated or sufficiently fed." The Immigration Officers have reported unfavourably upon the bodily or mental condition of eight children, and one of these children has been returned to England as insane. These reports show that for the most part children are placed out on the understanding that they will be boarded, clothed, and educated until they attain the age of fifteen years : after which time they are paid wages at the rate of three or four dollars per month. They also show that the homes in Canada connected with the various emigration societies are of great assistance in connection with the welfare and supervision of the children. Children who are

---

[1] Twenty-first Report of the Local Government Board, p. lxxxiv.

THE EMIGRATION OF CHILDREN 289

dissatisfied, ill, or in unsatisfactory homes, appear to be frequently received back into these homes, whence they are again placed out, after having received further training or medical treatment, as may be necessary.

In 1903 the Inspector of British Immigrant Children stated that 1675 boys and girls were brought into the Dominion during the year, and that the demand for them continued to be in excess of the supply.[1] In 1904 he wrote,[2] "2204 children were received. The demand has been steadily maintained. With the exception of an insignificant number, those on my inspection list are doing well, and few comparatively have been returned to England. The care and treatment of the children by their employers have been very satisfactory indeed." In 1905 the number of youthful immigrants increased to 2814. He then wrote: "There has been a fairly steady stream of juvenile emigrants this year, and notwithstanding this the total number of arrivals proved inadequate to the demand."[3] In 1906 immigrant children numbered 3258 souls. The inspector reported, "With the exception of an insignificant few they are doing well."[4] As additional testimony to the satisfactory position held by juvenile emigration, the following passage is quoted from the Canadian Sessional Papers:[5]

Started in a small way and promoted unostentatiously in the face of doubt, discouragement, and adverse criticism, child emigration to Canada has unfolded into an important factor in the annual Anglo-Saxon immigration into our Dominion. It is now generally conceded to be a real benefit not only to the children whose rescue from poverty and squalor it effects, but also to Britain's chief colony as well. Juvenile emigration assists in filling a gap in an important branch of our

---

[1] Report of Canadian Department of the Interior for 1902–3.
[2] Ibid., 1903–4, p. 138.
[3] Report of Canadian Department of the Interior, 1904–5, part 2, p. 135. [4] Ibid., 1905–6, part 2, p. 107.
[5] Op. cit., Vol. XL, No. 11, 1906, p. 135.

labour market, and numbers of farmers regard the influx of the so-called English home children as a veritable boon.

During the period 1888–1911 the major stream of juvenile emigration was directed to the Dominion of Canada; now, however, there seems to be a growing tendency to extend the movement to Australia and New Zealand. Chief among the plans which have been made for Australasian emigration of young people are those which owe their inception to Mr. Thomas E. Sedgwick. A season or two back he escorted fifty working lads from London and Liverpool to New Zealand, and there put them to work with farmers. "On our arrival in New Zealand," he writes,[1] " we found that the arrangements made by the Labour Department were incomparably the best ever devised by any State for their immigrants. Fifty of the most attractive of the two hundred and fifty offers of employment were reported on by the inspectors. After the boys had expressed their ideas as to North or South Island, sheep, cattle, or fruit-farming, and mates had been allotted to the same or neighbouring farms, parties were made up and sent in different directions, under the charge of labour officials, within a few hours of the arrival in Wellington; the whole distribution being accomplished without a hitch, and reflected the greatest credit on all concerned."

Mr. Sedgwick claims that his boys are protected as far as is humanly possible. The Secretary of Labour, acting under the written authority of the parents in each case, apprenticed the juveniles for three years [2] to trustworthy farmers. Under the indentures the employer was required to bank the wages, less a shilling a week, which was handed to the apprentice as pocket-

---

[1] In a pamphlet, *Junior Imperial Migration*, by T. E. Sedgwick, 26 Oriental Street, Poplar, E.
[2] Or until they reach the age of twenty-one, if such is a shorter period.

THE EMIGRATION OF CHILDREN 291

money. The boys undertook to repay the ten pounds which was expended on their fare, and this sum has been deducted from the bank-balances. In some cases the secretary has allowed a part of the savings to be sent home to assist the parents.

The Secretary of Labour is at liberty to cancel the indentures should he consider that a boy is not being properly treated, whilst the employer, in his turn, can request him to remove the lad in a fortnight, should he be guilty of such misconduct as would justify an employer in dismissing an ordinary servant. Any complaints of employers or employed are immediately investigated by the Department's officials, who are independent and unbiassed.

The scheme has, so far, proved successful, as the following report shows : [1]

> The boys had learnt quickly, settled well, were happy and content. They had grown much and improved in every way. The promise to give preferential consideration for the next party to nominees of those proving satisfactory, and the policy of leaving the success or otherwise of the experiment with the boys themselves put them on their mettle. Several cases of home-sickness were severe, but the bright sunlight, perfect climate, close association with animals and Nature, the amount to be learnt and variety of their duties, and the opportunities for enjoyment, such as riding, fishing, swimming, and shooting, in many cases did much to counteract this. The younger ones of sixteen or seventeen years settled more readily, as a rule, than did those of eighteen and nineteen, but all, with the exception of two absconders, eventually became acclimatised.

As to the value of juvenile emigration, a number of opinions exist. It is usually conceded, however, that if a person intends to settle in the Colonies at some future period of his life, the younger he goes the better. He may then arrive in the new surroundings before his character and habits have become set, and

---

[1] *Junior Imperial Migration*, p. 15.

whilst there is still time to mould himself to the altered conditions of life. With adults the metamorphoses demand a considerable amount of will-power, more very often than the individual possesses, and as a result he becomes a failure. With children, however, their plastic natures enable them to overcome the change with comparative ease, and consequently they make good emigrants. In the case of pauper children and waifs and strays, there are other benefits to be obtained by a recourse to emigration. These children frequently come from vitiated homes and surroundings from which it is absolutely imperative that they should be isolated. No better way of effecting this end can be suggested than by sending the yet untainted youngsters to the Colonies. Of course, it is not intended that boys and girls coming from dangerous environments should be shipped out of the country in their neglected condition; a thorough training in an approved home is imperative before they start.

Though the child seems to reap a number of advantages by being transferred to one or other of the overseas dominions, there is less evidence to show that the Mother Country is equally fortunate. We have a certain amount of sympathy for the witness who said, when giving evidence before the Commission appointed to consider Sir H. Rider Haggard's colonisation scheme:[1] " I think it would be better not to adopt a wholesale system of emigration, because the Canadian authorities very properly require the best material; they will not have feeble-minded, epileptic, or morally defective children. Therefore it would follow that if we emigrated pauper children wholesale we should be sending out of the country all the best of the children, and keeping the defective ones at home. The best of the pauper children who have no undesirable belongings should, in my opinion, be

---

[1] Report on Agricultural Settlements in the British Colonies, 1906, Vol. II, para. 1829.

THE EMIGRATION OF CHILDREN 293

retained and drafted as far as possible into the British Army and Navy, rather than be sent abroad to the Colonies." Mr. Holgate, writing in one of the Local Government Reports,[1] expresses almost similar opinions : " My own view," he says, " has always been that a system which undertakes to provide for the picked few, those who, being physically and mentally the best specimens of the class, are equally certain of a prosperous future in their own country, cannot be heartily supported by those who have to deal with the question as a whole, and who have to consider how to provide for all classes of children, whatever their bodily and intellectual capacities may be."

In considering the financial aspect of juvenile emigration, the question appears more satisfactory. At a meeting of the Fellows of the Royal Colonial Institute in 1904 it was estimated that by emigrating a pauper child a parish saves a sum equal to the cost of his keep for two years.[2] Thus an exodus of rate-supported children lightens the burden of the ratepayer.

It may be mentioned here that many Boards of Guardians refuse to consider schemes of emigration for children. They argue with much reason that once a child comes under their care they must be intimately associated with its welfare until it is old enough to look after itself.[3] As emigration would necessitate the transference of their control to some philanthropic or other body over which they could exercise no authority, they prefer to keep their youthful charges within the home country.[4]

---

[1] *Op. cit.*, Eighth Report, p. 152.
[2] *Proceedings of the Royal Colonial Institute*, Vol. XXXVI, 1904–5, p. 275.
[3] Mrs. Despard, speaking at the Royal Colonial Institute, March 28th, 1905.
[4] H. G. Kennedy, writing in the Eighteenth Annual Report of the Local Government Board, 1889, p. 141, says that though the value of emigrating pauper children is doubtful, there can be no doubt that to pretend to emigrate such charges is followed by highly interesting results.

As to the value of juvenile emigration, in so far as it affects the colony of reception, it is generally agreed that the advantages are many and the drawbacks few or none. The system is so regulated that only the fittest of children are given an entrance, those who in the future are likely to prove useful, industrious and self-supporting citizens. We know that many of the Colonies are eager to be provided with such youthful emigrants ; this alone is ample proof that the system is one that confers benefits on the receiving colony.

He says, " Among some of the populous Yorkshire unions, proposals to largely exercise the existing powers for emigrating pauper children to Canada were taken up seriously in 1888, but it turned out, when steps were actually begun to carry out this scheme, that the idea of sending the paupers away to a foreign land was most distasteful to the labouring classes and the project was abandoned, in consequence. In a few cases ' orphans ' of long standing turned out, when on the eve of departure, to possess parents in the aunt or uncle who had left the children chargeable for years to the rates, but whom the triumph of parental instinct constrained to claim their offspring when emigration was proposed."

CHAPTER XIII

THE ECONOMIC AND SOCIAL VALUE OF EMIGRATION AND IMMIGRATION

To what extent do emigration and immigration serve a useful purpose? This interesting problem of economic and social science has been frequently considered by departmental committees and reported upon by various commissions. It has been the subject of countless articles in all classes of periodicals and reviews, and has furnished points for debate in numerous political controversies. Abroad and in the Colonies it has by no means escaped attention, being the cause of much legislation and party strife. To answer this question it will be necessary to consider the value of emigration and immigration from three different standpoints: firstly, that affecting the Mother Country; secondly, that affecting the receiving country; and, thirdly, that which influences the individual personally.

Investigating, first of all, the influence which emigration has exerted upon the United Kingdom, we may safely claim that this migratory force has been productive of much good. During the early years of the nineteenth century the Census Records indicated a tremendous growth in the combined population of the three kingdoms. To this expanding population emigration acted throughout as a safety-valve. By clearing the market of some of the surplus labour it helped to maintain a normal condition of wages; it kept down food prices by lessening the demand for supplies, and relieved the poor-rate by removing from our shores people who would otherwise have become a public charge. Throughout the history of the nineteenth century we find that, whenever the prosperity of any trade has declined, the displaced workers have had recourse to emigration. An earlier chapter[1] has described the collapse of kelp-gathering in the north of Scotland, of hand-loom weaving in Yorkshire, of the serge trade at Devizes, Bradford-on-Avon and Warminster, of the cloth trade at Taunton, and of the crepe trade at Norwich; it has also dealt with the agricultural depressions in England, the disastrous potato famine in Ireland, and the distress which arose when arable was turned into pasture land. On all these occasions large numbers of workpeople were deprived of their means of livelihood, and by sheer need were forced to leave their native country and seek employment on the further side of the Atlantic.

A search through the annual reports of various trade unions published since 1850[2] reveals the fact that for many years these societies looked upon emigration as a favourable remedy for unemployment. The Secretary of the Flint Glass Makers' Association said on one occasion, when addressing the members: " If in a depression you have fifty men out of work, they will receive £1750 in a year,[3] and at the same time will be used as a whip by the employers to bring down your wages; by sending them to Australia at £20 per head you save £15, and send them to plenty, instead of starvation at home; you keep your own wages good by the simple act of clearing the surplus labour out of the market."[4] Accordingly an emigration fund became a constant feature with the more

---

[1] Chapter III.
[2] Such as those included in the Webb Collection of Trade Union pamphlets in the British Library of Political Science, London.
[3] Figures based upon the distress pay provided by the Society.
[4] See Sidney Webb *History of Trade Unions*, p. 183.

EMIGRATION AND IMMIGRATION 297

influential societies, but opposition from Colonial and foreign labour parties has had much to do with the stoppage of these trade-union grants.

Turning to the question of the Poor Law, it is universally admitted that the transposing of indigent British people to American shores has at times done much to relieve local expenditure. The Report on Emigration, published in 1826, gave numerous instances of cases where the rates fell consequent on the shipment to America of necessitous people. The following example is typical of many others. In April, 1826, a Kentish parish sent a number of its dependents to New York. The passage money from the London Docks to the United States amounted to £7 per person, exclusive of the landing fee of 4s. 6d.; the provisions for the voyage cost £3 10s.; incidental expenses averaged £2; and to this total of £12 14s. 6d. must be added a few extra shillings, to allow for the rail fare from Kent to the Docks. As a set-off to this sum, it was recorded that these people had been previously costing their union twenty pounds annually. Not only may we assess the gain produced by emigration in this instance as £7 per person during the first year of their departure, but we must remember that those who were sent out of the country belonged to a class which burdened the rates year after year. In being permanently rid of such people, the parishes were obviously able to effect a considerable saving.

A more recent instance of emigration acting as a beneficial measure is provided by the cathedral town of Norwich. This urban centre is peculiarly circumstanced, for, first, it claims to be situated further from a city of its own size than any other place of equal population in England, and, second, it is considered to be the centre of the widest agricultural district in the country. On these accounts it receives more than its full share of workers who wish to exchange a rural for a city existence. But while its population tends to increase abnormally, its industries do not display the same characteristic; moreover, the largest industrial concern in the locality is so organised that it provides "blind-alley" occupations for boys and girls. As a consequence, Norwich has more than its complement of unemployed adults. For a considerable while the situation was met, inadequately, we may say, by expending on casual relief a sum approximating a thousand pounds per week, but little or no lasting good resulted from this action. Finally, the Norwich Distress Committee and the Colman Company established a system of emigration whereby its dependents could start life afresh in Canada. So far, the results have more than justified the movement. The individuals seem to be prospering in their new homes, the emigration expenditure does not equal the sums spent on temporary relief, and the town is not demoralised by the presence in its midst of people deprived of work.[1]

In other ways it may be argued that emigration operates to the good of the forwarding community. Not only is local expenditure relieved by its timely and judicious use, as shown in the case of Norwich, but charitable institutions, such as hospitals, sanatoria, and asylums, all benefit by the removal of people who, though fit at the time of departure, gradually deteriorate when left to the harassing conditions of life in the old country. Emigration even relieves the expenditure connected with education, national insurance, and old-age pensions.

There is yet another manner in which the outflow of population from the United Kingdom has proved a boon, but this instance we mention with some diffidence. Until Canada and the United States took precautions to safeguard themselves against the coming

---

[1] A. Hawkes, Special Report on Immigration. Ottawa Government Printing Bureau, 1912, pp. 62–3.

EMIGRATION AND IMMIGRATION

of our human derelicts, it was the practice of parishes, societies, and countless charitably disposed persons to ship across the Atlantic the men and women who could not succeed at home.[1] Year by year the ne'er-do-wells were sifted from our population and provided with the money to reach North America. Those who could not find employment at home or who were unfit to work were sent off in thousands, without any thought as to their ultimate fate. It was no uncommon happening for magistrates to suggest emigration as an alternative for imprisonment, whilst even to-day barristers sometimes intimate that, if their clients are discharged, an undertaking will be given that they will be sent to America.[2] Writing in her work, *Life in an English Village*,[3] Miss M. F. Davies touches on this matter of selective emigration. "In 1830," she says, "the parish of Corsley, Wiltshire, shipped off at its own cost sixty-six of the least desirable of its inhabitants, about half being adults and half children.... The emigrants consisted of several families of the very class one would wish to remove, men of suspected bad habits who brought up their children to wickedness, whilst there were several poachers amongst them, and other reputed bad characters." One can almost imagine the disgust with which our American cousins welcomed such parties as came from Corsley! Looking at the practice, however, from a British point of view, it must be admitted that this selective process which tended for over fifty years to rid us of our degenerate population, though diplomatically indefensible, could only help to raise the general standard of those who remained behind.

Though on numerous occasions emigration has helped to thin out the surplus element of our growing population, it cannot be said that it has ever acted

---
[1] "Emigration is considered a riddance of diseased population."—*Edinburgh Review*, vol. 92, p. 493.
[2] Cf. Case tried at Maidstone Assizes on July 10th, 1911.
[3] *Op. cit.*, pp. 80–1.

as a harmful drain on our numbers. Certain Scotch writers, in the early part of the nineteenth century, predicted that if the exodus from the country were allowed to proceed, as indeed it has been, we should in time be confronted with the ills which usually visit a degenerate nation. Not only were such predictions wholly erroneous, but we may affirm that whenever emigration has proceeded from natural causes and not from such as are induced by political, military, religious, or industrial unrest, it has always been a healthful sign. Of recent French emigrants, the majority have gone from the eastern and southern departments, yet these divisions of the country maintain the strength of their population far better than does Normandy, which, during the last century, has furnished but few people for the colonies. The same may be said of Germany; her most populous districts are those from which emigration has proceeded freely. Even if we turn to Ireland, a country of exceptions and anomalies, we note that Munster is the province in which the strength of the population is most satisfactorily maintained, yet this is the area which has contributed more lavishly than any other towards the exodus to America. Writing on the effects of emigration, Paul Leroy-Beaulieu says:

> L'influence de l'émigration sur la santé du corps social, a-t-on dit avec esprit, est analogue à l'influence d'un saignement de nez sur la santé d'un homme : et comme un saignement de nez est également incapable d'affaillir un corps vigoureux ou de prévenir une apoplexie, de même l'émigration n'est susceptible ni d'énerver un grand pays ni de le préserver d'un superflu de population.[1]

So far, we have confined our attentions to discussing the beneficial aspect of the home exodus, but there is

---

[1] *La Colonisation Chez Les Peuples Modernes*, Tome II, p. 479.

EMIGRATION AND IMMIGRATION 301

a less satisfactory view to consider. Many authorities[1] hold that in numbers of cases where emigration has been urged as necessary, a more useful scheme would be to effect a redistribution of the surplus labour in the thinly populated areas of the Kingdom. The general movement of population has for the last hundred years proceeded from the agricultural areas into the towns.[2] As a result there is a constant cry of over-population and congestion in the urban districts, whilst an opposite condition holds in the country. The current Census Returns show that more than two-thirds of our total inhabitants dwell in the urban districts, whilst less than one-third are spread over the remaining areas. From these facts it seems that at the present time the congestion in the towns is an outcome of the depopulation of the country. Emigration, however, is now proceeding largely from the agrarian counties, and is, therefore, but a poor solution to the problem of unemployment, which demands such urgent attention in the populous towns.

Not only is there a significant move of the rural population into the urban areas, but it is a well-known fact that almost the whole of our alien immigrants settle there also.[3] Thus when the statistics report that, in 1910, emigrants numbered 1,659,801 and immigrants numbered 1,452,385, we may take it that only a small section of the first total had been recruited from the towns, but that almost all the latter had settled there.[4]

The problem of to-day, then, is how to absorb the

---

[1] Cf. Lord Eversley's paper read to the members of the Royal Colonial Institute, May 14th, 1907.
[2] A writer in the *Journal of the Statistical Society*, June, 1907, estimates the agricultural labourers to have numbered 1,904,690 in 1851; 1,803,040 in 1861; 1,423,860 in 1871; 1,999,820 in 1881; 1,099,570 in 1891; and 988,340 in 1901.
[3] See Whelpley, *The Problem of the Immigrant*, p. 9.
[4] Emigration and Immigration Tables for 1910. Government publication No. 180, p. 1, 1911.

superabundant town labour. The Colonies and the United States are beginning to look upon this portion of our emigration with a certain amount of disfavour and are discouraging it. They much prefer country-bred people to townsmen, as the former are more inclined to take up homesteads and to remain on them.

Some writers allege that our superabundant town dwellers could be distributed over the thinly populated country districts and employed there in some such occupation as intensive farming.[1] Lord Eversley has given it as his opinion that,[2] " It is in the direction of intense[3] cultivation in connection with small holdings, under the stimulus of ownership or of security of tenure, that we must look for a greater employment of labour on the land." Unfortunately the drawbacks which are involved in such a scheme as he upholds are very similar to those which hamper the progress of emigration. Much capital is needed to work the scheme, and townspeople are required to take up unfamiliar occupation in the country. Overproduction of perishable goods is, of course, an additional set-back to any scheme which is based on intensive culture at home.

The superabundant labour of the present time has been classified by Mr. and Mrs. Sidney Webb under four heads as follows :[4]

(*a*) People who have lately been in definite situations of presumed permanency; for instance, an engine driver, a cotton spinner, an agricultural labourer, a carman, or a domestic servant.

(*b*) People who normally in their own trades shift from job

---

[1] This form of occupation for townspeople has been constantly urged ever since the time it was suggested by the Hibernian Society. See Report on the Poor of Ireland, 1823, Vol. VI, pp. 201, 539.

[2] Cf. Lord Eversley's paper read to the members of the Royal Colonial Institute, May 14th, 1907.

[3] The original wording is preserved.

[4] *The Public Organisation of the Labour Market*, p. 164–5.

EMIGRATION AND IMMIGRATION 303

to job and from one employer to another, with more or less interval between jobs, but each lasting for weeks and perhaps months; for example, the contractor's navvy, the bricklayer, the plumber, the plasterer, and indeed all varieties of artisans and labourers of the building trades.

(c) People who normally earn a bare subsistence by casual jobs lasting only a few hours each or a day or two; for instance, the dock and wharf labourers, the market porters, and the casual hands forming a fringe around many industries.

(d) People who have been ousted, or have wilfully withdrawn themselves from the ranks of the workers; for instance, the man broken down by some infirmity or by advancing age, the habitual inmate of philanthropic "shelters," casual wards of the great cities and the professional vagrant.

By noting the various types of people included in this list we may see to what extent emigration may be used as a remedy for unemployment. In class (a) there are some people who might prove acceptable to Canada and the United States, especially the farm labourer, the domestic servant, and the carman who has a knowledge of horses. In class (b) there are fewer people who would be welcome; some of them could find work on the railroad constructions, and others, if healthy, would not be objected to if they forsook their own trades and took up agricultural pursuits. Class (c) is even less acceptable. Immigration authorities look askance at workers who form the fringe of their respective trades, as such people are already a burden in America. Men and women in this class, however, would be considered entirely on their individual merits. People in class (d) would be absolutely forbidden an entrance. Thus of all the members of our community who are at present unemployed only a small section would be able to benefit by any system of emigration to America which might be proposed.

Emigration has often been advised in cases where population has shown a rapid increase. Undoubtedly in the early part of the nineteenth century, when the means of locomotion were so primitive that labour could not easily follow the movements of trade, a wholesale exodus was useful in clearing the local congestions. This form of remedy was applied with success in Ireland, when the people became so numerous that the land could no longer produce sufficient for all their needs. But in ordinary cases of a gradual increase in population, such as England is at present experiencing, many authorities claim that there is no pressing need, on social grounds, for a general outflow. Thinly populated countries, we must remember, are by no means the most prosperous. The standard of comfort in our kingdom to-day is not lower than it was forty years ago, when our inhabitants were much fewer in number than they are now. As long as an abundant supply of raw produce is brought into the country, and, also, as long as serious overcrowding does not develop to such an extent as to jeopardise health, then an increase of population is a national gain and not a drawback.[1] On this point we may quote with advantage from Mr. Herbert Samuel's reservation in the Report issued by the Committee which sat to consider Sir H. Rider Haggard's emigration scheme.[2]

At the root of many of the proposals for State-aided emigration, he says, there appears to lie the theory that because there are persons unemployed England must be over-populated, and that if we could induce a proportion of our working-classes to remove to the Colonies, and at the same time stop foreign workmen from coming in, the problem of unemployment would be solved. But those who hold this view forget that, other factors being constant, the development of a country's natural resources and its foreign trade increases with the growth of its population and diminishes with its fall, that a smaller population may mean a smaller production and not a greater regularity of employment, and, conversely, that

---

[1] See Marshall, *Principles of Economics*, p. 400.
[2] See Mr. Herbert Samuel's reservation in the Report on Agricultural Settlements in British Colonies, 1906, p. 24.

EMIGRATION AND IMMIGRATION 305

an increase of population need not involve an addition to the ranks of the unemployed. Such, indeed, is the lesson of experience. An interesting table in a recent publication of the Board of Trade[1] gives the percentage of members of Trade Unions returned as out of work in each year from 1860 to 1903. In the first five years of that period the figures averaged 3·6 per cent. In the following forty years the population of the United Kingdom increased by twelve millions, or 40 per cent. But at the end of that time—in the last five years shown in the table—the percentage of unemployment, instead of having vastly increased through this great growth of population, was almost precisely the same—3·7 per cent, as it was at the beginning. An increase of numbers has not added to the degree of unemployment. A decrease of numbers does not promise to reduce it.

One grave objection to emigration is that it often robs a nation of the very people who are most useful at home. At the present time the restrictive measures enforced by Canada and the United States are so severe that only people of good physique and character can settle within their jurisdictions. The Mother Country in supplying emigrants is thus called upon to provide from her best stock, with the consequence that as the healthy and efficient people alone depart, the less healthy and physically imperfect grow in proportion at home. Under any circumstances such a procedure should be viewed with alarm, but when we remember that the physical standard of the English population is already suffering through the postponement of marriages and the limiting of families among the classes of the people who are best suited to rearing children, this selective process of emigration must be additionally weakening.[1] That

---

[1] Publication No. Cd. 2337, 1904, p. 83, British and Foreign Trade and Industry.

[2] Much valuable information bearing on this important question of national degeneracy may be obtained by a perusal of the Report of the Royal Commission on the Care and Control of the Feeble-Minded, published in eight folio volumes, 1908. Digests have been prepared by Mr. Dickinson and Mrs. Pinsent, both of whom were Commissioners.

the New World should endeavour to obtain the best people it can is obvious enough, but it is undoubtedly for the Mother Country to consider whether or no it can afford to be drained, year after year, of its finest stock.

Not only does emigration claim the strong and healthy, but it also attracts people at an age when they are at their maximum economic value. Most emigrants leave home when they are between eighteen and thirty-five, that is, after their country has reared them through the unremunerative period of childhood, and before they have had time to repay a tithe of the national expenditure incurred on their behalf. Marshall[1] estimated that the country spends an average of £200 in rearing each emigrant. He argued that the value of an individual, viewing him from his economic worth, is equal to the cost of rearing him. In estimating this cost, Marshall divided the population into five classes and put the figure for the lowest two-fifths of the people at £100 per head, for the next fifth at £175, for the next fifth at £300, for the next tenth at £500, and the remaining tenth at £1200. This gave an average of £300 *per capita*, a figure which is rather high, seeing that a small section of the emigrants are mere children, and have not yet grown to a productive age, and others are aged with little future in front of them. For this reason Marshall lowered the estimate to £200.

Dr. William Farr, of the statistical department of the Registrar-General's Office, determined an emigrant's value in another way. He said that a man's worth was the difference between his future earnings and his future cost of upkeep.[2] He took the case of an agricultural labourer as being synonymous with that of the emigrant, and calculated his future wages

---

[1] In his *Principles of Economics*, footnote on page 647.
[2] See *Journal of the Statistical Society* for 1853; also Mayo Smith, *Emigration and Immigration*, p. 110.

EMIGRATION AND IMMIGRATION 307

at the age of twenty to be £482, whilst his maintenance he reckoned at £248; his economic value was thus £234. As many agriculturists would be over twenty years of age and would therefore have a shorter expectation of life, Farr decided that the average value of all such people was £150. In reckoning the economic loss which such an exodus must mean to the country Dr. Farr said :[1]

> Valuing the emigrant as the agricultural labourers have been valued at home, taking age and service into account, the value of emigrants in 1876 was £175 per head. If we may venture to apply this standard to the whole period, it will follow that the money value of the eight million people that left England, Scotland, and Ireland in the years 1837–1876 was 1400 million pounds sterling, or an average of about £35,000,000 a year.

Dr. Farr, however, did not look upon this British exodus as a real loss to the country, for he added :

> It may be contended that emigration is a loss to the Mother Country. It seems so. It is like the export of precious goods for which there is no return. But experience proves that simultaneously with this emigration there has been a prodigious increase in the capital of the country, especially in recent years. Wages have risen and the value of the labourer has risen in proportion.

The economic value of an individual, as computed by Marshall and Dr. Farr, really depends, however, on the opportunity the individual has of finding remunerative employment. If he can secure adequate work in a sufficient amount, then he is worth some such value as was put upon him by these authorities. If, however, he has to accept inferior employment or less work than he can naturally accomplish, then his value is proportionately lessened. Lastly, if he is unemployed, his worth is of a negative quantity, for he

---

[1] In the Thirty-ninth Report of the Registrar-General, 1877.

is acting as a drag on the community. It must not be thought, however, that by emigrating all its unemployed the country would gain financially. The temporary fluctuations in the prosperity of trades cause a varying number of people to be employed, so that a margin of labour is a necessity. At different seasons of the year and even on certain days of the week the requirements of labour rise and fall; the butcher needs extra hands on Friday and Saturday; the baker on Friday night; the Post Office at Christmas time; the dock authorities on the arrival of a ship; the railway companies at August Bank Holiday, and so on. Our remarks above only apply, therefore, after a sufficient margin of labour has been deducted to meet these temporary exigencies.

A further argument against emigration is that the movement draws large sums of money from the Mother Country. To gain admittance to the United States every immigrant must now pay a head-tax of four dollars. As over 110,000 people left the United Kingdom for the United States in the year 1906–7, we see that, in this one season alone, a sum of no less than £88,000 passed out of the country to pay for this American tax. To enter Canada the immigrant must show that he possesses a certain stipulated sum, which varies according to his age and the season of the year. At a moderate estimate this sum might be placed at £3 10s.[1] The figures of British emigration to Canada stood at 114,859 for the season 1906–7, thus the amount of money transferred to the Dominion in

---

[1] All emigrants landing in Canada between March 1st and October 31st must possess $25 (£5 4s.) and children $12.50 (£2 12s.) each, and between November 1st and the last day of February $50 and children $25 each, and sufficient travelling money; except that the following need have sufficient travelling money only, viz. (1) farm labourers and female servants, if going to assured employment as such; (2) approved railway construction labourers who are guaranteed employment by railway contractors or companies; and (3) certain relatives of residents in Canada. Allowance for these excepted classes has been made in computing the average estimate of £3 10s. to the United Kingdom.

EMIGRATION AND IMMIGRATION 309

order to satisfy this enactment was over £400,000.[1] From these figures it is evident that the total displacement of British capital in the year under consideration was at least £488,000.

Not only must we take into account the sums which are legally demanded of our emigrants on submitting to American rule, but we must also mention those which are voluntarily carried away by them. Unfortunately no data can be given as to their amount, but by noting the purchases of land and property which many of them make on reaching their new destination we know that they must be considerable.

An attempt was made in 1856 to obtain an approximation of the sums brought by emigrants who disembarked at New York. With this view each person on landing was asked to disclose the extent of his funds. Some gave accurate details, but many of them, suspicious of the reason for requesting such information, evaded the answer and returned amounts much smaller than they really possessed. From the incomplete figures obtained in this way, it was computed that the average sum taken into New York by immigrants of all nationalities was $68.08.[2] Probably the Irish element at this date were in possession of a smaller average sum, but it is fairly certain that the English people possessed a greater capital amount than this.

It must not be asserted that these large sums are irreparably lost to the Mother Country. It is true that they are carried out of the kingdom and invested in American property, but they probably return to us sooner or later in the form of remittances and gifts to friends and relations at home. Important sums are annually sent back to the British Isles, and these help to cancel the amounts which departing emigrants take with them. For many years the Colonial Land

---

[1] Though this sum leaves the Mother Country, it is, of course, not lost to the Empire.

[2] Mayo Smith, *Emigration and Immigration*, p. 98.

A HISTORY OF EMIGRATION

and Emigration Commissioners attempted to assess the value of the returned remittances, and when this body was dissolved the Board of Trade continued the work. Finally, the task was abandoned, as the returns were found to be growing more and more incomplete and correspondingly less valuable. The following figures are selected from the annual reports of these bodies. Without being quite accurate they give some idea, however, of the amounts received by the Mother Country.

1850 .. £957,000 was sent back from various sources in North America.
1855 .. £873,000 ,, ,, ,,
1860 .. £576,932 ,, ,, ,,
1865 .. £481,580 ,, ,, ,,
1870 .. £727,408 ,, ,, ,,
1875 .. £354,356 ,, ,, ,,
1878 .. £784,067 ,, ,, ,,

It is interesting to compare the figures for any of the above-mentioned years with the volume of emigration during the same period. For instance, in 1878, the money returned to the United Kingdom was £784,067, whilst the exodus of people totalled 78,123. Thus we may say that each emigrant could have taken with him, in this particular year, a sum of ten pounds without the home country suffering any monetary displacement.[1]

Before leaving the question of finance we may add that the Mother Country recoups her loss in yet another way. Successful Englishmen, after having amassed a certain degree of wealth in the New World, are constantly leaving America to spend the remaining days of their existence in the land of their birth. They naturally bring with them the incomes of their savings, which thus help to strengthen the finances of the home country.

---

[1] As the emigrant in U.S.A. sends home more money than his brother emigrant in B.N.A., it is clear that if the two areas were dealt with separately, the sum to U.S.A. would be considerably greater than £10 and considerably less to B.N.A.

EMIGRATION AND IMMIGRATION 311

Our last indictment against emigration is that it absorbs a greater number of men than women, and therefore aggravates the disproportion which already exists between the sexes at home. Mulhall, in his *Dictionary of Statistics*, tells us that for every sixteen women who emigrate there are twenty-three men.

Not only does emigration take more men than women from the old country, where the latter predominate, but it also installs more men than women in the new country, where the former are in the majority. It thus disturbs the sex-balance in both the land of departure and that of arrival. In 1790 the United States Census reported that in the Republic there were five hundred and nine males to every thousand people. As immigration grew so the disproportion increased, for in 1900 the males were five hundred and thirteen per thousand. In Canada the excess is much the same, as the following figures show:—

	1871	POPULATION. 1881	1891	1901
Males	1,764,311	2,188,854	2,460,471	2,751,708
Females	1,721,450	2,135,956	2,372,768	2,619,607

Having dealt with the value of emigration as it is held to affect the United Kingdom, it is now necessary to speak of the influence which immigration has exerted upon the receiving countries, namely, Canada and the United States.

Of all the widespread changes which have taken place as a result of this movement, the first to claim our attention is that which deals with the effect of immigration on North American population. In 1765, two years after the close of the Seven Years' War and before the great exodus from Europe had commenced to make itself felt, the total population of Canada was given as 69,810.[1] The latest Census,

---

[1] Vide Census of Canada, 1870-1, Vol. IV.

that of 1911, estimated the figures to have reached 7,081,869. The first Census of the United States gave the population for 1790 as a few short of four millions. Now, according to the latest returns, the total, excluding the overseas possessions, is no less than 91,972,266. Knowing these figures, we are able to compare the amount of population in the North American Continent before the main flow of immigration actually commenced with the amount existing there to-day. In Canada the increase is from seventy thousand to over seven millions, whilst in the United States it is still more important, being from four to ninety-one millions. At first thought these figures seem to show a considerable increase due to the immigration movement, but on closer inspection the gain from this source is found to be somewhat less than is popularly imagined. We must remember that the natural advantages of Canada and the United States have always favoured the rapid growth of their own native population, so that a large native increase must be expected irrespective of any inflow of foreign people.

A way of estimating the amount of population, due to the inrush of Europeans, has been suggested by Dr. Edward Jarvis in the *Atlantic Monthly*.[1] His method is best explained by taking a concrete example. During the decade 1870–80, the white population of the United States increased by 9,815,981 people. There arrived during the same interval 2,944,695 immigrants. By 1880 these latter had lived in the United States an average of 3·7 years. Allowing them a reasonable increase during that period of 2 per cent per annum, the total number of immigrants and their descendants in 1880 may be computed as 3,162,502. On subtracting this number from the total increase of white people,

---

[1] *Op. cit.*, April, 1872, p. 468; also see R. Mayo Smith, *Emigration and Immigration*, p. 59.

EMIGRATION AND IMMIGRATION 313

6,653,479 is obtained as an estimate of the natural expansion irrespective of immigrants. This number is equal to an increase in ten years of 19·48 per cent among the native white population. In this way Dr. Jarvis found the percentage of increase for each of the decades between 1790 and 1870. He was thus able to compute the total amount of native white population living in the United States in 1870. By subtracting the figures so found from those given in the Census returns referring to the total white population, he obtained what was probably a very fair estimate of the share due to immigration. In 1870, he considered the white people of foreign descent to equal 11,607,394, and those of native Western European descent to equal 21,479,595. Carrying on his figures from 1870 to the present day, we obtain thirty millions as a fair computation of the number of white people now living in the United States who are either foreigners or who owe their origin to foreign parentage.

A yet more elaborate method of determining the amount of population which is due to European emigration was published by the United States Census Bureau in 1901. In a treatise entitled, "A Century of Population," the Registrar suggested[1] that to arrive at a satisfactory approximation it is necessary to classify the immigrants under three heads. Under the first he placed all immigrants and their descendants arriving prior to 1853 who were alive in 1900. The second group embraced the immigrants and their descendants who arrived between 1853 and 1870 who were alive in 1900. The third and last group was devoted to the immigrants with their descendants who arrived between 1870 and 1900, and who were still living in the latter year.

For the first group his figures were a million and a

---

[1] *Op. cit.*, p. 87.

half; for the second six millions, and for the third half a million, making a total of eight millions in all. These people were, it will be understood, contributions made by foreign stock to the so-called native element, and for our purposes must be added to the foreign stock as recognised in the returns. The foreign stock was computed in 1900 as amounting to 32,500,000 souls, thus the total amount due to immigration since 1790 was forty and a half millions.

Far more important than the actual numbers which govern the inflow of Europeans is the influence which these people exert and the work they undertake when they settle in the North American continent. Before immigration became popular the settled areas fringed the sea coast from Georgia to Nova Scotia, then followed the course of the St. Lawrence as far as the great lakes, and along the Hudson and Mohawk valleys.[1] The towns were few and generally unimportant. Industries were in their infancy, and agriculture was hampered by a lack of hands and suitable markets. The task of clearing the forest belts, of cutting canals, of making the highroads, of linking the centres of trade by means of railways, and of staffing the various industrial and agricultural concerns, has largely been the work of the immigrant arriving after the close of the eighteenth century. Without the assistance of his labour many of these great undertakings could never have been commenced, others would have had their progress considerably checked, and others again owe their very inception to the demand which he has created for them. Just how much of the progress is due to his efforts it is impossible to say, but a rough idea may be obtained by sharing the work between the native people and those of recent European descent, in proportion to

---

[1] Cf. Chapter VIII.

their numbers.[1] In Canada there are two native Canadians to every five European descendants, and in the United States the ratio is roughly as one is to two.[2]. From this we may surmise that in the former country the immigrant is responsible for five-sevenths of the national progress, and two-thirds of it in the latter. Mulhall, in his *Dictionary of Statistics*,[3] attempts to put a monetary value on the work of the immigrant, so far as Canada is concerned. "The agricultural capital rose," he says, "from 140 millions in 1861 to 343 millions in 1887, and as immigrants formed 30 per cent of the population during that time they are entitled to take credit for that share of the increase, say 61 millions. Agriculture constituting only 50 per cent of the wealth of Canada, the total accumulation due to the immigrants will be 122 millions sterling for the twenty-six years under consideration." The same writer, speaking of the value which immigrants have been to the United States, says:[4] "A group of two hundred persons settled in 1858 on the territory now known as the State of Colorado, and in 1880 there were 1220 miles of railway, 14 daily papers, 190,000 inhabitants, real and personal estate valued at nine millions sterling, and agricultural products worth £700,000 a year. In 1886 the value of the property in Colorado had risen to twenty-seven million pounds sterling."

It is interesting to note how the immigrants have distributed themselves in the search for work. Contrary to an opinion sometimes held, the majority of them have not become engaged as farmers or homesteaders. The settlement of the West has been

---

[1] Every white man in America is really an immigrant or a descendant of an immigrant, but we are here differentiating between the stock of those who formed part of the nineteenth and twentieth century exodus and their earlier prototype. [2] See figures given above.
[3] *Op. cit.*, p. 246. [4] *Op. cit.*, p. 246.

mainly carried out by native stock and not by European visitors.[1] The immigrants, however, have materially assisted in the exploitation of the mining industry in the New England states, in Nova Scotia, and New Brunswick; they have given an impetus to the manufacturing centres on the Atlantic seaboard; they have hired themselves as labourers to landowners, and they have invaded all constructional undertakings where manual work is necessary. The Census returns state that more than half the people employed in mining in the United States are immigrants; in the manufacturing and mechanical pursuits they monopolise a third of the work, and of the people employed by the various railroad companies at least a quarter belong to the foreign element. Mayo Smith[2] tells us that the foreign-born are represented to the extent of 45 per cent among the operatives in the cotton mills, of 36 per cent in the woollen mills, 33 per cent in the paper mills, and 36 per cent in the iron and steel works. Professor Emery of Yale University, in summing up the work of the immigrant,[3] says that the tendency of the foreigner, as far as the United States is concerned, is towards city life, mechanical and mining occupations, personal service, hand trades, and shopkeeping. Though these remarks apply almost wholly to immigrants in Canada as well as to those of the United States, it is necessary to point out that the former country is welcoming to-day a larger percentage of farmers and settlers than are taking up entries in the latter. This is merely due to the degree of settlement of the territories in those two divisions. Canada has still vast tracts of fertile lands for disposal, but similar areas are rapidly disappearing in the United State.

From the foregoing we see that immigrants who take up their abode in the North American continent

---

[1] Professor Emery in *Cambridge Modern History*, Vol.VII, .p 702.
[2] *Emigration and Immigration*, p. 95.
[3] *Cambridge Modern History*, Vol. VII, p. 702

are, for the most part, unskilled or skilled in the lower grades of labour. Roughly speaking, three out of every four declare themselves on passing the customs as having no particular occupation.[1] The resources of the non-British element are often small, sometimes being barely sufficient to satisfy the money qualification imposed by the authorities. On landing it is imperative that they should obtain work at the earliest possible moment, a factor which drives many who are fitted for something better to swell the ranks of the unskilled. Fortunately, in opening out these countries and in bringing them up to a pitch of European civilisation, large quantities of manual labour have been necessary; in fact, the progress of Canada and the United States at one time depended, in a direct ratio, on the number of hands that could be pressed into their services.

Though the unskilled type of immigrant has been extremely successful in the past, the openings for his rough handiwork are gradually growing fewer and fewer. Much of the elementary pioneer work for which he proved so useful is completed, machinery is supplanting him, and, in addition to this, his native prototype is multiplying sufficiently rapidly to supply local requirements. As a result of these conditions the invader from Europe is looking to the American factories as an outlet for his labours. In this quarter he is causing a serious disturbance in the level of wages. By living amidst surroundings and conditions which would be impossible for the average American he is able to undersell his competitors and to secure their employment. The Ford Investigation Committee of 1888, dealing with this question, reported that the inferior grades of immigration had done much towards lowering wages and the standard of living.

---

[1] This is partly due to the fact that wives, travelling with their husbands, usually declare themselves as of no occupation; also, that children are returned as having no occupation.

The report which this Committee issued told how the lower classes of Europe had crowded out the native Americans in certain industries, notably the cigar trade, the tailoring trade, and the shirt-making trade. Fifteen years before the enquiry was instituted 90 per cent of the people employed in these three trades belonged to the native population; at the time of the report the foreigners constituted 90 per cent of the workers and the natives only 10 per cent. Again, in 1873, the cigar makers in New York were earning eighteen dollars a week. On differences arising between employers and employed, foreigners were imported to take the place of the American workers, and the wages were simultaneously reduced. In 1888 the wages of cigar makers in this city averaged only eight dollars a week. In short, the report says, the tendency of alien immigration is to lower considerably the standard of wages which the American labourer has hitherto enjoyed.

Fortunately we may claim that the British immigrant rarely offends in this manner; his standard of life is much the same as that of his American brother workman, and it would be financially impossible for him to attempt underselling to any appreciable extent. There is one way in which the Englishman offends, however. Thousands of our skilled mechanics, stone-cutters, stone-masons, glass-blowers, locomotive engineers, etc., regularly visit the New England states in the spring. They do not go as contract men, for such is forbidden, but they depend on their skill and ability as passports for speedily finding them work. They earn good wages all through the season, most of which is remitted to their wives in England. When the slack period arrives they pack their grip sacks and go back home, only to return to the United States at the commencement of the following spring.[1] In this

---

[1] "Immigration Troubles," *Nineteenth Century*, October, 1891, p. 588.

EMIGRATION AND IMMIGRATION

way, they escape American taxation, perform none of the duties of citizenship, and they spend the bulk of their money outside the country in which they earn it. This practice, however, is not wholly unfavourable to the interests of the United States. Their labour creates wealth for its exchequer, they incur no expenditure incidental to the education of their children, and they stay at home and so cause no congestion during periods of industrial depression.

Beyond the influence which immigration has exerted on industry, labour, and the growth of population, there is yet to consider the effect of this force on the social fabric of the North American continent. Philosophers argue that the most virile races of the world are those which spring from a multitude of closely allied sources; if this be true, then Canada and the United States have reaped considerable advantage, ethnically, from the inflow of members of the various European races. Undoubtedly the North Americans, as a whole, are keen, thriving, and businesslike; whether or not these qualities are partly due to the outcome of a continuous intermixing with other races it would be impossible to say.

Whatever views may be held on this matter, however, it is generally admitted that a certain section of the immigrant population of to-day is a burden and a hindrance to social progress. We may support this contention by turning to the figures relating to pauperism, illiteracy, sickness, vice, and crime, which show clearly that these disabilities are far more frequent among the foreign element than among the native born people.[1] Some years ago the *Nineteenth Century* published an essay dealing with " Immigra-

---

[1] These disabilities need not be permanent, nor are they necessarily transmitted to the next generation. Under better surroundings much reclaiming may be effected.

tion troubles in the United States." The writer gave the following figures :—

(*a*) In Massachusetts the foreign element was 47·3 per cent of the total population.
(*b*) Of the convicts within this area the foreign element totalled 51·1 per cent.
(*c*) Of the prisoners the foreign element totalled 60·3 per cent.

Thus we see that although the foreign element did not equal a half of the total population, yet the foreign convicts exceeded a half of all the convicts, whilst the prisoners, presumably people who were serving short sentences, comprised three-fifths of all those who were incarcerated. It is in examining the figures affecting pauperism, however, that the burden of the foreigner is most plainly noted. The Secretary of State of New York, the same writer adds, reported that in the country poor-houses there were 9288 foreign-born paupers and 9172 native paupers. In the city poor-houses the figures were still more disquieting, for the foreign-born paupers numbered 34,167, whilst the native paupers only totalled 18,001. It is only by remembering that in this state the foreign people equal but a third of the whole population, that these items can receive adequate appreciation. If the data referring to sickness be examined also, the same conclusion is arrived at, namely, that the immigrant population is a burden to the community, supplying as it does the preponderating share of the inmates of hospitals and asylums. For detailed figures respecting this matter, the reader is referred to the chapter dealing with restrictive measures. With respect to illiteracy the various Census Reports tell the same tale : the foreigner, frequently the Irishman, is a great offender.[1]

---
[1] Three-fifths of the aliens in New York are unable to read.—Bryce, the *American Commonwealth*, p. 476.

In less tangible, but equally important, ways the immigrant has frequently proved himself to be a vitiating element of the community. In many quarters of New York City and the hamlets surrounding it, in Chicago, in the mining regions of Pennsylvania, in New Jersey, and in certain districts of Colorado, he has ousted the native inhabitant, and has established himself there in great colonies.[1] In these areas the foreign element is so strong as to permit of little or no assimilation of Republican ideals. Progress is slow and at times entirely wanting. Habits indicating a lack of civilisation are apparent on all sides, and the absence of a native population precludes the new settlers from appreciating their own shortcomings. These areas are strongholds of crime and disease, and the multiplicity of tongues[2] which are spoken within them make the spread of education a matter of much difficulty.

From the foregoing it is seen that the immigrant population of North America is often of an inferior social character to that of the native population. Yet we find that the political status of the male foreigner is frequently such that he can override the demands of the natural-born voter. It is well known that the Irish vote in the United States favours a policy of antagonism to Great Britain, and that the resident Germans largely control the actions of political leaders on liquor questions. These matters are made possible by the fact that in several states the immigrant is admitted to citizenship after a single year's residence, while he is still ignorant of the laws, language, and customs, and before he has had time to appreciate the honoured institutions of the land which receives him. As a rule, the lower types of immigrant are easily influenced by members of

---

[1] Bryce, the *American Commonwealth*, p. 474.
[2] In Pennsylvania the Bible Society has found it necessary to distribute its Bibles in forty-two different languages.

their own race, but they will give no thought at all to the arguments, good or bad, which are placed before them by people who are foreign to them. They seldom use their individual judgment, and so are the prey of designing party leaders and political agents. Happily this disability only clings to the first generation, for we find that the children of those who have expatriated themselves, when once they can speak the English language, show an intelligent interest in political matters and exercise due judgment in voting.

Before leaving this chapter there is yet to consider the effect of immigration on the individual. Does he or does he not benefit by severing his connection with the Mother Country and settling in either Canada or the United States? Though the question is one which has aroused much controversy it may be safely said that, as a rule, either he or his children gain by the change. In America the emigrant's outlook is wider; the workers are less cramped, labour is more plentiful, and social distinctions are not so irksome as in Europe.

A great quantity of literature has, from time to time, been printed describing the life of the emigrant, but much of it, unfortunately, has been written from a biased point of view. Some authorities who hold a brief for expatriation have only given prominence to the satisfactory issues of the question, whilst others, being afraid that a continual exodus would eventually depopulate the country, have confined their energies to depicting none but the worst aspects. This was the case with the *Quarterly Review* during the first two decades of the nineteenth century. To support its views this periodical published paragraphs of which the following is typical:[1] " I have taken much pains to inquire and have had the very best opportunities of ascertaining the unhappy fate of many of those

---
[1] *Quarterly Review*, vol. 9, July, 1813.

EMIGRATION AND IMMIGRATION 323

unfortunate people who have emigrated from Scotland, Ireland, and Wales. The account of their poverty, wretchedness, nakedness, and misery is almost too horrible to describe. Of money there is none to be obtained; what is carried out is soon expended, and when their clothes are worn out they have no means of replacing them. If they should obtain employment as labourers they can get no wages in money from their employers. If they obtain land they can get no wages in money for its produce."

In 1823 the same review printed the following extract:[1] " I called on my townsfolk, Jack Bellcare and his wife; both are disappointed. Jack left a comfortable home and dairy behind him and now works bareheaded on the road, cursing the hot climate. Friend John Steed, from Wisbeach, was grievously disappointed; nearly broken in spirit and pocket, he finds charity cold and friends few or none. English labourers and first-rate mechanics are seen working at the capital for the low price of half a dollar a day. Very few English farmers succeed; the best of them scarcely hope for more than a bare subsistence, consisting chiefly of bacon, Indian corn, and villainous whisky, without any of the little comforts they were accustomed to in England. The states of New York and Pennsylvania are best for an English farmer of any condition; but if he can by any honest means make both ends meet he ought to stay at home."

In view of the satisfactory reports issued by various Government authorities, we can only state that though these remarks may be true of isolated cases, they are not typical of the great army of people who emigrated in those early times. The Report on Emigration, issued in 1826-7, gives overwhelming testimony as to the benefits derived by the people

---

[1] From *Memorable Days in America*, by W. Faux, p. 112.

324   A HISTORY OF EMIGRATION

who went to live in North America ; so do the reports of the Colonial Land and Emigration Commissioners. In later times the Reports on Colonisation of 1889, 1890, 1891, and the Report on Agricultural Settlements of 1906, have all pointed to a similar issue. Were the testimony of the chief emigration societies obtained to-day, it would also go to prove that emigrants prosper as a result of their new surroundings. As a typical report we quote from the 1909 Year Book of the East End Emigration Fund :[1]

> It is with pleasure that we are able to write of our emigrants, even those who have not been long in Canada, that the majority of them have not only emerged from the initial stage of finding their feet, but have prospered greatly, have bought land, built houses and are rising into the higher grades of industry. Many of these successful ones write home for relations or friends, offering them house and board, and often work, until they can arrange for themselves.

Not only have we such documentary evidence as the foregoing to prove our contention, but in many minor ways it may be logically concluded that emigration tends to transplant the individual among favourable surroundings. If people who left their Mother Country to escape poverty were able to send home to their relatives an aggregate of fifteen million pounds in twenty-two years it seems a sure sign that prosperity attended their efforts. Yet this is the sum of money which came into the United Kingdom from former emigrants during the years 1847–69.[2] At the time of the great famine in Ireland, and during the various agricultural depressions in England, it cannot be gainsaid that by sending the sufferers to North America many were spared from disease and death. It is not, however, during such troublous

---
[1] *Op. cit.* p. 3.
[2] Thirtieth Report of the Colonial Land and Emigration Commissioners, 1870, XVII, p. 127.

EMIGRATION AND IMMIGRATION 325

times as these alone that emigration has rendered assistance. Every year it redeems thousands of men who for want of sufficient work in the Mother Country are gradually sinking deeper and deeper into poverty. By remaining at home they become demoralised and their chances slowly slip away from them, their ultimate fate being the workhouse. By emigrating, however, the fresh horizon of life gives them a new zest for work, and they soon develop into citizens of whom their adopted country is justly proud.

To-day the people most likely to derive benefit from emigration either to Canada or the United States may be roughly classified as farm labourers, domestic servants, and capitalists. For the farmer there seems a demand which increases with each season, whilst the wages obtained by them show a satisfactory upward trend.[1] For domestic service there are also unlimited opportunities. Not only do these workers receive fairly good wages, but the social status accorded to them in the country districts is far above that which they enjoy in the United Kingdom. For people with money who are willing to master the rudiments of American farming, cattle and horse breeding, market-gardening, fruit-growing, or store keeping there are also a multitude of opportunities.

Success, however, does not depend on the choice of occupation so much as on personal aptitude. A man who is fit and willing to turn his hand to the first opportunity which comes his way will rarely fail to succeed. Nevertheless, he must be ready to learn the American system of doing things, although he may feel that the Europeans employ a far better method. Canadians and their southern neighbours, it is well known, have a natural objection to English people of

---

[1] In Canada the wages for male farm hands averaged $347.10, and female hands $209.69 in 1910, as against $336.29 and $206.08 in 1909.—Census Bureau Returns.

the self-satisfied type, with the consequence that these seldom make headway.

The conjugal state of an immigrant has much to do with his ultimate success. The bachelor town worker possesses great advantages over his married brother. The former is mobile and can shift, when necessary, from town to town in search of suitable work, but the married man is hampered in his movements by his family, and therefore enjoys fewer chances of obtaining employment. Where homesteaders are concerned, however, the married immigrant shapes better than the unmarried. The bachelor is less able to settle down amidst the solitude of farm life, his nomadic nature often masters him, and frequently he is to be found quitting a prosperous homestead for the attractions of an urban existence. The married man, on the other hand, suffers less in this way, for his wife and children help to banish monotony, although the wife is frequently attacked with homesickness, and, in numbers of cases, persuades her husband to return to Europe. Two or three children prove a valuable asset to the married homesteader. These can be put to the lighter kinds of farm work during the busier part of the season, and in this way save the wages which would be otherwise paid to a hired labourer. More than three children, it need hardly be added, make serious inroads into the parental savings unless some of them are old enough to shift for themselves. In their case the ultimate benefits which fall to their lot greatly exceed those obtained by their parents.

Such is the value of emigration to the Mother Country, to the receiving country, and to the individual. To all three, there are positive and negative interests, but, generally, the former seem to outweigh the latter. The value of emigration, imperially, yet remains to be discussed.

CHAPTER XIV

PROBLEMS OF EMIGRATION

THE Board of Trade returns for 1912 state that emigration is drawing population from the United Kingdom at the rate of approximately three hundred thousand per annum :[1] in other words, one person out of every hundred and forty is destined to leave the Mother Country and settle within the Colonies or under the flag of a foreign Power. Most of these people are selected for their capacity for labour and high standard of health; they are mostly of an age when their economic worth is at its maximum, and they nearly all possess a certain amount of capital. A question of supreme importance is : " Can the Homeland afford to spare, in ever-growing numbers, these valuable members of its community ? "

It needs little argument to affirm that the migration of such people to foreign lands does involve a loss to the parent State unless the individual sets out to take up work in which his native country is directly interested. Unhappily this unprofitable migration is still very great, the total exodus of British subjects to foreign countries being 109,585 in 1901, 129,115 in 1905, and 148,399 in 1910.

Touching the outflow of British subjects to the Colonies the question is of a much more complicated nature. At the present time the United Kingdom stands in need of a strong population to face the competitive strength of Germany ; Canada is appealing for men not only to open out her industries, but

---
[1] The total emigration from the United Kingdom in 1911 was 272,996, balance outward.

also to guard against commercial and intellectual absorption by the United States, while the thoughts of Australia are turned towards Japan. Thus it is imperative that the great centres of the Empire should either maintain or increase the strength of their numbers.

How can this be done ? The only solution seems to lie in a recourse to colonial emigration. Population, we know, increases more freely in the Colonies than at home; therefore, if a number of the inhabitants of the United Kingdom are permitted to emigrate, it is logical to argue that the Empire will benefit numerically and, consequently, in military and commercial strength. But this giving of population by the Mother Country to her Colonies should not be done in a haphazard way, without any understanding or arrangement as at present holds. There should be a definite agreement between the various units of the Empire that all will band together in times of stress; this should be a fundamental axiom of Imperial agreement. As matters now stand the United Kingdom provides the Colonies with able and healthy stock at the rate of two hundred thousand a year, and in return has as yet no definite guarantee that her generosity will be repaid should external pressure force her to call for Colonial assistance. If we, in Britain, send the pick of our youth to people the dominions beyond the seas, and if, at the same time, we largely bear the burden of the Empire's defence,[1] then the dominions should be ready to give us the assurance that their support will be forthcoming whenever we require it. Of course, we feel that the bonds existing between the Mother Country and her Colonies are of a strong and sympathetic nature : we

---

[1] " Military and naval expenditure in the United Kingdom amounts to 29s. 3d. per head. In Canada it is only 2s."—The Secretary of State for the Colonies, Colonial Conference, 1902. It should be added, however, that at the moment of writing the question of Imperial defence is being considered by Canadian legislators.

have had ample testimony of late to prove that they are so, but none the less the situation is one that needs clearly defining, especially as " it is probably true to say, though it may not be generally admitted, that as each succeeding year adds conspicuously to the population of the young peoples of the . . . British Empire, the value of the Dominions to England increases in much greater proportion than the value of England to the Dominions."[1]

It is sometimes argued that the Mother Country is only too glad to get rid of a proportion of her population, seeing that those who go help to nullify the " surplus " which is said to exist at home, and that, in consequence, the Colonies need show no indebtedness, as they are already conferring a sufficient favour by opening their doors to this surplus. In many ways the home country does reap benefits from emigration. When her men and women return to their native land they bring with them fresh ideas and knowledge such as can only be learnt in a youthful continent ; the going and returning thus rejuvenates the old country and goes far towards banishing decay.[2] But it must not be thought that we are suffering at the present time from a congestion of population, nor that by lessening our numbers we shall reap material advantages. The strength of nations is largely reckoned by the extent of their people ; France, for instance, is troubled by a contracting birth-rate, whilst Germany points with pride to figures denoting popular expansion. Many authorities hold the view which a writer expresses in the following passage, quoted from a recent issue of the *Nineteenth Century* :[3] " By virtue of her

---

[1] Sir Charles Lucas, *Greater Rome and Greater Britain*, p. 174.

[2] " The ascendancy of Europe in the world, of Old World methods and standards, is no longer unchallenged. The future is largely for the " New Model " among peoples, and in the competition of the future it is all-important for England to have by her side British peoples built, for better or worse, on the New Model."—Sir Charles Lucas, *Greater Rome*, etc., p. 175.

[3] *Op. cit.*, " A Littler England." March, 1912, p. 494.

coal supply, which still ranks next to that of the United States in magnitude and cheapness of production, the United Kingdom can easily sustain a population very much greater than she now possesses. Practical proof of this is afforded by the fact that Belgium, another country which bases industry upon coal, has a population of 590 to the square mile, at which rate the United Kingdom would have about seventy-one million people instead of the forty-five million she now possesses."

In spite of these conditions, the same writer proceeds to show that while the population of the United Kingdom is threatened with decline that of the German Empire is still rapidly increasing, a most serious matter when considering questions of national defence. Though it is true that the German birthrate has fallen, it is still higher than ours, and Germany, instead of losing population by migration, is actually gaining immigrants on its balance inward. From the following table, based upon figures published by the Board of Trade in *British and Foreign Trade and Industry*,[1] it will be seen that Germany is beginning to take the place which used to be occupied by France in gaining people by migration.

AVERAGE ANNUAL LOSS OR GAIN BY MIGRATION
IN THE PERIODS NAMED

Period.	By United Kingdom.	By German Empire.	By France.
In the Sixties	−114,000	No record.	No record.
In the Seventies	− 92,000	− 78,000	+48,000
In the Eighties	−156,000	−131,000	+13,000
In the Nineties	− 58,000	− 35,000	+36,000
First 5 years of twentieth century	No record yet by this method, but about −100,000	+ 10,000	− 7,000

In spite of the obvious gravity of these matters we see no cause for apprehension in the extensive exodus to the Colonies: firstly, if the Colonies are prepared

---

[1] Cd. 4954 of 1909.

to assist the Mother Country in shouldering the burden of Imperial Defence, and, secondly, as long as the outflow does not exceed the natural increase, at home, of births over deaths.[1] We do see cause for apprehension, however, when the standard of the emigrants is considered. To-day the immigration laws of, say, Canada, are so severe that only the ablest and healthiest workers can secure an entrance into the Dominion. To draw each season some two hundred thousand picked members from our community must leave us physically and morally poorer. In one year the harm, truly, is imperceptible; in a decade, however, it must leave traces of an insidious character. It must not be thought that we are desirous of finding a home in Canada for any portion of our undesirables when we deplore the high standard of selection adopted by the Dominion immigration authorities, but we are desirous of pointing out that there are many grades of workers in the home country who are debarred an entrance to the Dominion, but who could perform valuable service in opening up the infant settlements of the West were they permitted to pass the authorities at Quebec. The truth is that the legislators of Canada, especially those representing the labour party, show an insufficient appreciation of the working-classes of the United Kingdom. But this is not the only fault committed by these politicians. Knowing full well that rural Britain is suffering from depopulation and that farm workers are becoming all too few,[2] they have permitted a drag-net to be spread over the agricultural districts of these islands in order that people may be enticed from us whom we can ill afford to lose. Their action points either to a lack of knowledge concerning our home economy or, what is far worse, to a disinclination to study the needs of the parent country.

---

[1] In 1910 this increase was eleven per thousand.
[2] Cf. the depopulation of the agricultural districts of Scotland.

In several ways the restrictive code of Canada presses severely, in our opinion, unnecessarily severely, on the intending emigrant from Britain. One stipulation requires that all men who seek an entrance into the Dominion and who receive assistance from charitable societies or public funds must take up farm work, in spite of any desire or aptitude they may personally possess for pursuing other occupations. The position is, therefore, as follows : If an emigrant has saved enough to pay for his own passage, and, in addition, can show a certain amount of ready-money on passing through the immigration sheds,[1] he is free to enter Canada and take up any calling he chooses; but if his own funds are supplemented with charitable or public assistance, then the Dominion demands that he shall become a farmer or a farm labourer. As though such an edict were not sufficiently drastic, the following letter appears to have been forwarded to all the most important aid societies by the Assistant-Superintendent of Emigration on April 20th, 1910 :

I beg to advise you that the regulations providing that no persons assisted financially by any emigration society, charitable organisation, or out of public funds can be permitted to land in Canada without the consent of this Office have been amended as follows : Hereafter, such consent can only be given to persons suited for, willing to accept, and for whom positions at farm work have been guaranteed from Canada, no matter whether they have the landing money or are going to friends and relations.

From this letter it is clear that the Dominion is determined to drive all assisted male emigrants on to the land, whether they be skilled workers in their own particular trades or not. Moreover, the authorities, in their haste to manufacture agriculturists, drafted the memorandum in such a way as to imply that a

---

[1] A sum ranging from $12½ to $50, according to age and season of entry.

PROBLEMS OF EMIGRATION 333

wife, who intended joining her husband, living, perhaps, in the centre of Montreal, but who accepted financial assistance from, say, the British Women's Emigration Association, could not go to him unless she were "suited for, willing to accept, and had a position guaranteed for her at farm work." Even domestic servants,[1] who, it may be said, are assisted in thousands to proceed to the Dominion, had, according to the inference drawn from this letter, to take up farm work.

Why the Canadian authorities have seen fit to tighten up these laws which primarily affect British workmen, it is hard to understand. One naturally wonders if the standard of the English emigrant has suddenly fallen, or whether people from the Mother Country are proving unduly burdensome in the Dominion. No such condition, however, appears to have arisen, for the Department of the Interior reported[2] in 1910 that "the class of immigrants from the United Kingdom is superior to what it used to be," while the following reassuring information is quoted from the report of 1908 : "The Deputy-Minister of the Interior declares that there are scarcely any grounds for the uneasiness manifested as to the large proportion of undesirables entering Canada from Great Britain." "It is true," he says, "that some immigrants are not immediately self-supporting, and are induced to come by the injudicious zeal of philanthropic societies, but those are few compared to the hundreds and thousands of British immigrants added to the population. The chief medical inspector reports that of 1002 immigrants who were refused entry, only 112 were British, or one-ninth of the total exclusions, although the British arrivals during the year (i.e. 120,182) were nearly one-half of the total immigration." In view of these statements, made by competent Canadian authorities, it seems only natural

---
[1] This section of the memorandum is now obsolete.
[2] *Canada Year Book*, 1910, p. xl.

to question whether or not the shutting out of these British workers from the Dominion factories is due to motives of real economic necessity or whether it is a party move of the labour organisations.

That it is clearly a case of labour pressure seems only too evident if the following quotation from *The Standard of Empire*[1] is to be given credence :

> A policy of restriction has been adopted by the Canadian Government against all classes of artisans wanting to emigrate to Canada. This has been done in the face of a general shortage of labour in most lines of manufacturing industries. The labour trust has made its influence felt. By maintaining a supply that will be at all times inadequate to the demand the agitators figure that their requests will be met, however extravagant they may be.
>
> This country (i.e. Canada) needs artisans, it needs carriage-makers, boiler-makers, machinists—men who can produce through their labour enough to make it profitable for employers to pay them three, four, or five dollars a day; this country needs these men as much as it needs farmers. Why should there be a discrimination against a man because his labour is not that of tilling the soil ? It requires all classes of men to make a nation. Through their energetic and aggressive advertising methods the Government have turned the stream of agricultural immigrants towards these shores. Must not the other walks of life be increased to keep pace with this development ? During the past three years Canada's population has increased by over six hundred thousand. Does not this call for more shoemakers, more canbinet-makers, more textile workers ? But whence are they to come ?

Again, the clause in the restrictive code of Canada, which provides for the deportation of people who become a public charge within three years of their landing, seems also open to exception. That the Dominion should safeguard itself against the unfair dumping within its confines of people who are already

---

[1] Under date of July 1st, 1910; this article originally appeared in *Industrial Canada*.

PROBLEMS OF EMIGRATION 335

or who are likely to become chargeable is clear to all, but it must be equally obvious that the Mother Country ought not to be held responsible for the moral and mental condition of her offspring for so long a period as thirty-six months after they have gone beyond her shores. In three years much that is unforeseen may happen, and the Dominion should be prepared, if it takes the immigrants, to take also the risks which are inherent to their very existence. As the regulations now stand there is nothing that we can find to prevent the authorities from shipping back to England a British workman who had met with a serious accident within the Dominion, and had been confined to a hospital for treatment, nor would it be a contravention of the Act to return to the Motherland a person whose reason had been suddenly impaired by prolonged exposure to severe climatic conditions. Whether the authorities would deport or not, were the above extreme cases to arise, is a matter which need not detain us ; the law allows for their deportation, and that in itself is sufficient ground for complaint.[1]

Certain distinctions which are made between charity found in England and Canada, for purposes of emigration, also seem to be of a vexatious character. According to the Dominion regulations at present in force a woman in the home country, who travels to Canada to join her husband, already settled there, may proceed as an ordinary passenger, although her husband has obtained charitable assistance within the Dominion to enable her to do so. If, however, the wife obtains the necessary assistance from a society or local body within the United Kingdom, then she must comply with many formalities before permission to sail is granted her by the Office of the Assistant-Superintendent of Emigration. Why, ask our British

---
[1] Cf. the deportation laws of the United States on this matter, vide Chapter VII.

aid societies, does home assistance stand in need of greater supervision than that advanced in the Dominion ? Whilst dealing with the question of the drain which is caused on this side of the Atlantic by the restrictive measures imposed by American powers, it is fitting to discuss, briefly, the various checks which our European neighbours have devised in order to arrest the outflow of their better-class population. The Swiss emigration laws are probably the most stringent in this matter. An Act of 1888 made it an offence at law to advertise in connection with trans-Atlantic passages ; to urge a man to leave his native land was also forbidden, whilst the indiscriminate selling of passenger tickets was checked by the provision of a limited number of licensed steamship agents. Thus emigration from Switzerland is, legally, free of all artificial stimulus.[1] In Germany, an enactment of 1897 forbade the departure of any citizen who had not completed his military training ; it appointed, also, a special staff of officials to regulate the emigration agencies. Later legislation prohibited advertising. The movement in Italy is practically in the hands of the Government, and no one can lawfully depart from trans-Atlantic ports without special permission.[2] Agents who work under State control are neither allowed to advertise nor use persuasion, whilst passage rates are kept somewhat high in order that they may not prove too attractive. Practically the same laws are enforced by Hungary as Italy, but, in addition, the Hungarian Government claims the right to name the routes by which all migrants are to travel. In Russia, the laws

---

[1] It is necessary to mention, however, that even these stringent measures are set at nought. Though advertising and persuasion are illegal, there is nothing to prevent a lecturer giving a discourse on the charms of colonial life and so instilling in his audience a desire of emigrating. We were present once at such a lecture in a little mountain village, and it was perfectly obvious that the one desire of the lecturer was not to educate his listeners, but to swell the tide of emigrants.

[2] J. D. Whelpley, *The Problem of the Immigrant*, p. 29 *et seq.*

PROBLEMS OF EMIGRATION 337

have been extremely severe since the time of the Japanese War. Permits for crossing the frontier are only granted when all military obligations are at an end, but large numbers of would-be emigrants escape across the borders under the guidance of ticket agents. In Belgium, the Emigration Commissioners have constituted themselves the sole judges as to the qualifications of those who shall be permitted to depart, a matter which complicates the work of the steamship companies. Of all these enactments there seems only one which might profitably find a place in the English statute book; that is the Swiss or German law which prohibits certain forms of advertising.

A second question of importance is, " Should the Home Government take an active part in forwarding emigrants and financing their movement ? " Certainly, if this were done the leakage to foreign States could be reduced to a minimum, and the flow to the less populous colonies strengthened—two matters which are of great moment. Personally, however, we feel that the State should confine its energies to regulating the flow, and should in no wise give financial assistance in creating it. Were an Imperial grant to be voted, private contributions would be immediately arrested, and the thousands of passage tickets which are annually sent over from America would probably contract into a few hundred. The taxes would be burdened, perhaps with little benefit, with the cost of this vote, and the type of people who would petition for support would be the very ones that are useful at home; those, in fact, who are leaving the country speedily enough without the aid of any artificial stimulus. In addition to these economic matters, there would always be a strong element of imposition to contend against. These are the factors as they concern us at home; there is also the colonial point of view to consider. Were a large Imperial grant to be voted to encourage emigration, the labour parties, which are extremely powerful in many of the overseas possessions, would feel alarmed at the consequences and would probably cry out for additional immigration restrictions. There would be little objection, on their part, however, to State-aided colonisation, as an influx of settlers would have no effect on the labour markets.

Were the Imperial Government merely to advance a loan in place of a grant in aid, some of the above objections would disappear; there would be fewer cases of fraudulent declarations, and there would be less likelihood of a curtailment of the provided passages. On the other hand, the Home Government would experience great difficulties in obtaining the repayments from North American and probably most other destinations, since many of the colonies have flatly refused on several occasions to give assistance by collecting such moneys. They feel bound to follow this course, as the male immigrant is admitted to the franchise after an extremely short period of residence and questions of repayment might easily be brought into political struggles. The wandering nature of emigrants, in general, would also make the collection of such sums a complicated business, whilst their recovery would be practically impossible from men and women who might be induced to retreat into a foreign State. In cases of death they would be lost entirely.

Though we feel that the Government would be ill-advised were it to grant free passages to any of the colonies,[1] we can see that much good would accrue

---

[1] It is interesting to compare the views of early and pre-Victorian organisers with those set out here. Elliot, the Agent-General for Emigration, said in 1837 that no direct aid should be given to help people to go: their safety in transit should be the only care of the Government. Lord Durham and C. Buller both held an opposite view. They claimed that the State should provide for, stimulate, and safeguard the exodus. Wakefield thought that assisted and free passages were necessary for the progress of a colony.

PROBLEMS OF EMIGRATION 339

were the Emigrants' Information Office to be assisted with a much more generous vote. Certain approved emigration societies might also be subsidised with State money.

What are the respective merits of emigration and colonisation : understanding by the former a movement from one land to another of people who intend to make their permanent homes in the country of reception, and by the latter not only the idea of movement to a new country, but also settlement on the land, usually in considerable numbers within a circumscribed area ?

Primarily it may be said that emigration is a much cheaper process than colonisation. An emigrant may be transferred from the Mother Country to his new home at a total outlay of something less than ten pounds ; a coloniser, on the other hand, will require at least a hundred pounds before he can start, and he would be well advised to wait until he could spend five to ten times this amount of capital.

Not only does the emigrant stand in need of less financial assistance than the coloniser, but the requirements for a successful issue are less exacting in his case. For him to succeed he must manage to fare decidedly better than he did at home ; for the colonist, not only must he make more headway than he did in the old country, but he must be in a position to save enough money to pay a fair rate of interest on his capital outlay, and should he wish at any time to dispose of his farm he must be able to do so without involving a pecuniary loss.

As long as the people who sail from our shores are energetic, desirous of making progress and fit in body, their success as emigrants should be assured, but many qualities in addition to these are requisite for the colonist. The colonist must also be in possession of a strong determination, ample self-reliance, perseverance, and a spirit unaffected by prolonged monotony. In favour of colonisation we may argue that the emigrant can only succeed when there is a demand for the class of labour which he can perform, whereas the ground idea of colonisation is that demand and supply go together. As long as land is available, and there is still enough in North America for many years ahead, the colonist can always find an outlet for his enterprise. Also, it may be urged, with much truth, that for a man with a large family of children who are past the age of schooling, colonisation is frequently more attractive than emigration.

The Departmental Committee which sat to consider Sir H. Rider Haggard's proposals discussed at length the relative merits of emigration and colonisation. Three main arguments, it reported,[1] have been urged in favour of colonisation as contrasted with emigration. Firstly, it has been said that circumstances may arise in which colonisation is possible but emigration impossible.[2] Secondly, it has been urged that colonisation enables assistance to be recovered, whereas money advanced for emigration is seldom recoverable. And thirdly, it has been said by some witnesses that there are certain classes unsuited for emigration but well suited for colonisation: farm hands, for example. But, proceeded the report of the Committee, we do not see that any of the arguments which have been brought forward in favour of colonisation in principle are convincing. On the other hand, the arguments in favour of emigration are many, and appear to us to be very forcible. Certainly there must be many persons unsuited for working as master farmers but suited for emigration. For instance, colonisation is hardly suitable for single women, large numbers of whom are now being successfully emigrated by such societies as the British Women's Emigration Associa-

---

[1] Pages 6, 7.   [2] Vide *supra.*

PROBLEMS OF EMIGRATION 341

tion. Again, it is clear, in any line of life, and especially in agriculture, that a man may be quite competent to act under orders, but not possess sufficient ability or experience to undertake the management of a business for himself. And if it be said that with a thorough preliminary training such men might become fitted, the answer is that such training is best obtained in Canada by working on farms for a year or two—and that is really emigration.

Considering finally, in its broadest sense, the position of such emigration as proceeds to the British Colonies, it may be claimed without fear of contradiction that the continuous and constant outflow of British subjects to our overseas possessions is a force of greater power than almost any other in the economy of our Empire. Colonial emigration has helped to build up an Empire, the numerical strength of which, counting only the white inhabitants, makes us one of the first-class Powers of the world. On quitting the home country for a colonial settlement our subjects neither lose their nationality nor we their reserve strength: they do not go forth to create keen industrial rivalry, as they would do were their destination a foreign country, but they settle where their energies still tell in favour of the Motherland. In explanation of this statement, it may be mentioned that the infancy of most colonies is spent in pursuing agricultural advancement; the people who are attracted to these areas are, therefore, occupied in adding to the resources of the home food supply. Were these men and women to go, however, to a more developed region, such as the United States, they might easily stimulate there an industrial competition such as would prove harmful to the Mother Country. In later stages of development the Colonies usually evolve industries of their own, but as long as they remain an integral part of the Empire the rivalry which they give rise to is of the same type as that which exists between Cardiff and Middlesborough. It is usually the case, however, that the Colonies develop specialities of their own which increase the total Imperial resources without encroaching upon those of the United Kingdom.

Colonial emigration opens up new fields for the investment of capital, and so brings about the potential increase of Imperial riches ; this, in turn, induces greater desires for national safety. To be safe to-day a nation must be strong, and its strength eventually depends on its capacity to pay for its armaments. Any new fund from which armaments or men can be derived is a source of national safety. It may be reasonably expected that the self-governing Colonies will take over more and more of their own defence, and will provide a contingent for Imperial defensive purposes. All creation of Imperial wealth makes for Imperial safety, and on Imperial safety depend those social reforms which all modern peoples have at heart, and which are the first things to be laid aside in time of war.

But colonial emigration does more ; it ensures for our nation a prestige which extends to all the continents of the earth. Such prestige in itself makes for safety, since it is probable, after what happened in the late South African War, that, should the need arise, the Colonies would make common cause with England, and an entity so large as the British Empire could not be attacked lightly.

Emigration has made our interests world-wide : no movement can be undertaken in any quarter of the globe without its reflection being cast, in some manner, upon the British Empire. Our pride of race has also been enhanced by this important movement, for the vigorous communities which are now proud to call themselves British are a tribute to our capabilities for reducing the undeveloped areas of the world to law, order, and prosperity. This has not been done by high-sounding phraseology, but by a steady stream of emigrants who have successfully transplanted the English type in such diverse quarters of the globe as Canada, South Africa, Australia, and New Zealand.

Colonial emigration, in short, provides a multitude of outlets for the genius of expansion and capacity for government which is so fundamental a feature of the British race.

APPENDIX I

Statistical Tables Relating to Emigration

TABLE I

DESTINATION OF EMIGRANTS SAILING FROM THE UNITED KINGDOM

Year.	British North America.	United States.	Australian Colonies and New Zealand.	Year.	British North America.	United States.	Australian Colonies and New Zealand.
1815	680	1,209	—	1840	32,293	40,642	15,850
1816	3,370	9,022	—	1841	38,164	45,017	32,625
1817	9,797	10,280	—	1842	54,123	63,852	8,534
1818	15,136	12,429	—	1843	23,518	28,335	3,478
1819	23,534	10,674	—	1844	22,924	43,660	2,229
1820[1]	17,921	6,745	—	1845	31,803	58,538	830
1821	12,955	4,958	320	1846	43,439	82,239	2,347
1822	16,013	4,137	875	1847[4]	109,680	142,154	4,949
1823	11,355	5,032	543	1848	31,065	188,233	23,904
1824	8,774	5,152	780	1849	41,367	219,450	32,191
1825	8,741	5,551	485	1850	32,961	223,078	16,037
1826	12,818	7,063	903	1851	42,605	267,357	21,532
1827	12,648	14,526	715	1852[5]	32,873	244,261	87,881
1828	12,084	12,817	1,056	1853	34,522	230,885	61,401
1829	13,307	15,678	2,016	1854	43,761	193,065	83,237
1830	30,574	24,887	1,242	1855[6]	17,966	103,414	52,309
1831	58,067	23,418	1,561	1856	16,378	111,837	44,584
1832	66,339	32,872	3,733	1857[7]	21,001	126,905	61,248
1833	28,808	29,109	4,093	1858	9,704	59,716	39,295
1834	40,060	33,074	2,800	1859	6,689	70,303	31,013
1835	15,573	26,720	1,860	1860	9,786	87,500	24,302
1836[2]	34,226	37,774	3,124	1861[8]	12,707	49,764	23,738
1837	29,884	36,770	5,054	1862	15,522	58,706	38,828
1838[3]	4,577	14,332	14,021	1863	18,083	146,813	50,157
1839	12,658	33,536	15,786	1864	12,721	147,042	40,073

[1] No reliable figures are available for Australia prior to 1821.
[2] Exodus increased owing to agricultural depression.
[3] Insurrection in Canada.
[4] Irish Famine and discovery of gold in California in autumn of 1847.
[5] Discovery of gold in Australia.
[6] Decrease in exodus owing to revival of trade and demand for men for Crimea.
[7] Increased prosperity in home agriculture.
[8] Civil War in United States.

APPENDIX I

Year.	British North America.	United States.	Australian Colonies and New Zealand.	Year.	British North America.	United States.	Australian Colonies and New Zealand.
1865	17,211	147,258	36,683	1889	38,056	240,395	28,834
1866	13,255	161,000	23,682	1890	31,897	233,522	21,570
1867	15,503	159,275	14,023	1891	33,752	252,016	19,957
1868	21,062	155,532	12,332	1892	41,866	235,221	16,183
1869[1]	33,891	203,001	14,457	1893	50,381	213,212	11,412
1870	35,295	196,075	16,526	1894	23,633	159,431	11,151
1871	32,671	198,843	11,695	1895	22,357	195,632	10,809
1872	32,205	233,747	15,248	1896	22,590	154,496	10,710
1873	37,208	233,073	26,428	1897	22,669	132,048	12,396
1874	25,450	148,161	53,958	1898	27,487	123,703	11,020
1875	17,378	105,046	35,525	1899	33,669	159,143	12,268
1876	12,327	75,533	33,191	1900	50,007	189,391	15,723
1877	9,289	64,027	31,071	1901	42,898	194,941	15,754
1878	13,836	81,557	37,214	1902	67,600	232,099	14,675
1879	22,509	134,590	42,178	1903	99,582	251,941	12,573
1880	29,340	257,274	25,438	1904	91,684	291,945	14,210
1881	34,561	307,973	24,093	1905	108,118	276,636	15,488
1882	53,475	295,539	38,604	1906	141,786	338,612	19,589
1883	53,566	252,226	73,017	1907	185,831	366,396	25,067
1884	37,043	203,519	45,944	1908	95,428	198,321	33,900
1885	22,928	184,470	40,689	1909	113,318	259,933	38,350
1886	30,121	238,386	44,055	1910	196,305	303,364	46,246
1887	44,406	296,901	35,198	1911	213,361	250,969	72,294
1888	49,107	293,087	31,725				

Table I gives the figures relating to emigration from the United Kingdom where the destinations have been either North America or Australia, including New Zealand. The latter division is merely given for comparison. Other destinations are not quoted, as being outside the province of this survey. The figures relate not to British subjects alone, but to the total exodus to the countries mentioned. It is true that the earlier figures were concerned almost entirely with men and women of our own nationality, but as the facilities of transport increased, the numbers gradually contained more and more of the foreign element. The accuracy which is displayed in the compilation of later figures must not be looked for in the earlier ones, as these, in many cases, were little more than rough estimates. It must be remembered that the Customs officials were responsible for the pre-Victorian returns, and no account could be taken by them of ships which did not obtain legal clearances before sailing. The sources of the above figures are (a) the Customs Returns, (b) the Annual

---

[1] Great distress in England.

Reports of the Colonial Land and Emigration Commissioners, and (c) the annual copies of tables relating to Emigration and Immigration ordered by the House of Commons. It should be noted that the foregoing table refers to the exodus from the United Kingdom and not to the volume of passenger traffic entering either Canada, Australia, or the United States. The latter may differ from the former owing to deaths or births happening during the voyage.

TABLE II

DESTINATION OF BRITISH EMIGRANTS SAILING FROM THE UNITED KINGDOM

Year.	British North America.	United States.	Australian Colonies and New Zealand.	Year.	British North America.	United States.	Australian Colonies and New Zealand.
1880	20,902	166,570	24,184	1896	15,267	98,921	10,354
1881	23,912	176,104	22,682	1897	15,571	85,324	12,061
1882	40,441	181,903	37,289	1898	17,640	80,494	10,693
1883	44,185	191,573	71,264	1899	16,410	92,482	11,467
1884	31,134	155,280	44,255	1900	18,443	102,797	14,922
1885	19,838	137,687	39,395	1901	15,757	104,195	15,350
1886	24,745	152,710	43,076	1902	26,293	108,498	14,345
1887	32,025	201,526	34,183	1903	59,652	123,663	12,375
1888	34,853	195,986	31,127	1904	69,681	146,445	13,910
1889	28,269	168,771	28,294	1905	82,437	122,370	15,139
1890	22,520	152,413	21,179	1906	114,859	144,817	19,331
1891	21,578	156,395	19,547	1907	151,216	170,264	24,767
1892	23,254	150,039	15,950	1908	81,321	96,869	33,569
1893	24,732	148,949	11,203	1909	85,887	109,700	37,620
1894	17,459	104,001	10,917	1910	156,990	132,192	45,701
1895	16,622	126,502	10,567	1911	184,860	121,814	80,770

Table II refers only to passengers of British nationality and contains no account of people of foreign descent who have embarked from ports within the Kingdom to the destinations stated. In neither case do the tables give the net emigration, that is to say, the balance outward over the inward movement; they merely give the numbers as handled by the shipping companies. Table II does not date back as far as Table I, as, in the earlier years, the total movement also approximated the outgoing of British emigrants, few foreigners embarking from our ports. The most remarkable feature of this table is the steady growth of Canadian immigration which in 1910 had outgrown that destined for the United States.

APPENDIX I

TABLE III

BALANCE OUTWARD OF EMIGRANTS OF BRITISH (AND IRISH NATIONALITY) TO CANADA AND THE UNITED STATES

Year.	Canada.	United States.	Year.	Canada.	United States.
1876	2,706	none[1]	1894	7,203	20,478
1877	2,033	603	1895	5,951	55,443
1878	4,448	20,654	1896	5,728	39,709
1879	14,455	71,758	1897	5,631	31,689
1880	16,214	140,052	1898	7,846	29,766
1881	18,151	146,323	1899	8,015	38,839
1882	34,344	153,435	1900	7,803	47,978
1883	37,164	144,870	1901	7,121	45,883
1884	22,273	93,814	1902	14,730	51,617
1885	10,517	80,083	1903	45,866	65,392
1886	17,578	99,801	1904	51,284	66,790
1887	25,177	143,183	1905	62,503	60,997
1888	26,036	131,955	1906	91,263	85,941
1889	19,627	97,379	1907	117,525	99,944
1890	12,995	77,673	1908	41,455	31,451
1891	12,578	87,587	1909	52,378	56,377
1892	13,944	87,341	1910	115,681	73,569
1893	15,573	81,521	1911	134,765	49,732

TABLE IV

BRITISH PASSENGERS WHO SAILED FROM THE UNITED KINGDOM TO NORTH AMERICA, GIVING INDIVIDUAL TOTALS OF ENGLISH, IRISH, AND SCOTCH

Year.	English to Canada.	Scotch to Canada.	Irish to Canada.	English to U.S.A.	Scotch to U.S.A.	Irish to U.S.A.
1853–60[2]	3,791	3,550	8,085	24,460	4,383	71,856
1861–70	6,589	2,434	4,008	36,511	7,667	69,084
1871–80	12,638	2,581	2,581	54,978	8,807	44,955
1881–90	22,222	3,519	4,451	90,919	17,816	62,660
1891–95	17,777	1,717	1,235	74,201	14,342	48,634
1896	12,802	1,563	902	48,434	10,535	39,952
1897	13,442	1,281	848	43,381	9,121	32,882
1898	15,975	1,658	1,065	42,244	7,372	30,878
1899	15,050	1,717	873	45,723	8,128	38,631
1900	13,819	1,703	888	49,445	11,504	41,848
1901	15,748	1,733	962	57,246	11,414	35,535
1902	20,985	3,811	1,497	58,382	12,225	37,891
1903	46,760	10,296	2,596	68,791	15,318	39,554
1904	54,051	12,715	2,915	76,546	17,111	52,788
1905	64,876	14,214	3,347	58,229	19,785	44,356
1906	88,099	22,278	4,482	76,179	23,221	45,417
1907	110,329	33,393	7,494	91,593	24,365	54,306

[1] Balance inward of 143. [2] Annual average between the years stated.

Year.	English to Canada.	Welsh to Canada.	Scotch to Canada.	Irish to Canada.	English to U.S.A.	Welsh to U.S.A.	Scotch to U.S.A.	Irish to U.S.A.
1908	56,490	1,308	16,705	4,088	48,414	1,427	14,720	31,518
1909	59,052	1,189	18,423	4,106	49,014	1,773	21,486	36,611
1910	106,131	2,137	35,570	6,367	60,481	1,646	27,918	41,019
1911	127,117	2,124	41,218	6,807	58,185	1,869	23,441	36,613

This table is valuable as it indicates the preference or non-preference which the various elements of the United Kingdom have shown in turn for Canada and the United States. The English, it will be seen, evinced a preference for the Republic in early times, but have recently overcome that preference. The Irish, on the other hand, have shown a keener appreciation for the United States than for the Dominion in each year recorded above. It may be noted that by adding together the English, Irish, and Scotch figures of any one year the total does not correspond with the estimate given in Table II for the same year. This is due to the fact that the earlier table in speaking of British emigrants refers not to English, Irish, and Scotch people alone, but to Colonials as well. No account of the nationalities of emigrants was kept before the year 1853.

TABLE V

COMPARISON OF BRITISH EMIGRANTS WITH AMOUNT OF POPULATION WITHIN THE UNITED KINGDOM

Period.	Population of United Kingdom. Estimated when necessary.	Average Annual Emigration during the Period.	Proportion of Emigration to Population.
			per cent.
1853–55	27,674,341	231,733	0·84
1856–60	28,391,544	123,497	0·43
1861–65	29,459,465	143,559	0·48
1866–70	30,696,335	170,807	0·56
1871–75	32,189,540	193,907	0·60
1876–80	33,929,039	141,876	0·42
1881–85	35,466,129	258,462	0·73
1886–90	36,891,538	253,245	0·69
1891–95	38,445,138	195,715	0·51
1896–1900	40,189,230	152,843	0·38
1901–05	42,702,947	117,363	0·27
1906–10	45,216,665	178,864	0·39

In the above table column two shows the population for the United Kingdom at various quinquennial periods between 1853 and 1910. (The period between 1853 and 1855 being one of three years only.) Column three gives the average

APPENDIX I

annual emigration during the same intervals, but refers to people of British birth only and to emigration not to North America alone, but to all places without Europe (all Mediterranean ports excluded). Column four gives the proportion per cent of such emigration to the total population. Though the actual figures governing the exodus from the Mother Country are gradually expanding, this table clearly demonstrates the fact that the growth of emigration is not keeping pace with the growth of population.

TABLE VI

OCCUPATIONS OF ADULT BRITISH EMIGRANTS WHO LEFT THE UNITED KINGDOM FOR NON-EUROPEAN DESTINATIONS (ALL MEDITERRANEAN PORTS EXCEPTED)

Occupation.	1901.	1902.	1903.	1904.	1905.
MALES—					
Agriculture	12,966	19,489	15,508	21,028	21,778
Commerce & profess.	18,146	21,971	14,865	13,577	13,380
Skilled trades	27,306	47,664	36,146	28,279	28,858
Labourers	43,276	74,224	36,671	41,333	41,568
Miscell. and not stated	50,107	51,213	37,477	34,915	33,563
FEMALES—					
Domestic & other service	27,060	26,726	15,817	21,345	18,337
Dressmakers and other trades	1,545	1,769	2,357	2,867	2,609
Teachers, clerks, and professions	667	633	1,698	1,737	1,351
Miscel. and not stated	76,198	95,388	66,815	70,275	65,982

Occupation.	1906.	1907.	1908.	1909.	1910.	1911.
MALES—						
Agriculture	25,473	26,446	15,184	21,128	24,174	33,232
Commerce, etc.	17,612	18,572	15,229	17,181	20,856	25,070
Skilled trades	39,285	46,642	28,070	32,971	48,361	48,585
Labourers	50,844	64,450	26,994	32,502	54,765	54,409
Miscel., etc.	40,717	51,737	43,379	42,902	56,162	65,018
FEMALES—						
Domestic, etc.	22,617	26,345	20,850	24,357	·31,526	36,397
Dressmakers, etc.	3,392	3,895	2,848	3,454	5,002	5,816
Teachers, etc.	1,656	1,812	2,165	2,225	2,769	3,751
Miscel., etc.	77,474	96,868	71,311	73,102	97,402	110,642

Table VI indicates, as far as ascertainable, the occupations of British adult emigrants who have quitted the United Kingdom for non-European destinations. Much difficulty was experienced when classifying the various occupations, and for this reason the numbers governing each class must only be accepted as approximate estimates. The Merchant Shipping Act of 1894 considers an adult as any person above twelve years of age. Thus this table contains an "occupation" record of every emigrant twelve years old and upwards. As many people under sixteen have no definite occupation we find that the "Miscellaneous and not stated" class is particularly heavy on this account. The numbers governing agricultural pursuits and domestic service seem unduly high in view of the home scarcity of such labour.

TABLE VII

NATIVES OF IRELAND WHO HAVE EMIGRATED VIA IRISH PORTS TO NON-EUROPEAN DESTINATIONS (ALL MEDITERRANEAN PORTS EXCEPTED)

Years.	Number of Emigrants.	Estimated Population.	Rate per 1000 of the Estimated Population.	Years.	Number of Emigrants.	Estimated Population.	Rate per 1000 of the Estimated Population.
1851 (from the 1st of May)	152,060	6,514,473	—	1881	78,417	5,145,770	15·2
				1882	89,136	5,101,018	17·5
1852	190,322	6,336,889	30·0	1883	108,724	5,023,811	21·6
1853	173,148	6,198,984	27·9	1884	75,863	4,974,561	15·2
1854	140,555	6,083,183	23·1	1885	62,034	4,938,588	12·6
1855	91,914	6,014,665	15·3	1886	63,135	4,905,895	12·9
1856	90,781	5,972,851	15·2	1887	82,923	4,857,119	17·1
1857	95,081	5,919,454	16·1	1888	78,684	4,801,312	16·4
1858	64,337	5,890,814	10·9	1889	70,477	4,757,385	14·8
1859	80,599	5,861,711	13·8	1890	61,313	4,717,959	13·0
1860	84,621	5,820,960	14·5	1891	59,623	4,680,376	12·7
1861	64,292	5,788,415	11·1	1892	50,867	4,633,808	11·0
1862	70,117	5,775,588	12·1	1893	48,147	4,607,462	10·4
1863	117,229	5,718,235	20·5	1894	35,895	4,589,260	7·8
1864	114,169	5,640,527	20·2	1895	48,703	4,559,936	10·7
1865	101,497	5,594,589	18·1	1896	38,995	4,542,061	8·6
1866	99,467	5,522,942	18·0	1897	32,535	4,529,917	7·2
1867	80,624	5,486,509	14·7	1898	32,241	4,518,478	7·1
1868	61,018	5,465,914	11·2	1899	41,232	4,502,401	9·2
1869	66,568	5,449,094	12·2	1900	45,288	4,468,501	10·1
1870	74,855	5,418,512	13·8	1901	39,613	4,445,630	8·9
1871	71,240	5,398,179	13·2	1902	40,190	4,432,274	9·1
1872	78,102	5,372,890	14·5	1903	39,789	4,413,658	9·0
1873	90,149	5,327,938	16·9	1904	36,902	4,402,182	8·4
1874	73,184	5,298,979	13·8	1905	30,676	4,391,565	7·0
1875	51,462	5,278,629	9·7	1906	35,344	4,388,006	8·1
1876	37,587	5,277,544	7·1	1907	39,082	4,377,064	8·9
1877	38,503	5,286,380	7·2	1908	23,295	4,371,455	5·3
1878	41,124	5,282,246	7·7	1909	28,676	4,371,570	6·6
1879	47,065	5,265,625	8·8	1910	32,457	4,368,568	7·4
1880	95,517	5,202,648	17·6	1911	30,573	4,375,468	7·0

APPENDIX I

The above table relates back to 1851, the time when Irish returns were first collected separately from those of the United Kingdom. From these figures it will be seen that the heaviest exodus from Ireland was experienced in 1852, the lowest in 1908. By comparing the fourth column in this table with the percentage column in Table V it will be seen that at any given time the percentage of Irish emigration is seldom less than twice that of the United Kingdom.

TABLE VIII

NATIVES OF IRELAND WHO HAVE EMIGRATED, SHOWING PROVINCE OF ORIGIN

Province.	Estimated Average Population.	Emigrants from May, 1851, to December, 1910.			Emigrants to every 100 of the Average Population.
		Males.	Females.	Total.	
Munster	1,392,058	745,334	713,905	1,459,239	104·8
Connaught	827,532	329,655	371,917	701,572	84·8
Ulster	1,784,509	657,038	533,156	1,190,194	66·7
Leinster	1,349,831	381,848	343,851	725,699	53·8
County unspecified	—	61,766	48,973	110,739	—
Total natives of Ireland	—	2,175,641	2,011,802	4,187,443	78·2

This table points out the districts of Ireland which have contributed most freely to the emigration outflow. Column two gives the estimated average population of the four provinces: these figures have been obtained by striking an average of the returns given in the Irish Census Reports of 1851, 1861, 1871, 1881, 1891, and 1901. The third and fourth columns distinguish between males and females. The excess of males is here indicated to be less than is popularly supposed. Column five shows that Munster has furnished more emigrants than it has average population, a most remarkable fact. Even in Leinster, the province with the least aptitude for joining in the exodus, the outflow has risen to more than half the estimated average population of the province. This table refers to natives of Ireland alone but to all destinations.

TABLE IX

NATIVES OF IRELAND WHO HAVE EMIGRATED, SHOWING TOTALS FOR EACH MONTH

Month.	1900.	1901.	1902.	1903.	1904.	1905.	1906.	1907.	1908.	1909.	1910.	1911.
January	995	1114	979	798	653	672	838	693	641	727	615	644
February	1843	1362	1064	1106	887	1067	984	1196	934	884	896	847
March	2464	2498	2352	2249	1947	4568	2622	2670	1881	1945	2358	2618
April	8443	8288	8392	8102	7441	6067	8451	7814	4163	6558	6888	7346
May	9254	6621	5940	7747	5013	4351	6150	6712	4228	4572	5459	5122
June	3813	2934	2620	2749	2429	2225	2567	3139	1664	2121	2739	2182
July	2246	1986	2278	2236	2201	1422	1760	2082	1234	1602	1861	1704
August	3519	3240	3591	3651	3387	2071	2628	3117	1634	1915	2243	1876
September	5493	4928	5600	5307	6196	3772	4081	4903	2850	3743	4530	3443
October	4287	4182	4844	3622	4412	2550	3140	4283	2396	2799	3322	3178
November	1920	1683	1729	1512	1625	1314	1372	1808	1077	1777	1123	1071
December	1001	777	801	710	711	597	751	665	593	633	423	542

Table IX indicates the varying disposition to emigrate on the part of the native Irish during each month of the year. As one would expect, April is the favourite month for leaving home. March and May also show a high exodus, but people who depart during the former month find that outdoor work, in the new countries, is not yet plentiful, whilst May emigrants often feel that April is more or less wasted if spent in the Old Country. September, it will be noted, is also a month of heavy emigration returns. This is due to the demand for harvesters. January and December are, naturally, months of low emigration. The above table refers to Irish people only. As English and Scotch people are more given to taking up seasonal occupations, such as farming, building, and doing certain forms of labourer's work than their Irish neighbours, it is reasonable to suppose that, in their case, the spring exodus would be still more marked than that shown in Table IX.

TABLE X

MONEY SENT BY SUCCESSFUL IMMIGRANTS IN NORTH AMERICA TO FRIENDS IN THE UNITED KINGDOM

Year.	Sums.	Year.	Sums.
	£		£
1848	460,000	1852	1,404,000
1849	540,000	1853	1,439,000
1850	957,000	1854	1,730,000
1851	990,000	1855	873,000

APPENDIX I

Year.	Sums.	Year.	Sums.
	£		£
1856[1]	951,000	1868	530,564
1857	593,165	1869	639,335
1858	472,610	1870	727,408
1859	575,378	1871	702,488
1860	576,932	1872	749,664
1861	426,285	1873	724,040
1862	381,901	1874	485,566
1863	412,053	1875	354,356
1864	416,605	1876	334,643
1865	481,580	1877	667,564
1866	498,028	1878	784,067
1867	543,029		

The above figures have been constantly referred to in previous chapters. They represent the total amounts received in the United Kingdom from immigrants in North America. Where passage tickets have been sent, their money equivalent is included in the above totals. It is impossible to differentiate between the sums emanating from English, Irish, and Scotch sources. It is known, however, that the Irish settlers have always been much more given to sending home financial assistance than either the English or Scotch, also that the United States Irish are more generous in this matter than Canadian Irish. The sums were only recorded between the years 1848 and 1878, but this system of providing for distant friends and relations has naturally continued. In 1910, for instance, 7263 steerage Irish emigrants were provided with American prepaid passages.

TABLE XI

(A) NUMBER OF EMIGRANTS OF BRITISH NATIONALITY WHO WERE DEPORTED OR REFUSED ADMISSION BY THE UNITED STATES

Year.	Adult Males.	Adult Females.	Children.	Total.	Year.	Adult Males.	Adult Females.	Children.	Total.
1888	35	39	14	88	1900	55	44	1	100
1889	45	38	16	99	1901	87	77	16	180
1890	19	35	3	57	1902	90	69	13	172
1891	59	65	43	171	1903	185	88	32	305
1892	97	85	40	222	1904	235	103	30	368
1893	121	81	39	241	1905	232	114	28	374
1894	115	56	8	179	1906	260	137	49	446
1895	155	67	10	232	1907	236	114	31	381
1896	101	54	14	169	1908	223	130	60	413
1897	74	44	9	127	1909	259	183	41	483
1898	81	46	7	134	1910	408	234	123	765
1899	79	40	16	135					

[1] The figures for 1856 and previous years are not given to the nearest pound.

(B) CASES WHICH LED TO THE REJECTION OF THE ABOVE EMIGRANTS BETWEEN 1897 AND 1910

Cause.	1897.	1898.	1899.	1900.	1901.	1902.	1903.
Violation of Contract Law	9	4	9	10	3	18	100
Paupers or likely to become	92	103	97	57	114	91	124
Disease	17	11	18	12	28	37	37
Idiocy or insanity	9	14	11	20	28	22	26
Convicts	—	2	—	—	1	2	1
Immoral	—	—	—	—	—	—	—
Returned with rejected emigrants	—	—	—	—	6	2	16
Other causes	—	—	—	—	—	—	—
Not stated	—	—	—	—	—	—	1

Cause.	1904.	1905.	1906.	1907.	1908.	1909.	1910.
Violation of Contract Law	43	16	20	30	21	8	21
Paupers or likely to become	248	253	286	206	214	264	569
Disease	28	27	33	23	20	41	39
Idiocy or insanity	42	64	97	112	113	123	98
Convicts	1	6	1	4	15	7	6
Immoral	—	—	—	—	4	18	18
Returned with rejected emigrants	5	5	6	6	20	22	11
Other causes	—	3	3	—	6	—	3
Not stated	1	—	—	—	—	—	—

(C) NUMBER OF EMIGRANTS OF BRITISH NATIONALITY WHO WERE SENT BACK TO THE UNITED KINGDOM BY THE CANADIAN AUTHORITIES

Year.	Adult Males.	Adult Females.	Children.	Total.	Year.	Adult Males.	Adult Females.	Children.	Total.
1900	2	—	—	2	1906	78	28	8	114
1901	5	1	—	6	1907	185	68	37	290
1902	1	1	—	2	1908	462	185	231	878
1903	23	1	—	24	1909	346	161	156	663
1904	29	6	1	36	1910	370	160	78	608
1905	49	2	1	52	1911	367	147	82	596

(D) CAUSES WHICH LED TO THE REJECTION OF THE ABOVE EMIGRANTS

Cause.	1900.	1901.	1902.	1903.	1904.	1905.
Paupers or likely to become	—	5	—	8	20	28
Disease	1	—	—	9	9	9
Idiocy or insanity	1	1	2	4	5	13
Convicts	—	—	—	—	—	1
Immoral	—	—	—	—	—	—
Inebriates	—	—	—	—	—	—
Returned with rejected emigrants	—	—	—	—	2	1
Other causes	—	—	—	—	—	—
Not stated	—	—	—	—	—	—

APPENDIX I

Cause.	1906.	1907.	1908.	1909.	1910.	1911.
Paupers or likely to become	69	153	663	470	365	313
Disease	16	24	43	35	53	56
Idiocy or insanity	24	89	100	86	107	94
Convicts	2	4	32	29	28	67
Immoral	—	10	5	14	16	16
Inebriates	—	—	29	8	9	3
Returned with rejected emigrants	1	9	5	16	19	36
Other causes	—	—	—	4	10	11
Not stated	2	1	1	1	1	—

By comparing Table XI (A) and (C) with Table II the deportation per cent of British emigrants may be found.

All the figures in the foregoing are quoted from official Government sources, as the Annual Reports of the Colonial Land and Emigration Commissioners, the reports of the Board of Trade, the old Customs returns, the Census reports, the annual copies of tables relating to Emigration and Immigration ordered to be printed by the House of Commons, and the Emigration Statistics of Ireland. Full particulars of each will be found in Appendix II.

APPENDIX II

Bibliography on Emigration from the United Kingdom to North America, 1783-1911

(A) OFFICIAL PUBLICATIONS OF THE HOUSE OF COMMONS[1]

ESTIMATE of the Sum required for facilitating Emigration from the South of Ireland to the Canadas and the Cape of Good Hope.

    1823 (401), XIII, 301.
    1825 (131), XVIII, 358, 361.
    1826-7 (160), XV, 227.

Report from the Committee on Emigration from the United Kingdom.

    1826 (404), Sess. Vol. IV.
    1827 (237, 550) Sess. Vol. V.

Report laid before the Colonial Department by Lieutenant-Colonel Cockburn, on the subject of Emigration, together with the instructions received from that Department, on January 26th, 1827, relating to Nova Scotia, New Brunswick, and Prince Edward Island.

    1828 (109), (148), XXI, 359, 379.

Numbers of persons who have emigrated from the United Kingdom to any of the Colonies of Great Britain.

    1820 to 1830-1830 (650), XXIX, 435.
    1825 to 1832-1833 (696), XXVI, 279.

---

[1] Explanation of references as given officially: The date of the year, with the figures between parentheses, thus, 1852 (in 190) denote the Session and the Number according to the Sessional List at the foot of each paper. The roman numerals and figures following them, thus: LIII, 37 point out the Volume and MS. page of the Sessional Collection, as arranged for the House of Commons.

APPENDIX II 357

Reports from Commissioners for Emigration to the Colonial Secretary.

1831–2 (724), XXXII, 209.

Act passed in North America for levying a Tax on Emigrants. Circular from the Colonial Office recommending the same.

1831–2 (730), XXXII, 197.

Canadian Waste Lands.

1832 (March 30th), No. 334.

Correspondence with Governors, etc., of British Colonies in North America and Australia, relating to Emigration.

1833 (141), XXVI, 299.

Various Tables relative to Emigration.

1836 (in 512), XI, 744.

Disposal of Lands in British Colonies.

1836 (August 1st), No. 512.

Report from the Agent-General for Emigration from the United Kingdom, April, 1838.

1837–8 (388), XL, 1.

Number of Persons who have emigrated from the United Kingdom to British North America, United States, etc., between 1832 and 1836.

1837–8 (137), XLVII, 175.

Report of the Earl of Durham on Affairs of British North America.

1839 (3), XVII, 1.

(This report has recently been published as Vols. II and III of Sir Charles Lucas' *Lord Durham's Report*.)

Representations to Her Majesty's Government from the London Highland Destitution Relief Committee.

1841 (in 333), VI, 273.

Correspondence relative to Emigration to Canada.

1841 (298), XVI, 369.

Letter respecting proposed Emigration of certain Female Paupers from the Parish of St. Marylebone.

1841 (294), XXI, 395.

358 A HISTORY OF EMIGRATION

Report of the Agent-General for Emigration on applicability of Emigration to relieve Distress in Highlands, 1837.

1841 (60), XXVII, 229.

Despatch from the Governor-General of British North America transmitting the Annual Reports of the Agents for Emigration in Canada, 1841.

1842 (373), XXXI, 1.

General Report of the Colonial Land and Emigration Commissioners:

1842	(567), XXV, 55.		1857–8	(2395), XXIV, 401.
1843	(621), XXIX, 15.		1859	(2555. Sess. 2), XIV, 159.
1844	(178), XXXI, 11.		1860	(2696), XXIX, 1.
1845	(617), XXVII, 83.		1861	(2842), XXII, 1.
1846	(706), XXIV, 1.		1862	(3010), XXII, 1.
1847	(809), XXXIII, 131.		1863	(3199), XV, 247.
1847–8	(961) (961–11), XXVI, 1, 41.		1864	(3341), XVI, 477.
1849	(1082), XXII, 1.		1865	(3526), XVIII, 383.
1850	(1204), XXIII, 55.		1866	(3679), XVII, 359.
1851	(1383), XXII, 333.		1867	(3855), XIX, 121.
1852	(1499), XVIII, 161.		1867–8	(4024), XVII, 787.
1852–3	(1647), XL, 65.		1868–9	(4159), XVII, 119.
1854	(1833), XXVIII, 1.		1870	(C. 196), XVII, 111.
1854–5	(1953), XVII, 1.		1871	(C. 369), XX, 335.
1856	(2089), XXIV, 325.		1872	(C. 562), XVI, 639.
1857	(2249. Sess. 2), XVI, 33.		1873	(C. 768), XVIII, 295.

Between 1873 and 1877 the Commissioners issued an annual "Colonisation Circular."

Correspondence relative to Emigration since the last Papers, also correspondence relative to the Sale of Colonial Lands, since the date of the last Despatches laid before Parliament. Part I, British North America.

1843 (291), XXXIV, 171.

Reports by the Emigration Agents of Canada, New Brunswick, and New South Wales, to the Governors of these Provinces.

1843 (109) XXXIV, 9.

Return of Ships, their Name and Tonnage, employed in carrying Emigrants, since the passing of the Colonial Passengers' Act: and also correspondence respecting certain Emigrant Ships.

1844 (503), XXXV, 261.

APPENDIX II 359

Correspondence relating to the Emigrant Ships—*Catherine* and *John and Robert*—conveying Emigrants to Cape Breton and Canada.
>1844 (in 503), XXXV, 261.

Papers relative to Emigration to the British Provinces in North America.
>1847 (777) (824), XXXIX, 19, 63.
>1847-8 (50) (932) (964) (971) (985), XLVII, 1, 303, 373, 431, 457.
>1849 (1025), XXXVIII, 9.
>1851 (348), XL, 297.
>1852 (1474), XXXIII, 559.

Number of Persons who have Emigrated at the Expense of the different Poor Law Unions in Ireland in 1844, 1845, and 1846, giving an account of the Emigrants.
>1847 (255), LVI, 199.

Indexes to Reports of Commissioners, 1812-1840.
>1847 (710-IV), LVIII, Part IV, 1.

Indexes to Reports of Commissioners, 1828-1847.
>1847 (710. I), LVIII, Part IV, 1.

Reports from the Commissioners to the Colonial Office, respecting Emigration to the British North American Colonies.
>1847-8 (in 50), XLVII, 1.

Memorials addressed to the Board of Trade, recommending the Deportation of Unemployed Operatives, with a view to the cultivation by them of Cotton in the British Colonies.
>1847-8 (in 586), LI, 247.

Statements, Tables, etc., respecting Emigrants from the United Kingdom in the years 1846, 1847, 1848, and 1849.
>1849 (in 507, II), XVI, 1019.

Account to January 5th, 1849, of Sums advanced by the Public Works Loan Commissioners for the purpose of Emigration, under the provisions of the Act 4 & 5 Will. 4, c. 76, showing the Interest paid, Principal paid and remaining unpaid.
>1849 (in 165), XXX, 361.

Expenses at the Depots or other Establishments for the Reception of Emigrants, during the years 1847 and 1848 respectively.
>1849 (244), XXXVIII, 1.

Number of Emigrants from Great Britain and Ireland respectively to Colonies and Foreign Countries in each year 1839 to 1848 inclusive, distinguishing Cabin from Steerage Passengers, and showing the Number embarking at Liverpool.
1849 (in 558), L, 403.

Despatch, transmitting Report from the Chief Emigration Agent at Canada for the year 1849, and Documents showing the facilities afforded to Emigrants from Europe for reaching the interior by the completion of the St. Lawrence Canals.
1850 (173), XL, 1.

Laws concerning the Commissioners of Emigration of the City of New York.
1851 (in 632), XIX, 1.

Abstract of Acts for the Regulation of Passenger Ships.
1851 (in 632), XIX, 1.

Abstract from Clerks of Unions of the Number of Emigrants sent out or assisted to Emigrate, by Boards of Guardians in Ireland, in pursuance of the provisions of the Irish Poor Relief Acts, from May, 1850, to March, 1851.
1851 (in 1381), XXVI, 547.

Letter from Lord Hobart to the Colonial Land and Emigration Commissioners, enclosing letter from Mr. Vere Foster, detailing the Treatment of the Passengers on board the Emigrant Ship *Washington* on the passage to New York : with the Answer returned by the Commissioners.
1851 (198), XL, 433.

Correspondence between the Boards of Guardians of St. Pancras and the Poor Law Board, relating to the Emigration of Children to the Bermudas.
1851 (243), XL, 411.

Number of Poor Persons who have been authorised to Emigrate and Sums which the Poor Law Board have authorised to be raised or borrowed for the purpose in the year 1851.
1852 (in 1461), XXIII, 1.

Number of Vessels which have sailed from Ports in the United Kingdom with Emigrants on Board, during the Five Years, 1847–1851, distinguishing whether such ports are under

APPENDIX II

the Superintendence of an Emigration Officer or not: with the Number of such Ships which have been Wrecked or Destroyed, and the Number of Lives Lost.

1852 (245), XLIX, 55.

Reports relative to the Mortality on board the emigrant ships *Bournduf, Wanata, Marco Polo,* and *Ticonderoga.*

1852-3 (205), XCVIII, 335.

Reports within the six months ending January 31st, 1854, on the loss of vessels carrying emigrants to America and Australia.

1854 (178), XLVI, 429.

Correspondence in relation to the recent outbreak of cholera on board the emigrant ship *Dirigo.*

1854 (492), XLVI, 463.

Number of Passenger Ships that cleared from ports in the United Kingdom under the Passengers Acts, 1852 and 1855, yearly since 1853, with their tonnage, Port of destination, and number of passengers carried.

1860 (350), LX, 431.

Return for 1860, 1861, 1862, and first six months of 1863, showing the number of emigrants who have left the United Kingdom for the United States, British North America, the several colonies of Australasia, South Africa, and other places respectively: distinguishing the native country of the emigrants. Also a return showing the emigration for the years 1815 to 1863 (first six months).

1863 (430), XXXVIII, 19.

Number of Emigrants, natives of Great Britain or Ireland, who have left the United Kingdom for the British Colonies or the United States of America, during the ten years ending December, 1867.

1868-9 (397), L, 487.

Circular despatched to the Governors of different Colonies on the subject of emigration.

1870 (179), XLIX, 595.

Local Government—Reports of Commissioners. (Many of these Annual Reports contain matter relative to Emigration to North America, such as Expenditure by Guardians.)

1872 (C. 516), XXVIII, 1.
(Annually after 1872.)

Return showing names of the Colonial Land and Emigration Commissioners: the instructions originally given to them and their functions: also prices of land in the United States and the Colonies: number of acres sold or otherwise disposed of, in each of the agricultural Colonies and in the United States in 1868, 1869, and 1870, with the price, etc.

1872 (154), XLIII, 377.

Statistical Tables relating to Emigration and Immigration from and into the United Kingdom in the year 1876, with report to the Board of Trade thereon.

1877 (5), LXXXV, 621.
(Annually after 1877.)

Emigration Statistics of Ireland for the year 1876.

1877 (C. 1700), LXXXV, 643.
(Annually after 1877.)

Reports with regard to the Accommodation and Treatment of Emigrants on board Atlantic Steamships.

1881 (C. 2995), LXXXII, 93.

Correspondence on the subject of Emigration from Great Britain to the Colonies and the proposed formation of an Emigrants' Information Office.

1886 (C. 4751), XLV, 525.

Report on the Emigrants' Information Office for the year ending March 31st, 1888.

1888 (C. 5391), LXXIII, 25.
(Annually after 1888.)

Memorandum of arrangements with the Canadian Government, the principal land Companies, etc., for starting a Colonisation Scheme for the Crofters and Cottars of the Western Highlands and Islands of Scotland.

1888 (C. 5403), LXXX, 293.

Correspondence respecting a Scheme of Colonisation referred in 1887 for the consideration of the Colonial Government.

1888 (C. 5361), LXXIII, 1.

Correspondence in the case of Mr. R. Vesey Stoney, J.P., relative to charges of Improper Administration of Public Funds, in connection with the State-aided Emigration from Mayo: with the Local Government Board Inspector's Report thereon.

1888 (88), LXXXIII, 85.

Report from the Select Committee on Colonisation.
> 1889 (274), X, 1.

Report from the Select Committee on Colonisation.
> 1890 (354), XII, 1.
> 1890-1 (152), XI, 571.

First Report of the Commissioners appointed to carry out the Scheme of Colonisation in Canada of Crofters and Cottars from the Western Highlands of Scotland.
> 1890 (C. 6067), XXVII, 237.
> (Annually until 1906.)

Report of the Departmental Committee into the management and working of the Emigrants' Information Office.
> 1896 (C. 8256), LVIII, 183.

Reports, Maps, Tables, and Appendices relating to Migratory Agricultural Irish Labourers for 1900.
> 1900 (Cd. 341), CI, 483.

Report on the Salvation Army Colonies in the United States, and at Hadleigh, England, with Scheme of National Land Settlement, by Commissioner H. Rider Haggard.
> 1905 (Cd. 2562), LIII, 359.

Report by the Departmental Committee appointed to consider Mr. Rider Haggard's Report on Agricultural Settlements in British Colonies.
> Vol. I. 1906 (Cd. 2978), LXXVI, 533.
> Vol. II. 1906 (Cd. 2979), LXXVI, 579.

Memorandum on the History and Functions of the Emigrants' Information Office.
> 1907 (Cd. 3407), LXVII, 457.

Precis of the Proceedings of the Imperial Conference.
> 1911 (Cd. 5741).

(B) ARTICLES IN PERIODICALS

1802. An Inquiry into the Causes and Effects of Emigration from the Highlands.—*Edinburgh Review*, Vol. 1, Oct., 1802, p. 61.

1805. Observations on the Present State of the Highlands of Scotland.—*Edinburgh Review*, Vol. 7, Oct., 1805, p. 185.

1808. A Statistical and Historical Inquiry into the Progress and Magnitude of the Population of Ireland.—*Edinburgh Review*, Vol. 12, July, 1808, p. 342.
1818. Birbeck's Notes on America.—*Edinburgh Review*, Vol. 30, June, 1818, p. 123.
1819. Sketches of America.—*Quarterly Review*, Vol. XXI, No. 41, Jan., 1819, p. 124.
1820. Emigration to Canada.—*Quarterly Review*, Vol. XXIII, July, 1820, p. 373.
1823. Memorable Days in America.—*Quarterly Review*, Vol. XXIX, No. 58, July, 1823, p. 338.
1824. Restraints on Emigration.—*Edinburgh Review*, Vol. 39, June, 1824, p. 315.
1826. Irish Absentees.—*Quarterly Review*, Vol. XXXIII, March, 1826, p. 465.
1826. Emigration.—*Edinburgh Review*, Vol. 45, No. 89, Dec., 1826, p. 49.
1828. Third Report upon Emigration from the United Kingdom.—*Edinburgh Review*, Vol. 47, Jan., 1828, p. 205.
1828. Emigration Report.—*Quarterly Review*, Vol. 36, No. 74, March, 1828, p. 539.
1828. Ireland : its evils and their Remedies.—*Quarterly Review*, Vol. 28, July, 1828, p. 53.
1834. Secondary Punishments—Transportation.—*Edinburgh Review*, Vol. 58, Jan., 1834, p. 336.
1835. Immigration.—*North American Review*, Vol. 40, April, 1835, p. 457.
1838. Emigration from the United Kingdom ; abstract of Official Reports, 1838 (by R. W. Rawson).—*Journal of the Royal Statistical Society*, Vol. 1, July, 1838, p. 155.
1846. Proposals for Extending the Irish Poor Law.—*Edinburgh Review*, Vol. 84, Oct., 1848, p. 267.
1848. The Irish Crisis.—*Edinburgh Review*, Vol. 87, Jan., 1848, p. 229.
1849. Some particulars of the Commercial Progress of the Colonial Dependencies of the United Kingdom during the twenty years, 1827–46, by J. T. Danson, Esq.—*Journal of the Royal Statistical Society*, Vol. XII, Nov., 1849, p. 349.

APPENDIX II

1850. Return of the Trades or Callings of the Emigrants who arrived at the Ports of Quebec and Montreal during the Year 1849.—*Journal of the Royal Statistical Society*, Vol. XIII, May, 1850, p. 183.

1850. Return of the Number of Emigrants embarked, with the Number of Births and Deaths during the Voyage and in quarantine; the total Number landed in the Colony; . . . with the number of souls from each Country. . . .—*Journal of the Royal Statistical Society*, Vol. XIII, Aug., 1850, p. 275.

1850. Emigration and Industrial Training.—*Edinburgh Review*, Vol. 92, No. 188, Oct., 1850, p. 491.

1850. Comparative Statement of the Number of Emigrants arrived at the Port of Quebec since the year 1829 inclusive.—*Journal of the Royal Statistical Society*, Vol. XIII, Dec., 1850, p. 364.

1854. Emigration from Great Britain and Ireland in each year from 1843 to 1852, inclusive, and the destination of the Emigrants.—*Journal of the Royal Statistical Society*, March, 1854, Vol. 17, p. 72.

1854. European Emigration to the United States.—*Edinburgh Review*, Vol. 100, No. 203, July, 1854, p. 236.

1855. Pauperism and Crime in the United States of America, by the Rev. Robert Everest.—*Journal of the Royal Statistical Society*, Vol. 18, Sept., 1855, p. 229.

1859. Emigration from Great Britain and Ireland in each year from 1843 to 1858, inclusive, and the destination of the Emigrants.—*Journal of the Royal Statistical Society*, Vol. 22, Sept., 1859, p. 427.

1862. On the Utility of the Colonies as Fields for Emigration, by H. Merivale.—*Journal of the Royal Statistical Society*, Vol. 25, Dec., 1862, p. 491.

1862. Emigration, 1815–61.—*Journal of the Royal Statistical Society*, Vol. 25, Dec., 1862, p. 537.

1864. Ireland.—*Edinburgh Review*, Vol. 119, Jan. 1864, p. 279.

1864. The Canadian Emigrant Route across the Continent: in the Commercial Progress . . . of Central America, by Henry Y. Hind.—*Journal of the Royal Statistical Society*, Vol. 27, March, 1864, p. 94.

366   A HISTORY OF EMIGRATION

1869. Emigration to Canada, 1863–68.—*Journal of the Royal Statistical Society*, Vol. 32, Sept., 1867, p. 333.
1872. On the Colonies. Part V, Emigration, by A. Hamilton. —*Journal of the Royal Statistical Society*, Vol. 35, March, 1872, p. 115.
1872. Immigration, by Edward Jarvis.—*Atlantic Monthly*, Vol. 29, April, 1872, p. 454.
1877. The Immigrant's Progress, by William H. Rideing.— *Scribner's Monthly*, Vol. 14, Sept., 1877, p. 292.
1880. Ireland: her Present and her Future.—*Edinburgh Review*, Vol. 151, Jan., 1880, p. 99.
1880–87. Emigration and Immigration in the years 1879– 1880–81–82–83–84–85–86 (Mr. Griffen's report to the Board of Trade).—*Journal of the Royal Statistical Society*. In Vols. 43–50, inclusive.
1881. Irish Emigration, by J. H. Tuke.—*Nineteenth Century*, Vol. 9, Feb., 1881, p. 358.
1881. Transplanting to the Colonies, by W. M. Torrens.— *Nineteenth Century*, Vol. IX, No. 49, March, 1881, p. 536.
1882. Why they Come, by Edward Self.—*North American Review*, Vol. 134, April, 1882, p. 347.
1882. With the Emigrants, by J. H. Tuke.—*Nineteenth Century*, Vol. 12, July, 1882, p. 134.
1883. Why send more Irish to America? by Professor Goldwin Smith.—*Nineteenth Century*, Vol. XIII, No. 76, June, 1883, p. 913.
1884. Evils incident to Immigration, by Edward Self.—*North American Review*, Vol. 138, Jan., 1884, p. 78.
1884. Immigration into the United States, by Armand Liégeard.—*Journal de la Société de statistique de Paris*, Juin, 1884. (A Translation to be found in the *Journal of the Royal Statistical Society*, Vol. 47, Sept., 1884, p. 496.)
1884. State-directed Emigration, by Lord Brabazon.—*Nineteenth Century*, Vol. 16., Nov., 1884, p. 764.
1885. State Aid to Emigrants, by J. H. Tuke.—*Nineteenth Century*, Vol. 17, Feb., 1885, p. 280.
1887–8. Practical Means of Extending Emigration, by W. Hazell.—*Royal Colonial Institute Proceedings*, Vol. XI, 1887, p. 49.

APPENDIX II

1888–9. Colonisation, by W. Gisborne.—*Royal Colonial Institute Proceedings*, Vol. XX, p. 53.
1888–92. Emigration and Immigration (continued) in the years 1887–88–89–1890–91–92.—*Journal of the Royal Statistical Society*. In Vols. 51, 52, 54, 55, 56.
1889. The American Field for Emigration.—*Chambers's Journal*, Vol. 66, Dec., 28th 1889, p. 820.
1890. Canadian Immigration and Emigration.—*Journal of the Royal Statistical Society*, Vol. 53, 1890, p. 476.
1890. Recent Experiments in Colonisation, by Arnold White. *Contemporary Review*, Vol. LVIII, Nov., 1890, p. 655.
1890. L'émigration Européenne, Par Eugen von Philippovich.—*Revue d'économie politique*, Vol. 4, 1890, p. 341.
1891. The Restriction of Immigration, by H. C. Lodge.—*North American Review*, Vol. 152, Jan., 1891, p. 27.
1891. Immigration Troubles of the United States, by W. H. Wilkins.—*Nineteenth Century*, Vol. 30, Oct., 1891, p. 583.
1891. La Politique des Etats-Unis relative à l'émigration. Translated by J. Chartrou.—*Revue d'économie politique*, Vol. 5, 1891, p. 29.
1892. Our National Dumping-Ground: A study of Immigration, by B. Weber and C. S. Smith.—*North American Review*, Vol. 154, April, 1892, p. 424.
1892. The Immigration Problem in America.—*Westminster Review*, Vol. 138, July, 1892, p. 65.
1893. Shall Immigration be Suspended? by W. E. Chandler. *North American Review*, Vol. 156, Jan., 1893, p. 1.
1893. Why Immigration should not be Suspended, by H. C. Hansbrough.—*North American Review*, Vol. 156, Feb., 1893, p. 220.
1893. The Census and Immigration, by H. C. Lodge.—*Century Magazine*, Vol. 46, Sept., 1893, p. 737.
1894. How We Restrict Immigration, by Joseph H. Senner.—*North American Review*, Vol. 158, April, 1894, p. 494.
1895. Immigration and Naturalisation, by H. S. Everett.—*Atlantic Monthly*, Vol. 75, March, 1895, p. 345.
1895. Canadian Immigrants, by A. Paterson.—*National Review*, Vol. 25, May, 1895, p. 399.

1896. Restriction of Immigration, by F. A. Walker.—*Atlantic Monthly*, Vol. 77, June, 1896, p. 822.
1897. Should Immigration be Restricted ? by S. G. Croswell.—*North American Review*, Vol. 164, May, 1897, p. 526.
1897. Immigration and the Educational Test, by P. F. Hall. —*North American Review*, Vol. 165, Oct., 1897, p. 393.
1900. Our Immigrants and Ourselves, by K. H. Claghorn.— *Atlantic Monthly*, Vol. 86, Oct., 1900, p. 535.
1901. The Changing Character of Immigration, by K. H. Claghorn.—*World's Work*, Vol. 1, Feb., 1901, p. 381.
1901. Among the Immigrants, by A. Henry.—*Scribner's Magazine*, Vol. 29, March, 1901, p. 301.
1902. Immigration's Menace to the National Health, by T. V. Powderly.—*North American Review*, Vol. 175, July, 1902, p. 53.
1902. Americans in the raw. The High-tide of Immigrants : their strange possessions and their meagre wealth ; what becomes of them, by E. Lowry.—*World's Work*, Vol. 4, Oct., 1902, p. 2644.
1902. In the Paths of Immigration, by J. B. Connolly.— *Scribner's Magazine*, Vol. 32, Nov., 1902, p. 513.
1902. The Weak Spot in the American Republic, by J. Weston.—*Nineteenth Century*, Vol. 52, Dec., 1902, p. 905.
1903. In the Gateway of Nations, by J. A. Riis.—*Century Magazine*, Vol. 65, March, 1903, p. 674.
1903. What shall we be ? The Coming Race in America, by Gustave Michaud.—*Century Magazine*, Vol. LXV, March, 1903, p. 683.
1903. Head Tax on Aliens.—*United States Treasury Department Decisions*, Vol. 6, April 29th, 1903, p. 372, and Vol. 6, May 7th, 1903, p. 407.
1903. Military Colonisation, by Major-General T. Bland-Strange.—*United Service Magazine*, Vol. XXVII (New Series), No. 894, May, 1903, p. 149.
1903. British Emigration : an appeal to England, by D. Mills.—*Empire Review*, Vol. 6, Nov., 1903, p. 434.
1904. A Million Immigrants a Year. (i.) Efforts to restrict undesirable immigration, by H. C. Lodge. (ii.) The

APPENDIX II

need of closer inspection and greater restriction of immigrants, by F. P. Sargent.—*Century Magazine*, Vol. 67, Jan., 1904, p. 466.

1904. Is the New Immigration Dangerous to the Country? by O. P. Austin.—*North American Review*, Vol. 178, April, 1904, p. 558.

1904. The Restriction of Immigration, by R de C. Ward.— *North American Review*, Vol. 179, Aug., 1904, p. 226.

1904. International Control of Immigration, by J. D. Whelpley.—*World's Work*, Vol. 8, Sept., 1904, p. 5254.

1905. Emigration: an International Affair, by J. D. Whelpley.—*Fortnightly Review*, Vol. 77, Feb., 1905, p. 317.

1905. The Emigration of State Children, by C. Kinloch-Cooke.—*Empire Review*, Vol. 9, April and June, 1905, p. 208 and p. 456.

1905. Emigration and Colonisation. Proposed New Authority, by C. Kinloch-Cooke.—*Empire Review*, Vol. 9, May, 1905, p. 305.

1905. Control of Emigration in Europe, by J. D. Whelpley. —*North American Review*, Vol. 180, June, 1905, p. 856.

1905. A State-aided and State-directed Scheme of emigration and colonisation, by C. Kinloch-Cooke.— *Empire Review*, Vol. 10, Aug., 1905, p. 1.

1905. A Canadian's Criticism of the Dominion Immigration Policy, by E. C. Nelson.—*Empire Review*, Vol. 10, Aug., 1905, p. 47.

1905. The Attitude of Labour Towards Emigration, by C. Kinloch-Cooke.—*Empire Review*, Vol. 10, Dec., 1905, p. 412.

1905-6. Our Emigration Plans, by "General" Booth.— *Royal Colonial Institute Proceedings*, Vol. XXXVII, 1905, p. 138.

1906. The Sons of Old Scotland in America, by H. N. Casson.—*Munsey's Magazine*, Vol. 34, Feb., 1906, p. 599.

1906. State-aided Emigration: A National Programme wanted, by Sir C. Kinloch-Cooke.—*Empire Review*, Vol. 11, March, 1906, p. 97.

1906. Work and Wages in British Columbia.—*Macmillan's*

Magazine, Vol. 1 (New Series), No. 6, April, 1906, p. 440.
1906. The Irish in America, by H. N. Casson.—*Munsey's Magazine*, Vol. 35, April, 1906, p. 86.
1906. The English in America, by H. N. Casson.—*Munsey's Magazine*, Vol. 35, May, 1906, p. 209.
1906. The Welsh in America, by H. N. Casson.—*Munsey's Magazine*, Vol. 35, Sept., 1906, p. 749.
1906. Pending Immigration Bills, by R. de C. Ward.—*North American Review*, Vol. 183, Dec., 1906, p. 1120.
1906. The Medico-Economic Aspect of the Immigration Problem, by T. Darlington.—*North American Review*, Vol. 183, Dec., 1906, p. 1262.
1907. Emigrants for Canada, by E. J. Prior.—*Macmillan's Magazine*, Vol. 2 (New Series), No. 15, Jan., 1907, p. 185.
1907. The Chinaman in British Columbia.—*Macmillan's Magazine*, Vol. 2 (New Series), No. 15, Jan., 1907, p. 208.
1907. The Human Side of Immigration, by J. G. Brookes.—*Century Magazine*, Vol. 73, Feb., 1907, p. 633.
1908. The Gentleman Emigrant, by Brian Bellasis.—*Empire Review*, Vol. XV, No. 89, June, 1908, p. 368.
1908. The Menace to Canadian Unity, by Louis Corbally.—*National Review*, Vol. LI, No. 304, June, 1908, p. 563.
1908. Outlook for the Homesteader in Western Canada, by W. H. Belford.—*Empire Review*, Vol. XV, No. 90, July, 1908, p. 441.
1908. Imperial State Aid to Emigration, by C. E. T. Stuart-Linton.—*Empire Review*, Vol. XVI, No. 92, Sept., 1908, p. 142.
1908-9. Imperial Emigration and its Problems, by Dr. Arthur.—*Royal Colonial Institute Proceedings*, Vol. XL, 1908, p. 314.
1909. British Emigrants and Canada, by Sir Clement Kinloch-Cooke.—*Empire Review*, Vol. XVII, No. 99, April, 1909, p. 210.
1909. Imperial Labour Exchanges, by Sir Clement Kinloch-Cooke.—*Empire Review*, Vol. XVII, No 101,

APPENDIX II

June, 1909, p. 360; and Vol. XVII, No. 102, July, 1909, p. 444.

1909. Emigration and the Poor Law Report, by Sir Clement Kinloch-Cooke.—*Empire Review*, Vol. XVIII, No. 103, Aug., 1909, p. 23.

1909. The Passing of the Promised Land, by C. M. Harger.—*Atlantic Monthly*, Vol. 104, No. 4, Oct., 1909, p. 461.

1910. Canada: Far West (Emigration Possibilities), by Lady Thomson.—*Empire Review*, Vol. XVIII, No. 108, Jan., 1910, p. 395.

1910. An Imperial Colonisation Scheme, by Rev. R. L. Gwynne.—*Empire Review*, Vol. XIX, No. 110, March, 1910, p. 109.

1910. Canada or Australia? A Question for the Intending Emigrant, by W. E. Graham.—*Empire Review*, Vol. XIX, No. 111, April, 1910, p. 145.

1910. Some Aspects of Farming in Western Canada, by Philip Larcom.—*Empire Review*, Vol. XIX, No. 112, May, 1910, p. 265.

1910. An Emigration Policy and Juvenile Emigration—Heredity and Environment.—*The Times*, May 24th, 1910, pp. 33 and 45.

1910. On a Canadian Farm, by Mrs. Lloyd-Jones.—*National Review*, Vol. LV, No. 328, June, 1910, p. 611.

1910. The Emigration Conference and Thoughts on the Emigration Conference, by A. R. Colquhoun.—*United Empire*, Vol. 1 (New Series), No. 7, July, 1910, p. 510.

1910. Canada's Exclusiveness, by Sir Clement Kinloch-Cooke.—*Empire Review*, Vol. XIX, No. 114, July, 1910, p. 371.

1910. Canadian Colonisation: A Suggestion, by William Pearson.—*United Empire*, Vol. 1 (New Series), No. 8, Aug., 1910, p. 561.

1910. The Public Lands of the United States, by Morris Bien.—*North American Review*, Vol. 192, No. 658, Sept., 1910, p. 387.

1910. Canada's Experimental Farms, by Elizabeth Walmsley.—*Empire Review*, Vol. XX, No. 116, Sept., 1910, p. 110.

1910. A Plea for Englishmen in Canada.—*National Review*, Vol. LVI, No. 331, Sept., 1910, p. 84.
1910. The Land Movement and Western Finance, by C. M. Harger.—*North American Review*, Vol. 192, No. 661, Dec., 1910, p. 746.
1910. The Imperial Problem, by the Duke of Marlborough.— *United Empire*, Vol. 1 (New Series), No. 12, Dec. 1910, p. 838.
1911. Needed—A Domestic Immigration Policy, by Frances A. Kellor.—*North American Review*, Vol. 193, No. 665, April, 1911, p. 561.
1911. Canada and the Immigration Problem, by Professor Stephen Leacock.—*National Review*, Vol. LVII, No. 338, April, 1911, p. 316.
1911. State Control of Emigration, by Holcombe Ingleby.— *Empire Review*, Vol. XXII, No. 128, Sept., 1911, p. 92.
1911. Pour les émigrants—A bord des Trans-atlantiques, by Césarina Lupati.—*Le Monde*, Vol. 1, No. 5, Oct., 1911, p. 679.
1911. Emigration and Immigration, by Sir Clement Kinloch-Cooke.—*Oxford and Cambridge Review*, No. 16, Oct., 1911, p. 168.
1912. A Littler England.—*Nineteenth Century*, Vol. 71, March, 1912, p. 494.

The following periodicals are largely devoted to emigration matters :—

The Board of Trade Labour Gazette (Monthly).
The Canadian Labour Gazette (Monthly).
The Coloniser (Monthly, London).
Canada (Weekly journal, published in London).
Canadian News (Weekly, London).
The Imperial Colonist (Monthly, organ of the British Women's Emigration Association).
The Standard of Empire (Weekly, London) ; also

A quarterly poster exhibited in all Post Offices of the United Kingdom, published by the Emigrants' Information Office.

APPENDIX II 373

(C) MISCELLANEOUS PUBLICATIONS

(NOTE.—In the case of certain works, difficult to obtain, it has been thought advisable to quote the Press Marks of the British Museum Reading Room.)

1797. Sur les prévénus d'émigration.—B. M. F. 745 (8).
1802. Antidote contre une brochure sur l'émigration (Paris).—B. M. 879, b. 19 (7).
1805. Observations on the Present State of the Highlands of Scotland, by Thomas Douglas, fifth Earl of Selkirk.
1809. Transactions in the Red River, by Thomas Douglas, fifth Earl of Selkirk.
1820. A few Plain Directions for persons intending to proceed as settlers to Upper Canada.—B. M. 798, d. 11.
1829. A Letter from Sydney, by Edward Gibbon Wakefield.
1832. The Emigrant's Guide: containing practical and authentic information.—B. M. 10470, aa. 19.
1833. Hints and observations on the disadvantages of Emigration to British America.—B. M. 8275, aa. 1 (3).
1833. England and America, by E. G. Wakefield.
1834. Letters and Extracts of Letters from settlers in Upper Canada.—B. M. 1103, F. 45 (4).
1834. South Australian Association. An outline of a plan of a proposed colony, by E. G. Wakefield.
1834. The Emigrant's Informant, or a guide to Upper Canada.—B. M. 10470, bb. 21.
1843. Emigration. Who should go. Where to go to. How to get there.—B. M. 1390, h. 18.
1844. Lands in Canada West to be disposed of by the Canada Company.—B. M. 1880, C. 1 (152).
1847. The American Loyalists, by Lorenzo Sabine.—B. M. 10880, d. 67.
1848. Emigration in its practical application to individuals and communities, by J. H. Burton.—B. M. 1157, F. 6 (3).
1849. A View on the Art of Colonisation, by E. G. Wakefield.
1852. The Emigrant's Handbook, being a guide to the various

fields of emigration in all parts of the globe, by J. Cassell.—B. M. 10002, C. 26.

1859. Emigration to Canada. The Eastern Townships of Lower Canada.—B. M. 10470, a. 48 (1).

1861–1891. Annual Reports of the Commissioners of Emigration of the State of New York; published irregularly between 1861 and 1891 in 39 volumes. Reports deal with the years 1847 to 1890.

1869–1891. Statistics of Immigration into the United States between 1869 and 1891; published in the Annual Reports of the Chief of the Bureau of Statistics (Treasury Department) on the commerce and navigation of the United States.

1869. History of Upper Canada, by William Canniff.—B. M. 09555, d. 8.

1870. Immigration and the Commissioners of Emigration of the State of New York, by Friedrich Kapp.

1871. What Emigration really is, by a resident in Canada.—B. M. 10470, bbb.

1879. Essays of Travel, by Robert Louis Stevenson (Chapter I).

1884. The Story of the Settlement, by T. Sheffield; published at Grahamstown (referred to in Chapter X).

1886. Emigration and the Malthusian Craze, by Justitia.—B. M. 8282, de, 24 (5).

1886. Land in the United States (John Hopkins University Studies, Vol. IV).

1886. Canada: its History, Productions, and Natural Resources (published by the Department of Agriculture, Ottawa; revised periodically).

1887. Emigration and Immigration. Report of the Consular Officers of the United States (Bureau of Foreign Commerce) 49th Congress 2nd Session, House Executive Document, No. 157.

1889. The Ford Committee Report. A Report to regulate immigration into the United States, Jan. 19th, 1889. 50th Congress, 2nd Session, House Report, No. 3792.

1890. Emigration and Immigration, by R. Mayo Smith.

1891. De la Colonisation chez les Peuples Modernes, par Paul Leroy Beaulieu.—B. M. 8154, dd. 5.

APPENDIX II

1891. Studies in Statistics, by G. B. Longstaff.
1892. Laws of the American Republics relating to immigration and the sale of public lands (United States).—Bureau of the American Republics, Bulletin No. 53, July 21st, 1892, 52nd Congress, 1st Session, Senate Executive Document, No. 149, pt. 4.
1894. Immigration and Alien Contract Labour Laws (United States).—Report from the Committee on Immigration. June 7th, 1894, 53rd Congress, 2nd Session, House Report, No. 1040.
1897. Canada (The Story of the Nations Series), by Sir J. G. Bourinot.
1898. E. G. Wakefield, by R. Garnett; in the Builders of Great Britain Series, Vol. 4.
1904. Canada and the Empire, by E. Montagu and B. Herbert (Chapter II).
1904. Edward Gibbon Wakefield et sa doctrine de la Colonisation systematique, par A. Siegfried.
1905. The Problem of the Immigrant, by J. D. Whelpley.
1906. Emigration: Colonisation Proposals, by "General" Booth.
1906. The Canadian War of 1812, by Sir C. P. Lucas.
1908. Waste Humanity, by F. A. McKenzie (Salvation Army Press).
1908. The Emigration Snare, by Miles Birkett (John Ouseley, publisher).
1908. Aims and Methods of Charitable Organisations promoting Emigration to Canada from the British Isles (published by the Minister of the Interior, Ottawa).
1909. The Public Organisation of the Labour Market, by S. and B. Webb.
1909. History of Canada, 1763–1812, by Sir C. P. Lucas.
1909. No English need Apply, or Canada as a Field for the Emigrant, by Basil Stewart.
1909. The Surplus: a pamphlet dealing with the emigration work of the Salvation Army.
1909. A Study of the Population of Manhattanville, by Dr. H. B. Woolston (Columbia University Publications, Vol. XXXV, No. 2).
1910. The Public Domain and Democracy, by Dr. R. T.

Hill (Columbia University Publications, Vol. XXXVIII, No. 1).
1910. Information for British Teachers regarding Schools work in Canada (published by the British Women's Emigration Association).
1910. Pamphlet on emigration to the United States.—*Emigrants' Information Office Handbook* (revised occasionally).
1910. Emigration Statutes and General Handbook, compiled by W. B. Paton, M.A.—*Emigrants' Information Office Handbook* (revised occasionally).
1910. Circular on the Emigration of Women.—*Emigrants' Information Office Handbook* (revised occasionally).
1910. Statutes of Canada, 1910.—9-10 Edward VII, Vols. 1-11 (Acts of the Parliament of the Dominion of Canada, Vol. 1, Public General Acts).
1911. Junior Imperial Migration: pamphlet by Thomas E. Sedgwick (26 Oriental Street, Poplar, London).
1911. Scots in Canada, by J. M. Gibbon (a popular account of Scotch emigration to Canada).
1911. A Key to Empire, compiled by the Staff of the *Empire Magazine*.
1911. Historical Geography of the British Colonies.—Lucas, Vol. 5, Part 3, Canada, by J. D. Rogers.
1912. Canada Handbook, compiled by W. B. Paton, M.A.—*Emigrants' Information Office Handbook* (revised annually).
1912. Lord Durham's Report on the Affairs of British North America, by Sir Charles P. Lucas (3 vols.).
1912. Canada To-day (annual of the weekly journal *Canada*).
1912. Immigration and Labour, by Isaac Hourwich (Putnam).

(D) STATUTES OF THE REALM RELATING TO EMIGRATION

43 Geo. 3, c. 56.	Passenger Vessels.
56 Geo. 3, c. 83.	Passenger Traffic.
58 Geo. 3, c. 89.	Attendance of magistrates on board vessels.
59 Geo. 3, c. 124.	Passenger Vessels.
1 Geo. 4, c. 7.	Customs.
4 Geo. 4, c. 84.	Passenger Vessels.
4 Geo. 4, c. 88.	*Ibid.*
5 Geo. 4, c. 97.	Artificers going aboard.
6 Geo. 4, c. 116.	Passenger Vessels.
7 and 8 Geo. 4, c. 19.	*Ibid.*
9 Geo. 4, c. 21.	Passengers in Merchant Vessels.
4 and 5 Will. 4, c. 76.	Poor Law Amendment. Emigration.
5 and 6 Will. 4, c. 53.	Merchant Vessels.
1 and 2 Vict. c. 56.	Poor Relief. Emigration.
3 and 4 Vict. c. 21.	Passenger Ships.
3 and 4 Vict. c. 78.	Canada (Clergy Reserves).
5 and 6 Vict. c. 107.	Passengers in Merchant Ships.
6 and 7 Vict. c. 92.	Poor Relief. Emigration.
7 and 8 Vict. c. 101.	Poor Law Amendment. Emigration.
8 and 9 Vict. c. 14.	Passenger Ships.
10 and 11 Vict. c. 31.	Poor Relief. Emigration.
10 and 11 Vict. c. 103.	Passengers' Act.
11 and 12 Vict. c. 6.	Passengers to North America.
11 and 12 Vict. c. 110.	Poor Law Amendment. Emigration.
12 and 13 Vict. c. 5.	Relief of Distress. Ireland.
12 and 13 Vict. c. 33.	Merchant Vessels.
12 and 13 Vict. c. 103.	Poor Law Amendment. Emigration.
13 and 14 Vict. c. 101.	*Ibid.*
14 and 15 Vict. c. 1.	Passengers by Sea.
15 and 16 Vict. c. 44.	*Ibid.*
16 and 17 Vict. c. 84.	Passengers' Act Amendment.

18 and 19 Vict. c. 119.	Passengers.
19 and 20 Vict. c. 9.	Public Money. Emigration.
26 and 27 Vict. c. 51.	Passengers' Act Amendment.
29 and 30 Vict. c. 113.	Poor Law Amendment. Emigration.
33 and 34 Vict. c. 95.	Passengers' Act Amendment.
35 and 36 Vict. c. 67.	Local Government Board. Emigration.
39 and 40 Vict. c. 61.	Poor Law Amendment. Emigration.
44 and 45 Vict. c. 49.	Land Law (Ireland) Act.
45 and 46 Vict. c. 47.	Arrears of Rent (Ireland).
46 and 47 Vict. c. 43.	Tramways and Public Companies (Ireland). Emigration.
47 and 48 Vict. c. 28.	Ibid.
51 and 52 Vict. c. 41.	Local Government Act. Finance of Emigration.
52 and 53 Vict. c. 29.	Passengers' Act Amendment.
54 and 55 Vict. c. 23.	Emigration.
55 and 56 Vict. c. 52.	Canada. Public Loans.
57 and 58 Vict. c. 60.	Merchant Shipping.
61 and 62 Vict. c. 37.	Local Government (Ireland) Emigration.
4 Ed. 7, c. 15.	Emigration of Children.
5 Ed. 7, c. 18.	Unemployed Workmen.
6 Ed. 7, c. 48.	Merchant Shipping Amendment.

INDEX

A

Adelaide, wealthy immigrants' visit to, 234
Advertising emigration, 61, 62, 63
Age of emigrants, the, 305
Agents, emigration, appointed by Government, 85
Agreement with colonies, necessary, 329
Agricultural colleges, 174
Agricultural depressions, 47, 49
Agricultural labourer, weekly wages of, 45, 53
Agricultural settlements, Report on. (*See* Haggard, Sir R.)
Agriculture, Department of, 174
Aid from Government, for emigrants, 98
Aim of Passengers' Acts, 106
Albany settlement, 229
Alberta, 188, 194, 223, 267, 268
Allan Line, 65
Amalgamated Society of Engineers, 84
Amount of population due to emigration in N.A., 313
Anchor Line, 71
Apprentices, parish, 272
Arable turned into pasture land, 3
Arnold White, Mr., 239
Arrears of Rent Act, 73, 92, 95
Arrival, condition of emigrants on, 107
Artificers to leave Great Britain, persuading, 180
Assiniboia land, 194
Atlantic crossing, deaths during, 102
—— miseries of, 101
—— rations for, 102, 104

Atlantic transport, Royal Commission to enquire into, 114
Attractions which draw settlers from their lands, 240
Australia for colonisation, 249
Australian Land Act, 21

B

Barnardo's Homes, 33, 80, 284, 285.
Barr Colony, 69, 243, 252
Belgian emigration laws, 337
Belgian glass-blowers, 145
Benefits obtained by the individual immigrant 322
Bermuda, 276
Birth-rate of Germany and France, 331
Blind-alley occupations, 298
Bonds, regulations for, 103, 125, 133, 134
Borough councils, powers of certain, 94
Bow River settlement, 247
British and Colonial Society, 65
British Columbia, 195, 223, 266, 268
British Welcome League, 170
British Women's Emigration Association, 80, 258, 259, 260, 261, 262, 264
Brokers, licences for, 113, 125
Buller, Charles, 22, 23
Burden of immigrants to New York, 133
Burden of immigration, 320
Burden to local rates in U.S. of immigrants, 106
Burdett Coutts (Baroness), 59
Burns, Mr., on emigration, 35
Burrows, Capt., petition of, 277

379

INDEX

C

Canada ceded to Great Britain, 1
Canada Company, 193, 216, 217, 218
Canada, cost of immigration to, 99
Canada for colonisation, 248
Canadian Agricultural, Coal, and Colonisation Co., 225
Canadian colonisation schemes, 27
Canadian Immigration Act, 246
Canadian immigration, from U.S., 187
Canadian Manufacturers' Association, 262
Canadian Pacific Railway, 62, 175, 185, 194, 195, 225, 247
Canadian Settlers' Loan and Trust Co., 80, 225
Canvassers, Dominion, 168, 169
Cape Breton Isle, 5, 7, 69, 192
Cape Colony, 228, 274.
Carleton (Governor), 209
Castle Garden, 118, 165
Cathcart, Lady Gordon, 73, 236, 251, 253
Character of emigrants, 305, 261
Character of women emigrants, enquiry into, 261
Charitable assistance, 335
Charitable bodies, 75, 159, 169, 170, 171
Charity Organisation Society, 76, 77
Child emigrants, condition on landing, 274
— — inspection of, 283
— — success of, 288, 289
Child emigration, rules for, 282, 284, 287, 290
Children, demand for, in the colonies, 275, 286
Children, emigration of. Views of Mr. Holgate, 293
Children's Emigration Societies, 284, 286
Children, when to emigrate, 285, 292
Church Army, 76, 78, 171
Church Emigration Society, 33, 78
Classification of unemployed, 302
Cleanliness, orders in council for, on voyage, 110

Clearances in Scotland, 45
Clergy Reserves, 215, 216, 217
Coal and population, relation of, 331
Cockburn (Colonel), 18, 193, 227, 253
Cold Bath Fields Prison, 273
Colleges, agricultural, 174
Colmer, Mr., opinions of, for successful colonisation, 253
Colonial Land and Emigration Commissioners, 25, 71, 98, 109, 119, 121, 220 (note), 234, 256, 257, 275, 309, 324
Colonisation and emigration compared, 339
Colonisation circular, 26
Colonisation Committee, 30, 69, 94, 95, 167
Colonisation schemes, faults in early, 252
Commercial Colonisation Co., 80, 225
Commission (Government) on Emigration, 1831, 21
Committee of 1826-7, 39
Compagnie Générale Transatlantique, 139
Congested Districts Board, 96
Conjugal state of immigrants, 326
Connecticut, emigrants to, 6
Consolidation of farms, 42, 44
Constitutional Act, 1791, 209
Continental emigrants embarking at British ports, 22
Contract labour, 144, 156
Co-operative emigration by trade-unions, 83
Correction, House of, 273
Cost of emigration, 230, 243
Cost of steerage passages, 127 (note)
Cotton Spinners' Society, 84
County Councils, powers of, 94, 96
Coutts, Baroness Burdett, 59
Crime and immigration, 320
Crofters' colonisation scheme, 86, 240, 242, 243
Crown Lands Department, 68, 220
Crown Reserves, 214, 215
Cunard Line, 71, 120
Currency in B.N.A. and U.S. compared, 180

INDEX

D

Deaths during Atlantic passage, 102
Debarred from emigrating, people, 140, 147, 150
Defence of Empire, 328, 330
Demand for immigrants in excess of supply, 158. (*See also under* Child emigration)
Deportation of immigrants, 154, 155 (note), 334
Depressions in agriculture, 47, 49
Desert Land Act, 204
Destination of immigrants, 188. (*See also* Ch. VIII)
Disbanded soldiers, 193
Disease and immigration, 320
Dispersal of immigrants at ports, 165, 166, 167, 168
Directors of the Poor, as emigrators, 274
Dishonest parents and child emigration, 293 (note)
Distress committees, 36, 97
Dr. Barnardo's Homes. (*See* Barnardo's Homes)
Domestic service in Canada, 264, 265, 325, 333
Dominion Land Act, 74, 224, 225
Doyle's enquiry, 279
Dressmakers in Canada, 266
Durham, Lord, 22, 25, 107, 108, 134, 160, 177, 178, 197, 219

E

Early immigrants, ignorance of, 181
East End Emigration Fund, 33, 65, 76, 77, 324
Embarkation routine, 128
Emigrant and Colonist Aid Corporation, 234
Emigrants' Information Office, 29, 31, 35, 36, 265, 339
Emigration and colonisation compared, 339
Empire, defence of, 328, 330
English and Welsh Local Government Act, 94
English emigration, 2, 4, 40, 48, 49, 57, 58, 86, 88, 89, 97.
Erie Purchase, 198

Ethnical view of immigration, 319
Eversley, Lord, on intensive farming, 302
Excursions for home-seekers, 188
Experimental farms, 173
Exportation of machinery forbidden, 57
Extent of early emigration, 14

F

Fares of Atlantic passage, 65, 127
Farm labour, 325, 332
Farms, demonstration, 33
Farms, experimental, 173
Farm workers in Britain, drain on, 331
Farr, Dr., on the value of an emigrant, 306
Faults in past colonisation schemes, 252
Federation of societies, proposed, 76
Female Middle-Class Emigration Society, 257
Feudal changes in Scotland, 64
Fielding's emigration scheme, 235
Figures relating to emigration, 14, 26, 35, 38, 47, 50, 52, 55, 88, 97, 136, 176, 183, 187, 228, 259, 269, 289, 327
Financial assistance for emigrants, 263, 275, 280, 281, 297
Ford, Mary, case of, 279
Foreign competition in trade, 58, 60
Franchise and immigration, 321
Frauds practised by emigrants, 167
Frauds practised on emigrants, 113, 114, 116, 164, 165
Free grants of land, 3, 218
Free passages, 24, 43, 338
Free rail tickets to destination, 167
Free soil democracy, 203
Further Amending Act, 91, 92, 256

G

German emigration laws, 336
Germans in north-west states of U.S., 190

INDEX

Glass-blowers from Belgium, 145
Glengarry, 5
Goderich, Lord, 210, 218
Gordon Cathcart (Lady). (*See* Cathcart)
Gore, Governor, 216
Gourlay, 216
Government control of emigration, 337
Government grants for emigration, 85
Government reports. A source of information, 16
Graduation Land Act, 200
Grahamstown settlers, 229
Grants of land to irresponsible people, 219
Grosse Isle, 108, 161
Growth of population, 295
Guardians, emigration by, 146
— money spent by, 88, 89, 90, 93
— powers of, to emigrate, 91

H

Haggard, Sir Rider, 32, 169, 244, 292, 304, 324, 340
Hand-loom weavers, 53, 54, 55, 73
Head-tax, 134, 136, 137, 139, 141
Highland Society and emigration, 102
Holgate, Mr., on emigrating children, 293
Home helps, 264
Home-seekers' excursions, 188
Homestead Act, 203, 204, 205, 207
Homestead entries, 226
Homestead fees, 226
Hospitals, immigrant, 134, 159
Hospital treatment of immigrants, 149, 155, 161, 162, 166
Hubbard, Miss, 258
Hudson Bay Co., 223
Hungarian emigration laws, 336

I

Ignorance of early immigrants, 181
Illinois Railroad Co., 205
Illiteracy of immigrants, 320
Ill-treatment of child emigrants, 280
Immigrants sending for relations and friends, 182
Immigration Commissioners, Board of, 135
Imperial Conference, 34, 35
Imperial Defence, 328, 331
Imperial emigration, 341
Imperial Home Reunion Association, 171
Indians, settlements of, 191, 201
Industrial disturbances, effect of, on emigration, 53
Industrial expansion of Canada, recent, 184
Industries and immigration, bureau of, 163
Information on early reception, sources of, 158
Inman Line, 71, 138
Inspection of child immigrants, 283
Inspection of vessels, 123
Insuring immigrants, 133
Interior, Dept. of, 168
Ireland's (Bishop) immigration assistance, 235
Irish Church Temporalities Fund, 95
Irish emigration, 2, 4, 18, 27, 40, 68, 70, 91, 93, 98, 229, 235, 256
Irish famine, 25, 50, 86
Irish in New England States, 190
Irish labour in Great Britain, 54
Irish poor, enquiry into state of, 20
Irish Poor Relief Extension Act, 51
Irregular sailings, 103
Irresponsible people, grants of land to, 219
Irrigation, 205
Italian emigration laws, 336

J

James, emigrant ship, 105
Journey, miseries of the, 101, 113, 115, 117, 125, 158, 159, 165, 167
— mortality on the, 110, 117, 119, 122

INDEX 383

Juvenile emigration, value of, 291
Juvenile offenders, 273

K

Kafirs in pay of British emigrants, 229
Kelp industry, 48
Kentucky, immigrants going to, 198
Killarney settlement, 241, 243
King William's Town settlement, 238

L

Labour, contract, 144, 156
Labour, farm, 325, 332
Labour in Lanark, 54
Labour, the necessary margin of, 308
Lanark, labour in, 54
Land grants, 3, 20, 206, 212, 219
Land grants to Talbot's immigrants, 11 (note)
Landing arrangements at New York, 118, 164
Landing, condition on, of child emigrants, 274
Land Law Act, 95, 96
Land, purchases in instalments, 199, 224
Lands reserved for public services, 200
Land surveys, 179
Land systems, 197
Lazy emigrants, 33, 229
Lewis, Miss Jane, 257
Licences for brokers and others, 113, 125
Loans offered by the State, 339
Loans to emigrants, return of, 258, 259, 338
Local Government Board, 88, 89, 90, 95
Local Loans Act, 95
London Female Emigration Society, 255
London Society of Compositors, 81
Low-class immigrants, 321
Lower Canada, land, 207, 208
Loyalist migration, 5, 6, 12, 208

M

Machinery, exportation of, forbidden, 57
Macpherson, Miss, 278
Manitoba and North Western Railway, 225
Manitoba land, 194, 223, 241, 266, 268
Manitoba, wheat-growing in, 185
Margin of labour, the, 308
Marshall on the value of an emigrant, 306
Mary Ford, case of, 279
Medical examination of emigrants, 124, 148, 150, 286
Medical report on immigrants, 333
Medical tax, 139, 161
Mennonites, 246
Merchants Shipping Act, 123, 126
Miami Land Co., 198
Military colonists, 13, 228
Milliners in Canada, 266
Miseries of the journey, 101, 113, 115, 117, 125, 158, 159, 165, 167
Mississippi Valley. Settlement of, 190
Mohawks, land of the, 194
Monetary assistance for women emigrants, 260
Monetary worth of immigration, 315
Money in possession of emigrants, 70, 308, 309
Money required to be in possession of emigrants, 308
Money spent by Boards of Guardians, 88, 89, 90, 93
Montreal, Lord Durham on, 178
Morals and Atlantic crossing, 129
Morning Chronicle, extract from, 276
Mortality on journey, 110, 117, 119, 122
Movement of settlers, the, 190
Murray (Governor), 209

N

Napoleonic wars, effect of, 12, 46, 57
National Council of Women of Canada, 263
National Debt of U.S., 198

INDEX

New Brunswick, 4, 6, 18, 135, 178, 192, 211, 223, 266, 268
New immigrants, work undertaken by, 195
New Jersey, 321
New South Wales, 275
New York, burden of immigrants in, 133, 139
New York landing arrangements, 118, 164. (*See also* Castle Garden)
New York State, illegal act of, 138
New Zealand, 249, 290
North-West Land Co., 27, 74, 80
Norwich and emigration, 297
Nova Scotia, 4, 6, 18, 178, 191, 193, 211, 223, 268
Nugent's, Father, immigration scheme, 235
Nurses in Canada, 266, 267

O

Occupations of emigrants, 316
Ohio Land Co., 198, 202
Ontario, 5, 193, 221, 223, 266, 268
Opportunities for women in Canada, 270
Ossington, Lady, 239
Outlook of immigrants, 322
Overcrowding on emigrant ships, 107, 112
Overseers of the poor and children, 272

P

Pace settlers, value of, 252
Page, T. W., on causes of emigration, 66
Parish apprentices, 272
Parishes, English, powers to grant money, 86
Parish relief, 48
Passage tickets, fraudulent, 113, 115
Passengers' Acts, 24, 106, and Ch. V generally
Pasture from arable land, 3
Pauperism and immigration 320
Peel's, Mr. Thomas, immigration scheme, 232
Pelican Lake, settlement at, 241

Pennsylvania, 6, 190, 198, 321
People debarred from entering B.N.A., 150; from U.S., 140, 147
Physically unfit immigrants, 149, 150
Physical standard of emigrants, 305
Pilgrim Fathers, 13
" P " marked on emigrant ships, 103
Poor (Irish). (*See under* Irish)
Poor Law Amendment Act, 50, 86
Poor Law and congestion of population, 41
Poor Law Commission, 1908, 34
Poor Law emigration, 256
Poor Law Relief Act, 87, 91, 93, 256
Poor Law, relief to, by emigration, 297
Population, effect of emigration on, 300, 311, 312
— effect on emigration, 38, 40, 273
— growth of, 295
— need for, in the Empire, 327
Potato crop and Irish emigration, 52
Potter's Joint Stock and Emigration Co., 80
Pre-emption Acts, 202, 205, 207
Preference of immigrants for U.S., 176, 179, 181, 182
Prepared settlements, 235, 247
Prescott, General, 210
Prince Edward Island, 4, 18, 210, 268
Progress in U.S. and B.N.A. compared, 177
Prosecutions of shipmasters, 113
Public lands of the Dominion Act, 221
Public services, land reserved for, 200
Purchase of Land Act, 96

Q

Quarantine, 107, 108, 129, 143, 160
Quarantine at Grosse Isle, 107
Quebec, 6, 192, 193, 223

INDEX 385

Quebec Act, 209, 211
Quebec, arrival of emigrants at, 107, 156

R

Ragged schools, London, 275
Railroad companies and land, 205
Rankin, Sir J., 75, 76, 238
Rate-wars and Atlantic fares, 65
Rathbone, Mr., 28
Rations on voyage, 102, 104, 112, 124
Redemptioners, 71
Redistribution or emigration? 301
Red Star Line, 71
Relief to the body-politic, emigration a, 298
Remittance men, 299
Remittances from immigrants, 51, 324.
Repayments of loans, 338
Report of 1826-7, 16, 17, 42, 53, 208, 232, 317, 324.
Report on Agricultural Settlements. (See Haggard, Sir R.)
Resources of immigrants, 317
Restrictions, absence of, on immigration, 131
Restrictions of to-day, 132, 140, 150
Restrictive Laws, policy of, 331, 332, 334, 336.
Rider Haggard, Sir. (See Haggard, Sir R.)
Robinson, Mr. Peter, 166, 193, 229, 251.
Roman Catholic emigration, 235
Royal Highland emigrants, 4
Royal Proclamation of 1763, 208
Royal William, 120 (note)
Rules for proper conduct of immigration to U.S., 141, 147
Rum, island of, congestion in, 40, 73
Russian emigration laws, 336
Rye, Miss, 257, 278

S

Safety valve, emigration a, 295
Sailings of vessels, irregular, 55

Sail ousted by steam, 120
St. Pancras Union, emigration by, 276
Saltcoats settlement, 242, 243, 253
Salvation Army, 32, 76, 79, 171, 245, 246
Samuel, Mr. Herbert, on population and unemployment, 304
Saskatchewan, 188, 194, 223, 267, 268
Savings of former emigrants, spent in U.K., 310
Scheduled districts, 96
Schools in Canada, 267
Scotch emigration, 2, 3, 4, 5, 6, 8, 39, 40, 49, 59, 64, 69, 98
Seasonal immigrants, 319
Sedgwick, Mr. T., 290
Seducing artificers to leave Great Britain, 180
Seigneuries, 179
Seigneurs and land, 207
Selective process of emigration, the, 305, 329
Self-government for Canada, 22
Self-Help Society, 76, 77
Selkirk, Lord, 8, 10, 64, 69, 194
Sending home for relations and friends, 70, 71
Sending immigrants inland, 138
Settlement of North America, 314
Sex balance, disturbance of, 257, 311
Shaughnessy, Sir T., 247
Shipmasters and prosecutions, 113
Shipping companies, 126
Ships bearing letter " P," 103
Shipwrecks, 119, 170
Sliding scale of admission tax, 136, 137
Small farmers, hard lot of, 42, 46
Societies, emigration, 24, 33, 51, 64, 65, 76, 7 8, 79 80, 170, 171, 234, 255, 257, 258, 262, 263, 284
Societies, work of, 25
Society of Friends, 51
Soldiers, disbanded, 193
South Africa for colonisation, 248

INDEX

South African Colonisation Society, 33
South Australia, 275
South Australian Act, 21, 233
Staff of emigration officers, 118
Steam power, introduction of, 561
Steam replaces sail, 120
Steerage, cost of, 127 (note)
Stoke Prior Colonial Training College, 261
Stone and Timber Act, 204
Strongholds of low-class immigrants, 321
Successful colonisation, to effect, 253
Success of colonisation schemes, 250, 251
Suppression of Juvenile Vagrancy, Society for, 274
Supreme court, decision against New York, 138
Swan River Colony, 232
Sweetman's, Mr., emigration, 236
Swiss emigration laws, 336
Symmes, John Cleves, 202

T

Talbot, Colonel, 11, 166, 193, 214
Teachers in Canada, 266, 269
Tennyson settlement, 240
Timber Culture Act, 204
Tooke on prices, 46
Townships, shape of, 199, 222
Townspeople discouraged to emigrate, 302
Trade, foreign, competition, 58, 60
Trade unions, 80, 81, 82, 83, 296
Trade unions and co-operative emigration, 83
Trade unions and emigration of "victims," 84
Tramways Act, 73, 96
Transport of emigrants, unrestricted, 101, 104
Treasury grant, 159
Treasury loans, 19
Treasury, stipulations regarding governmental loans, 28
Treaty of Peace, 1763, 1
Tuke, Mr. J. H., 73, 76
Turner, Professor, quotation, 196

U

Unassisted and assisted emigration, relative proportions, 68
Underselling by immigrants, 318
Undesirable immigrants, 136, 137, 140, 141, 144, 147, 149, 150, 299
Unemployed, classification of, 302
Unemployed Workmen Act, 31, 97
Unemployed and emigration, 304
Uniformity, lack of, in immigration laws, 134
Union Chargeability Act, 87
Union of Saddle and Harnessmakers, 82
United Loyalists, 192, 193, 209, 211, 212, 214
United States, emigration to B.N.A., 187
United States and British colonisation, 250
United States, national debt, 198
Unprofitable emigration, 327
Unskilled emigrants, 317
Unsound supplies of provisions, 116
Urban centres, pressure in, 60, 301
Urban life of Irish immigrants, 183
Urban overcrowding, 60, 301

V

Value of an emigrant, the, 306
Value of emigration to women, 268, and Ch. XIII
Value of juvenile emigration, 291
Van Diemen's Land, 233
Vansittart's, Mr., emigration, 228
Vere Foster, Mr., 116, 257, 259
Vessels, inspection of, 123

W

Wages of agricultural labourer, 45, 53
Wages of women in Canada, 265, 266, 268, 269
Wages, standard of, lowered by the immigrant, 318
Wakefield, E. G., 20, 22, 233, 234
Wealthy immigrants' visit to Adelaide, 234

INDEX

Weavers, 53, 54, 55, 73
Webb, Mr. and Mrs. Sidney, classification of unemployed, 302
Western movement, 196
West Ham Distress Committee, 65
Wheat-growing in Canada, 183, 185
Wolseley Settlement, 238
Women and colonisation, 341
Women emigrants, of two classes, 255

Women, opportunities for, in Canada, 270
Women's Emigration Society, 258
Women's National Immigration Society, 263
Women's wages in Canada, 265, 266, 268, 269
Wortley Hostel, 261

Y

Youthful qualities learnt from home-comers, 330